(Dis)Forming the American Canon

African-Arabic Slave Narratives
and the Vernacular

Ronald A. T. Judy

Foreword by Wahneema Lubiano

University of Minnesota Press
Minneapolis
London

Published by the University of Minnesota Press
2037 University Avenue Southeast, Minneapolis, MN 55455-3092
Printed in the United States of America on acid-free paper

Judy, Ronald A. T.
    (Dis)forming the American canon : African-Arabic slave narratives and the
vernacular / Ronald A. T. Judy :   foreword by Wahneema Lubiano.
        p.   cm.
    Includes bibliographical references and index.
    ISBN 0-8166-2056-3 (hard   :   alk. paper). — ISBN 0-8166-2057-1 (pbk.   :   alk. paper)
        1. American prose literature—Afro-American authors—History and criticism—
Theory, etc.   2. American prose literature—Arab American authors—History and
criticism—Theory, etc.   3. Slaves' writings, American—History and criticism—Theory,
etc.   4. Slavery—United States—Historiography.   5. Afro-Americans in literature.
6. Arab Americans in literature.   7. Narration (Rhetoric).   8. Canon (Literature).
9. Autobiography.   I. Title.   II. Title: Disforming the American canon.
PS366.A35J83   1993
810.9'896073—dc20   92-3888
                                                                              CIP

The University of Minnesota is an
equal-opportunity educator and employer.

This book is dedicated to my father and grandfather, who gave me a *kunya* already marked with distinction— I place them both like a seal upon my heart, like a seal upon my arm. Indeed, love is strong as death itself.

Contents

Acknowledgments

This book is the result of some effort on my part, and much support from colleagues and students. Wlad Godzich presented me with the challenge and value of undertaking a project of this magnitude. Among those colleagues whose theoretical reflections have sustained me in thinking, as well as provoked me to thought, are Didier Coste, Terry Cochran, Gitahi Gititi, Lisa Frank, Roy Kay, Kathryn Murphy-Judy, and John Wright. Those of my students at Macalester College, Swarthmore College, and Carnegie Mellon University who have contributed immeasurably to this project through their resourceful probing are Carla Scott, Joseph Raza, Triyana Silton, John Krinsky, Marianne Hartigan, Mathew Henson, and Geoffrey Sauer. The writing of this book was made possible by the generous support I received at various stages of my research from the University of Minnesota Graduate School Dissertation Fellowship in 1987, Macalester College Hewlett-Mellon Predoctoral Fellowship in 1988, the Minority Scholar-in-Residence Postdoctoral Fellowship Program at Swarthmore College in 1989, and the Faculty Development Office at Carnegie Mellon in 1990. This book's completion, however, would not have been possible without the material and moral support of my family, and the invaluable service performed by Laura Westlund and Sabah Ghandour in its editing. I take full responsibility for all errors and faults found within these pages.

A Note on Transliteration

In the transliteration of Arabic I have by and large followed the Library of Congress convention, except in the following particulars. I do not capitalize the definite article *al*, even in the case of proper nouns such as *al-Ghazalī*, except when it begins a sentence. In those instances where the definite article *al* is followed by a word beginning with one of the "sun letters," I have followed the Arabic convention of pronunciation, according to which the *l* of the definite article is integrated into the following letter. As a result I transliterate *as-sunna* instead of *al-sunna*, and *ar-Risala* instead of *al-Risāla*. With the exceptions of Ben Ali and Job ben Solomon, I have made slight modifications in my transcription of the Arabic proper names of the authors of Arabic slave narratives so that they are readily identifiable with the way they have come to be spelled in most texts. Accordingly, Abu Bakr Al-Saddiq becomes Abū Bakr as-Ṣiddiqi; Abdul Rahahman (Abd al-Rahman Ibrahima) becomes ʿAbd-ur-Raḥmān; and Omar Ibn Said becomes ʿUmar ibn Said. As for Job ben Solomon, because this spelling is a complete anglicization that displaces even the Fulani pronunciation (Ayuba Suleiman Diallo), I have arabized it as Ayyūb ibn Suleimān Diallo. I have not modified the proper name Ben Ali at all, re-marking the anonymity of the author of the manuscript called *Ben Ali's Diary*.

Abbreviations Used in Citations of Kant's Work

Chapters 4 and 5 of this book contain numerous citations from the work of Immanuel Kant. These citations refer to both the original German and the English translations of Kant's work. German citations of *Kritik der reinen Vernunft* are from the edition by Raymund Schmidt (Hamburg: Felix Meiner Verlag, 1926); English citations of this work are from *Critique of Pure Reason*, trans. Norman Kemp Smith (New York: St. Martin's Press, 1965). Following convention, citations from *Kritik der reinen Vernunft* and *Critique of Pure Reason* are located by the pagination of the first edition of 1781 (A) and/or the second edition of 1787 (B). A or B will appear just before the page number in the parenthetical citations when the reference is to a passage that is one edition but not the other. German citations of *Kritik der Urteilskraft* are from the edition by Karl Vorländer (Hamburg: Felix Meiner Verlag, 1924); English citations are from *Critique of Judgment*, trans. Werner S. Pluhar (Indianapolis: Hackett, 1987). German citations from *Beobachtungen über das Gefühl des Schönen und Erhabenen, Metaphysische Anfangsgründe der Naturwissenschaft*, and *Prolegomena zu einer jeden künftigen Metaphysik, die als Wissenschaft wird auftreten können* refer to *Kants Werke*, ed. Ernst Cassirer (1764; Berlin: Bruno Cassirer, 1914); English citations of these works are from, respectively, *Observations on the Feelings of the Beautiful and Sublime*, trans. John Goldthwait (Berkeley: University of California Press, 1960); *Metaphysical Foundations of Natural Science*, trans. James W. Ellington (Indianapolis: Hackett, 1985); and *Prolegomena to Any Future Metaphysics*, trans. James W. Ellington (Indianapolis: Hackett, 1977). Parenthetical citations that appear in chapters 4 and 5 from the *Kritik der reinen Vernunft*, *Critique of Pure Reason*, *Kritik der Urteilskraft*, and *Critique of Judgment* employ the following abbreviations.

KrV	*Kritik der reinen Vernunft*
CPR	*Critique of Pure Reason*
KU	*Kritik der Urteilskraft*
CJ	*Critique of Judgment*

Foreword

Wahneema Lubiano

What concludes this study is Ronald Judy's declaration that the textual indeterminacy of an African-Arabic American slave narrative allows it to elude the philosophical, philological, historical, canonical, and intentionality readings that would grasp at it and prove its undoing. Unlike the overdetermined Douglass and Equiano narratives, too plainly revealed to us by African American canon-formation gestures or by the imperialism of Kant's reasoning, *Ben Ali's Diary* finally protects itself from corruption by its mysteriousness, its status as enigma, and its impenetrability. Just like a woman; or a dream of the perfect woman: always almost available, always just out of reach; except that mystery or enigma has never proved to be a resistance for women.

But a woman is not a text? Nonsense. We speak here of the failure of categories and never mind their always already weakened imperatives. If a slave narrative can prove the undoing of Kant's Negrophobia, if a literary discourse can rock the foundation of something as material, as political and politicizing as the academy, then the ephemerality and inefficacy of mythic gender is a useful analogy for the limitations of textual indeterminacy as a privileged mode of resistance for emergent studies.

But I pun ahead of myself. Where do I begin with a book that so eloquently and elegantly pounds yet another nail into the coffin of a metaphysics of presence? This is a study that offers so very much: a surgical critique of Kant's inability to "reason" away the Negro's being; a mapping of the means by which Douglass's narrative strips Kant's veil of rationality away from the xenophobia that undermines his project; a sustained analysis of one of Black studies's founding moments and its relation to the incredibly "interested" nature of academic knowledge production, circulation, and legitimation; an evisceration of Allan Bloom, his genealogy, and his progeny; an engagement with the reconstructionists' intervention in African American literary studies; a serious—and often productive—reading of the Douglass and Equiano narratives; and finally, the recovery of an African-Arabic American slave narrative and the deconstruction of its literary history. I might be forgiv-

en, in the face of such riches, my hesitation over picking at certain problems, certain lacks, in the study. But the issue of emergent studies is too important a rallying point, too cathected a nexus of epistemology, politics, and aesthetics, for any of us to leave alone.

Judy recapitulates the founding moment of Black studies at Yale as an intervention into the knowledge factory, a possibly radical intervention that he contrasts to another founding moment: that of American studies, whereby an economic and political elite, already inscribing its dominance on the world and "reading" the terms of that control from its material and political dominance, established a fitting cultural myth for itself. The moment of Black studies is the frame for Judy's exploration of the canon-formation gestures of Robert Stepto and Henry Louis Gates, Jr., that cohered in *Afro-American Literature: The Reconstruction of Instruction*. This project, like Black studies itself, was intended as an emancipatory project that provided the background for the larger project of "making" an African American literary canon. Judy presents Black studies, African American literary discourse, and the new African American canon as the academic equivalents of the slave narrative's intervention into the discourse of "being."

Again, where does one begin with a book that, among so many other interesting and provocative things, is a thorough challenge to Kant's organization of beingness? And as well a challenge to the comfort involved in the work of recovery of marginalized texts? And the introduction of little known and fascinating texts?

Judy's work begins by recounting a history of a particular African American literary studies moment of reconstruction, the two-week seminar held by the Afro-American Studies Program of Yale in June 1977 entitled "Afro-American Literature: From Critical Approach to Course Design," which later evolved into the text *Afro-American Literature: The Reconstruction of Instruction*. That moment—like the October 1966 International Colloquium on Critical Languages and the Sciences of Man at Johns Hopkins, marked by French intervention into the North American conflict over the humanities, and the establishment by Daniel Gilman in 1876 of the institutional model for the humanities in the North American research university—makes visible the institutionalization of intellectual interventions on the epistemological battleground of the academy. A kind of genealogy, this account is the background for Judy's engagement with Frederick Douglass's narrative, a narrative central to

African American literary canon formation and the textual site for Judy's working out of an argument that insists that "resistance through canon formation is legitimated on the grounds of conservation, the conservation of authenticity's integrity." This insistence then prepares the ground for Judy's challenge to the African American slave narrative's hegemony in African American literary studies, a challenge that would be a corrective to what he terms the idealist conservatism of the Douglass text's centrality. The challenge text is the African-Arabic American slave "narrative," *Ben Ali's Diary*.

The object of focusing on *Ben Ali's Diary* as a specific case of narrative indeterminacy in African-Arabic American slave narratives is to provoke different thinking about the African American because Ali's non-representationality cannot be deployed to argue modernity's privileged discursive mode: subjectively grounded narrative writing. For Judy, the linguistically foreign (Arabic), heterographic (with its irregular spellings) manuscript is linguistically daunting, yet its linguistic indeterminacy is not itself sufficient cause for not reading Ali's manuscript as an augmentation (of canon-formation project). Its inability to be deployed as an agent of identity definition or even to be recognized as a narrative prevents its insertion into a discourse predicated on "knowing," on decipherability. If *Ben Ali's Diary* is merely an assemblage of graphic markings, intriguing scribbles on the page that cannot be fixed to a determinate source, an abstract consciousness, it cannot be deployed as an instance of narrativized subjectivity.

To make his argument that the representative African American slave narrative, Douglass's *Narrative,* can dispose of the limitations of Kant's "reason" but cannot threaten the hegemony of "knowing," Judy pays more attention to the *content* of the African American slave narrative—because it is "knowable"—and does a more *formal (linguistic)* analysis of the African-Arabic narrative. He then uses his linguistic analysis to argue that the formal qualities of the African-Arabic American narrative make it a more nuanced and complicated text than the *content* of the Douglass narrative. He treats the African American slave narrative as though it means only what it says it means, and then uses the indecipherability of the African-Arabic American manuscripts as evidence of their ambivalence or indeterminacy. Further, he argues that Henry Louis Gates's theory of "signifyin(g)," the basis for a reformed African American canon, is weakened because signifyin(g) has some reference—however attenuated—to a knowable referent. This "knowability" marks

for Judy the entrance of the African American slave narrative into the
hegemonic discourse of reason even as it unseats Kant's particular reign
of reason.

Judy uses Gates's readings of the African American narratives to set
the terms of his own argument about those narratives' limitations without paying much attention to the possibility of other readings of those
texts. He does this because he wants to unseat Gates, and while his interesting challenge to Gates opens up the discourse of African American
literary canon formation, it also flattens the texts on which Judy focuses
(which he argues explicitly and implicitly Gates does) in order to do so.
For example, while I do not want to argue in support of Gates's or anyone else's articulation of the slave narrative as "authentic" representation of African American literariness, I think that to argue that the
Douglass text's deconstruction of Kant's "Negro" is idealist only is to
ignore the complicated relationship that the African American slave narratives had to an abolitionist political *movement*. Judy makes that argument by marginalizing the intervention of those texts into the political
terrain on which they were produced. That is to say, by arguing that the
slave narrative's resistance is domesticated by the conservative nature of
canon formation is to ignore the reality of hegemonic discursive formations. I think it might be useful here to look at Ernesto Laclau and Chantal Mouffe's salient reminder that at "any moment—and especially in
periods of organic crisis" there are themes that "operate as necessary
surfaces of inscription within which *any* hegemonic alternative has to be
constructed" (92).[1] They go on to argue that "intellectual transitions
rarely take the form of complete breaks; there is rather a much more
subtle game of continuities and discontinuities" (93).

Notwithstanding what I see as the problem of Judy's critique of the
relation of African American slave narrative to the discourse of challenges to epistemology at the site of canon formation, Judy's dispatch of
Kant is surgical and economical. The African American slave narratives—especially that of Douglass—graph the scope of the slave writers'
ambitions and provide Judy with the tool by which to explode Kant's
"Negro Problem." Kant can't think the Negro within the terms of his
Critique, which doesn't stop the momentum of his Negrophobic nightmare. The fear and desire that cannot be contained by "reason" produce
the nightmare that reason then dehumanizes. Douglass's narrative, a
politically cognizant act on his part and an intellectual tool in Judy's
analysis, is a transaction in the domain of epistemological politics.

The limitation of Douglass's text's agency is, however, for Judy, its "idealist" nature. A misreading, I think, but a necessary misreading in order for Judy's analysis to produce the more literarily ambivalent and thus politically resistant African-Arabic American slave narrative text, Ben Ali's manuscript. First, Judy reads Gates reading Douglass, then he takes the Douglass narrative at its word when it describes itself as the means by which Douglass found himself or knew himself to be a man, and, finally, by virtue of his understanding of the social realism of the Douglass text, argues that its political work depends on the text's presentation of itself as the means by which a black man writes himself "into being." The ground of Judy's readings of Douglass, his analysis of Gates's theory of vernacular "signifyin(g)," and his understanding of "idealism" all constitute fecund ground for engagement and debate.

It is the strength of Judy's study, his brilliant close reading of Ben Ali's manuscript, however, that presents me with the most productive site of engagement. For in addition to the work of the text's and its context's deconstruction, Judy vaults onto much more cathected ground when he argues that the indeterminacy of the Ali manuscript is its register of resistance. He argues that because the Ali manuscript is undecipherable, it interrupts the containment possibilities attached to more "legible" texts. Ali cannot be discussed within the terms of a hegemonic discourse, thus the manuscript serves as a marker for the destabilizing possibilities of emergent literary production because it "not only linguistically but also historically" circulates "beyond the received notion of the Western Doctrine of the Sign as event" (from Judy's epilogue)—it is a text that defies signification. That defiance marks its resistance.

I am uneasy with the notion that a text, produced within a social formation, either completely acquiesces in or completely resists the terms of its circulation in and of itself. If it cannot be completely "known" within the terms of their discursive formations, still its status as "unknown" cannot produce a political effect outside of some agent's deployment of it, within specific circumstances. To suggest that the lack of referent for the formal qualities of a text is resistance is to suggest that the university, established by Judy as a site for epistemological challenge, for example, can be balked, can be challenged, can be corrected, by mystery; that commodity circulation depends upon understanding and explanation. The state does not need a bayonet, it is true, to intrude

itself in the cultural domain, but neither does it need to make consistent arguments for categorical imperatives, or to construct determined meanings for cultural productions, or even to regulate circulation, in order to produce its political effects.

Judy ends his work by looking at Nelson George's *The Death of Rhythm and Blues* and rightfully pointing to George's error in holding that "the attachment of circulatory value equals the dissolution of cultural production." But Judy is on shaky ground when he maintains that circulatory value signals the dissolution of "authentic" production value.

Authenticity is both a political project, in that it is produced as a strategic response to the real power differentials between dominant and marginalized groups, played out on the cultural terrain with political, economic, and social stakes, and also—like the idea of a virtuous woman—the production of hysteria around purity and boundary maintenance. I return again here to Laclau and Mouffe: "Radical contextualization of meaning, when it is coupled with the recognition of the unstable character of all context, means that there is no meaning that contains in itself the guarantee against its own corruption" (95).

If the division between the socially produced groups African American and European American were not a boundary of historical, political, and social salience, then the relation of cultural object to group "being" would not matter. Authenticity is produced by circulation, not dissolved by it; absent the threatening presence of a dominant group, there would be no originary status, no necessary group "belonging" to protect. Authenticity is produced as a value precisely because of the existence of circulation. If Euro-American dominance did not threaten the cultural "being" of African Americans—a threat that is reified not only in terms of cultural production but in terms of the gendering of "blackness" itself and the constant perceived "need" to claim, for example, the women of the group, the children of the group, the style of the group, whatever—then cultural production would not be the "thing" in constant danger of being usurped. Authenticity is gendered by virtue of its relation to that which has to be protected so that the group might know itself *against a particular social, political, and historical threatening reality*. It is a site for anxiety about corruption, about containment, about penetration.

Not only is Nelson George wrong in holding that "the attachment of circulatory value equals the dissolution of cultural production" (which Judy correctly recognizes as a mistake), he is wrong also in arguing for

"authenticity" pre-circulation: authenticity is not a *value* to-the-group outside of dominance or hegemony. Something is authentic *against* some (possible) appropriation by other forces, by others. If the division between African American culture and non-African American culture were not a boundary of historical/political/social salience, then relation of cultural object to group specificity wouldn't matter. This is congruent with Judy's reading of George, but Judy stumbles in tying "authenticity" to production from a historically produced hybrid group. African Americans are not only subaltern, they are hegemonic subjects with all that implies—including the blurring of the line between the cultural production of a dominant and a marginalized group. If "complete subordination" is impossible, as Judy argues, then so is "complete insubordination"—or authenticity.

Further, Judy makes the claim that emergent studies/cultures are "beyond the state." I disagree. Perhaps they are not completely within reach of the state's formal disciplinary apparatuses, but what of the state "within"? Culture is a terrain on which the state operates without formally disclosing its presence[2] if only by means of its reproduction—in mediated ways—in the imaginary of even marginalized subjects.

Which, obviously enough, brings me back to where I began and to both an obvious presence and an obvious absence in this work: gender. "Being" is a category that marks a subject. What is marked there? What is the language of marking? And for whom?

For Judy, the concept of "the Negro" is "an empty concept, a purely formal invention of the mind." I would add only that it also marks desire and fear, and, chimera or not, such marking is a political force—discursively so and in the realm of raw events of power. Therefore, Douglass's slave narrative is not simply a "writing into being" but a "writing into being *for*" or "writing into being *to*," a politically cognizant act, an entrance into the graphic symbolic not simply as a textual making or a reminder of human "being" but as a transaction in the domain of politics with an object of address: the contestation over power, over rights, over participation in a political economy.

In other words, a slave narrative is not just for the slave; it is for the discourse. That is to say, as Fanon puts it, "it is implicit that to speak is to exist absolutely for the other," "to speak a language is to take on a world, a culture" (38).[3] The "meaning" or "intention" of the Douglass text is not a thing in and of itself—to believe it to be so would be to fall into the trap of idealism. It is a negotiation in an ongoing struggle.

Judy reads the Douglass text as insufficient to the work of problematizing the identity model and argues that Ben Ali's text escapes that limitation. But just as slavery rested on more than the slaveholder's "reasoning" about the slave's "identity"—it rested also on the *desire* of those in power, the psychosexual pleasures of "othering" as well as the imperatives of profit—so too does the identity model rest on more than reduction to itself as the necessary site of politically epistemological challenge. And this dynamic of "othering" brings me to the incredible absence in this text that I referred to earlier: the absence of an acknowledgment or critique of the gendered nature of the discourse of "reason," the language of Douglass's deconstruction of Kant's "Negro," the parameters of slave-narrative discourse and their un-self-conscious enshrinement of Douglass's remaking the category of Negro or African American humanity into Negro or African American "manhood." The progeny of this remaking are with us still.

When Douglass's narrative marks manhood as that which the slave lacks, when the language of reason is resonant with those things that historically women lack, when the terms of a study of Kant's rationality and its implosion, the founding of Black studies and African American canon formation, and the circulation of value (with its tainting and corrupting possibilities) are the climax (pun intended) of the study, then I am staggered by the absence of a certain self-consciousness here, in the midst of theoretical discourses constantly reformulated by the interventions of feminisms. To what exactly do we attribute this study's silence?

Being is a set of terms—a male new set of terms; "making a man" is "being" on male grounds, for neither Kant's nor Douglass's humanness makes "female" humanness possible. And if Ben Ali's manuscript's indeterminacy has feminist implications, then their articulation in Judy's work is sotto voce indeed.

Judy not only doesn't comment on the masculinist language and imaginings of the texts or the discourse of reason, he doesn't make an argument for why gender does not have to be addressed, and I mean gender not only in terms of what is left out—because apparently it did not occur to Judy to take up gender as something to consider even if only to dismiss its importance—but what of a gender critique of Douglass and his text's articulations? Being (and its critique) is finally not just being on new terms but being on male terms both new and not new. Remember, the slave narrative is about staking one's ground as a man in order to assert humanness. Or, as in the case of Judy's argument

for Ben Ali, that particular narrative—resistant to decipherability—might also resist gendering. If this is so, I want to hear it said, see it written. And then perhaps a reader might take up the argument that I began earlier: is mystery an epistemological politics?

Chapter 1

Introduction
Critique of Incorporation

> From our degenerate literary art, as also from that itch for scribbling of
> our learned men which has now reached such alarming proportions,
> wells forth the same sigh: Oh that we could forget ourselves! The
> Attempt fails: memory, still not suffocated by the mountains of printed
> paper under which it is buried keeps on repeating from time to time:
> "A degenerate man of culture! Born for culture and brought up to non-
> culture!"
> —Friedrich Nietzsche, *On the Future of Our Educational Institutions*

The cue for the title of this book comes from a particular intervention
into the corpus of academic American cultural history. Around fifteen
years ago, in June 1977, the Afro-American Studies Program at Yale University hosted a two-week scholarly seminar entitled *Afro-American
Literature: From Critical Approach to Course Design*. The seminar was convened under the auspices of the Modern Language Association's
Commission of Minority Groups and the Study of Language and
Literature, with sponsorship from the National Endowment for the
Humanities. In retrospect, this seminar was a propitious event in the
institutional history of the humanities in the United States. Occurring at
Yale when it did, it was instrumental in opening up a space in academe
for the intellectual agenda that has come to be known as "canon formation." The particular project of canon formation that emerged from the
Yale seminar established the strategic importance for Afro-American
cultural studies to delineate the genealogy of its thought as a means of
nullifying the interdiction placed on it in the authorized historiography
of American culture. In this sense, the canon formation project articulates a body of work that contradicts, and so disrupts the integrity of, the
dominant discourse of American cultural history. It *(dis)forms* the
American canon, which from its inception has been a story of the unilinear transmission of *Reason*[1] from Europe to the Americas, by articulating
the multifarious possibilities of expression that constitute the historical
legacy of this "New World."

1

In large measure this introduction is an explanation of how I come to designate this contradiction as *(dis)formation.* Starting with an exposition of the historical moment in which the Yale seminar happened, I situate Afro-American canon formation as the institutional site where the agendas of Afro-American studies and poststructuralist critical theory meet. This explanation is only the propaedeutic of the project envisioned in this book. The chief lesson of the Yale seminar is how Afro-American canon formation opens up a moment in the contentious debate over American cultural history in which it becomes possible to think culture differently, if at all. The particular case for thinking differently presented in this book is the literary trace of the hybrid African-Arabic culture that came to the Americas with enslaved Africans. The earliest known record of this trace is from the first half of the eighteenth century (1731). Recognizing this trace as an aspect of American cultural history, however, means engaging the 1977 Yale seminar.

I

Undoubtedly, the twenty-nine scholars from select universities and colleges in the northeastern and Atlantic states who gathered together in New Haven in June 1977 were acutely aware of the potential of the moment. As a seminar explicitly devoted to matters of literary theory and pedagogy that was hosted, and for the most part organized, at Yale, it fell under the shadows of two important academic movements in the United States: Afro-American studies on the one hand, and what has since become known as the poststructuralist theory boom of literary criticism on the other.

The theoretical stakes are readily discernible in the intellectual agenda expressed in the seminar's proceedings, published by the Modern Language Association in 1979 as *Afro-American Literature: The Reconstruction of Instruction.*[2] In his Introduction to the proceedings, the seminar's principal organizer and director, Robert Stepto, Jr., states that the seminar's objective was to yield a literary understanding of Afro-American literature in order to reconstruct its modes of instruction. That aim was to be in tandem with Geoffrey Hartman's pursuit of a literary criticism highly attentive to the problematics of methodology entailed in reading as an institutional praxis.[3]

Such a theory-centered project was well in line with the intellectual agenda that had emerged out of the International Colloquium on

Critical Languages and the Sciences of Man, held at Johns Hopkins eleven years earlier in October 1966. The colloquium's significance as the instantiation of "theory's" intervention into the North American conflict over the humanities is well enough known, as is the particular role that Jacques Derrida's colloquium paper played in that intervention. I will not rehearse the details of either here, except to remark how the title of Derrida's paper, "La structure, le signe et le jeu dans le discours des sciences humaines" ("Structure, Sign, and Play in the Discourse of the Human Sciences"), underscores the historic significance of the intervention's taking place when and where it did.

It was at Johns Hopkins in 1876, after all, that Daniel Coit Gilman established the institutional model for the humanities in the North American research university according to Wilhelm Dilthey's concept of *Geisteswissenschaften* (the human sciences), in which difference in methodology is the basis for the classification of knowledge. Perhaps it would be more accurate to state that at the moment of Derrida's intervention, Johns Hopkins, in its division of intellectual labor into disciplines of science and disciplines of liberal arts, arranged the latter more in accordance with Ernst Cassirer's application of Erich Rickert's *Kulturwissenschaften* (cultural sciences), which supplements classification by method with classification by subject matter. *Kulturwissenschaften* was well suited for the ascendancy of abstract formalism in the human sciences: the legitimation of a formalist methodology is its own capacity to represent its object field as the effect of its activity. And there was no better institutional site than Johns Hopkins to mark the instantiation of structuralism as an authoritative methodology in the United States. Derrida's paper ironically undermined this supplementation of Dilthey, and so too structuralism, by foregrounding the question of the historical nature of methodology, that is, the historicity of all intellectual work.

It was the inescapability of this very question about the historical nature of methodology that defined the theoretical project of the 1977 Yale seminar on Afro-American literary theory. Although Johns Hopkins may have been the site of a particular, one might say monumental, formulation of the question, it found even more elaborate articulations in numerous other institutions. By 1977, Yale figured prominently among those institutions as a hotbed of poststructuralist theory, a reputation due in large measure to the presence on its campus of Geoffrey Hartman, Harold Bloom, Paul de Man, and J. Hillis Miller.

Not only was a great deal at stake theoretically in the Yale seminar's proposing an Afro-American literary theory and history, but there were considerable political stakes as well, with respect to the academic status of Afro-American studies. The institutional politics of Afro-American studies subtending the 1977 seminar involved the seminar's sponsorship by the Yale Afro-American Studies Program, whose own institutional history stretched back to the tumultuous spring of 1968 when Yale held an extraordinarily ambitious symposium called *Black Studies in the University*. The extraordinariness of *Black Studies in the University* was made plain when the provost of Yale, Charles Taylor, Jr., opened the symposium by acknowledging the authority of the imperative that the university "must do justice . . . to the black man's share of American history, American politics, economics, and art."[4]

That imperative had been directed at Yale by the Black Student Alliance (BSA). To be sure, such an imperative in and of itself could no longer be regarded as truly extraordinary. Other universities, such as Columbia, Morgan State, San Francisco State, Howard, and Harvard, had already been recent scenes of student demonstrations and similar demands for a more relevant instrumental curriculum. What made the Black Student Alliance's imperative unique was its situating the problem of Black studies within the institutional context of the university. The BSA organized and successfully solicited financial and intellectual sponsorship for an academic symposium, gathering together university scholars, administrators, and students, as well as community activists and a grant-giving foundation (the Ford Foundation). The symposium, in its organization and the intellectual rigor of the papers read at it, was to serve as ample demonstration of the academic validity of Black studies. In the words of Armstead L. Robinson of the Black Student Alliance, responding to the repeated comments of surprise from Yale faculty about the "scholarly weight" of this symposium on Black studies organized by a group of Black students: "Our achievement is remarkable, among other reasons, because it proves that students can do this type of work."[5]

It also proved, to Yale at least, that the inclusion of Black studies in the university was not merely a bowing to external political pressure, but entailed recognizing substantial authentic scholarship. The symposium's success in convincing Yale of this was primarily due to the conceptual framework in which Black studies was situated, a framework that the university and the BSA could agree upon: intellectual rigor and

scholarly authenticity. The key question to be pondered by the symposium was, as Taylor put it, "What is the intellectual significance of focusing a part of our curriculum consciously and directly on the black
experience?" With Taylor's public acceptance of the authority of the
Black Student Alliance's imperative, Yale demonstrated that the problem of Black studies could be effectively addressed by the university in
properly academic terms.

In this same vein, both Taylor and Robinson concurred that the university as a social institution is responsible for the development and
transmission of knowledge. Where they differed (a difference implicit
in the very question of intellectual significance and rigor) was about the
nature of that knowledge. For Taylor it was the knowledge on which
understanding depends. For Robinson it was the knowledge of historical difference in understanding, a knowledge on which just action
depends. Taylor's knowledge-dependent understanding recalls Dilthey's distinctive cognitive process (*Das Verstehen*), which is based on
the deciphering of physical expressions (*Ausdruck*): the physical manifestation of Spirit (*Geist*) as the *ideology* of "culture," its mental content,
not in the narrow sense of psychology, but as the "cultural world."
Robinson's dispute with this notion of understanding concerned its
assumption that the activity of deciphering expressions is itself culturally neutral and apolitical.

Taylor's and Robinson's difference over the nature of legitimate
knowledge echoes what has remained the fundamental contention
between universities like Yale and the oppositional constituencies like
the Black Student Alliance, which emerged in the universities after the
Second World War. This is the continuing dispute over the function and
configuration of cultural studies, which finally is a dispute about what
culture is. The symposium participant who drew attention to this dispute was McGeorge Bundy, then president of the Ford Foundation and
the former dean of Harvard's Faculty of Arts and Sciences. Bundy pointed out that the question of including Black studies in the general curriculum entails an unavoidable challenge to the enshrined notion that
the delineation of academic disciplines results wholly from a rigorous
methodological "understanding."

Bundy's way of putting the issue vividly exposes the stakes
involved. He begins by recognizing the symposium at Yale as an expression itself, legible in terms of an established institutional grammar for
defining instituting moments. Yale's financial as well as its institutional

support to the public posing of the question, Is Black studies a valid academic subject?, is a pronounced indication that it already has been accepted that it is. The crucial question before the symposium, then, was not whether there was a subject, but to what purpose was there a subject? The question of purpose enables a distinction between the political view of historical events, "what one has as an explicit point of view for the purpose of achieving a given political result," and the historical view of events, "the way one goes about the assessment and analysis of evidence." Bundy deploys this distinction in order to make the case that the university's historical obligation to knowledge is not political but historical (*Black Studies in the University* 173). That is to say, the legitimate grounds for instituting a scholarly field is the fact that the object field of study (in this case the Black experience) is valid in itself because it is a great part of the experience of mankind, and not the fact that the studies serve as a means for providing "a sense of purpose, identity, and direction" (173). In fact, when a field is instituted on the validity of its objective historical status, ipso facto, studying it provides a means for acquiring purpose and identity. The legitimacy of an academic field is determined by the nature of its subject matter, and in Bundy's assessment of the Black studies case, the subject matter is "the History of Thought" (*Geistesgeschichte*). This is not meant in the humanist sense of a foundational body of classical works. On the contrary, Bundy is careful to point out that he is talking about the specific historical objectification of the Black cultural experience, as well as its ideology. If there is any humanism entailed in Bundy's cultural anthropology, it is the German Romantics' *Humanität*, as opposed to the Renaissance ideal, *humanitas*, which Timothy Dwight so vigorously enforced during his tenure as president of Yale (1795-1817).[6] Although Bundy does not discuss the Romantics' investment in *Humanität* in these terms, his comments directed at Karenga's call for a politically grounded Black studies make it quite clear that what is at stake is the integrity of knowledge's organization according to a profound commitment to the History of Thought, and to culture in that sense.

This is not to suggest that in his view of culture Bundy is a New Humanist in the vein of Irving Babbitt, Norman Forester, Paul Elmer More, and John Sherman, reacting against the scientifically oriented philosophies of culture. The History of Thought for Bundy is a liberating project whose range extends far beyond the narrow historical restrictions of Western culture. Yet, in his argument that Black studies

are valid because they are "a great part of the experience of mankind," there is an implicit hypostatizing of culture as a universal concept, so that the specificity of Black expression can be read as converging with the expressions of other specific cultures at a conceptual plane superseding their historical specificity. That specificity is not lost but is subsumed under the totalizing work of Dilthey's human sciences. Bundy does not deny the political nature of Black studies, but rather he insists that the task of the scholar is to approach any cultural studies with the appropriate methodological rigor. His hypostatization of culture occasions the privileging of the interpretative moment and the abstraction of that moment from its own institutional and political conditions. This is not cynicism. Bundy's aim is to shift registers in the debate about Black studies. The Black experience in the Western Hemisphere is unquesionably a valid object for scholarship as a historical cultural expression; this argument has been won. What remains is to realize its scholarship in properly academic terms of field. It is in the question of the properly academic that Bundy finds the political aspect of knowledge, and that is the question of determining the legitimate ground for delineating disciplines.

Accordingly, the very event of the Yale symposium opened a Pandora's box with far-reaching consequences. With insight into the obvious, Bundy remarked: "There will be more acts like this, and it is certain . . . that these studies begun here will be imitated or matched elsewhere" (174). Seemingly in validation of this assessment that the favorable results of the symposium were a foregone conclusion, Yale College faculty authorized the establishment of the Afro-American Studies Program on 12 December 1968. Bundy's certainty about the Yale symposium's institutional significance was based on an understanding of how knowledge is appropriated and circulated within the university economy and of Yale's prominence in that economy. This is why he could claim Yale's symposium as the beginning of the politics of the question of knowledge.

What the Yale Black Student Alliance did in 1968 was open the box on mostly latent and only occasionally exposed differences in the university between the attitude that holds "politics" and "learning" to be wholly separate, and that which knows them to be in an uneasy symbiosis. The fact that the latter view must be learned through the work of administering the university underscores Bundy's reading of the university as a cultural expression. In this regard, he charges the emergent

Afro-American Studies Program with the politics of demystifying the ideology of culture invested in the university. In other words, the legitimate grounds for Afro-American studies should be the very politics of social responsibility that Taylor and Robinson held in common, which recognizes the university as a participatory institution of civil society. Bundy obviously knew when as well as where he was. In 1968 Yale was setting a trend for the university: the appropriating professionalization of cultural studies.[7]

By the summer of 1977, the danger of overt professionalism's appropriation of the political agenda of Afro-American studies was great enough, specifically in the field of literary studies, to precipitate an intervention, which took the form of the Yale seminar. A summary glance at the status of Afro-American literary studies—even at institutions like Yale and Harvard where there were strong emerging programs and departments of Afro-American studies—prompted Stepto, in another 1979 publication, to echo the principal concern that had led to the Yale seminar's conception and execution:

> [There is] a . . . premise [which] argues that Afro-American literary history chronicles the incorporation—but not the integration—of an aberrant literature into the literature of mainstream American (or more broadly, Western) culture. Among the implications of this premise is the idea that once a literature shifts its point of reference from the environs of a subculture (Afro-American) to that of a dominant culture (American), the literature itself develops in sophistication, from pre-form (slave narrative, for example) to form (autobiography, etc.). Such a view of Afro-American literary history often occasions the abandonment of Afro-American historiography in favor of what may turn out to be a rather peculiar and essentially synchronic view of American letters as an unwieldy whole.[8]

This was not a critique of the concept of literary history per se, as much as it was a complaint about the pedagogical practices which resulted from the historicism so prevalent in postformalist (i.e., post–New Critics) American literary history. Such a complaint focused attention somewhat on a specific academic problem: can Afro-American letters be subsumed under the Romantic notion of literature that has always been the determinate notion in the U.S. university, without undermining the aesthetic categories informing that notion?

At first glance, this is not even a very interesting question, let alone a radical provocation to thought. And that assessment could hold, were it just a question of whether or not select works of Afro-American writing

could fit under the category of literature. After all, the instances of Ralph Ellison's, Toni Morrison's, and Zora Neale Hurston's works being accepted as examples of "literature" are apparent indications that inclusion is facile enough. It merely requires an extending of the literary circle, not a rethinking of the concept of literature itself. Of course, first glances tend to be superficial, and the particular fashion in which these three writers' works have been included—they are emphatically qualified as examples of specifically good "black" and "black women's" literature—exposes a structural tension that makes inclusion appear anything but facile. Arguably these qualifications mark the historicity of production specific to these works in a way that accords with Stepto's challenge to the premise of incorporation. Yet in that marking they also tell another history, one which designates the field in which their specificity is inscribed: the institution of Romantic philology as the basis for the study of modern language literatures in the United States. More pointedly, they tell a story about the unfulfilled agenda of American literary studies, the attempt initiated by Vernon Louis Parrington, influenced by Hippolyte Taine, to ground a national identity in a literary historiography of culture.[9] This agenda became crucial to the instituting of American studies at the end of World War II.

Under scrutiny, then, the focal point of Stepto's dispute with incorporation is a critique of the dominant historiography's assumption of theoretical dominion. This critique calls for a twofold recognition: first of the aesthetic and historical value of Afro-American literature for American literary studies, and second that the struggle over Afro-American literary criticism is fundamentally a struggle between literary theorists of radically variant cultural and historical perspectives over the power to determine the requisite principles for describing the authoritative methodologies of literary and cultural analysis. The crucial problem subtending the agenda of the Yale seminar in 1977, as well as Stepto's critique of the incorporation premise, was the problem of how to teach and who could teach Afro-American literature in the U.S. university. Should it be integrated into the existing pedagogical modes and subsumed under the dominant categories of aesthetic production? Or should it be constituted as a discrete field of study because of the irresolvable aesthetic difference between it and general American literature?

Consider the moment at which the 1977 Yale seminar was convened, in the wake of the Black Art Movement's insistence on a radical aesthetic alterity, which threatened to result in the almost complete expulsion of

Afro-American literature from academia. Charles T. Davis of Yale had
tirelessly fought to mitigate this threat by pointing out that the conception of Afro-American literary expression advocated by Addison Gayle
and Amiri Baraka was identical to that of the Romantics and therefore
situated the movement well within the purview of Western academic
authenticity. Although Davis was not among the official participants of
the seminar, his call for a more critical theoretical engagement with
Afro-American literary expression was echoed in Henry Louis Gates,
Jr.'s abstracting workable traces of linguistic-based analyses of literature
out of the Black Art Movement's polemics of "race and superstructure"
(in particular the theories of Stephen Henderson, Houston Baker, and
Addison Gayle).[10] In so doing, Gates re-marked the terms with which
the seminar provocatively revisited the fundamental, and by now practically paralyzing, problem of Afro-American studies' authenticity in relation to the human sciences. The provocation came with the principal
proposition subtending the seminar: that the material and historical circumstances of those cultural discourses previously excluded from the
university are distinct enough from those of the institutionally sanctioned knowledge to justify a unique critical discourse and professional
practice of reading.

What Bundy anticipated in 1968 as the inevitable, but in no way
minuscule, step from the instituting of an Afro-American Studies Program at Yale to the emergence of an academic discipline, had already
moved on by 1977 into the very struggle over the preconditions for reor-
ganizing knowledge that he wanted to preempt. While the lines in this
struggle were rather acutely drawn for the 1977 seminar in terms of the
challenge Afro-American literary studies posed for the disciplines of
English and American studies, the issues at stake concerning the nature
of knowledge involved many other fields and disciplines besides. In
particular, Feminist, Chicano, and Native American studies were also
threatening the structural integrity of language and literature departments organized around the concept of national culture. Still, the emerging field of Afro-American studies has proved to be an issue central to
the general crisis of knowledge that has come to describe the field of
humanities in the North American university. What was discovered at
the 1977 Yale seminar was that this struggle is between the ideal of a
universal science of culture, Bundy's totalizing human sciences, *Geisteswissenschaften*, and what I deliberately choose to call (for reasons that
will become apparent throughout this book) a rigorous nonteleological

cultural critique. Perceiving that the overdetermined conditions for the tension between the human sciences and Afro-American studies lie in the very configuration of the university, and its history in the United States in particular, the Yale seminar participants announced the immediate issue at hand to be organizational agency—the rules of the game, as it were.[11]

For many, such an assault on the rules of the game is horrendous and lamentable, in that it leads to the corruption of the standards of knowledge that in their view have made a pluralistic civil society possible. Among those who have a great deal invested in the connection between standards of knowledge and civil society, Allan Bloom is credited with having been one of the first to identify definitively the chief culprits of this assault on the foundations of civil society. Bloom accuses nihilistic (read Nietzschean) deconstruction, also known as poststructuralism or postmodernism, and the instituting of Afro-American studies in the late 1960s. By his account Afro-American studies stands for a traumatic rupture, an explosive dissonance between the discourse of universal human momentum, progress, opportunity, and *isonomia* (equality under the law); and the political-economic discourse of commodity distribution, or class division. This rupture, or rather its exposure, whose emblem is for Bloom the frightening spring of 1968 at Columbia, constitutes the site of social dissolution.

In the spring of 1968 Bloom could only speculate on how Afro-American studies would change his beloved university and hope that this change was reversible. Still, the situation had become critical, warranting a decision: either the rupture must be corrected or its obfuscation in history must be effected. The first option, which was Bundy's call, requires a comprehensive revision of existing social relations, based on the conviction that maintaining the autonomy of educational institutions from political and economic interest is the sine qua non of legitimate cultural formation and dissemination. The second option, which is Bloom's, recognizes the rupture as a distant apocalyptic event (what happened at Columbia in the spring of 1968 revealed the future demise of humanist standards of excellence), which is then reinscribed as the primary cause for a reactionary revisionism. The problem plaguing both of these options is that, as Bundy remarked at the 1968 Yale symposium, the institutional fact of Afro-American studies keeps getting in the way. What this fact means with regard to Bloom's project of revision is that contradicting the revelation of 1968 requires something far more compli-

cated than just returning to the teaching of those cultural texts, those artifacts, which were the wellspring of *humanitas*. Insofar as Bundy's call for a more inclusive humanities presupposes the universal legitimacy of the Enlightenment privileging of Reason, it too requires something far more complicated than just progressive methodologies capable of extending the ideal of *Humanität* (humanness) to include "non-Europeans."

Appreciating how the theoretical agenda of the 1977 Yale seminar foregrounds these complexities in a way that forecloses on the concept of culture as totality requires a history of *humanitas* in North America, an account of the university as a social institution. Properly done, such an account would approach the magnitude of Hofstadter and Smith's history of American higher education. As this is far beyond the scope of my project here, I offer a brief exploratory sketch instead.

From the founding of the collegiate system in North America, beginning with Harvard in 1636 (chartered in 1650), William and Mary in 1693, and Yale in 1701, the liberal arts college has functioned as the guarantor of civil society through its regulating the collocation of the discourses of political power and knowledge. The liberal arts college was the conservator of culture in North America. In the view of Cotton Mather, without the establishment of colleges in New England, "darkness must have soon covered the land, and a gross darkness the people."[12] Because these first colleges were *studia generalis*, or resorts of scholars through which licensure was legitimated, regulation was achieved through a classical humanist curriculum of *studia humanitatis*.[13]

After the American Revolution of 1776, and the establishment of the state according to the Enlightenment principles of republican rule by law, there was concern about the inadequacy of this curriculum, as well as the overt sectarianism of the collegiate system. Provision was made for a federal, or public, education west of the Alleghenies through the Ordinance of 1787, under the Articles of Confederation. This ordinance reserved a plot of land for education in every prospective township. This same concern for making provision for public education, as a way of liberating knowledge from sectarian dogma, was expressed in the movement for the chartering of state universities. Among the chief proponents of public education were Benjamin Rush,[14] Thomas Jefferson, George Washington, and James Madison, all of whom, except Jefferson, agitated for the chartering of a national university. The aspira-

tion for a national university never came to full fruition, but there was success at the state level, principally in the Western and Southern frontier states. Georgia led the way with the chartering of the University of Georgia in 1785. In 1789 North Carolina chartered the University of North Carolina. The University of Tennessee followed in 1794, and the University of South Carolina in 1801. This flurry of university charters did not, however, mean an immediate push for curriculum reform. On the contrary, in curricular organization each of these universities looked very much like Harvard and Yale, the chief difference being that they were founded by the state and not by private religious sects.[15]

By the first three decades of the nineteenth century, however, there was sufficient desire for curricular reform to give birth to widespread student unrest, the most spectacular being the Harvard revolt of 1823. The students' principal demand was for an education that provided a functional, practical knowledge that was immediately translatable into marketable praxis (as opposed to the anachronistic Greek and Latin lessons they were required to take). In addition to the students' demand for instrumental knowledge there was agitation for curriculum reform from another quarter. The collegiate system had absorbed an influx of the first group of American professors to receive their Ph.D.s at German universities, chiefly at the University of Göttengen, where research-oriented study, along with the emerging Romantic conception of historical philology, was strong. This group of New American professors, as they were called, included George Ticknor, Edward Everett, Joseph Green Cogswell, and George Bancroft. At the same time that the students were demanding instrumental knowledge, these young professors sought to achieve the professionalization of knowledge as *Wissenschaft:* the rigorously defined methodological production of knowledge. Such professionalization was viewed as the means to achieving the complete independence of teaching (*lehrfreiheit*) and study (*lernfreiheit*) from ideological constraint.

Ticknor was perhaps most notable among the group of New American professors. On his appointment as the Smith Professor of French and Spanish Languages at Harvard in 1819 (the first endowed professorship in modern languages in the United States), he struggled to enact curriculum reforms aimed at realizing an American university analogous to those in Germany. Unable to solicit wide support for his reforms among Harvard's faculty and administration, he was allowed to organize his professorship along whatever lines he saw fit. This he did,

preparing two separate courses of lectures in French and Spanish literatures. But after sixteen years of protracted agitation for change, Ticknor resigned his chair in 1835.

Throughout his efforts at Harvard, Ticknor's conception of the university found reinforcement in his friend and colleague Thomas Jefferson, as well as a connection with the idea of the instrumentality of knowledge. Jefferson, who had been campaigning for some system of public education in Virginia since 1779, finally succeeded in convincing the state to charter the University of Virginia in 1824. Conceived along the same lines of curricular reform proposed by Ticknor at Harvard, the University opened in 1825 and reflected Ticknor's and Jefferson's conception of the modern university in its structure of eight professorships, or schools, including modern languages ("French, Spanish, Italian, German and the English language in its Anglo-Saxon form"), as well as modern history and geography.[16]

If Ticknor's efforts at Harvard and Jefferson's University of Virginia exemplified the struggles for *Wissenschaft* and instrumental knowledge in the U.S. universities and colleges, the exemplary expression of reactionary resistance to both these drives was Jeremiah Day's 1828 Yale Report. In the view of the Report, both professionalization in scholarship and instrumental knowledge were subversive of the traditional objectives of liberal arts education in precisely the same way. Both meant a trivialization, if not outright abandonment, of classical humanities studies, and so amounted to the corruption of the nation's moral fiber through the subversion of its connection to the history of ethical and aesthetic values (embodied in the humanist canon of Greek and Latin literary works) on which civility in its fullest sense depends. Day's Report rather successfully defended the liberal arts curriculum against these dangerous tendencies as that which provides "the *discipline* and the *furniture* of the mind,"[17] but this defense of the classical humanities curriculum did not have lasting influence.

There was an effective response to the Yale Report by October 1830 in New York City at the Convention of Literary and Scientific Gentlemen, which laid the foundations for the short-lived University of the City of New York. By 1839 Day's own Yale had allowed English into its liberal arts curriculum, prompting him to remark: "It might soon be necessary to appoint an instructor in whittling." In 1850, Benjamin Silliman helped establish the Sheffield Scientific School at Yale, and Francis Wayland led Brown University to modify its curriculum, introducing

new subjects and a limited elective program. Between 1852 and 1863, the University of Michigan began to move concretely toward a full-fledged university system under Henry Tappan. Influenced by Tappan's work at Michigan, Andrew White used the Prussian institutions of Berlin and Göttingen as his models in the organization of Cornell University, which was chartered by Ezra Cornell in 1865 under the first Morrill Land-Grant Act of 1862 (which provided every state establishing an agricultural college with 30,000 acres of public land per member in Congress). These movements toward academic professionalization and instrumental knowledge reached their culmination with the incorporation of Johns Hopkins University in 1870, or, more precisely, with the appointment of Daniel Coit Gilman as its president in 1876. Gilman made Johns Hopkins a model research institution where the human and physical sciences (*Naturwissenschaften*) flourished as disciplined methodologies.

While the Morrill land-grant universities posed a threat to the hegemony of the collegiate liberal arts college in education, they also provided it with considerable relief from the encroaching marketplace. With a deliberate eye toward instrumental education, universities like Wisconsin, Minnesota, Michigan, California, Cornell, and Johns Hopkins became the new sites of marketable technical knowledge, leaving the liberal arts colleges to pursue classical humanities studies. Eventually even the colleges were compelled to respond to market forces, with particular institutions, like Yale, Harvard, Amherst, Rutgers, William and Mary, and Princeton, becoming research universities with graduate programs. Those liberal arts colleges whose curriculum reforms were constrained to the inclusion of modern language and literatures, history, and technical subjects became effectively the Lower Faculties of the private and public universities, providing the preparatory studies needed for the more advanced professional training only to be gotten at the universities.

By the end of the Civil War, the historical mission of the collegiate system, the conservation and dissemination of classical ethical judgment and aesthetic discrimination, had either been displaced by that of research and knowledge production, or had become little more than undergraduate education. The liberal arts colleges' losing hegemony over the apparatus and organization of knowledge, was coterminous with the autonomy of the humanities (*studia humanitatis*) from the general economy of the marketplace, as the privileged sphere of intellectual activity. Studying humanities in the liberal arts colleges was the luxury

of those who were not compelled to train themselves for the market-place.

It may indeed be ironic that at precisely that moment when the humanities were no longer required to respond to the demand for relevance, studies in modern languages and literatures achieved in the liberal arts colleges what had been sought at the beginning of the nineteenth century: curricular reform grounded in philological methodology. By the time David Star Jordan initiated the country's first degree in English language and literature at Indiana University in 1885, the study of modern literature and languages had already become devalued in market terms as surplus knowledge, taking a backseat to history, business, and the quantitative social sciences.

This is not to suggest that the general devaluing of humanities in the marketplace was tantamount to a loss of cultural value. On the contrary, it signals an even sharper distinction between the inherent worth of ideas (as products of intense intellectual activity) and the exchange value of instrumental knowledge. Accordingly, the humanities' value as culture is in its capacity to resist, or transcend fluctuating political and economic structures. That is to say that in the research university, organized according to the methodological division of labor, culture could no longer be construed as the accumulated knowledge of the human experience contained in an ideal body of classical works. Instead it is taken to be the variegated expression of the complexities of human experience, where that experience is thought of as constituting a totality, through time, and culture as the History of Thought (*Geistesgeschichte*) is best understood through rigorous methodological assessment, i.e., through *Geisteswissenschaften*.[18]

With the redividing of intellectual labor between the university and the liberal arts college, the social function of liberal arts education became conservative *mimesis* (masterful reproduction of the sanctioned expressive forms of high culture) and *oikonomia* (careful stewardship of high culture as a whole). The social function of the university was *techné* (the production of instrumental knowledge). In accordance with the humanities' distinction between *mimesis*, *oikonomia*, and *techné*, the division of labor between the master, steward, and technician of the house has to be represented in the division of social classes. This view was reflected subsequently in the New Humanists' assessment of the distinction between university and college education: "the state schools could train America's body—fertilizer and railroad men—while the Eastern

schools saved its soul."[19] The greatest crisis for the liberal arts occurs when both *mimesis* and *oikonomia* become subordinate to *techné*.

As a social institution, then, the university in the United States remains true to its institutional genealogy, being, like the colleges before it, the guarantor of civil society through its regulating the collocation of the discourses of political power and knowledge. Rather than dissolving with the ascendance of the research university over the liberal arts college, this function of regulation becomes the professionalization of the human sciences: the turning of ardent methodological study into culture as bureaucracy. This is indeed the point at which Gilman's Johns Hopkins emerges. It is also the point where Bundy's version of the story ends, with the recognition of professionalism of *Geisteswissenschaften* as a constitutive activity of the university, and as the hallmark of serious intellectual work in culture.

Undeniably, the history of the university in the United States which I have told so far, because of its narrative character (i.e., the sequential order in which I have portrayed events), falls within the mode of the very history it tells. That is, the story's central issue, the contradictory pull within the American university between the competing ideas of "useless" and "productive" intellectual work, is also its narrative framework. Where it falls within the confines of its own central issue is in the view that the collaboration of Afro-American studies with theory somehow enables the delineation of the distinctive, the culturally specific aspects of Afro-American literature and culture.[20] This view seeks the legitimation of Afro-American studies in terms of its having an inherent "worth" as cultural knowledge. As long as the approach to Afro-American studies is predicated on a response to the demand for a demonstration of either its instrumental value or cultural worth, Afro-American studies will remain firmly within "Western" modernity's organizational model of knowledge.

It was in the context of trying to see beyond this organizational model of knowledge that the twenty-nine gathered at Yale in 1977. What issued from this gathering was an imperative for some kind of theoretical rigor in the handling of Afro-American literature. That imperative became the basis for an intellectual as well as an institutional agenda, a school of thought about Afro-American literary history and theory which extended well beyond the geographic limits of the Yale campus in New Haven and the two-week time span in June 1977—so much so that

much of the subsequent theoretical writing in Afro-American literary studies can be said to share a certain affiliation with the Yale school of Afro-American literary theory.

The defining concerns of the Yale school agenda are presented in the eleven papers of the published proceedings, *Afro-American Literature: The Reconstruction of Instruction*. Seven of the eleven are theoretical interventions of a sort (three of them close readings of Frederick Douglass's 1845 slave narrative): three are by Gates, two by Stepto, one by Sherely Williams, and one by Robert O'Meally.[21] Among these seven interventions, Gates's and Stepto's readings of Douglass's slave narrative stand out; they are in the only section of the book that bears explicit reference to theory (its title is *Theory in Practice*). Concluding the introduction to this section, Dexter Fisher, Stepto's co-editor, remarks that if, as Gates claims, "' 'a literary text is a linguistic event,' it is this 'theory' that is put into 'practice' in the essays on Douglass."[22] The question is whether or not this theory extends the boundaries of the humanities far enough to enable a different thinking about culture.

There is significant variance in methodological approach between Stepto's and Gates's readings of Douglass's 1845 slave narrative. Stepto grounds his reading in Northrop Frye's concept of generative mythology, placing him far closer to the formalism of New Criticism than to the poststructuralist problematizing of master narratives that plays so vibrantly in Gates's reading. Yet, despite this difference in methodology, both their readings are exemplary of three central ideas that issued out of the Yale school of Afro-American literary theory. First, they are demonstrations that Afro-American literature can withstand critical scrutiny. Second, they are demonstrations that close readings of Afro-American texts yield their linguistic (and cultural) wealth. And third, they suggest that through such sustained critical reading it becomes possible to delineate an Afro-American literary history as a field of substantial scholarship, to engage in a project of canon formation. The Yale school begins that delineation of its canon with the slave narratives, maintaining that the slave narrative was the archetype for all subsequent Afro-American literary forms. To be sure, the idea that there is a particularly Afro-American literary tradition and criticism whose genesis can be found in the narrative strategies of slave narrative was not altogether new. It had already been expressed by Arna Bontemps in 1966.[23] For Bontemps, Afro-American cultural "experience" was known through its

canonical texts, which, when taken together, will to the Afro-American literary tradition what is regarded as its received *textual experience.*

The authority of this extraordinary scholar notwithstanding, the specific forms and history of the mediated Afro-American textual (discursive) experience were first explored in detail in the theoretical writings of the Yale school, which discovered in the slave narrative not only the historical emergence of Afro-American literary history, but also the history of Afro-American theorizing of experience.[24] In the texts of the slave narratives the concerns of history and theory meet. Once slave narratives have become invested with this kind of theoretical and historical importance, the question is, On what terms are the texts of slave narratives to be read, and to what extent are those terms demonstrably inevitable?

This is not a simple question. Behind the question about the critical terms by which slave narratives are to be read, there is a more fundamental historical one: What is heterogeneity? A less obscure and, in a fashion, more preemptive way of putting this question is, What is it about the organization of knowledge and its relation to social formations of power in bourgeois society that necessitates diversity's being conceptualized only in terms of hierarchy, of the supposedly empowering inclusion of the disparate periphery into the ordered center? Why is the process of that empowerment currently conceived of in terms of resistance, either the resistance of the periphery to centralist expansion, or the center to peripheral intrusion? In any event, resistance through canon formation is legitimated on the grounds of conservation, the conservation of authenticity's integrity.

Keeping to the somewhat staid terms of dialectic development in which the issue has been formulated, there are two competing perspectives. From the centralist perspective, heterology—when articulated as the fragmentary analysis of fragments, the discursively sited, and hence unstable, analysis of human discursivity—is the threatening of authentic culture by the periphery. From the perspective of the periphery, such heterology *is* authentic culture in its most mundane-cum-material expressions. Not only are the conjunctive operations of discourses of knowledge and power that so define the way in which academic fields get authenticated implicated in the academic instituting of Afro-American studies, but so is the instability entailed in the nature of academic work. That instability is discernible even in the university's function as conservator.

Within the configuration of the university, every academic field or discipline must, at minimum, delimit its object field, as well as present a body of theories pertaining to that field, in order to achieve institutional authority. Those fields that fail to delimit a unique object field or to generate theories attendant to the object of that field are regarded as being highly unstable. Unable to define a coherent methodological approach to a unique canon of texts, they cannot attract students who, trained in that methodology, assure the field's continued maintenance and growth. Such unstable fields are continually subject to institutional assault on the grounds of illegitimacy or scholarly inauthenticity, and subsequently they are always at risk of collapse, with the residue of the field becoming appropriated by other associated disciplines.

The Yale school's articulation of an emergent Afro-American literary theory can be viewed as an attempt to forestall the field's imminent collapse by not only delimiting a unique object field (an Afro-American literary canon), but also theorizing about the unique means by which its object field is delimited. In this way, the authority of Afro-American literary studies does not derive from the objects themselves, as it were (these, it is admitted, can be and are appropriated by other fields), but from specific rigorous methodology of approaching the objects, from theory. In other words, in order to become a viable academic discipline, Afro-American literary studies must define its normative object of analysis, i.e., Afro-American literature, in a specifically Afro-American way. Its institutional authority must be gained through the determination of a set of theories and methodologies, capable of recognizing in Afro-American literary expression the materialization of the uniquely Afro-American experience in the West.

In this view, the object field—i.e., the texts—has no necessary ontological status, but issues from specific historical discursive practices and aesthetics. Remarkably enough, the Yale Afro-American Studies Program that Bundy predicted would make plain just how dead Classical humanities were, went him one step further and announced the closure of the *Geisteswissenschaften* which he so confidently proclaimed to be the hope for a new social order. In picking up Bundy's challenge to make the academic politics of field their work, the Yale school discovered that the authorization of institutional knowledge, in the form of fields, is always historical and arbitrary. Although this discovery does not lead to a total abandonment of the "work" of art, it does amount to a total abandonment of the Romantic idea of the mystique of

the "work" of art. Interjecting the slave narrative into the privileged site of literary expression achieves, in effect, a *(dis)formation* of the field of American literary history. If artistic form is invariably heterogeneous, then is not historical consciousness also heterogeneous? And, if this is so, then isn't the rug pulled from underneath the Romantic conception of literary history as reflecting the historical development of American consciousness, recognizing itself through sequential periods of expression finally culminating in totality and the closure of history?

The careful elaboration that these questions require is the principal work of the first part of this book. What is important at this moment, though, are the implications of the text's loss of ontological status. Pursued to its logical extremes, the project of canon formation undermines the grounds on which the institutional authority of the human sciences rests: the History of Thought. More precisely, what is at risk is the conception of writing as cipher, as the transparent representation of experience. Among the most enduring lessons of the Yale school, chiefly through the work of Gates, is the recognition that Afro-American slave narratives exploit this conception to the point of problematizing it, in order to achieve freedom from objectification, in order to gain the vernacular corpus.

II

While it has become almost a cliché to state that Afro-American slave narratives constitute a process of emancipation through writing, to conceive of this process as a function of linguistic indeterminacy has yet to become widely accepted. What I attempt in this book is a first move along the way toward such thinking, by focusing on the problematics of legibility which arise when attempting to read a particular, purportedly autobiographical, Arabic slave narrative. That narrative was written in the first half of the nineteenth century by one Ben Ali who was enslaved on Sapelo Island, Georgia, and it is commonly known as *Ben Ali's Diary or Meditations*. Although I argue for the inclusion of *Ben Ali's Diary* in any scholarly attempt to describe an American literary history, my aim is not to delimit a new field of literary study that could be called "Afro-Arab-American" or to fix a new definition of "the literary." Instead, I attempt to describe how a nonrepresentational concept of literariness is involved in Ben Ali's text, so that a different sort of literacy is at stake in it than that which preoccupied the Yale school.

At first glance, the Ben Ali manuscript presents a particular problem of reading for no other reason than that it is linguistically foreign for all scholars of American cultural history except those who are at least literate in Arabic. Yet not even that literacy assures the manuscript's easy accessibility because of the predominance of its heterography. Those irregular spellings demonstrate no rule of thumb, no readily discernible pattern of representation, and even the literate Arab or Arabist finds the manuscript a somewhat daunting case of linguistic indeterminacy. This indeterminacy, however, is not sufficient cause for not reading *Ben Ali's Diary* as an augmentation of Afro-American canon formation.

Ben Ali's Diary may be the longest Arabic slave narrative known to exist in North America, but it is not the only or the most famous one. It would be somewhat naive to assume that the mere "rediscovery" of this or any other New World Arabic slave narrative would necessarily occasion a reassessment of the problems of linguistic variance and opacity, or signal the emergence of new possibilities in the conceptualization of the hybridity of the purported Afro-American literary canon. In point of fact, neither has occurred. So far, what has been rediscovered has also been recovered in the name of coherent continuity.

In 1984, Allan Austin in his *African Muslims in Antebellum America* sought to introduce some of these Arabic texts to the academic field of American studies. One year later, in *The Slave's Narrative*, Henry Louis Gates, Jr., situated the New World Arabic slave narrative within the field of Afro-American canon formation by beginning his documentation of the chronological development of slave narratives with an anonymous review of Thomas Bluett's *Memoirs of the Life of Job the Son of Solomon* (Ayyūb ibn Suleimān), which appeared as an advertisement in *Gentleman's Magazine* in 1750.[25] In these *Memoirs* Bluett recounts Ayyūb's story of his upbringing as a prince in Bundu, a Fulani-dominated emirate neighboring Futa Toro; his involvement in wars and slavery; his own capture and enslavement near the Senegalese coast while returning to Bundu, having himself just sold slaves to the English; his enslavement in Maryland in 1730-31; and his subsequent struggle to freedom in England. The focal point of Gates's interest in the *Memoirs* is its account of how Ayyūb eventually acquired his manumission through demonstrating literacy in Arabic by writing a letter to his father while in Maryland. In *Figures in Black* (1987), Gates identifies Ayyūb ibn Suleimān's 1731 Arabic epistle to his father as the first successful attempt of an African slave in the West to write himself free.

Others besides Austin and Gates have attempted to categorize and include these Arabic texts according to one or another of the prevalent concepts of American literary history. Two historians are notable: Foster Grant, who recounts Ayyūb ibn Suleimān's enslavement in Maryland and subsequent struggle to freedom in England in his *Fortunate Slave*, and Terry Alford, whose *Prince among Slaves* is an account of the famous 'Abd-ur-Raḥmān of Futa Djallon who was enslaved in Mississippi.

In *Fortunate Slave*, Grant tries to appropriate the significance of Ayyūb's literacy to humanist interests. Yet, from this humanist perspective he cannot quite come to terms with an indigenous African slave economy. He must somehow define Ayyūb's own participation in the slaving economy of Bundu as an aberration, and attribute it to what he perceives as an external influence: Islam. In Grant's account, Islam is the intractable order of the Other that will not stay put in either time or place. It is the same everywhere at every time, a monolithic force of destruction. Using the same currency of humanist ambivalence toward Islam, Alford represents Islam as a marginal social phenomenon in West Africa, occurring chiefly among the aristocracy. Consequently, 'Abd-ur-Raḥmān's literary outpouring is portrayed in terms of aristocratic nobility and tragic fall. Alford has forgotten the popular rural basis of Islam in Futa Djallon during the eighteenth and nineteenth centuries. Such a popular Islamization did not support court schools, but established popular centers of learning, such as Timbo. By the beginning of the nineteenth century, 60 percent of the population in Futa Djallon and Bundu was literate in Arabic.[26]

Nonetheless, as a result of the attempts made by Grant, Alford, Austin, and Gates to radically translate these Arabic texts into the canon of English-language New World slave narratives as rarities, their inclusion in that canon has marked the degree to which American cultural history is in fact a multilinear and multifilial affair. Including *Ben Ali's Diary* in the canon of New World slave narratives occasions an interpolation that destabilizes the very concept of canon as consisting of a set of collectible literary texts, organized according to a representational theory of language. The heterography of Ben Ali's narrative also problematizes the conception of orthography that presupposes a necessary relationship between grapheme and phoneme, or at least a parallel structuring that is sublated by thought's hierarchical relationship to material expression (whether oral or literal). It is my contention, more-

over, that when a manuscript like Ben Ali's Arabic diary is deemed autobiographical it challenges the conception of a unilinear Western History of Thought in an even more radical way than that of the Yale school. As an illegible autobiographical diary, Ben Ali's writing gestures the literariness of being that discombobulates the foundational claims of both literacy and being. Instead of bringing emancipation through literacy's intervention into being, Ben Ali's slave narrative brings forth signs whose materiality resists abjection through Reason.

The objective, then, in focusing on *Ben Ali's Diary* as a specific case of narrative indeterminacy in African-Arabic American slave narratives is to provoke a different thinking about the supposedly peripheral status in modernity of what must now be referred to as the African American.[27] If the Ben Ali manuscript is to be recognized as an emancipating intervention into the territory of modernity, then this emancipation is achieved in a manner incomprehensible for the framing of what is supposed to be modernity's privileged discursive mode: subjectively grounded narrative writing. Consequently, attempting to read Ben Ali's Arabic slave narrative prompts a study of the conditions of knowledge determining the field of modernity, and within that field a specific order of cultural studies (*Kulturwissenschaften*).

The thesis that I develop throughout this study is that Ben Ali's narrative occasions the generation of paralogisms that, although anticipated by both the most theoretical History of Thought (Kant's) and the most ambitious History of Thought (Hegel's), are incomprehensible enough to preempt any gesture at systemic totality. Something Kant, perhaps, appreciated better than Hegel.[28]

I have divided this work into two parts. Part I consists of three chapters, which function as expositions of the conditions of knowledge determining such cultural studies as African American studies. Chapter 2 begins by discussing the methodological qua political stakes involved in the inclusion of African American literary studies as an autonomous field within the American university, and then probes the ideological investments in the correlation of writing, experience, and literary history as an inevitable consequence of the Yale school's project of canon formation. In the service of that project, the work of the Yale school exploits the slave narrative's capacity for producing a heuristic effect. The institutional construction of slave narratives as an authentic field of knowledge betrays not only the arbitrary nature of knowledge's institutionalization, but also the problematic nature of knowledge as either an

objective field of inquiry or a subjective activity of reflection. Gates in particular, in insisting on reading the slave narrative as a direct response to Kant's understanding of "the Negro," challenges the idea that the crisis of the humanities in the university—resulting from the failure of modernity to attain its ends—can be addressed by a return to Kant's aesthetics. Tacitly accepting de Man's assessment that the current crisis in theory results from the Kantians' (particularly Schiller's) misreading of the *Critique of Judgment*, Gates carries us, by way of Ralph Ellison, to a mode of thinking art very much in line with Schelling's.

Schelling's *Philosophy of Art* is an extension of the critical field of aesthetics opened up by Kant's *Critique of Judgment*. Schelling concurred with Kant's project of setting aesthetics firmly within the parameters of critical inquiry on the basis of knowledge divorced from the aggregate of art objects, but he differed from Kant with regard to the radical separation of the phenomenal and the noumenal. For Kant, aesthetic judgment is not subsumable under a concept of Understanding, and so cannot be objectively validated or realized. It is discursivity at work, entailing the purely formal operativity of thought (apperception). Exceeding Kant's restriction of philosophical inquiry to discursive matters (i.e., delimiting what can be spoken about with absolute conviction), Schelling sought instead to describe everything absolutely. For Schelling, the Absolute (Ideal) appears within things in the world. Hence his insistence that there are degrees of the empirical in aesthetic judgment, that the Real and Ideal are synthesized in art. Beauty is defined as the "concept perceived in concreto."

In contrast to Kant, Schelling's view of art as the absolute's realization required him to develop an attendant concept of discursivity as a universal history of progression, in order to account for disparity and change in the form of art. Along these lines, Schelling, like Hegel, insisted on the essential propriety of art's being studied by philosophy. Yet Schelling's concept of art is not, like Hegel's, built around the logic of dialectic progression, according to which art moves through time and space toward the ultimate *telos* of the Absolute Spirit's emergence, which achieves the closure or end of art itself. Instead, Schelling identifies art with the emergence of the Absolute Spirit; only art can represent materially the synthesis (*Indifferenz*) of knowledge and action, of that which is known in thought and that which constitutes form in expression. Philosophy's concern with art is with the necessary phenomenal expression of the Absolute, emanating directly from the Absolute.

The soundness of the philosophy of Art, in the abstract, stems from art's, in the concrete particular, entailing the Ideal. Hence, the methodological study or science of Art first of all means the historical construction of art in all its particular material forms. The philosophy of Art cannot be merely reflection on the abstraction of form in thought. It must also reflect on the material history of formal development, tracing in the history of form the History of Thought.[29]

Albeit in less absolute terms, the same correlation of the histories of form and thought operates in Gates's grounding his reading of slave narratives as "the attempt of blacks to *write themselves into being*" on the correlation of language-use and presence (*The Slave's Narrative* xxiii; emphasis in the original). On these same grounds the Yale school's project of African American canon formation entails a disciplined activity of reading specific historical linguistic traces, the historiography of African American literary expression, in order to find in them a history of African American thought.

Chapter 3 takes up this activity within the framework of Gates's assertion that tracing the formal development of slave narratives will reveal the *literary* history of African Americans' coming into being. This assertion functions as a critique of Western modernity's association of literacy and self-reflective cognition. Insofar as that cognition is the linchpin of civil society, Gates's assertion extends into a critique of the legitimating discourses of bourgeois social order: epistemology and anthropology (particularly ethnography) together constitute the authoritative historiography of thought. Reading a selection of slave narratives (those of Briton Hammon, Albert Gronniosaw, Ottobah Cugoano, and Olaudah Equiano) against this historiography, in accordance with the Yale school's project of writing a counterhistoriography, I argue that the Yale school runs the risk of slipping back into philology, a sort of phenomenology of language.

It is to the Yale school's credit that in recognizing the slave narrative's expressions as material traces of cultural history it recalls Schelling's critique of what Kant's aesthetic had become in Hegelianism. That recognition, however, fails to loosen literary expression in particular and language in general from their subservience to the History of Thought.

Chapter 4 is an exposition of how Kant's conceptualization of the Negro leads to such a release. It also explores the consequence this has for understanding linguistic referentiality. The point of departure is

Frederick Douglass's complaint in his 1845 slave narrative about the cost of knowledge. Almost reaffirming the motto ignorance is bliss, Douglass proclaims the imperative to action that his long-sought-after knowledge places on him. Douglass realized this imperative, in part, in the act of the slave narrative as an effective response to slavery that focuses thought on the relationship between experience and expression, being and writing. In doing so he defines two basic situations of indeterminate linguistic referentiality. The first entails the foregrounding of the wholly literary nature of subjective expression: where the realization of autonomous subjectivity is determined to be an effect of writing, then writing is recognized as emancipatory. The second concerns the importance of the conception of an emancipatory writing and the complex relationship between knowledge and power that emerged in modernity, achieving its greatest proportions in the Enlightenment concept of subjective freedom.

Douglass's thinking about himself as a free man in terms of the relationship between experience and expression calls attention to the connectedness of Kant's conception of the Negro and his thinking about indeterminate linguistic referentiality. Establishing that tie requires that Kant's *Critique of Pure Reason* be read in a way that is at odds with the spirit of Anglo American Kant scholarship, which resembles dogmatism in its allergy to form as merely an accidental attribute. In becoming too much a science (*Wissenschaft*) of the symbolic, as a consequence of the neo-Kantian reaction against the vulgar positivism to which Schelling's formalism leads, much of North American Kant scholarship has neglected the fact that the problem of formal lawlessness (*unrechtmäßig*) both enables and betrays Kant's architectonic. What is discovered in the movements of Kant's thinking the Negro is the indeterminacy constitutive of every narrative, an indeterminacy that is marked as paralogism and that is to be ameliorated (never negated) through its rhetoricization (its becoming the grounds for a rule of designation, or *Wortbestimmung*). Kant's thinking the Negro affords us a glimpse at the high risks involved in the notion that language can say any experience, and that any language oriented toward meaning is intentional in its description of objective meaning. For Kant, both objective consciousness and the subjective experience of this consciousness are realized only in discourse. Kant's rule of designation, therefore, is not simply subjective nominalism. It is primarily a critique of the conception of the subject as an expression of its own intentionality.

Part II consists of four chapters, each of which is an account of how specific texts exhibit the same indeterminacy of discursivity exhibited in Kant's conception of the Negro. Chapter 5 continues the exposition of the problem of paralogism in Kant, focusing this time on the *Critique of Judgment*. The pretext for this exposition is an interview given to Theodore Dwight in 1845 by Lamen Kebe, a slave in Georgia who was literate in Arabic. Kebe, also known as "Old Paul," was originally from Futa Djallon, where he was part of an African Muslim intelligentsia and had been a school administrator for some years prior to his capture. He provided Dwight with a bibliography of the texts used in higher education in Futa Djallon. That bibliography is substantial enough to provide a glimpse of the organization of Muslim knowledge in West Africa during the last half of the eighteenth century. In providing his booklist, Kebe was quite explicit about his desire to underscore the West's failure to know Africa.

Bringing attention to Africa as a problem of nescience in this way, the enslaved Kebe articulates the issue of the African's status in Western modernity as a problematic of the Enlightenment conception of subjective freedom from the phenomenal bonds of nature. This subjective freedom from nature lies at the crux of Kant's project to designate the structural possibilities of cognition. By concentrating in his *Critique of Judgment* on the purely transcendental faculties operative in aesthetic experience, disengaged from concern or interest in any particular object of aesthetic judgment, Kant could display the genealogy of cognitive agency, the discursivity of thought, as functioning in full autonomy from nature. Kebe's re-marking the historical limitations of that agency before Africa offers an insight into how Kant's discovery of the irresolvable indeterminacy of discursivity preempts any successful theoretical comprehension.

This is where *Ben Ali's Diary* comes in. When the objective of theory is to achieve a model of reading that can give an adequate account of even those forms that its own logic cannot anticipate—an abstract logic of form, as it were—then a text like Ben Ali's poses the danger of an almost insurmountable obstacle to signification. Not because it defies reading (it does not), but precisely because it betrays the arbitrariness of any formalism, particularly one that claims to define thinking. Once the project of discovering the foundation of cognitive agency is forsaken, which is what Kant's discovery of discursivity's indeterminacy entails, then *Ben Ali's Diary* can be recognized as something else besides a virtu-

ally unreadable text, or a challenge to rethink signification along more material historical lines. It is the challenge to rethink materiality, as well as the historical.

In chapters 6, 7, and 8 I attempt to take up the challenge of the Ben Ali manuscript. Chapter 6 reviews the numerous failed attempts to decipher *Ben Ali's Diary*. The overbearing problem of the text's illegibility and Joseph Greenberg's insistence that the manuscript is not a diary have not problematized its classification as an autobiographical text. How can Ben Ali's manuscript still claim to be autobiographical, to be a diary? And if it is, what sort of story of the self is it? It has no purposiveness, no tale of subjective development, but is merely an assemblage of graphic markings, intriguing scribbles on the page that cannot be fixed to a determinate source, an abstract consciousness. In such an instance, where the assertion of subjective singularity represents a problematic of reading both historical inscription and reference, what is the basis for the very possibility of the subject's rhetorical figuration?

In order to address these questions, in chapter 7 I regard the Ben Ali manuscript as something of an analogue so as to achieve a critical translation of the major portion of the manuscript. This prompts an experimental cartography of Ben Ali's writing as graphic markings which evoke a theory of signs first articulated in the Islamic *'ilm-ul-kalām* (the science of discourse). The experiment turns on the problem of signification that writing provokes: How is it possible for a symbol to not directly represent an objective referent and thus not be configured (in a constellation of symbols) as a relay or a mediating code between modeling systems of culture and experience, yet enable the expression of meaningful messages? How can a symbol that has no referent enable the expression of meaning for messages? These questions involve the three cardinal terms of my experimental cartography: signification, representation, and referent. In offering this translation I address the relationship of translation to reading, through an exploration of the way in which the indeterminacy of narrative challenges the conception of graphic signification as the representation of thought.

Chapter 8 recognizes the Ben Ali manuscript as an index of the indeterminacy of linguistic signification that engenders interpretation and enables reading. In this sense, the institutional praxis of reading is the *periphrasis* of linguistic indeterminacy. With the Ben Ali manuscript, the periphrasis of indeterminacy becomes a moment of collaboration, if not troublesome convergence, a specific point of departure (*Hinausgriff-*

punkt) for reading slave narratives that moves toward thinking culture and cultural production as something other than either the sum total of Western thought about being, or the residual effects of an abstract "History of Thought." The aim in pursuing this question of institutional reading at the chosen site of the Yale school, the New World slave narrative, is to engage the articulated history of a specific cultural work so as to think the work of history, the subject, in a way that does not reclaim representation. In the wake of the Yale school project of Afro-American canon formation, the most compelling question of cultural studies becomes this relationship between the history of work and the work of history.

Pittsburgh, 22 November 1991

Part I

Writing Being: The Slave Narrative as the Original Text

Chapter 2

Critique of American Enlightenment
The Problem with the Writing of Culture

νυν δ' οτε παντα δεδασται.
But now when all has been allotted.
—Choerilus, *Perseis* (Rhetoric 429)

Revolution in Historiography

Henry Louis Gates, Jr., concludes his preface to *The Slave's Narrative* with the remark that "[John] Blassingame's work relates to our work in [literary] criticism, in an ideal relation of text to context" (vii). This, after already dedicating the book to Blassingame, in honor of what Gates and his collaborator, the late Charles T. Davis,[1] termed "the revolution in historiography . . . effected in [Blassingame's] *The Slave Community*."[2] To state the obvious, Gates wants to make a point in emphasizing the importance of Blassingame's work on slave narratives. Or rather, he wants to make two points. One is that since the publication of *The Slave Community* in 1972, slave narratives have become the focal point of theoretical discussions on the historiography of the antebellum South.[3] The second point is more subtly articulated and has to do with the nature of historiography, with American literary theory's relationship, in particular, to the concept of history.

Regarding the first point, when John Blassingame published *The Slave Community* in 1972 he was breaking with an American historiographical tradition, prevalent since Ulrich B. Phillips.[4] According to that tradition, slave narratives were, in the majority, heavily edited by white amanuenses, and therefore not authentic autobiographies. Even when the editorial interpolation is minimal or nonexistent, the narratives are discountable, because they are so wholly a form of deliberative discourse—abolitionist propaganda—that they are too subjective to provide an accurate account of "historical reality." Blassingame's fracture was multiple. Not only did he write a social history of the antebellum Southern slaves' collective mentality and culture, the complex symbolic economies and social institutions they constructed as Africans forced into slavery, but he based that history on the study of seventy-six Black autobiographies and memoirs, slave narratives. *The Slave Community*

was not susceptible to the argument of abolitionist editorial interpolation in that of the seventy-six Black autobiographies used in the study
fifty (66 percent) were written by manumitted slaves and had no abolitionist amanuenses.[5] In fact, in using these narratives to write *The Slave
Community* Blassingame follows a long-established historiographical
opinion, using the oldest of the three appropriate source materials of history: the written document.[6] Accordingly, he uses both literary and
official documents in writing his history, establishing the authenticity of
the seventy-six slave narratives (literary documents) by contrasting their
material with "several hundred" white planters' autobiographies, along
with official written records in the form of plantation records and agricultural journals, as well as the travel accounts of Whites considered
nonparticipants in the peculiar institution (*The Slave Community* viii).[7] In
the resulting ternary depiction of slavery—autobiographies/official
records/travelogues—autobiographies, whether Black or White, are
handled as verifiable documents of history.

The Blassingame revolution in historiography that Gates and Davis
refer to is the establishment of the slave narrative as an authentic document of history. Yet Blassingame's work was not so much a revolution
in historiography as it was an extension of its field of work. If he broke
with one particular American historiographical tradition—viz., the big-
oted refusal to look at all the evidentiary sources of slave history—he
adhered quite rigorously to another. In his "Critical Essay on Sources,"
which is appended to *The Slave Community*, Blassingame argues that if
"historians seek to provide some understanding of the past experience
of slaves, then the autobiography must be their point of departure; in
autobiography, more clearly than in any other source, we learn what
went on in the minds of black men. It gives us a window into the 'inside
half' of the slave's life" (227). He continues to recommend black autobiographies (slave narratives) as especially important sources for the
study of the historical development of the slave's personality: "There is
generally so much ego involvement in the autobiographies that they are
invaluable for studies of black self-concepts" (227). No matter that slave
narratives, or any other autobiography, are by definition testimonial,
and so deliberative. In fact, it is because it is deliberative discourse that
the narrative provides information about the psychology of the slave,
how the slave experienced reality as given. Blassingame recognizes the
shortcomings of so deliberative a discourse. Nonetheless, the "systematic analysis" of the slave narratives as source material is made possible

"by applying the rules of evidence rigidly"; their verification is possible by investigating several independent sources (literary and official). In answer to the anticipated question of the slave narratives' usefulness as source material for history—"Are they representative?"—he asserts that slave narratives

> are just as representative as other kinds of literary material. . . . Like most personal documents, the autobiography provides a window to the larger world. . . . When autobiographies are accepted both as records of the unique experiences of each individual author and as eyewitness accounts of several slave communities they are clearly representative. (230)

A far more crucial question than representation for Blassingame is reliability. The reliability of slave narratives is no greater or less than that of any other literary document. A benefit of reading slave narratives is that they shed some more light on what happened in slavery, but the principal reason for their study is that they are verifiable documentation of how the slaves experienced slavery (*The Slave Community* 229–38). The object of such reading, then, is not to discover the history of events, but to trace the historical transcription of African American experience in literature. In their reliability and representativeness slave narratives are *the* documentary history of the collective African American experience of America in slavery. When utilizing the seventy-six Black autobiographies to write the history of slavery, Blassingame does not treat these texts as transparent representations of the "historical reality" of slavery. Instead, the texts are read as the historically first transcribings of the particular African American experience of that reality, the historical beginning of recording "an authentic black voice in the text of Western letters."[8] That "record" constitutes the economy of signification through which the historical experience is transmitted. Here is the revolution in historiography that Gates and Davis refer to. *The Slave Community* breaks with the established historiography's stance in relation to the document; it has given up trying to determine whether the document in itself is telling the truth or its ultimate expressive value. In so doing it breaks away from historiography's ideology of the past, and exposes that past as ideological.[9] History may inevitably be the working of the document, the specific way in which it is constituted as a document, as a record of experience, but for Blassingame the document is no longer an inert material through which what was said, done, and experienced can be reconstituted. It is the enabling of the transcribing of experience, the

writing of African American history, which is found "in the black texts themselves," in the recurring topoi and tropes which constitute the shared modes of figuration found in the slave narratives.

This brings us to the second, more subtle point of Gates's preface, American literary theory's relationship to the concept of history. Blassingame's work on slave narratives has been attended by explorations into what theoretical model of reading is the appropriate basis for the analysis of slave narratives. Such explorations were central to the 1977 Yale seminar on African American literary theory, which effectively established a school of thought about linguistic-based theories of literary history. In any event, after 1977, almost all the prominent theories of reading slave narratives have entailed language-based structuralist or poststructuralist typologies in which the signifying value of the linguistic figure is apprehended in textual experience. In keeping with these prominent modes of analysis, any viable exploration of the slave narrative must correlate the linguistic codes and rhetorical figurations particular to the narratives, with the general problems of representing experience in linguistic expression.[10] These language-based theories of reading slave narratives presuppose the general theories of signification which have come to be known as the "literary theory boom."[11]

Still, even if African American literary theory is engaged with "literary theory" to the extent that one is not conceivable without the other,[12] its approaches to the general problems of signification have been from the premise that there is a particularly African American representation of experience operative in the slave narratives. The linguistic codes and rhetorical figurations of slave narratives operate in discernible patterns as encodings, ciphers, of the processes by which the slaves effect a realization of conscious self-reflection—and thus autonomous subjectivity—by transcribing experience in writing. It is important that the belonging-togetherness of African American literary theory and the theory boom be underscored, in order to focus attention on what is at stake in the necessity to delineate an appropriately African American literary theory: the continued integrity of the humanities as an authentic institution of knowledge. The interrelatedness of the necessities of African American theory and "theory" has some historical weight (which I addressed in chapter 1), precisely because in the final analysis it is the question of the institutional status of difference that is the overarching frame of reference for the contestation over theory which has so unsettled the university.

A variety of conceptions and methodological approaches to the issues of signification since the Yale seminar have generated equally numerous figurative taxonomies, varying in both definition of the determinate figure (metaphor as opposed to catachresis) and topoi, as well as institutional agenda. Yet, for all the differences between these methodologies, there is an agreed-upon project of historicizing the African American experience through interrogating its textual transcription. Accordingly, much that for nearly seventy years has been painstakingly gathered by scholarship under the name of African American culture—the authenticity of oral testimony, the sustaining structures of "folk" tradition, even the movements of music—in the past twenty years has begun to slip under the truncating effect of motto: "canon formation." Adhering to this motto has meant the critical writing of the history of African American culture from the slave narrative on. Because the focus of so much of the critical work on slave narrative of the past twenty years has been the delimitation of a legitimate African American critique through this writing of history, the stress has fallen on articulating theories of reading that enable the discovery of the agency driving African American historiography. Insofar as this agency is to be found in the linguistic structures of the slave narratives, it is not a first cause, but the necessity of narrative form.[13] The two members of the Yale school to have most consistently and successfully influenced theories of reading slave narratives are Robert Stepto, Jr., and Henry Louis Gates, Jr. Both Stepto and Gates have continued their efforts to delineate out of the slave narratives a literal history of African American culture.

Stepto, for example, in his 1979 book *From Behind the Veil*, strives to derive an African American historiography (which is contrapuntal to the dominant American historiography) from his rhetorical readings of slave narratives.[14] The determinate figure of this historiography is what Stepto terms the metaphor of authenticity, whose genealogy he traces in the dialectical development of "pregeneric myths" (narrative topos employed in the early slave narrative) culminating in the generic 1845 *Narrative of the Life of Frederick Douglass, an American Slave, Written by Himself*. Stepto appropriates this usage of pregeneric myth from Northrop Frye, who in *Anatomy of Criticism* talks about four narrative pregeneric elements of literature which he calls *mythoi* or generic plots.[15] As with Frye, Stepto's pregenerics are analogues of topos, functioning as the "canonical or mythic stories which delimit the *temenos* of Afro-American culture." The argument is that the determinate pregeneric

myths of the slave narratives not only existed prior to literary form, but they eventually shape the forms that comprise African American culture's literary canon (*From Behind the Veil* ix; *The Reconstruction of Instruction* 17). The first text of that canon is the slave narrative, and the primary pregeneric myth for the slave narrative is the quest for freedom and literacy. Abstracting out of the body of slave narratives the linguistic evidence of how each narrator sought to achieve literacy and through demonstrating it in writing freedom, yields the history of African American literature's formal development, and concordantly the history of its literary culture. Stepto charts four distinct phases of narration in the slave narrative: Basic Eclectic, Basic Integrated, Generic, and Authenticating Narratives.[16] Douglass's 1845 *Narrative* marks the emergence of the pregeneric myth into identifiable generic forms, i.e., autobiography (Douglass's *My Bondage, My Freedom*, 1855, and *Life and Times of Frederick Douglass*, 1881 and 1892). In this way Douglass's work spans two formal developments of African American literary history: the Generic and Authenticating Narratives.

Identifying Frederick Douglass's slave narrative as an exemplar of the authenticating slave narrative is not capricious. By locating the precise moment when African American literature emerges as a generic form in Douglass's 1845 text, Stepto makes the birth of African American literature coincide with Matthiessen's golden period of American literature, and situates his own theory of African American literary history in such a way as to effect an interpolation into the *temenos* defining authoritative American literary history. Moreover, through that interpolation Stepto designates the arbitrary basis of the dominant historiography's instituting moment by proffering the slave narrative as a rhetorical intervention into the narrative Romantic historiography of American culture, occasioned by Matthiessen's *American Renaissance*. Because that designation is very limited, exclusively African American, the interpolation proves to be quickly and easily appropriated into the very instituting processes Stepto seeks to problematize. The dilemma of this particular critique is that in order to achieve a successful intervention into American literary scholarship, it articulates the same concept of the literal writing of culture informing Romanticism, historicism: the notion that the historiography of cultural production traces the historical emergence of a specific cultural identity. Paradoxically, this liability is rooted in the key concept of Stepto's project, the metaphor of authentication. Be that as it may, the terms of this liability are rather instructive.

Granting that authentication means that African American literary history is constituted by a progressive dialectic, in which the pregeneric myth is the thesis, against (in the fullest sense of the word) which the authors in Stepto's genealogy create their literary works. Once the myth is set in motion with the slave narrative, it searches for its literary forms of expression by arrogating to its meaning particular generic properties—"notably the properties of autobiography, fiction, and to a lesser degree historiography" (*From Behind the Veil* ix). Throughout this search the myth both assumes and does not assume the properties of the genre it arrogates to itself. In the exchange between the pregeneric myth's meaning and the generic properties, the myth's formal expression is achieved in a way that neither completes its meaning nor preempts it through formal closure. As a result, the historical continuity of literary-based African American cultural studies issues from the myth's meaning never becoming identified solely with one genre. Accordingly, tracing the consequential literary forms enables the critical literary historian "to gain a clearer view of how some slave narrative types become generic narratives, and how, in turn, generic narratives—once formed, shaped, and set in motion by certain distinctly Afro-American cultural imperatives—have roots in the slave narratives" (*From Behind the Veil* 5-6). In that tracing, though, form is subordinated to meaning, which is always denotative: any generic or procreative aspects entailed in the (pre)generic myth find expression in the uncompleted dialectic of form and meaning. As a consequence, the African American literary texts, which become cultural documents, are little more than the surplus value produced in this exchange.

Nor can this superfluousness be ameliorated by a mediating metaphor of tension, say that of genius and genius loci.[17] Where the slave narrative is understood as the inception of a protracted struggle for literacy, genius figures a particularly parochial history, the African American struggle for a recognized subjective identity beyond a slave economy; genius loci is the specific articulations of that struggle. Stepto rearticulates Geoffrey Hartman's figure of genius/genius loci so that the ascending American literary criticism—particularly New and Practical Criticisms—is figured out as the genius, and his own articulation of the African American literary history is figured out as the genius loci. Delineated in the genius of the pregeneric myth, the particularly African American experience functions in the linguistic codes and rhetorical strategies of slave narratives. This could hardly be stated more clearly

than in the opening section of chapter 2 of *From Behind the Veil*, where the anomalous generic nature of Booker T. Washington's *Up From Slavery* (is it slave narrative or autobiography?) affords Stepto the occasion to debunk three theoretical premises that "have had fairly disastrous effect upon Afro-American criticism and historiography," the third of which is the premise of incorporation (see chapter 1).

Nonetheless, Stepto fails to heed the admonition that literary critics must avoid historicism.[18] In the figure genius/genius loci, he takes what he had carefully shown to be a historical development, African American literature, and recognizes it in terms of periods of formal development which unfold as the effects of a necessary and universal dialectic of progress. The outcome is the uniquely African American literary forms of expression constitutive of African American literary history. Literary history is privileged over literary chronology, because it enables a teleology: the development of historical consciousness, which develops "through the course of historical and linguistic time" (*The Reconstruction of Instruction* 2). This lapse into historicism is all the more fatal for a project one of whose stated objectives is to effect a problematizing intervention into the Romantic reading of literary history as a determinate pattern of journey. If Stepto has succeeded in demonstrating that the Romantic position is in fact in continuity with the Enlightenment, with respect to its assumption of theoretical dominion, he has done so only to the extent that he has also succeeded in demonstrating that his own project is legitimated on the same theoretical grounds. At the level of Stepto's analysis, African American historiography is virtually absent; he makes no mention of the efforts of William G. Allen (1849), V. F. Calverton (1929), or Vernon Loggins (1931) to write the history of African American literature. Nor, in all fairness, did the scope of his project require that he do so. At the level of his own methodological formulations, however, historiography, i.e., the authoritative transcription of experience as a developmental story, is what is most clearly at stake. As a result, the emergent African American literary theory is a sanctioned activity of reading that is capable of discovering and confirming laws of cultural expressions in the relations of signs.

Gates too is concerned with the academically dominant historiography of American literature with regard to slave narratives. Yet, recognizing that Stepto's metaphor of authenticity causes the slave narrative to fall fully within the dominion of American *Literaturwissenschaft*, he has African American literary historiography emerge concordantly with

African American literature, being directly overdetermined by the same primary pregeneric myth of the quest for literacy and freedom. Through this inversion of the myth's terms Gates gains an assessment of the relation between historiography and literary expression that problematizes the distinction between literary and literary theory. In that assessment both are a collection of signifying practices that constitute the texts of the literary canon on the basis of a theory of the sign. That theory is a representational doctrine of signs, where language is the labor of culture and where to delineate the economy of that signifying practice is to delineate the parameters of an African American culture through the study of its linguistic structures, its literary forms.

In keeping with this, the question of how slave narratives ought to be read cannot be answered definitively merely by even the most extensive exercise in close reading. What is required instead is a structuralist reading that approaches the narratives not only as repositories of cultural history, but also as literary texts whose marginality to the canonical texts of Western culture results from the modalities that culture has used to define itself. What is required is a way of reading narrative form historically. An early attempt at this occurs in Gates's reading of the opening paragraph in the first chapter of Douglass's 1845 *Narrative*, where he employs the structuralist model of binary opposition (Jakobson, and Lévi-Strauss) in order to reveal in the text's pattern of juxtaposing opposites a "profoundly relational type of thinking in which a strict barrier of difference or opposition forms the basis of a class [identity]" (*The Reconstruction of Instruction* 223). The principal juxtaposition of opposites is slave/horse (ignorance), which is placed in binary opposition to master/knowledge. The difference between horse and knowledge is subtended by that between nature and culture. That opposition, in turn, is carried to its logical extreme, producing oppositional modes of interpretation. Difference in interpretation ironically subverts the master's claim to total knowledge, because it dichotomizes meaning. There is no necessary connection between signifier and signified. That irony is brought to a sort of fruition in the conclusion of the second chapter in Douglass's *Narrative*, where he reflects on the difference between the slaves' and the masters' interpretations of slave music. The fruit this yields for Gates is the "first [critical] charting of the black hermeneutical circle and which we could take again as a declaration of the arbitrary relation between . . . the signifier and the signified" in its description of thought's nonverbal embodiment as a perception peculiar to "members of a specific [African

American] culture" (*The Reconstruction of Instruction* 230). Douglass's *Narrative* reveals that "not only is meaning culture-bound . . . but how we read determines what we read, in the truest sense of the hermeneutic circle" (230). The point of such an approach is to reveal those meanings of slave narratives which have been hidden or marginalized by the enforced bias of historical representation, to discern in the linguistic and rhetorical codes of slave narratives the relation of text to context, of experience to linguistic expression. As Gates puts it, "the slave narrative represents blacks' attempt to *write themselves into being*" (*The Slave's Narrative* xxiii); not as creatures, but as self-conscious subjects. This suggests that what the slaves write themselves into is *Being*, which is constituted textually; and that the history of *Being* is discernible through the exploration of formal aspects of the text, the narrative and rhetorical strategies which make it up (xxiii–xxiv). The exploration of the formal linguistic and rhetorical structures of slave narratives discovers the literary means by which African American culture developed a representation of self-reflective subjectivity as a process of translating experience.

Read in these terms, the slave narrative does indeed appear to be a "countergenre . . . set in motion by the mode of the Confession" (Gates, *The Reconstruction of Instruction* 214), the critical study of which has at least two institutional effects. First, once the repressed meanings of the narratives have been discovered, it becomes possible to track their transmission into subsequent forms of African American literary expression, thus delineating a viable field for African American theory. The second effect is that this field becomes the focal point for a literary history whose paramount achievement will be the formation of a negative canon: an African American canon which desedimentizes the logic of cultural literacy—i.e., the transparent relationship of writing to thought—subtending the institutional marginalization of African American literature in the university. The paradigm of that African American canon is the slave narrative, whose definitive characteristic is its declaring the arbitrary relation between the signifier and the signified. Whatever comes to be designated under this paradigm as the African American literary tradition must fail to function as a given; rather, it is continually recreated through acts of reading that fabricate, according to shifting methodological parameters, its genealogy of constitution.

Gates traces that genealogy through a very specific tropology of "Signifyin(g)," which serves both as his object of analysis and as the method by which he delineates the field of analysis.[19] In the course of

tracing the theoretical implications of that genealogy, he invokes the writing of the eighteenth-century African-Prussian philosopher, Antonius Gullielmus Amo, on the proper methodology of criticism and hermeneutics. Amo's views on critical method are found in his "Essay Concise and Exact on Criticism, Interpretation, Method: The Art of Disputation and Other Matters Dealt with in Logic," which was published in 1738 in addendum with his *Tractatus de arte sobrie et accurate philosophandi* (*Treatise on the Art of Philosophizing with Sobriety and Accuracy*).[20] In this essay Amo writes the following on criticism:

> Criticism is the *habitus* of the contemplative intellect, whereby we try to recognize with probability the genuine quality of a literary work by using appropriate aids and rules. In so doing, certain general and particular points must be considered. . . . In general, every critic must be a polyhistor and must know many languages. In a more special sense he must be versed in those things that are the special objects for critical contemplation. . . . It is the interpreter's task (1) to exercise due attention and (2) contemplation, (3) so that he has the argument of the theme before his eyes. . . . All the rules of contemplation must be applied. (233-34)

The significance of this quote for Gates's conception of Afro-American literary theory is found in the relationship between the two words that define criticism for Amo: *habitus* and contemplative intellect. As an addendum to the main body of his *Tractatus*, Amo's comments on criticism presuppose the definition of terms elaborated in the text. Amo was not a philosophical system builder, and his *Tractatus* is a rationalist treatise in logic that, generally speaking, follows Christian Wolff's view of logic as the art of demonstration.[21] The *dispositio* of Amo's *Tractatus* is in the scholastic manner, covering concepts (intentionality, *ens*, subjectivity, objectivity, and so on), judgments, and the syllogism. It also connects logic with ontology and contains considerable psychology, which was one of Amo's central intellectual concerns. In keeping with his Wolffian tendencies, the law of identity is the basis of all knowledge in Amo's philosophy, whose general aim is the proper derivation and application of the principles of cognition. That is to say, Amo is concerned with intentionality, which is the conscious faculty of the mind by which objects (*ens*) are determined, and, more to the point, with distinguishing between cognitive and effective intention (the former is concerned with rational objects—ideas, discourse, cognition; (the latter with phenomenal objects).

Amo defines *habitus* as an effective aspect of intention, an activity of cognition rendered nigh on reflexive by repetition. *Habitus* is a cognitive disposition of readiness toward specific activities of thinking; it is a faculty of mind. Criticism is a faculty of the contemplative intellect: *habitus mentis contemplativis.* The contemplative intellect, or contemplation, is the faculty of the mind that comes into play subsequent to perception, whether sensuous or purely rational (attention and representation, respectively, in Amo's terms). The cognitive mode of contemplating is the operation of the mind that consists of acts of ratiocination uninterruptedly connected until an adequate and determinate idea is reached. In this regard, criticism is taken to be a doing of contemplation, a term whose derivation from the Latin *contemplatio* is not altogether fortuitous. The Latin *contemplativus* is a form of the noun of action, *contemplatio,* derived from the transitive verb *contemplor,* which is a compound of the prepositional prefix *cum/con* and the verb *templor,* whose substantive is *templum.* The latter is a term of auguration, referring to a square space on earth and in the heavens that is delimited by the augur; in the interior of this space he is silent and interprets the omens. The derivation *contemplativus* is the Latin translation of the Greek *theoretikos,* which is derived from the verb *theorein,* a coalescing of *thea,* "the outward look or aspect, in which something shows itself," and *horao,* "to look at something closely, to contemplate or survey." *Thea* is the goddess related to *Alethia,* "the unconcealment from out of which and in which that which presences, presences" (this is translated as *veritas,* verity = truth). *Ora* signifies the respect, honor, and esteem we bestow. In this sense, *theorein* means "the beholding [looking] that watches over truth."

Those individual citizens of the Greek polis who were designated to act as legates on certain formal occasions—such as the Pythian games and commissions of *hierpoioi* ("those who presided at various ceremonies," like the feast of Hephaestus, sacrifices at Eleusis for the consecration of the first fruits, or the festival of Dionysus)—were as a group called *theoria,* and as individuals *theoros.* The *theoria* performed the act of seeing as official ascertainable knowledge, thereby providing the basic material, the object, for discursive activity. The *theoria,* particularly in its function as *hierpoioi,* was designated by and from the *Boule* ("the great Council of the communes of demes"). By the sixth century B.C. in the Athenian democracy, it was the *Boule* that sent to the *Ecclesia* ("the Assembly of the People") *probouleumata* ("the reported deliberations of the *Boule*"), which served as the basis for the decrees of the *Ecclesia.* A

decree always supposed a *probouleumata*, whether explicitly mentioned in the decree or not. All *probouleumata* relied on *theoria*. As to *aesthesis*, any woman, slave, or child was capable of the simple act of seeing something, yet because they were not citizens of the polis they were not legitimate viewers of the polis, ergo their "seeing" was of no factual (discursive) consequence. The authenticity of omnipotence by which the *Boule*, and consequently the *theoria*, could determine the factual was derived at last from the *nomos*.[22] In the sixth-century Athenian *Boule*, *nomos* acquired the meaning of political law, thereby displacing the *themistes* ("the supernatural principles that the *patria* [clan] gained through its king as transmitter of the divine patronage"). Hence the praxis of theory is an issue of *isonomia* ("equality of apportionment" or "equality under the law"). When the philosophers introduced the problematic of identity in the light of *isonomia*, *theorein* as legitimated *aesthesis* became distinguished from *aesthesis* ontologically. *Theorein*, then, was a praxis, but rather than being a private act of a cogitating individual, it designated a very public one.

Through the *theoria*, events became socially and democratically validated, requiring vision to submit to public judgment and argumentation in order to become a discursive property of the polis. From this moment the criteria for the validity of an argument could no longer be its content (as that is particular) but rested upon the form of the vision: the *elenchos*, "dialectic." *Theorein* was no longer necessary but rather it was calculable, and *aesthesis* had no standing. This situation was exacerbated if not initiated by the introduction of the principle of noncontradiction, "being is, not being is not," which enables ontology.

In his *de Anima*, Aristotle attributes the saying "all things are full of gods" to Thales, the first Milesian of Greek Ionia concerned with a "philosophical" account of Being in the universe, or ontology. For Thales, Being was of theology and independent from subjectivity: it was not totally apprehensible, but invisible and a mystery. To this extent we imagine that Thales's assertion that water was the origin of all being, of all phenomenal things, was the first attempt to determine the Being of being, meaning the first principle or origin of existence, the primary agency by which Being is in the world. For the pre-Socratic Greeks it was this Being that looked at man, and not man that conceptualized it. By the same token, the experiencing of phenomena, being in the world, was not a discarding of the sensation of the senses; rather, it was to be saved or collected, *legein*, in *logos*. In its verbal form, *legein* underscores

that a dynamic process was at stake in the ancient Greeks' conception of things. The collecting was a mediated understanding of the totality of Being that was achieved through the eye (seeing) and the ear (hearing), and whose object was the first principle, termed *Logos* by Heraclitus, who along with Pythagoras and Parmenides was the most influential of the Milesians on Socratic thought. Here *Logos*, as the substantive of the verb, is the abstraction of the operation of collecting, that which becomes collecting, the collecting of *tà phusikà*, nature, for which there was no question of its being conceptualized, except through the attentive form of dialectic. The legitimate activity of dialectic is to collect Being.

Refined by Plato and Aristotle, dialectic lays the basis for the determination of knowledge of truth through the liberation of the individual (subject) from the traditional hegemony of Being. It achieves this liberation through the establishment of *theoria*'s hegemony over knowledge, a hegemony justified by its capacity to reveal the idea of the totality's conceptualization, to collect in an authorizable, i.e., verifiable way. Plato named the aspect or outward look in which presence shows what it is, *eidos*. In the common language of Attica *eidos* meant the outward aspect that a visible thing offers to the physical eyes (the eye as an organ). Yet Plato removed the *eidos* from the purview of the organ, making it that which will never be perceivable by the physical eye. With Plato *eidos* became the nonsensuous essence of what is sensible to the eye as well as the other sensory organs. To have seen this idea, this aspect, *eidenai*, is to know.

In this sense, *theoria* is not in opposition with praxis, but rather with *aesthesis*, now understood as the "sensible perception/the sensation of sensing."[23] With Aristotle, *theoria* became abstract and cognitive contemplation of invisible, indivisible Being. It was of the order of a rational discourse built on the principle of noncontradiction, of identity; *aesthesis*, on the other hand, became the locus of deceptive perception. By the time the Athenians had abandoned the multiplicity of the social and the sensible for the discourse of uniqueness and unity, i.e., logic, any discourse that served the principle of noncontradiction was identical to itself and hence was legitimate. The final occultation of the sociopolitical dimension of *theoria* was achieved by the ontological move that placed it into the field of the real as the ideal, and *aesthesis* into the field of the sensible as illusion. Thus theory and the aesthetic were irreparably set at odds.[24]

In a similar fashion Amo's *habitus* of contemplative intellect is a cognitive activity that is distinct from the activity of perception, or even representation. The fundamental distinction is the ancient one of *aesthemata* and *noemata*, "things perceived and things known." Contemplation as ratiocination is a kind of *poiesis* ("knowledge involved in creating or producing something") whose objects are first principles (*Tractatus* 172-74). Still, as activity it remains abstract. As a translation of *theoretikos*, *contemplativus* negates the historical activity of *theorein*. What it collects is nothingness (see *Tractatus* 170).

Read this way, Gates's epigraphic paraphrase of Amo's theory cannot be the reference point for an African American theory that aims at regarding the work of African American culture-writing. An African American theory formulated from Amo's theorizing on criticism would be an Idealist theory. Yet the argument that enables such a reading of Gates also denies it. Amo's definition of criticism as *habitus mentis contemplativis* rests upon a metaphysical distinction between the factual and the ideal (*Tractatus* 95-104). There can be no doubt that Gates conceives of the history of Blacks' writing themselves into being as entailing something other than merely that which is grounded in the sensationalist notion of the factual. But if an ontology of culture is involved here, it is not idealist. Gates does not maintain that culture is a transcendental ideal category of Being. His claim is not that theory realizes the thing in itself as sui generis, but rather that what is knowable and true is sayable: one can indeed say it in language. Language does not stand by itself as an ideal referent; the word must come to the assistance of the word. Hence referentiality is based on the ability of language to refer to itself, which is why Gates's theory will discover its agency in the texts themselves. The result is that one can have one's metaphysics and eat it too. This is achieved at considerable price, because it is a metaphysics of language, and one of the supreme linguistic illusions is to believe that deictics or signatures anchor us to something solid: they only help us believe that we negotiate the drift and flux. Gates is fully aware of this cost and manages to defer its payment by trading in linguistic referentiality.

The conceptual focus of this dedication to reading slave narratives is a certain preoccupation with mimetic representation, and with discovering in that representation the basis for a cultural canon. The point is to read the representation of the institution of slavery in the slave narrative

"in the sense of mimesis."[25] It seems that using theory to explicate the Black experience found in the slave narratives enables insight into the fact that "both modes of mimesis, of the literary representation of reality, as well as modes of reading, or interpretation, [are] complex responses to concrete social situations and to received modes of discourse."[26] As in his previous reading of Douglass's 1845 *Narrative*, even if it is viable to categorize all literary representation as one or another form of mimesis, this is not done in the service of a notion of semiotic transparency and literary verisimilitude.[27] The representativeness in Frederick Douglass's creation, manipulation, and transformation of a public self is anything but mimetic in the sense of a more realistic representation of reality.[28] If the unified identity of Douglass's autobiographies is wholly a narrative effect, then his representativeness, in the sense of mimesis, must be the enabling narrative function.[29] Thus, the degree to which a text is viewed as mimetic is determined by the variables of discursive context (viz., text-milieu). In the case of Douglass, representativeness is the only narrative mode for the single and sufficient reason that narration, whether oral or written, is a fact of language, and language signifies without imitating. According to this conception of the rapport between writing and reading, Frederick Douglass was indeed the "Representative Colored Man," because he achieved a form of presence through the manipulation of rhetorical structures within a modern language. Learning to read the slave narrative as the beginning to write African American culture requires recognition of this correlation of language use and presence.

The slave narrative, which is always language centered, i.e., a restricted grammatical universe of reference whose primal referents are abstracted from material existence (they are linguistic signifiers), is incapable of "showing" anything beyond itself. That is because within any given economy of literal narrative representation there are only words, such that mimetic representation means words imitating words. In this sense mimesis in the slave narrative's representation of slavery implies something of the representativeness of the slave narrator vis-à-vis the "experience" of slavery as well as his relationship to other slaves. Simply put, the inscribed narrator, Douglass's autodiegetic "I," is a figure of speech. Gates is quite explicit on its being a figure of relations in absentia, a trope, a discursive function that masquerades as an index for the self-conscious experience of phenomenal reality.

Mapping Signifyin(g)

Gates's tropology of the literal African American experience owes a great deal to Ralph Ellison's thinking on the textual nature of experience. Conveniently enough for Gates, that thinking is focused on the slave narrative. Contrary to a frequently held, though sorely misinformed assessment, Ellison was not of the opinion that there was no specifically African American literary experience. His view was simply that it was a formally heterogeneous experience, drawing from diverse literary antecedents as well as a vast array of oral folklore and tradition. As for its own particular defining characteristic, for him it is spatio-temporal movement, both physical geographical and historical wanderings, as well as metaphysical displacement. His name for this characteristic of African American culture is "the patterns of movement." Ellison used this phrase in response to a question put to him by Steve Cannon about the formal similarities between the narrative of *Invisible Man* and the slave narrative. His rather lengthy response presents succinctly the issues of experience, identity, and literary history involved in the dispute about slave narratives.

> Frankly, I think too much has been made of the slave narrative as an influence on contemporary writing. Experience tends to mold itself into certain repetitive patterns, and one of the reasons we exchange experiences is in order to discover the repetitions and coincidences which amount to a common group experience. I wouldn't have had to read a single slave narrative in order to create the narrative pattern of *Invisible Man*. It emerges from experience and from my own sense of literary form, out of my sense of experience as shaped by history and my familiarity with literature. However, one's sense of group experience comes first because one communicates with the reader in terms of what he identifies as a viable description of experience. You project your vision of what *can* happen in terms of what he accepts as the way things *have happened* in the past, his sense of "the way things are." Historically, we were trying to escape from slavery in a scene consisting of geographical space. First to the North and then to the West, going to the Nation (meaning the Indian Nation and later the Oklahoma Territory), just as Huckleberry Finn decided to do, and as Bessie Smith states in one of her blues. Of course, some of us escaped south and joined the Seminoles and fought with them against the U.S. Geography forms the scene in which we and our forefathers acted and continue to act out the drama of Afro-American freedom. This movement from region to region involved all of the motives, political, sociological, and personal, that come to focus in the struggle. So, the movement from South to North became a basic pattern for my novel. *The pattern of move-*

ment and the obstacles encountered are so basic to Afro-American experience . . . that I had no need of slave narratives to grasp either its
significance or its potential for organizing a fictional narrative. I would
have used the same device if I had been writing autobiography.[30]

Ellison's thinking about the slave narrative's role in African
American literary history is diametrically opposed to that of Arna
Bontemps, who argued that all of the major African American writers,
Ellison included, are indebted to the slave narratives.

Consciously or *unconsciously*, all of [the major Black writers] reveal in their
writing a debt to the narratives, a debt that stands in marked contrast to
the relatively smaller obligations they owe the more recognized arbiters of
fiction or autobiography. . . . If not all of them had read slave narratives,
they had heard them by word of mouth or read or listened to accounts
these had inspired. Thus, when they put pen to paper, what came to light
like emerging words written in invisible ink, were their own versions of
bondage and freedom. (Quoted in *The Slave's Narrative* xx; emphasis in the
original)

Because the evidence of that debt is revealed in the very structural
patterns of the texts produced, these texts constitute the realm of literary
experience. However, Ellison's presumption of difference in perspective
between the moment of experience and reflexive expression suggests a
conception of experience that is somewhat more syncretic than
Bontemps's. Initially this difference appears to stem from Ellison's maintaining a notion of a phenomenal experience that is distinct from the idealized experience found in the literary text and that is subtended by the
radical autonomy of the individual. Such is the common understanding
of Ellison's view, for which he was soundly condemned by the Young
Turks of the Black Art Movement because of his apparent privileging of
autonomous subjective consciousness over the collectively expressed
will. Further consideration, however, disabuses us of this impression.

Ellison's denial does in fact rest upon his sense that there is a distinction between the material aspects of experience and the modalities in
which that materiality is expressed in repetitive forms or patterns constitutive of literary experience. But this does not preclude creative
exchange between the two. A common group experience is discovered
in the exchange of experiences as expressive forms: both the individual
and the general stories are ineffable, being formal effects of expression,
but the individual story is somewhat less ineffable than the general,
somewhat more immediate in its transcribing of the successive collisions

with material circumstance. It follows, then, that the expressive form ("the narrative pattern") of *Invisible Man* is Ellison's articulation of his individual sense of experience as shaped by history (common experience) in accordance with his familiarity with particular literary forms. Because the dominant pattern for his novel, the movement from South to North, is a form of expression that is basic to the African American group experience (which Ellison encountered personally), there is no imperative for reading in the narrative expression of *Invisible Man* an exclusive formal indebtedness to slave narrative.

Avoiding the danger of confusing these formal effects of expression with the material effects of experience is achieved through understanding how common group experience emerges as a formal effect within an exchange of expressive forms. In that exchange, group identity is sought in the commonplaces of the repetitive expressions of experience in its concrete reality. The multiple expressions of the experiences of life are linked reflectively in the consciousness as the collection of repetitions and coincidences "which amount to a common group experience." In asserting that "I would have used the same device if I had been writing autobiography," Ellison holds the self-conscious immediacy of experience to be the origin of expression, as opposed to a redetermining pattern of expressive forms (like the slave narrative). The possibility of subjective expression is not found in its entirety ready-made within a prescribed economy of textual polyvalence, nor is it found completely beyond the parameters of such an economy in the raw materiality of phenomenal experience. Expression is articulated in the margin between experience and textual polyvalence. Thus, the origin of *Invisible Man*'s expression is found in writing as an effect of negotiating between a manifold of both experience and literary form.

Together the extraliterary experiences and the expressions of literary form shape what both author and reader will mean. Even though there is a movement in support of authorial intention pervading Ellison's appeal to the conscious use of style and experience that puts considerable emphasis on subjective intention, he does not deny the effect of collective expression. Rather, consciousness is an effect of representation in collective expression and, to that extent, stands before and beyond it. "I" always supersedes "us." This invocation of the notion of individual autonomy and the integrity of the minority against majority opinion, however, does not serve as the grounds for legitimating the uniqueness of individual expression. Nor does Ellison jump to the proposition that

there is some determinate subjective agency that is untouched by the manifold of experiences and mediates between them. By that same token he does not arrive at the conclusion that whatever mediation does occur will produce the *same* collective construct. Instead, what he attempts is a descriptive mapping, a cartography, of the historical traces of the movement between consciousness of experience and expression. That cartography is the focal point or the organizing perspective for highly disparate discourses. As such, it engenders the possibility of a multiplicity of collectives and their expressions becoming the purest form of manifesting the experience of the human possibility of being-in-the-world. "Authorial intention" is a figural site on the map for the indeterminacy entailed in the conjunction of historical experience and literary expression.

This indeterminate intentionality is what Gates discovers in the geospatial phrase "pattern of movement," correctly noting that it is the primary figure of Ellison's literary theory, as well as a primary Afro-American trope for the translation from the particular to the general. It is precisely this pattern of movement that the art of the slave's narrative willed to the Black textual tradition, making it possible both for us to transcend the chaos of individual memory, since these collective texts constitute the beginnings of the African American canon, and for the trope itself to inform Black novels, which emerged in the nineteenth century directly from the slave narrative.[31]

Undoubtedly collective experience offers the potentiality for the communicating of subjective experience along familiar lines of experience. That potentiality constitutes the collective memory. Both collective expression and subjective consciousness occur as narrative effects in a specific rhetorical movement, making perspective their historical site: the position from which exteriority and interiority are viewed through verbal deictics. The experiencing of phenomenal materiality is thought of as sublated by the narrative ordering of things under the effects of the work of writing. In that case, experience is not only transcribed into narrative agency but it is the issue of that transcription. In this regard, the question of coincidence in formal expression is a totally textual matter.

In claiming that the "pattern of movement" is constitutive of Afro-American experience, Ellison's own concern for literary history is disabused of the arbitrary distinction between fiction and nonfiction when it turns to issues of narrative structure, in spite of the explicitly stated commitment to authorial intention. Entailed in the geospatial figure of the movement from South to North is a reversal that parodies and

reconfigures, but does not overcome, Bontemps's thinking about the slave narratives.[32]

Chiasmus is a principal narrative feature of *Invisible Man*. Ellison readily admits that the ironic reversals driving the text are informed by a very specific discourse peculiar to African American culture, the discourse of "signifying," which he defines in terms of varying aspects of parody. Ellison has written considerably about signifying and its function in his novel. In the essay "On Bird, Bird-Watching and Jazz," signifying is the satirical riffing in jazz, again involving a formal parody of the melody (in the case of Ellison's Bird example it was "They Picked Poor Robin," which in the novel is the call in which the invisible man recognizes his own history). In the same essay he defines it as a ritual naming.[33] Ellison elaborated on this second sense of signifying in his review of Leroi Jones's *Blues People* when he characterized the title of Lydia Maria Child's book, *An Appeal in Favor of That Class of Americans Called Africans*, as "a fine bit of contemporary ironic signifying"—signifying here meaning, in the unwritten dictionary of American Negro usage, "rhetorical understatements."[34] Later on, in the 1972 publication of the short story "And Hickman Arrives," signifying is the formal parody of call and response, where the response innovatively extends the structural expressive parameters of the call's text.[35] Parody, satire, irony, and understatement: what these all have in common as aspects of signifying is naming as rhetorical substitution, or periphrasis.

If Ellison's "pattern of movement" is taken as signifying, what is it a periphrasis of? Most obviously he is signifying the conceptual basis for Cannon's question to him: the assumption of a formal transparency between texts that happen to be produced by African Americans. Yet by reformulating the issue in terms of the problematics of literary expression's relationship to historical experience, Ellison resites the dispute at another register. The dispute over the formal influence of slave narratives is recast as the dispute over the possibility of delineating a literary history of American culture.[36] In that dispute, Gates is right on the mark when he calls Ellison "our Great Signifier" (*Figures in Black* 244), for two reasons: first, because of Ellison's "naming things by indirection and troping throughout his works"; and second, because of what Ellison names throughout his works, that being the genealogy of his novel.

Taking into account *Invisible Man* and the numerous excerpts from his novel in progress,[37] the bulk of Ellison's published work has been literary criticism directed in large measure at informing literary scholars

and critics, as well as the public at large, how to read *Invisible Man* in relation to the rest of American literature. This has involved him in protracted and recurrent debates with literary scholars and critics of all stripes, from the school of the New York Intellectuals (like Irving Howe) to Black Aestheticians (like Addison Gayle and Stephen Henderson), over the authentic version of American literary history.

This question of authenticity is not merely about the authenticity of the Afro-American novel, it is also about the determinate conditions that make literature in general and American literature in particular the site where historical and cultural experience is both represented and constructed. That is to say, the question of the genealogy of African American literary forms cannot be approached simply on the basis of a predetermined extraliterary agonistics between Black and White worlds. Understanding any American novel means coming to terms with the complex history of America as a philosophical and social revolution; it means understanding the intimate connectedness of American literature to the political and social history of American Democracy. In this regard, it is the drive of the novelist to

> re-create reality in the forms which his personal vision assumes as it plays and struggles with the vividly illusory "eidetic-like" imagery left in the mind's eye by the process of social change. Life for him is a game of hide-and-seek in which he is eternally the sometimes delighted but more often frustrated "it." . . . For, as with all fictive arts, the novel's medium of communication consists in a "familiar" experience occurring among a particular people, within a particular society or nation (and the novel is bound up with the notion of nationhood), and it achieves its universality, if at all, through accumulating images of reality and arranging them in patterns of universal significance.[38]

It is expected then that the genealogy that Ellison names is a hybrid complex one. It entails the blues, which he, in accord with Albert Murray and Edgar Hyman, has seen as the manifold complexity of narrative strategies and rhetorical operations through which Afro-Americans subverted the nihilistic aspects of their enslavement, creating a rich culture of human endurance, and which comprehends a wide range of musical form of expression from shouts to jazz and rock and roll. It also entails the authorized literary canon, including such names as Richard Wright, Henry James, André Malraux, T. S. Eliot, and Stephen Crane, but the names most recurrent in his naming of literary ancestors are those that F. O. Matthiessen identified as the five classic

authors of American literature: Emerson, Thoreau, Hawthorne, Whitman, and Melville.

Ellison insists on his right to claim all of these as constituting his genealogy, an entitlement which he had to defend not only against the visceral condemnations of the Black Aestheticians who tagged him a cultural Judas, but also against the patronizing rejoinders of White literary theorists whose canon of American literary history has marginalized if not outright excluded Afro-American literature. Like Irving Howe and Lionel Trilling, he sees literature as mirroring social reality, and because that mirroring operates through the symbolisms of narrative form, literary criticism has to involve literary and aesthetic, as well as sociological, historical, and moral perspectives. It was this combination that made the New York Intellectuals' critical praxis, as Vincent Leitch puts it, a distinctive mode of American literary criticism, whose nearest equivalents were the cultural criticism of the Frankfurt school and that practiced by F. O. Matthiessen. This commitment to a literary theory that balanced aesthetics and the political was explicitly declared by Philip Rahv in the summer 1943 issue of the *Partisan Review* (a principal publication forum for the New York Intellectuals): "We could never agree to 'subordinate' art and literature to political interest."

Yet, Ellison's chief criticism of the New York Intellectuals was that when reading Afro-American literature they lost sight of their own methodological imperatives and produced inadequate readings which reduced Afro-American literature to reflections of narrow ideological posturing. When it came to the writings of Wright, Ellison, and Baldwin, Howe and Trilling did "subordinate" literary art to racial politics. Howe went so far as to maintain that the criterion for authentic Afro-American literature was fear and violence, to strike a blow at the white man.

The situation was not at all any better with academic literary criticism. When *Invisible Man* appeared on the literary scene in 1952, there were no acknowledged American classics written by Afro-Americans in the canon that was studied and taught in the emerging American studies programs and departments around the country, not even at Harvard. The reasons for this absence lie with the circumstances of American literary studies' institutionalization in the wake of F. O. Matthiessen's landmark book *American Renaissance*.[39]

With the publication of Matthiessen's *American Renaissance* in 1941, the academic study of American literature became institutionally authorized qua productive within the U.S. university.[40] This does not mean that

American Renaissance marked the invention of American studies; that role is usually reserved for Parrington's *Main Currents of American Thought*. Instead, Matthiessen's book marked the instituting of American studies as an academic field, delimited according to a specific thematic tension which could be studied in terms of periodic development: the tension between rebirth and influence.[41] The productivity of the field was almost immediately evident. In numerous universities at the end of World War II, there was a rapid growth of courses entitled "American Renaissance" (or some cognate thereof), resulting in a flourish of Ph.D.s in English specializing in American Renaissance. This growth culminated in the emergence of American studies programs and departments at places like the Universities of Minnesota and Pennsylvania in the mid-1950s.

For Matthiessen the period bracketed by the years 1845 and 1860 was the time in which American literature achieved a renaissance analogous to the Renaissance of Europe, giving rebirth in literature to the humanists' ideal of *humanitas*. This figure of a particularly American literary rebirth of *humanitas* was paralleled by Matthiessen's giving rebirth to Coleridge's Romantic conception of literature as a heterocosmos. In this light, Matthiessen bemoaned the poor taste of the masses as explanation for the greater popularity of sentimental novels, like Sara Payson Willis Parton's *Fern Leaves from Fanny's Portfolio* (which sold 100,000 copies its first year, as opposed to Melville's most successful novel, *Typee,* which, in spite of numerous reprints, never approached that figure even by the author's death in 1891), echoing Nathaniel Hawthorne's 1855 complaint to George Ticknor that popular American readership had been "wholly given over to a damned mob of scribbling women" (quoted in Matthiessen x). His stance on the slave narratives was not much better. He ignored them altogether. Although he maintained that "the one common denominator of my five writers, uniting even Hawthorne and Whitman, was their devotion to the possibilities of democracy" (ix), there is no mention in the 661 pages of *American Renaissance* (Matthiessen's appended chronology included), not even a footnote or an aside, to Frederick Douglass's *Narrative of the Life of Frederick Douglass, an American Slave, Written by Himself.* Perhaps this was because the sales of Douglass's *Narrative* far outstripped those of Melville's *Typee,* putting it in the same class of vulgar literature as Parton's novels. After all, Douglass's *Narrative* had gone through nine editions by January 1848, and had sold 30,000 copies by 1850. Then again, could it be that Douglass showed insufficient devotion to the possibilities of democracy?[42]

These absences notwithstanding, *American Renaissance* intended to present a canon of American cultural heritage for all the people, a canon whose importance had been established by "the successive generations of common readers" (x). The American Renaissance it portrayed was to stand as an idealized period of cultural unity and community spirit just prior to the disintegration of the Civil War. The implied objective was to define literary expression as an evasion of a political, social, and possibly moral dilemma. This objective is reflected in the tension between Matthiessen's complaint about an aesthetically crude public (represented by the poor sales of the period's "masterpieces") and his idealization of the writings of his five privileged authors as embodying the true spirit of American reconciliation and revolutionary zeal.

Such an idealized canon could not help but fail to address the political issues in force in the period just before the Civil War (Arac 163). This same failure extends to Matthiessen's immediate political agenda of presenting the American Renaissance as exemplary of the transformative powers of the popular will. Both the definition of the period's literary success in his five authors and the pursuit of this political agenda required that the problematic of slavery be deleted. It was necessary for the depiction of ultimate literary success in the age of Emerson and Whitman that the Democratic party's commitment to slavery (culminating in the passing of the Massachusetts slave law in 1850) be deleted as the cause for Emerson's turning to the Romantic concept of literary expression as transcendental (and hence compensating what he knew to be the political moral failure of the revolution). The success of Matthiessen's political agenda also required that the crisis of social dissolution precipitated by the importance of slavery to the American Constitution be deferred until after 1860, making the Civil War stand as the delimitation of the fall *after* the Renaissance.

Such a delimiting of a period of literary development in isolation from historical issues, which are devalued as too nonliterary to warrant analysis, occasions an overall periodization of American literary history. Through the definition of specific themes, which were supposed to be representative of the paramount ideas informing American culture, Matthiessen could fix American cultural history to a very limited geographical area (Boston, Concord, and New York) and explain progressive transformation (change) temporally. In this manner a redemptive secession of New England from the problematic social space and history of slavery is achieved. Because the area does not entail slavery as a

viable economic institution, being an area of "free states," the whole troublesome issue can be banished from the page, erased from the story. It became possible to have an American literary history (and also cultural history) that begins with the Puritans and culminates with the Renaissance without including an Afro-American writer. This means that for the period between 1845 and 1860 no slave narratives or autobiographies are accounted for, in spite of the fact that Douglass's 1845 slave narrative was published in Boston. This omission legitimates the reintroduction of the Civil War into American cultural history as a traumatic break with the enshrined tradition of liberalism, brought about by forces and interests that are extrinsic and antipathetic with that tradition. In summation, Matthiessen's figure of rebirth occasioned the instituting of a narrative Romantic historiography of American literature that sought to discover in the formal analysis of privileged literary expression the history of American culture. But in order to achieve a coherent history, something that required a stable object field, the exclusion of Afro-American literature was necessary.

Ellison's geospatial figure of movement stands in direct opposition to Matthiessen's figure of rebirth and the periodization model of American literary history. In order to make good on his own entitlement as an American author, Ellison has to effect an intervention of Afro-American literature into the authorized canon of American literary history, so that the story of American literary history paralleled the story of American cultural history that he knew, which was altogether broader than what Matthiessen portrayed. He gains this intervention through the figure of movement as the key to American literary history, which he revisits in numerous guises: patterns of movement, migration, and Heraclitus's axiom "geography is fate."[43] Geographical displacement proves the most effective tactic of intervention, because no matter where the nation went, it took the problem of slavery with it. This was boldly made evident in the aim of the party of Jackson, the Democratic party, to defer the need to settle the slavery question and ultimately to prepare for the success of slavery by geometrically increasing the slaveholders through imperial expansion.

But of even greater importance is how Ellison recognizes in Emerson's own valuation of "the Negro as a symbol of Man" the legitimate grounds for making movement the determinate model of American literary history. He underscores this legitimacy by attributing that valuation to Romanticism (*Shadow and Act* 32). If the Afro-American

is truly, in Emersonian terms, the most genuine American, then the history of African American literature is essentially American literary history, and that history cannot be fixed to one geographical area but is an ongoing syncretic process whose dimensions are historically spatial. In choosing to achieve that intervention by asserting the importance of symbolism and historical development as geography, Ellison makes the very problem which Matthiessen had sought to exclude from literary history the force *of* literary history.

In the wake of Ellison's intervention, American literary history can no longer be portrayed as a series of literary successes interrupted momentarily by an intrusive trauma whose effects will eventually be overcome through a diligent return to the aesthetic ideals that informed the anterior success of the American Renaissance. Instead, it is presented as a complex arraying of literary efforts to address an intractable problem in the hope of compelling social action. This is how Ellison is able to appropriate the Emersonian theory of literature as social action in a manner that subverts Matthiessen's usage of that same theory in the service of displacement and political evasion. That appropriation is particularly evident in the insistence that American literature springs from the national consciousness provided by the unique American experience.[44] Yet, as a master namer, Ralph Waldo Ellison has been very careful to devalue his affiliation with Ralph Waldo Emerson. In so doing, he is fulfilling Emerson's credo of originality, as well as sharing in his anxiety of influence (*Shadow and Act* 144–66). This he must do, in order to acquire some comfort in the role that he seems destined to assume as an African American writer: that of Emerson's Genuine Man.

To call Ellison "our Great Signifier" is naming with ironic understatement. Ellison not only signifies but *Signifies*; he functions as the reference for intense contestation over the relationship between Afro-American literature and authorized versions of American literary history. As a polemical opposite of Bontemps, Ellison has one foot in the arena of Afro-American literary theory and its struggles to delineate an authentically Afro-American literary history; as a prominent American novelist who insists on his incorporation within the official pantheon of literary figures, he has the other foot in the arena of American studies.

If the spatial coordinates of indeterminate movement entailed in Ellison's "patterns of movement" displace the temporally centered American literary history conundrum of collective influence versus individual genius (along with its associated dyad of subject/object), then

recognizing the slave narratives as the prototypic text of Afro-American literary development operates as a "deconstructive" reading of the authorized version of literary history as national culture.

Understanding experience thus goes beyond the subjective intentionality of meaning. In the representation of experience in history, an agreement is found that exceeds the subjective consciousness of the author: the author is neither the agent of the experience nor of the form of expressing or representing it. This does not mean that the author is reduced to an ahistorical transparency (viz., the literary genius) through which cultural truths are projected onto an autonomous literary work. Even though in an autobiography like the slave narrative, the phenomenal author is associated with the narrator's autodiegetic "I," that association is through the signature of the proper noun: Douglass, the slave author—the historical African American—is connected to his discourse through the personal name and is able to declare what he irreducibly is by naming himself.[45] The *proper* name itself is only a "mark" of a doubtful "outside-of-the-text"; it "stands" for the author who can never be "there" except as a sign. This does not mean burying the critic's participatory role in the constitution of the document as an object of reflection beneath a pseudoautonomous taxonomy of the text. Because theory is a constituting form, where language, or rather rhetorical play, is what constitutes the document as a critical object, there can be no doubt that all players in the field, both writer and reader, participate in the determination and transmission of the literary image. The critical name is no less or more an index of narrative agency than is the authorial. Rather than revealing the ultimate, as in supralinguistic, subjective determinate of narrative agency, the proper name functions as an index of the connection of two economies of signification: that of the world represented in the critical narrative (reading) and that of the world of writing and publication.[46] Reading slave narratives is writing slave narratives; and writing slave narratives is emancipatory.

The point is that just as there is never an "outside-of-the-text," there is never an "inside-of-the-text," especially with regard to ideological interests of aesthetic values. Even the most pronounced particularity of the critic remains constructed within a prior matrix of possible meanings and expressions. Perhaps this makes it easier to see that African American theory, after 1977, is concerned with the event of the formative synthesis of experience, the intending of the objective field of consciousness, which Husserl termed *noesis*. It is concerned with the

description of literary images as *noemata*, that is, as objects constitutive of the field of experience.[47]

The distinction implied in Blassingame's and Ellison's work, and which the Yale school of African American theory elaborates, between the slave's intentional act of consciousness (to tell the story of the experience of slavery) and the intentional autonomous or heteronomous object of experience that confronts consciousness (the historical event of slavery), suggests that there is something heterogeneous about referentiality. The distinction between judgment of fact and judgment of value is sublated by a more fundamental distinction between the event of experience and the significance of experience, between the operation by which we synthesize perceptions and the operation by which we attribute meaning to the synthesis. Meaning is an effect of linguistic structures, which constitute worlds of reference, totalities of beings for whom experiences are possible.[48] Thus, awareness of historicity is always retrospective, whereby the determinate condition for gaining meaning is the reader's awareness of the historical (cultural) authenticity of the movement that takes place between the reader and the text.[49]

This is a rather tight hermeneutic circle, which displaces a meaning grounded in subjective intentionality for one grounded in the operations of linguistic referentiality. Linguistic codes and rhetorical figures function as signs of the historical process that mitigates experience, thus legitimating their treatment as traces of a signifying practice whose study will provide the contours for writing the history of culture.[50] To be sure, there are two questions being raised here, one of history as the archeology of the document, and one of culture as the writing of history. Both these questions conjoin at one site, the cultural document. That conjunction founds this site. In order for writing to be the transcription of experience, the problems of historicity and meaning, of document and culture, must become almost indistinguishable.

The gist of the motto "canon formation," then, is the imperative to write culture, to collect together the documentation of the emergence and development of African American identity. A tenet of this writing of culture is that this identity is textual. It is disclosed by the activity of reading linguistic traces; an activity which, as argued in the following chapter, still runs the risk of slipping back into philology.

Chapter 3

Writing Culture in the Negro
Grammatology of Civil Society and Slavery

> We must understand this correlation of language-use and *presence* if
> we are to learn how to read the slave narrative within what Geoffrey
> Hartman calls its "text-milieu." The slave narrative represents the
> attempt of blacks to *write themselves into being*.
>
> —Gates, *The Slave's Narrative*, xxiii

The statement that "the slave narrative represents the attempt of blacks
to *write themselves into being*" is the motto for a deft and profoundly ele-
gant critique of Western modernity's insistence on the putting-together
of reflection and the grapheme. Its deftness is in making understanding
the connectedness of writing and Being a prerequisite for reading slave
narratives, and then reading slave narratives as initiating the sustained
African American critique of that connectedness. Its elegance is that the
profoundness of the critique is in direct proportion to the fundamental
profundity of Western modernity's discovering the authentic trace of
liberated autoreflective consciousness only in writing. What I want to
understand in this chapter is how recognizing the slave narrative as the
beginning of African American literary history puts into jeopardy the
knowledgeable tradition of *la pensée de libertinage érudit*. That is to say,
that in reading the slave narrative as a historical documentation of the
African's capacity for self-reflective consciousness, Gates problematizes
Western modernity's dominant typology of signs: that economy of
signification in which there is a necessary relationship between literacy
and reflective consciousness.

The definitive features of this typology were first systematically legitimated in Descartes's attempt to think the relation between apperception
and being in the world as the conceptual relation of (*Ego*) *cogito me cogitare* (I think myself thinking). In Descartes's thinking of this relation,
apperception is identified with the writing of determinate universal
structures (mathematical algorithms) of cognitive reflection. Those structures, which are the principles of his system, guarantee legibility and
ground all legitimate adjudication of true knowledge in the conscious
processes of the cogito. With that guarantee Descartes articulates a sys-

tematic story of consciousness's connexity with a specific symbolic economy, in which that economy's dissemination occurs through a particular
order of liberating erudition: the liberal arts and sciences. But Descartes
only begins the story; others elaborate it into an ever-expanding symbolic economy.

Sir Francis Bacon had perhaps an even keener sense of the social
import of liberal arts erudition. *The New Organon* (1620) reveals by its
very title the progressive identification of reality as a closed system
whose processes operate according to an inner logic. This book also
reveals the degree to which the new erudition was bound to the old
logic of identity, to the defining of affirmation through negation:

> Let a man only consider what a difference there is between the life of men
> in the most civilized province of Europe, and in the idlest and most bar-
> barous districts of New India; he will feel it be great enough to justify the
> saying that "man is a god to man," not only in regard to aid and benefit,
> but also by comparison of condition. And this difference comes not from
> soil, not from climate, not from race, but from the arts. (Book I, Aphorism
> CXXIX)[1]

When Bacon declares that the differences between men are ultimately
grounded not in inherent or physiological capacities, but rather in the
arts, he is concerned with the legitimate conditions for knowledge of
nature. Realization of these conditions is hindered by false notions, characterized as the four classes of idols in possession of the human understanding: idols of the tribe, whose foundation is in human nature; idols
of the cave, founded on the peculiarities of nature and education of the
individual; idols of the marketplace, formed through the intercourse and
association of men with each other; and idols of the theater, which have
immigrated into men's minds from various dogmas of philosophy and
from wrong laws of demonstration. The idol at play in New India is that
of the cave. This is clear in Bacon's locating the occurrence of difference
in thought between New Indian and European not in nature but in education, in particular liberal arts education, which is proposed as the sole
correct entrance to the understanding of Reason that will reveal natural
law.

The difference between the New Indian and the most civilized
European is that the latter is liberated from Idolatry through proper
education. Because this emancipation enables the founding of a civil
society that is grounded in Reason's capacity to bring to light the universal natural law, proper education in Reason is a precondition for partici-

pation in that society. This idea of civil society's grounding in Reason legitimates the view that political rights are determined by *literacy*. This is not simply a question of writing's indicating thinking: thinking is naturally indicated in language. Writing indicates the difference between natural and civil thought. Civil thought is social, and civil society emerges from the compact of reflectively conscious individuals to form a collective through which each individual's natural rights are assured only insofar as they do not infringe on those of others; those natural rights are observable only through "preexisting civil laws" embodied in the literal history of civil society and concretized in its arrangement of "the power of coercion." Accordingly, what distinguishes civilized man from natural man is the material realization of reflection: natural man lacks education, the arts and sciences. Civil education, becoming appropriately literate, is the means to civility. Bacon is echoing an argument for emancipating humanist erudition that was by then well rehearsed.

At the emergence of Western modernity, with Descartes's discovery of the certainty of cogito, the focus of knowledge turned away from viewing the world as the material manifestation of one divine order or law, to viewing man as the subject for whom the world appeared. The world became a manifold of being collected in sentience, which had to be organized according to some a priori principle. That principle was Reason, which sought to discover at first the mechanical basis for nature's order, i.e., natural law. Natural law is reflected in the order of civil society, which results from the collectivity of self-reflectively conscious individuals. The precondition for civility, self-reflective consciousness, is realized only through civility, achieved only through Reason. Reason becomes the sole grounds for achieving knowledge of both nature and man, therefore Reason would liberate man from doxa. This is the moment when proper erudition is that which establishes the dominion of Reason, whose principal currency is writing (a currency whose growth in circulation was enhanced by technological advances in reproduction: movable type printing). Failure to trade in Reason's currency becomes grounds for the assumption that Reason was lacking. Lacking Reason becomes grounds for legitimate exclusion from the natural rights of man.

One of the earliest English American tracts, Morgan Godwyn's *The Negro's and Indians Advocate*, published in 1680, serves as an example of the discourse of Right's overdetermination by Reason.[2] Godwyn's text is a religious tract written against the slaving practices of the Virginia

planters. He argues that the Negro of the New World is a human, subject to the same immutable laws of nature that govern the human condition in accordance with the divine order, and hence admissible into the *congregatio fidelium*.[3] The first proposition of chapter 1 of the *Advocate* is that *"naturally* there is in every Man an equal *Right to Religion"* (9; emphasis in the original throughout). The second proposition is that *"Negro's* are Men, and therefore are invested with the *same right"* (9). It is in his argument for natural rights that Godwyn proves himself to be truly an Enlightenment man. The natural right of man to religion is the inherent capacity, which is a "special Privilege peculiar to him [as Man]," for having the notion of a deity, a Universal Order. Man could *"be subject* to Laws or *Discipline"* and raised above the herd of brutes only through this "prerogative of *Reason* implanted in his soul, the only proper apt seat for *Religion"* (11). And if it is the soul of man alone, in exclusion to his corporal aspects, that is because religion is an exercise "where in the mind and Understanding only are concerned." The body is abstracted from the operations of the Understanding as a "secondary" and "subservient" agent. To be subject to Laws means to be subject to the imperfections of conscience; to have a prospect of happiness, or be apprehensive of future dangers and contingencies, all of which are moral faculties peculiar to the *"Rational Being"* (11). For Godwyn, to be religious is a natural right of humans, because to be religious requires that one be reasonable, which is a faculty peculiar to all humans. Again it is the exposition of the capacity for Reason that secures rights. The Negro demonstrates the "most clear *emanations* and results of *Reason,* and therefore the most genuine and perfect characters of *Homoneity* . . . [in their] *Risibility* and *Discourse* (man's *peculiar* Faculties), and employment of *Reading* and *Writing"* (13). Consequently there can be no doubt that they are indeed fully human, and so imbued with all the natural rights that are associated with humans.

The gist of Godwyn's critique of the Virginia planters is not that they dehumanize the Negro, but that they wrongly do so, by limiting the scope of the law. Natural science is natural science, and the Negro too falls within its purview. The crucial question that Godwyn addresses, and rebukes the planters for neglecting, is, How are these creatures to be subsumed under the law? For Godwyn, the problem is one of misrepresentation, of, if you will, poor science. When represented in the appropriate terms of the law, by being held accountable to it, the Negro is

quite obviously human. The proof is in the collected traces of the Negro's Reason in writing.

Viewed along the line of thought whose trajectory is traceable from Descartes through Bacon and Godwyn, the written slave narrative has a specifically heuristic humanizing function. Because Reason is the hall-mark of humanity, and because literacy is a determination of Reason, in writing the slave becomes reasonable. In so doing the slave narrator pro-vides an exemplary demonstration of the Negro's humanity. At first glance this humanization in writing operates on the assumption that the Negro's worth as a human transcends the Negro's exchange value as a commodity. This assumption follows Godwyn's abstracting of Reason from the material body. More careful consideration of the terms of that humanization—Reason in writing—raises some troubling questions. If the determination of Reason is comprehended according to modernity's transcription of the material world of lived experience into a meaningful system of reference, then what determines that system? In other words, can any writing function as the expression of universal Reason? What happens when the writing is illegible, and how is its illegibility deter-mined? Another way of phrasing this question is, What is Reasoned writing?

These questions touch at the very heart of Western modernity's writ-ing about the connexity of literacy and Reason. Expositing the crisis they map in that body of work is the dedicated concern of this entire book, but what is of interest with the specific issue at hand, the humanizing function of the slave narrative, is the way in which only certain modes of expression, certain languages, possessed the capacity to represent human being.

As Janhneinz Jahn has pointed out, Africans were writing in Euro-pean languages as early as the first half of the sixteenth century (e.g., the Portuguese *autos* of Afonso Álvares against Chiado), with the Latin pan-egyric poetry of Juan Latino (1516–1606) being a celebrated example of erudition.[4] Yet neither Álvares's nor Latino's writing aimed at demon-strating the humanity of the Negro or establishing a distinctly "Negro" literature.[5] The Latin writings of the eighteenth-century African-Prussian Antonius Gullielmus Amo were like Juan Latino's in the sense that they demonstrated no attempt to articulate a distinctive Negro liter-ature. Amo's work also differed from Latino's in two important aspects: it was produced at the height of the Enlightenment, when the Negro's humanity was put into question, and in at least one of his published

writings, *De jure Maurorum in Europa* (a dissertation on the rights of Blacks in international law; see note 21 of chapter 2), Amo challenged the validity of that questioning. While the balance of his known work— the already-mentioned *Tractatus de arte sobrie et accurate philosophandi* (see chapter 1), and his *dissertatio inauguralis, De humane mentis apatheia seu sensionis ac facultatis sentiendi in mente humana absentia* (1734)—shows no telltale signs of his Africanness, at the time he wrote them the simple event of an African writing in a European language was in radical con- tradiction to the established understanding of the Negro's ontological status—but the contradiction had to be in a European language.

By the second half of the eighteenth century, there was an outpour- ing of such contradiction in the English language in varying form. In 1760 Briton Hammon dictated his captivity narrative, *Narrative of the Uncommon Sufferings and Surprizing Deliverance of Briton Hammon*. Phillis Wheatley's *Poems on Various Subjects Religious and Moral* appeared with some fanfare in 1773. Only three years earlier, in 1770, the slave narra- tive that Albert Gronniosaw dictated to a young lady of Leominster was published as *A Narrative of the Most Remarkable Particulars in the Life of James Albert Gronniosaw, An African Prince, as Related by Himself*. The *Letters* of Ignatius Sancho were published posthumously in 1782. Ottobah Cugoano's *Thoughts and Sentiments on the Evil of Slavery* was published in 1787. There is some dispute as to whether or not Cugoano produced this narrative wholly on his own, but there is no doubt that his friend Olaudah Equiano was the sole author of the 1789 slave narrative *Narrative of the Life of Olaudah Equiano, or Gustavus Vassa, the African*. Be that as it may, Gronniosaw's, Cugoano's, and Equiano's works are among the earliest slave narratives. The phenomenal growth in produc- tion of such English-language slave narratives had, by the first half of the nineteenth century, established the slave narrative as a particular genre of writing, and English as the principal European language in which the Negro was written into humanity.[6]

Identifying English as the principal European language in which the Negro was written into humanity still does not fully answer the ques- tion—What is Reasoned writing? Getting a better answer to this ques- tion requires a closer reading of the humanizing Negro-writing, beginning with the two earliest English-language slave narratives, Hammon's *Uncommon Sufferings* and Gronniosaw's *The Most Remarkable Particulars*. Amanuenses or no, these two narratives describe the rhetori-

cal terms by which subsequent slave narratives, up until that of Frederick Douglass (1845), achieve humanization in writing.

In Hammon's *Uncommon Sufferings*, the African slave is represented as a lost soul who, by a divine act, is brought to an awareness of subjective identity and emancipation through a conversion. Converted from the baseness of material exigency to the consciousness of spiritual grace, the slave as object becomes the Christian subject. Subjective identity recognizes itself in the consciousness of being *in* the world while never being *of* the world; it emerges through the fundamental rupture between *physis* and *nomos*. This was also evidenced in the sixteenth-century Mexican Inquisition confessions of African slaves, as well as the confessions of Negro criminals in the New England colonies during the seventeenth and eighteenth centuries. Both of these examples offer an exposé of the terrible effect of stepping outside of the civil law. What is terrible about the penitents and criminals of these texts is not their articulating subjective identity as emerging (explosively) in the experience of freedom from the alienation produced in the economy of slavery. What is terrible is the appearance of a subject whose freedom implies a release from the legitimation of social relations in general. Confession, in effect, mitigates the terror by defusing it along a linear path of spiritual development, according to which the subject of freedom is marked as the primitive state of a nature incomprehensible to Reason: the African slave who is outside of the civil law is beyond the natural law reflected in Reason, and an un-Reasonable nature is a terrible nature. Hence, the trauma of slavery not only inscribes identity as subjection to the law, it also presents the possibility of its expression in natural resistance, which is remarked as the effect of the slave's having some residual experience of an African materiality that remains unthinkable. Granted, this concept of the conversion echoes somewhat Augustine's conversion in the *Confessions*, but the slave narrative converts the view of grace in the *Confessions*. If nothing else, Hammon's sufferings are of a Reasonable nature, demonstrating that the autonomy of human identity is in *nomos*. Grace is in becoming a subject of the law of The Book, from inscribing the self in the law: it is the dwelling in *logos*. In this primary form, experience in the slave narrative is articulated as the pursuit of recognition of one's humanity through writing.

But what exactly does it mean to pursue the recognition of one's humanity through writing? In Gronniosaw's *The Most Remarkable Particulars* it means that "writing" is conceived of as emancipatory. Gron-

niosaw employs the figure of his desperate desire for literacy—the ability to read the Bible—to mark the means by which he overcomes his spiritual dilemma brought about by his confusion concerning the "true religion." The confusion resulted from an inability to understand the graphic and verbal codes of literacy, an inability directly linked to a cultural lacking. When Gronniosaw first encounters the Bible he has already been stripped of the material trappings of his African culture.

> When I left my dear mother, I had a large quantity of gold about me, as is the custom of our country. It was made into rings, and they were linked one into another, and formed into a kind of chain, and so put round my neck, and arms, and legs, and a large piece hanging at one ear, almost in the shape of a pear. I found all this troublesome, and was glad when my new master took it from me. (8)[7]

Whatever significance the gold had had in Africa, it had acquired an altogether other exchange value now, evincing that whatever economy of symbolic exchange Gronniosaw had acquired currency in before, he too had lost that particular significance for another. In Gronniosaw's narrative, slavery is transcribed as the event of the alienation from all African significance. Thus stripped, he was "washed, and clothed in the Dutch or English manner." Appearance aside, however, he could not even identify codes, let alone decipher them. Aware that what grammar he knew was useless to him now, he resorts to a radically naive empiricist aesthetics: things are what they appear to be. So when he experiences his new master's reading out loud for the first time, Gronniosaw can only trust in what he sees:

> [My master] used to read prayers in public to the ship's crew every Sabbath day; and when I first saw him read, I was never so surprised in my life, as when I saw the book talk to my master, for I thought it did, as I observed him to look upon it, and move his lips. I wished it would do so with me. As soon as my master had done reading, I followed him to the place where he put the book, being mightily delighted with it, and when nobody saw me, I opened it, and put my ear down close upon it, in great hopes that it would say something to me; but I was very sorry, and greatly disappointed, when I found that it would not speak. This thought immediately presented itself to me, that every body and every thing despised me because I was black. (8)

Achieving literacy is something of a compensation for the displaced African symbolic economy. In exchange for the lost materiality of Gronniosaw's Africanness, he seeks to gain access to an economy of

signification which initially seemed inaccessible at the thought that the one material trace of his Africanness which could not be removed barred his entrance.[8] With this thought Gronniosaw conflates understanding with recognition: the canonical text of Western letters did not recognize him because he was black, hence he could not understand it—it didn't talk to him. Through acquiring literacy forty-five years later, and dictating the story of it in his narrative, Gronniosaw achieves at least a portion of the recognition he sought. The Bible functions in Gronniosaw's narrative as a metaphor for Western literacy and culture, and even for humanity. Accordingly, when Gronniosaw acquires the ability to read the Bible, "to make the book talk to him," he acquires recognition of his humanity. He will write his face into the tradition of Western letters. But if the face that Gronniosaw writes is black, it is absolutely not black African.[9]

This alienation from Africa is a response whose necessity cannot be assessed except in terms of the economy of slavery. Let us say that this is an economy of development and substantial expansion which inscribes consciousness in the framework of the object's abject commodification. Gronniosaw's conception of writing marks it as symptomatic of the very obfuscation of materiality at play in his narrative, the very denial that blackness has any real bearing on one's being. In his writing the Christian Negro displaces the pagan African. That is, in Gronniosaw's autoconversion from a black African to the literate Negro master, experience is realized only in its legitimate representation, which is underwritten by a more authoritative perspective: Gronniosaw did not "write" his narrative himself but dictated it to an amanuensis. In attempting to gain emancipation through literary expression, Gronniosaw wants to effect an interpolation into Western modernity's economy of signification where literacy equals Reason equals culture and civility. But if writing is the visible sign of Reason, then he is not quite there yet.

Getting there was achieved in 1787, seventeen years after the publication of Gronniosaw's narrative, by another African author, Ottobah Cugoano (also known as John Stuart). Not only did Cugoano get there by writing and publishing his *Thoughts and Sentiments on the Evil and Wicked Traffick of the Slavery and Commerce of the Human Species*,[10] but he did so in a way that parodies the articulation of the civilized Christian Negro. Cugoano acknowledges the Western claims of priority in liberal education, only to subvert the moral value of those claims and translate literacy from a sign of Reason to one of colonial annihilation. His slave

narrative is the first to use the mastery of letters explicitly to indict slavery as a perverted economic and moral order that is only one in a long list of disgraceful acts perpetrated by the Europeans against the peoples of Africa, Mexico, and Peru in the name of civilization. To drive the point home, Cugoano provides a story of "the base treacherous bastard Pizarra" (Pizarro) and the massacre of the Incas, which recalls the account of the Spaniard's conquest of the Incas by Garcilaso de la Vega (1539–1616), *The Royal Commentaries of the Inca*. In Cugoano's account of this story Father Vicente Valverde, chaplain to Pizarro's expedition, is attempting to convince the Great Inca, Atahualpa, that Pope Alexander had the authority to grant dominion over Peru to the Spanish monarchy:

> [Atahualpa] observed [in response] that he was Lord of the dominions over which he reigned by hereditary succession; and, said, that he could not conceive how a foreign priest should pretend to dispose of territories which did not belong to him, and that if such a preposterous grant had been made, he, who was the rightful possessor, refused to confirm it; that he had no inclination to renounce the religious institutions established by his ancestors; nor would he forsake the service of the Sun, the immortal divinity whom he and his people revered, in order to worship the God of the Spaniards, who was subject to death; and that with respect to other matters, he had never heard of them before, and did not then understand their meaning. And he desired to know where Valverde had learned things so extraordinary. In this book, replied the fanatic Monk, reaching out his breviary. The Inca opened it eagerly, and turning over the leaves, lifted it to his ear; This, says he, is silent; it tells me nothing; and threw it with disdain to the ground. (78-79)

Cugoano employs the literacy which Gronniosaw identified with emancipation and civility as the determinate figure, the signature, of ignorance, violent enslavement, and genocide. His parodying misapplication of the figure of the Bible and civilization to acts of wanton violence and misappropriation, is not simply a revisionist historiography; it is an instance of catachresis. This is a catachresis directed at the West's claims of possessing the sole means of access to transcendent propriety. In his retelling of Atahualpa's story, Cugoano parodies those claims of propriety by ironically naming the players: the Spanish, the Inca, and himself. In his naming, the latter two are identified with the transcendent spirit of morality and, in the case of the Inca, with the authority of ownership that had prior claim.

> [Atahualpa] was Lord of the dominions over which he reigned by hereditary succession . . . he could not conceive how a foreign priest should pre-

tend to dispose of territories which did not belong to him, and that if such a preposterous grant had been made, he, who was the rightful possessor, refused to confirm it. (78)

Told thus, there is clearly a conflict of at least two heterogeneous economies of signification, two conflicting domains of propriety, and the contention is over whose terms will decide the issue. This contention cannot be resolved by the higher order of a third party, because there is already a radical difference between the Spaniards and Incas over who really knows the higher order, which is the point that Cugoano has Atahualpa make. The resulting violence of the Spaniards does not achieve a resolution to this difference by appealing to the higher truth, but achieves resolution by terror and enslavement. The Spaniards are labeled with the lie of bastardy.

Here Cugoano is ironically naming the moment when Western modernity is born of a crisis in legitimacy whose sign is the problem of discursive indeterminacy: the inability to adjudicate between equally effective yet mutually exclusive symbolic economies. That moment is the encounter with a "New World," populated by sentient cogitating beings, an encounter by which Europe would identify itself. The fact that the New World was on this world, and that its beings' thinking was so familiar while so alien in its ordering, provoked a crisis of enough magnitude to require a stabilizing comprehensive discourse on the natural order of things. What Cugoano's story brings to the fore is how the resolution of the crisis engendered by the New World was keyed to the formulation of a universal order or judgment by which proper dominion could be determined. On this account, the exchange between Valverde and Atahualpa that Cugoano recalls is an evocation of the engendering moment of the "New World" encounter. Valverde's invocation of papal bulls before Atahualpa was only a particular expression of an already-complicated body of scholarly and juridico-theological disputes over the legitimate grounds for claiming property rights. The terms of order in these disputes came to inform the economy of slavery and thus the production of the Negro. This is why Cugoano employs the story: to subvert that production by exposing its legitimating terms as self-contradictory. In order to better appreciate the depth of Cugoano's cutting parody of the terms of order by which the Negro is produced, I now make a slight digression into the engendering moment of the "New World" encounter evoked by Cugoano's story.

The Grammar of Civility in the New World

The focal issue in these scholarly and juridico-theological disputes was the concept of dominion. Ostensibly the key questions concerning various Spanish claims of dominion over the New Indies, along with its attendant rights, were: What determined dominion? On what authority could dominion be dispensed? Once its determination and dispensation were described, what rights of exploitation derived from dominion?

The problem of legitimate dominion over the "discovered" lands was an issue of investiture, which is why the 1493 bulls of Pope Alexander IV, in which he granted Spain and Portugal full dominion over both the lands and the people of the "New World," was only the opening highly contested word in a protracted struggle for power. Alexander IV's bulls situated the issue squarely in the juridico-theological discourse of the emerging post-*reconquista* European state. So rather than resolving the issue of legitimate dominion, he placed it on ever-shifting grounds of the legitimation of sovereignty.

By the close of the fifteenth century, Spain's possessions in the Indies were limited to a handful of Caribbean islands—mainly Hispañola, Cuba, Jamaica, and Puerto Rico—and a few, mostly coastal, mainland settlements in Nicaragua and Brazil. While the cultural and material circumstance of the peoples who inhabited these regions presented certain problems, none of these posed any serious difficulties concerning the legitimacy of Spanish dominion and the sovereign rights of the Castilian crown over the lands and peoples of the Indies. Although the only explicit justification given in Alexander IV's bulls for Castile's temporal dominion was the propagation of the Christian religion, as far as the Castilian crown was concerned dominion conferred absolute sovereignty. In accordance with this understanding, in September 1501 the Catholic Monarchs, Isabella and Ferdinand, appointed Fray Nicolás de Ovando *Comandero de Lares* (royal governor). Isabella's 1501 *cédula* (instructions of government) to Ovando, and her subsequent instructions of March 1503, was the first attempt to determine the legitimate nature of Spanish dominion over the Indies. Her 1503 instructions, in particular, formed the basis of Spanish Indian relations for some time to come:

> I command you, our said governor, that beginning on the day on which you receive my letter you will compel and force the said Indians to associate with the Christians of the island and to work on their buildings, and to

gather and mine the gold and other metals, and to till the fields and produce food for the Christian inhabitants and dwellers of the said island;
and you are to have each one paid on the day he works the wages and
maintenance which you think he should have . . . and you are to order
each cacique [chief] to take charge of a certain number of the said Indians
so that you may make them work wherever necessary. . . . This the Indians
shall perform as free people, which they are, and not as slaves.[11]

In establishing that the Indians were free people subject to the
Spanish Crown, Isabella legitimated their forced labor. Ovando understood this legitimacy with rather wide latitude, and he petitioned for
and received permission to establish in Hispañola the Castilian institution of *encomienda*, which effectively enslaved the native population of
the island.[12] The *encomienda* so devastated the Indian population that it
raised questions about the legitimacy of the Spanish dominion. Those
questions led to Ferdinand's agreeing in 1512 to summon a junta, a
council of theologians and jurists to deliberate on the matter. That council was convened on 27 December of that year in the city of Burgos,
whose bishop, Juan de Fonseca, was the minister in charge of Indian
affairs.

The Burgos Junta resulted in thirty-five articles of law governing the
affairs of the Indies, known as the Laws of Burgos. Those laws provided
juridico-theological legitimation for Spanish claims of dominion over the
Indians in a way that would eventually lead to the interdiction of feudal
authority in the Indies. The Junta resolved the issue of legitimate dominion within the logic of *lex* (or *ius*) *divina*, "divine law," and so staved off
any crisis for the idea of universality of the law. At the same time, in its
function as a royal mechanism of legitimation (an office of royal bureaucracy), the Junta was an instantiation of the emerging absolute sovereignty of the crown.[13] From Isabella's financing of Columbus's first
mission, to the Castilian monopoly of the Indies trade and exploration,
the "new lands" were a part of the formation of the absolute state. In the
unilateral articulation of the Burgos laws for the Indies the crown actualized its omnicompetence.

The Burgos Junta successfully argued that the inhabitants of the
Caribbean islands lacked the material and symbolic signs of civilization,
which rendered them legally subject to the state's jurisdiction. To make
its point, the Junta adopted John Mair's argument that the Aristotelian
categorical concept of natural slaves was sufficient grounds for adduc-
ing the Indians' status as subject to Spain's dominion. Applying Mair's

reading of Aristotle to the conquistadores' *relaciones* (narratives of exploration and conquest) of the Indians' natural bestiality, the Junta
classified them with the animals as *irrationales* (irrational creatures)
belonging to men absolutely as members of an inferior species. The consequence was a theological cum juridical argument that legitimated the
conquest and employment of Indian labor under King Ferdinand, and
also preserved the integrity of the universality of the law. For the Burgos
Junta, the discovered Indies, or Americas as they were called after 1507,
were "new lands," but their discovery did not yet involve the encounter
with a "New World," a *Mundus Novus*. The island and coastal cultures
were different from that of Spain, but they did not offer a logical conundrum in the form of a way of being that fit the classical criteria for being
considered human and civil—*polis, civitatis, techne,* and *ratio*—but which
clearly functioned in accordance to a law that could not be comprehended by Christian notions of either human or divine legislation.

Such a "New World" along with the conundrum emerged between
1518 and 1522, when the Aztecs were encountered. In November 1522
the second letter of the five *Cartas de relación* written by Hernán Cortés to
the Holy Roman Emperor Charles V, was published by Jacobo
Cromberger, who also published the third letter in March 1523, and the
fourth in 1525.[14] Cortés wrote these letters as a consequence of his having sailed to Mexico for the purpose of colonization, against the express
wishes of the governor of Cuba, Diego Velázquez. Velázquez was the
deputy to the hereditary admiral of the Indies, Diego Colón
(Columbus's son), who was the emperor's representative, so Cortés's
disobedience to Velázquez was potentially tantamount to disobedience
to the Crown.

To preempt this appearance of disobedience to the emperor, Cortés
sought directly from Charles V the legitimacy for his decision to conquer
Motecuçoma's domain. This he achieved by first appearing to respond
to the demand of his crew to establish formally a *comunidad*, the Rica
Villa de la Vera Cruz, in order to guarantee that the emperor's interests
were enforced. This "demand" was made in accordance with the *Siete
Partidas* of Alfonso X (the thirteenth-century Castilian compilation of
law), by whose precepts the law could only be set aside by the demand
of all good men of the land, who formed a community in organic unity
with the king against threats to his interests through the expression of
popular will. In the instance of Vera Cruz, the threat was posed by the
perceived inadequacy of Velázquez's orders to Cortés, whose thirty

items of instruction dealt principally with searching for Juan de Grijalva's fleet and establishing trade relations with the people of Yucatán. This appeal to feudal law ran the risk of Cortés's being associated with the *comuneros*, who in 1520 were forming corporations in opposition to Charles's claim of sovereignty. Cortés's innovation, immediately upon invoking the feudal code to legitimate the *comunidad*, was to submit the Villa de la Vera Cruz to Crown authority.

As a formal municipality bound directly to the Crown's interests, the Villa de la Vera Cruz appointed Cortés as *alcalde mayor* (the head of the *concejo*, the civic council) and captain of the royal army. One of Cortés's first acts as *alcalde mayor* was the appointment of two *procuradores* (representatives) of Vera Cruz, Alonso Hernández de Puertocarrero and Francisco de Montejo, who were charged with presenting the *comunidad's* case to Charles V in person in order to gain the imperial charter for Vera Cruz and so establish it as the legitimatizing imperial agency of Yucatán. In pursuit of this objective, Cortés wrote his famous *Cartas.*

So much of the substance of Cortés's five letters to Charles V is dedicated to the legal and quasi-legal legitimation of his enterprise, in which he employs Latinate constructions and faint echoes of classical writers like Livy and Aristotle, that certain scholars of the conquest have attributed to him rather extensive university training.[15] It would be far too ambitious to take up here the complicated dispute over whether or not, or to what extent, Cortés's epistolary style was influenced by classical learning; however, I am not altogether persuaded by the argument that the occurrence of Latinate constructions in Cortés's *Cartas* is merely a matter of conventional modes of address (Pagden xlvii). It would seem that imputing a rhetorical objective to the *Cartas* and, further, that this objective prescribed or otherwise determined their formal mode of expression, implies that Cortés had a deliberative familiarity with at least juridical discourse. The "masterfulness" of that familiarity may be determined by his successful employment of the tropes of jurisprudence to legitimate his position. Indeed, the lack of self-conscious literary devices in the *Cartas* (Pagden xlvii), though possibly indicating an absence of formal university learning, is not at all unexpected at the moment in which a central thrust of the humanist learning emerging in the universities of Bologna and Salamanca was toward *translatio:* the vernacularization of forms in order to address contemporary (modern) events. In any event, because of the conditions under which Cortés was writing (the double imperative of providing juridical legitimation and

ethnographic description within a unitary narrative), his style is often disjunctive, clumsy, and verbose (Pagden xlvii). This same stylistic eclecticism foregrounds the relationship between social formation (the emergent imperial bureaucracy) and discursive order in the face of what was a crisis in knowledge, that is, a crisis in the legitimate grounds of social formation.

In this sense Cortés's *Cartas* marked the emergence of the New World Spanish state, whose civil autonomy was derived not entirely from imperial and papal legitimacy, but in large measure from material exigency.[16] As an early modern text *Cartas de relación* is exemplary of the problematic relationship of experience and expression on which the empire's juridico-theological discourse of sovereignty would turn and flounder, and which is evoked by Cugoano's recounting of Garcilaso de la Vega's Atahualpa story. The principal interest of this discourse was in determining the language (i.e., the authorized codes) of legitimacy, something much more accessible to reading when the juridico-theological response engendered by Cortés's *Cartas de relación* is taken into account.

What Cortés published in 1522, by way of legitimation, was the accounting of an obviously civilized society that practiced in recognizably civil manner what were equally recognizable as unnatural acts. This emergence of communities that were so clearly the work of true men, but so profoundly different, precipitated a crisis of relativity, an unquestionably empirical challenge to the idea of universality. What was declared as discovered and possessed in the name of the emperor would undo the emperor. Cortés's *relaciones* about the civility of the Aztecs required that the question of dominion in this situation be more closely studied than it had been at Burgos in 1512. The Aztecs presented a case which could not be brought into accord with the precepts of Mair's argument. In order to preserve the integrity of the claims of an absolute unified world under one God, it had to be established whether or not the Aztecs were a new or alternative world, or an aberration of the known world. The situation, which came to be called "the affair of the Indies," presented a dilemma for the Spanish claim of dominion. Because Cortés based those claims on direct corporate (*comunidad*) subjugation to imperial rule, thereby circumventing feudal authority, he established New Spain as an imperial domain. Yet, the way in which he did this is crucial in that it laid the ground for future American claims of legitimate rebellion against the Spanish state. Cortés submitted to the emperor's sover-

eignty in accordance to the law; in this way Charles V's absolute sovereignty is derived from the law. In a fashion not unlike Henry de Bracton's, Cortés recognized that while the king has no equal in his realm, he is subject "to God and the law, since law makes the king . . . there is no king where will rules and not law."[17] Cortés's whole strategy, and the rhetorical success of his *Cartas*, was based on this understanding of the absolute universality of the law. At stake in the question of dominion was sovereignty based on the sanctity of the law.

The idea of the universal unity of the world under one law was perhaps most eloquently expressed and rigorously defended in sixteenth-century Spain by the Thomist movement that was called the School of Salamanca. The School of Salamanca's speculation on the Aztec situation was new and different from the Burgos Junta's in two ways. First, it was different in form and circumstance of expression, being a series of scholarly lectures that were not explicitly solicited by the state. Second, it was more sophisticated than the Junta had been in its employment of Thomist humanism in its analysis of the dominion problem.

The first of the School to provide extensive analysis of "the affair of the Indies" was its founder and principal teacher, the Dominican Francisco de Vitoria, in his *relectio De indis*. For Vitoria, the issue of Spanish dominion over the Aztecs was a question of *dominium rerum* (rights of property). In the Thomist theory of natural law, men had *dominium* over their goods (*bona*), their actions, their liberty, and to a certain extent their bodies. Civil society was based on the actualization of these property relations between persons, things, and actions. Yet, the absence of civil society is not legitimate grounds for denying *dominium rerum*, because the latter are natural rights, implanted by God at the creation in *cordibus hominum*, and hence a part of God's law in nature, *ius naturale*, and not God's grace. Accordingly, the resolution to the problem of Spanish dominion was not to be found either within the limits of papal jurisdiction or of Roman law. Instead, it was to be discovered in the determination of whether or not those Spanish claims could be asserted in a manner that did not violate the Indians' *dominium*.

Ideally, Spanish dominion over the Indies should be legitimated on the basis that it preserves and protects the Indians' *dominium rerum*. In other words the questions as to whether or not Indians were men, and if so, as to what sort of men they were, and how they could be categorically accounted for, were to be broached from within the frame of reference of Thomist *respublica christiana*, in which the theory of Rights is abstract-

ed out from the Aristotelian exegesis of the "true Gospels," the primacy of the normative behavior of Christians, and the rightness of the juridico-political and social institutions of Christian Europe. The hypostatization of this frame of reference as the expression of a universal illumination granted to all men, whether pagan, Muslim, or Christian, was the characteristic feature of Thomist humanism from early on. In fact, under the name of Reason the theory of natural law was an instrument of cognition that allowed man to see the world as it is. Vitoria's innovation was the way in which he managed to argue not only for the Indians' humanity but for their civility as well, yet still preserve the integrity of the one true world. He achieved this by underscoring a crucial lacking on the Indians' part.

In keeping with the Thomist theory of natural law, Vitoria assumes only four possible valid reasons for denying that the Indians had possessed true dominion over their affairs, in order to legitimate depriving them of natural rights: either they are sinners, infidels, foolish (*amentes*), or irrational beings (*irrationales*). The first two possibilities are rejected because one implied the heresy of Wycliffe and Hus—all true dominion must be from grace (this was the English heresy in which Wycliffe argued that the right of investiture was not in the province of either imperial or papal authority)—and the other was disputed by the ethnological information provided through the *relaciones*, which clearly established the Indian's complete ignorance of the one true religion. Vitoria discards the remaining two reasons on the basis of the same ethnological data, because it demonstrates not only that the Indians are humans and not animals, but that they possessed a certain rational order in their affairs. What then could be the legitimate grounds for the Spanish claims of dominion?

This question is further complicated by Cortés's ethnographic data, which described a culture with extensive evidence of rationality and civility: a material culture capable of constructing cities of stone, urbanization (society based on the *polis*), sophisticated and hierarchical social organization, commerce, juridical institutions, and above all highly ritualized religious practice. For Vitoria, *dominium* is a right natural to man because of his rationality, which man has by nature as a creature of God. Rights as such could only be defined objectively as that allowed under law. Forfeiture of the natural right of *dominium*, then, would require that the Indian was truly irrational and so in violation of the law of nature. In the face of the overwhelming evidence of the Indians' rationality and

civility, even the two most frequently cited acts of abomination held against the Indians, cannibalism (in the case of the Caribs) and human sacrifice (in the case of the Aztecs), were viewed by Vitoria as no more than singular temporary aberrations of reason and so not evidence of true irrationality, which made them insufficient grounds for denying the Indians possession of *dominium*. The argument that *dominium* is an inalienable right of man by virtue of his rationality, which is a law of nature, contradicted the Aristotelian theory of natural slavery, and undermined the Burgos Junta's justification of Spanish *dominium* over the Indians on the grounds that they were irrational. Yet, if the Caribs' anthropophagy and the Aztecs' practice of human sacrifice were not explainable in terms of the Indians' irrationality, how could they be explained? This is the critical question that Vitoria resolves in a fashion meant to escape the moral and epistemological dilemma engendered by the conquests.

Vitoria based his answer to this question on analogy: the Indians are like children. As *dominium* is a natural right independent of objective property, children can be said to have *dominium*, although they may not exercise it properly. In this state of improper use, children are not irrational, but they are unrational, their reason is potential. Instead of being natural slaves, the Indians are a class of natural children, much like European peasantry. As is apparent in their material culture and social structures, the Indians are undoubtedly heirs to the state of true reason, but as is also apparent in the social institution of human sacrifice, they do not yet possess the full requirements of civil life.

Simply put, the Indian was undoubtedly subject to a "poor and barbarous education" [*relectio De indis*, cited in Pagden, *Fall of Natural Man* (Cambridge University Press, 1987), 97]. In this way Vitoria could classify the Indian as being an analogue of children and the European peasant, whose ignorance derives from the lack of "speculative intellect," of cognitive reflection that came from education. The Indian demonstrated a clear capacity for reason, but acted unreasonably because of a failing in habituation. The implications of this analogy with children and peasantry were far-reaching: Pope Paul III asserted in his bull of 1537 that the Indian was fully qualified for admission to the *congregatio fidelium*. The infantilization of the Indians, however, did not legitimate Spanish *dominium* in America. According to Vitoria, the claim of Spanish *dominium* could not be based on *ius naturale*; instead, a more likely source of

legitimacy was *ius gentium* (the law of nations), which for him was a positive and not a natural law.

As a nation,[18] the Spaniards had three rights under the law: the right of travel (*ius peregrinandi*), the right of communication (*ius communicatio*), and the right to preach their religion without interference (*ius predicandi*), which also permitted the Spaniards to wage just war against any tyrant in defense of the innocent. Vitoria granted that under the law of nations the Spaniards had the right to land and trade in the Indians' domain, and to propagate Christianity to whomever would receive its message. If the Indians opposed the Spaniards in the exercise of these rights, then there were legitimate grounds for just war against them. In this case conquest would be a legitimate redress for the injury of violating Spanish rights. In the absence of such injury, war was not justified. As the Indians had never injured the Spaniards—in spite of Cortés's depiction of the *noche triste* of 30 June 1520 as a rebellion against Spain— Vitoria was led to conclude that the Castilian crown had absolutely no grounds for claiming *dominium rerum*.

Failing to find any legitimate basis for the Spanish possession of the Indies, Vitoria refrained from calling for wholesale abandonment of the colonies on the political grounds that such a withdrawal would jeopardize the interests of the emperor and nobility. This conclusion left the crown with only a very limited *dominium iurisdictionis* (political dominion) in regard to the Indians' being like children. Because the purpose of that *dominium* would be to secure the Indians' own *dominium*, however, it was a precept of charity and could not entail coercion.[19] Thus, the only right under law the Spaniards had in the Americas was *ius predicandi*, the right of propagation and protection of the innocent; but that right did not confer the property rights of *dominium rerum*. Legitimate Spanish dominion was limited to political sovereignty, principally in the form of a missionary vocation of enlightenment and the protection of the Crown's subjects. That political sovereignty would become the basis for the School of Salamanca's subsequently arguing, in tandem with Bartolomé de Las Casas, that the Indians were free subjects of the Crown, and as such had full rights to its protection.

The one crucial deficiency of the Indians which legitimated Spanish dominion was the absence of a literati. For Vitoria, the absence among the American Indians, even the Aztecs and Incas, of arts and letters, the liberal arts on which cognition thrived, did not result in their forfeiting claims of possessing dominion, but it did mean that they had no knowl-

WRITING CULTURE IN THE NEGRO   83

edge of truth, which gave the Spaniards a legitimate right to enter the Indians' domain. Vitoria recognized the Indians' humanity, and even their capacity to cogitate, but this recognition was not that of alterity in cogitation (a difference in thinking).[20] Thinking as a part of man's essence is held to be that which enables the distinguishing of good from evil, but it does so according to a universal order that translates the *prima praecepta* logically into secondary precepts that function as the basis for all codes of social behavior. The moment in Western history when the recognition of alternative worlds becomes possible—in the Spanish encounter with the Aztecs—is also the moment when humanism achieves hegemony.

Perhaps the most crucial aspect of Vitoria's argument is the underlying crisis in aesthetics it seeks to resolve. Indian civilization presents a moment of experience that resists schematization. A certain effect of the exotic is brought about by the Spaniard's ability to fully experience things and events which he cannot understand but still must act upon. He cannot act on the grounds of his reasoned understanding, so he acts on the grounds of the experience, from which he will retrospectively justify his actions by transcribing the experience into received legitimate (juridical) forms of understanding. That which is incomprehensible in experience becomes comprehensible in writing. Cortés's epistles to Charles V serve as excellent examples of this. His transcription underscores the fact that the experience is not immediately subsumable under the categories of Reason, yet those same letters leave Reason intact to recuperate it in the wake of practical achievement, conquest of the "New World," thereby revealing a fundamental difference between the processes of experiencing (*aesthesis*) and those of comprehending.

Of course, this is not a problem that Vitoria could conceptualize well enough to thematize it, nor had he any need to. After all, there remained for him the optimistic doctrine of the soul, of the Universal Order, which promised eventual and inevitable understanding of these things. There was purpose.

Still, as Cugoano's recounting of the Spaniard's conquest of the Incas would have it, this moment of encounter with the New World, the very moment in Western history when the recognition of alternative worlds becomes possible, is the moment when that possibility is precluded by the correctness of Reason and the ignorance of the affectivity of experience. It is also the moment when Reason, without the knowledge, or at least the acknowledgment, of its adherents, loses all hope of ever com-

prehending the world in terms of one universal law, which is why Cugoano's catachresis is so revealing. At its inception, modernity is caught by a malaise, whose pathology is undetermined until it reaches the point of crisis that we find ourselves in at this point, when contravening action is virtually inconsequential to the outcome.

Cugoano's 1787 narrative makes it all too plain that the sense of crisis surrounding the possibility of multiple true worlds, which was brought about by the publication of Cortés's encounter with the Aztecs, is rendered no less acute by the lapse of nearly three centuries. At the back of Descartes's identification of cognition with algorithms, Bacon's hypostatization of science, and Godwyn's expression of the Negro's familiarity of countenance and discourse (the figuration of "our Negro's" bodies), sits the same totalizing universality of law, of *ius naturale* (natural law) found with Vitoria. Cugoano's narrative shows that what is really at issue in the writing of African American culture is not the humanity of the Negro (who with the first slave narrative no longer is a transcendental abstraction, but has become a material embodiment of that which exceeds the boundaries of our reasonable truth), but the universal comprehension of reality, of what it is and how it functions. When the "Indian" and the "Negro" appear as human, but function in ways that violate fundamental precepts of reality, they threaten not only a multiplicity of perspective, but a multiplicity of worlds as well.

This multiplicity of worlds is what modernity has sought to annihilate all along, particularly in its often-articulated readiness to recognize manifold worlds as no more or less than the plurality of the forms of human experience. The trick is that the conditions of experience remain constant and universal.[21] Heterogeneity is removed from reality as a flaw, an aberration of the universal and homogeneous totality of truth. In the proto-Enlightenment arguments of Bacon and Godwyn, this truth is achieved through the free use of Reason, that is, Reason freed from dogma and prejudice. The recognition of alterity as being merely superficial variations in Reason is meant to be liberating, precisely in that it frees perspective from being grounded in dogma and opinion, leaving it to seek legitimacy instead in the disinterested and inescapable (and to that extent universal) determining conditions of the world. These alternatives are recognized as such within the parameters of a universal natural law (here natural law is barely distinguishable from the laws of nature). The crux of the matter is how to represent the Negro as being demonstrably human within terms of the law.

The Horrible Labor of Self-recognition

It is one thing to conceive of New World African American slave narratives as constituting a process of emancipation through writing; it is another thing to conceive of this process as a function of modernity's grounding of subjective emancipation through reasoned thought's material expression in writing. In the latter case the productive figuration of the slave narrative is read as a praxis grounded in the subsuming of lived experience under thought. It is important not to forget or obfuscate the fact that this is a purely rhetorical figuration. A cure for such forgetfulness is offered in the 1789 slave narrative of Olaudah Equiano, *Narrative of the Life of Olaudah Equiano.*[22]

Equiano's narrative, like those of Hammon and Gronniosaw, represents the slave as being brought to an awareness of subjective identity and emancipation by a conversion that is achieved through his enslavement. Unlike the other tellings, however, in Equiano's narrative this conversion is a fundamental violation of his being and a challenge to his humanity: it is horrible. Much has happened already in Equiano's narrative by the time he gets to the issue of English-language literacy: his capture, the reunion with and final separation from his sister, and the Middle Passage. When he reaches England in 1757 at nearly twelve years of age, he has fully imbibed, along with his readers, the horror of enslavement. The awe that he feels toward things Western is tempered by a healthy dose of anguish. It is in his description of his stay in Falmouth that he turns his attention to the matter of literacy.

> I had often seen my master and Dick employed in reading; and I had a great curiosity to talk to the books, as I thought they did; and so to learn how things had a beginning: for that purpose I have often taken up a book, and have talked to it, and then put my ears to it, when alone, in hopes it would answer me; and I have been very much concerned when I found it remained silent. (43-44)

This telling is in striking contrast to that of Gronniosaw. It is presented in a very anecdotal manner, lacking the anguish that filled Gronniosaw's encounter with the Bible. For Equiano this is a quaint story, one that tends to flesh out the characterization of a bewildered and terrified twelve-year-old boy. But the word "beginning" plays a crucial role here. It is important to keep focus on when and where Equiano narrates this story, as well as when and where the tale takes place.

Equiano recounts this story at the beginning of chapter 3 of his *Narrative*, a chapter of important beginnings. It begins with the story of Equiano's being sold in Virginia to Lieutenant Michael Henry Pascal of the royal navy, who was captain of a merchant ship bound for England called *Industrious Bee*. During the thirteen-week voyage from Virginia to England, Pascal imposed on Equiano the name Gustavus Vassa, marking the beginning of his final English identity.[23] That voyage was also the beginning of Equiano's friendship with the young American who was his first White friend and teacher, Richard (Dick) Baker. As Equiano tells it, his moments of observing Pascal and Dick reading and his attempts to make a book talk to him occurred sometime in the spring of 1757, during his first time ashore in England at Falmouth. Reading is an activity associated in Equiano's mind with "the wisdom of the white people in all things" (43). Although he will want to make books talk from then on, he will not even begin to learn to read and write until the winter of 1759, having spent two years at sea with Pascal in the royal navy. Thus, Equiano's literacy does not begin with his acquiring the practical skill to read, but with his having the will to read. This finding of will is the beginning of his acculturation through literacy, for in reading he finds his soul: in February 1759, just as he began his schooling, Equiano was baptized Gustavus Vassa at St. Margaret's Church, Westminster. Equiano finds salvation, if not an end to his sufferings, by making the book talk for him, so that he too could "learn how things had a beginning." In fine, with this anecdote about wanting to talk to books like Pascal and Dick, Equiano determines his mastery over books and remarks that all things significant have a beginning in *his book*.

The most significant beginning, however, the beginning of his reflecting on his subjective reflexivity, had already been achieved at the start of chapter 2, when Equiano's autobiographical "I" establishes the narrative's identification with the young Igbo boy whose family life was full of bliss and civility. By presenting Gronniosaw's desire to make the Bible talk to him as a small joke, "see here how funny I was to think such a thing," Equiano reinforces both that identification and his authority.

Equiano effects identification in a very prosaic fashion, catching the reader up in the pathos of the twelve-year-old boy's fear. Identification is not achieved with statements like "I was born" or "We live in such and such a way"; instead, the emergence of Equiano's self-reflective con-

sciousness, which the reader comes to identify and know as human, occurs with such statements as "I wept with fear and anguish for my sister," and "I was terrified ... and quite overpowered with horror and anguish ... " This emergence is found in a moment of terrible conversion, as he writes in the dedication of his narrative:

> By the horrors of the slave trade I was first torn from all the tender connections that were naturally dear to my heart; but these, through the mysterious ways of providence, I ought to regard as infinitely more than compensated by the introduction I have thence obtained to the knowledge of ... a nation which ... has exalted the dignity of human nature. (3)

The dedication determines the psychological investment of the narrative. This is a figurative narrative of subjective recognition, in which the ultimate issue of slavery is enlightened freedom. At the heart of his narrative of self-recognition—its incentive, as it were—are the violent material circumstances of Equiano's enslavement in the New World (as distinct from his capture and enslavement in Africa). These circumstances are literally transcribed in the dedication as an event of terrible momentum, an effect, the experience of which threatens to exceed the descriptive capacity of the eloquently figured free subject. Equiano designates this effect as "horror."[24] His use of this term recalls its etymology as an anglicization of the Latin *(h)orrour:* a shuddering with terror and repugnance, as well as the symptom of a disease. This horror is what Equiano calls the effect of experiencing an already-lost African body. That experience is a symptom which is literally legible, and submits to a representation that allows for the lost African body to be ameliorated by an ethical, aesthetic, and finally theoretical knowledge which is manifested in a work, a book, whose signatory is conscious of its being "wholly devoid of literary merit."

Narrative of the Life of Olaudah Equiano is an unliterary literary work that is the production of "an unlettered African." Addressing it to *"the Lords Spiritual and Temporal, and the Commons of the Parliament of Great Britain,"* Equiano wrote in the dedication of his narrative:

> I am sensible I ought to entreat your pardon for addressing to you a work so wholly devoid of literary merit; but, as the production of an unlettered African, who is actuated by the hope of becoming an instrument towards the relief of his suffering countrymen, I trust that *such a man*, pleading in *such a cause*, will be acquitted of boldness and presumption. (3; emphasis in the original)

The work of writing is to offer relief through the resurrection of the demised body as representative trace. Horror is not the synecdoche for slavery, it is the synecdoche for the logic that requires a man to validate his humanity through literacy, that makes writing the sole avenue to humanity. Horrible labor. Writing is the work that inscribes him as an instrument toward the relief of scriptural suffering, that abstracted trace of bodily demise. In writing, Equiano's subject somehow transcends and imposes itself on the materiality of existence, making it a legible experience. Through this portrayal of his narrative subject's ability to read at both a latent and a manifest level (specifically in presenting his subject's latent reading of the meaning of the book he manifestly reads his own story), Equiano demonstrates "his true mastery of the text of Western letters and the text of his verbal representation of his past and present selves" (Gates, *Signifying Monkey* 157). Equiano's writing is the act of narrative self-fashioning: it is autobiography.

In working to write himself into being, Equiano demonstrates a subjective identity recognizing itself in the fundamental rupture between *physis* and *nomos*. There is a sorting of emphasis in this recognition: Equiano's barely perceptible shifting of the terms of the slave narrative conversation about subjectivity away from its focus on the homeostasis of presence in voice toward the fluidity of identity in the graphic inscribing of perspective. Tracking this fluidity becomes the question of writing the history of culture. What Equiano's slave narrative has in common with those of Gronniosaw and Cugoano is the figuration of self-reflective consciousness as a compulsion, a forceful momentum toward subjective recognition. Yet with Equiano, once that recognition has been achieved, the compulsion is sustained toward an even keener recognition of the fundamental problematic of identity at its core: the identity of an African subjectivity. A discernible productive figurality or tropology is at work in Equiano's text, which effects a figuration of the self within the field of modernity as a problematic of legitimation in order to desedimentize the logic of transcription that perpetuated the horrors of the transatlantic structure.

As a history of intellectual development, Equiano's slave narrative tells a story of an emerging subjectivity's triumphant struggle to discover its identity. This is a dialectic struggle in which negation produces positive identity, along the line of trail and tribulation, sympathetic development, awakening, and emancipating death. The death that is emancipating is the negation of the materiality of Africa. Writing the

slave narrative is thus a *thanatology*, a writing of annihilation that applies the taxonomies of death in Reason (natural law) to enable the emergence of the self-reflective consciousness of the Negro.

In writing the death of the African body, Equiano gains voice and emerges from the abject muteness of objectivity into productive subjectivity. It should not be forgotten that the abject muteness of the body is not to not exist, to be without effect. The abject body is the very stuff, the material, of experiential effect. Writing the death of the African body is an enforced abstraction. It is an interdiction of the African, a censorship to be inarticulate, to not compel, to have no capacity to move, to be without effect, without agency, without thought. The muted African body is overwritten by the Negro, and the Negro that emerges in the ink flow of Equiano's pen is that which has overwritten itself and so become the representation of the very body it sits on.

It is no wonder then that in Equiano's narrative his enslavement in Africa is the primary instance of transcribing the material world of lived experience as trauma in order to ground culture in a narrative act of assemblage (*narratio*). Through transcription Equiano is able to attribute procreative meaningfulness to the negative black body. This proves to be writing's grounding in the acknowledgment of a very specific bifurcation of consciousness in modernity: the splitting of perception and apperception as two heterogeneous activities of the mind. The slave narrative is thus modernity's emblem of the problematic determination of the "field" of lived experience in thought. Self-reflectivity is presented as a dynamic effect in writing, whose presenting as self-reflection *in* writing is a regulative principle *of* writing.

This bifurcation, generally associated with the Enlightenment, informed the attempt to theorize the cognitive conditions of the relationship between self-consciousness and nature, and that theorizing strove for a proof of thinking's transcending nature.[25] To suggest that Equiano's highly literary autobiography is a specific response to this project of Reason, which strove to emancipate thinking from the imperatives of scientific management, is at least to situate the slave narrative in close proximity with the project of Romanticism. After all, that literate autobiography that would become the emblem of Romanticism, the self-liberated, sentient, thinking subject, appears first and foremost with Rousseau as the marginalized response to the Enlightenment. There is something of a "family resemblance" between Equiano's narrative, in its

dedication to exhibiting consciousness through the exaggerated exposition of his feelings at experiencing slavery, and Rousseau's *Confessions* published only eight years before.[26] It is as if Equiano were echoing Rousseau's conception of natural man, and the corrupting tendencies of culture.[27] Yet, what is perhaps most striking about Equiano's story of self-reflective consciousness produced through struggle between the individual and the social order is how it echoes Rousseau's definition of consciousness in *Emile*, as the "dual relation to oneself and one's fellow man."

This regard for thought about experience focuses on the objective function of writing as the constant betrayal of the reflectivity of theoretical thinking, that is, thinking about thinking. In Rousseau's writing theoretical discourse is a specific economy of signification that has as its first referent the instance of signification itself. Writing is to become an emancipating praxis, an aesthetic moment which remains grounded in representation. Through his writing, Rousseau can assert the radical singularity of his enterprise—his subjectivity—in order to subvert the metaphysics of Enlightenment. It may be said, however, that even though the singularity of his enterprise in writing his subjectivity presents a particular problematic of reading both historical inscription and reference, meant to subvert the metaphysics of Enlightenment, he writes his self on the basis of self-reflective consciousness's rhetorical figuration as a tropological field.

In that regard, it is Rousseau's autobiographical writing that echoes the slave narrative, beginning with Briton Hammon's *Uncommon Sufferings* of 1760. Hence, Equiano's narrative can only appear to be echoing Rousseau, but unavoidably does echo Gronniosaw and Cugoano. The slave narrative achieves a subversive intervention into the Enlightenment concept of the history of culture as writing, by beginning the writing of a history of culture. Recognized as marginal responses to Enlightenment, slave narratives present a particular problematic of reading both historical inscription and reference. Even so, the question of identity remains crucial. What kind of identity (self-centered or cultural/collective) is at the root of slave narrative? And what does self-centered or cultural/collective mean as an option?

In the context of the New World slave narrative, where the principle of identity is regarded as the first law of thought, to endeavor to reflect on this principle is to propose a violation of propriety. As a matter of

course, then, there is no need to argue the propriety of beginning with an act of theft, a stealing away, a profound disregard for propriety that gives forth the very principle of identity that is sought after.[28]

The law of identity is expressed by the common formula *A* is *A*. It states not only that every *A* as such is the same, but rather that every *A* as such is the same with respect to itself. In the state of being oneself there is embodied the relationship "with," an existential connectedness. Thus we have a mediation, a connection, a synthesis, a unification into a oneness. Because of this circumstance, identity appears with the character of unity throughout the history of Western thinking, and is looked upon as the first law of thought, or principle of inference. Read in these terms, the earliest slave narratives (by Hammon, Gronniosaw, Cugoano, and Equiano) are stories of subjective development through the transcription of thinking, the demonstrated capacity to realize Reason. More pointedly, the objective in writing the Negro's traces of Reason is to displace difference out from the Negro, to abstract Negro identity out from the material difference of phenomenal being into the liberating discursivity of thought.

In the liberating discursivity of thought, cultural identity transcends matter, and differences in thought and culture are explainable in terms of deviating illusion.[29] What is the nature of such a culture? Equiano provides a clear direct answer: it is a written compensation for a lost material Africa. Africa in this culture of writing is a productive trace, an abstraction whose only materiality is its graphic representation. Graphically represented Africa becomes the imaginative referent that grounds a specific body of intellectual work (i.e., the European-language writing of Africans) as culture. This culture of writing is an archetypical form that can be sustained through the continued circulation of African representations. Culture as an archetypical form is quantifiable only as a totality that transcends materiality. It is a quantifiable totality that is forever possible in the pure quality of form, the purely formal quality of thought's relationship to materiality. Culture is the work of self-reflective consciousness in thought. This thought of culture is actualized as Reason in history: the experiencing of phenomenal materiality is sublated and collected according to thought's ordering of things in the written text under the sign of subjective identity. Culture is *Geist*. At issue, finally, is the discursiveness of the process.

Writing Culture as Nonrecuperable Negativity

It turns out, then, that the assumption of the Negro's transcendent worth as a human presupposes the Negro's being comprehensible in Western modernity's terms. Put somewhat more crudely, but nonetheless to the point, the humanization in writing achieved in the slave narrative required the conversion of the incomprehensible African into the comprehensible Negro. The historical mode of that conversion was the linguistic representation of slavery: the slave narrative. By providing heuristic evidence of the Negro's humanity the slave narrator begins to write the history of Negro culture in terms of the history of an extra-African self-reflective consciousness. The trajectory of thought drawn from Hammon's and Gronniosaw's celebrations of Christian spirituality becomes a project of *Geistesgeschichte* by the time it reaches Equiano.

From here it can be seen that asserting the slave narrative to be the paradigm form of African American literature leads to an almost inevitable return to philology, and investment in *Geisteswissenschaft*. After all, the struggle of the Yale school concerns methodology: the appropriate language of critical analysis for African American literature. The traditional subject of philology, since its emergence in the late eighteenth century, has been the study of the supplanting of one normative dialect over another, of the discovery of a primal fundamentally homogeneous linguistic sphere of reference.

Behind the reading of the slave narrative as self-reflective, drawing attention to itself with its conspicuously complex and enigmatic codes, stands the same moral imperative that Paul de Man discovered as striving "to reconcile the internal, formal, and private structures of literary language with their external referential and public effects."[30] It cannot be unexpected, then, that the inordinate attention which the Yale school's project of canon formation focuses on the formal properties of slave narratives should generate the legitimate grounds for an *intrinsic* African American formalism, one which pays close attention—reads—the cultural specificity of its literary expression. That attention has to acquire the rigor of method, and so ought to entail a respect for its texts, in the sense of attentive responsiveness and responsibility.

On the other hand, not only in spite of but also because of the attempts of the Yale school of African American literary theory to assure valid interpretation through an ethical ethnic formalistic criticism (which is legitimated by the necessity to read the text carefully in accor-

dance with intrinsic forms of literature), form becomes a solipsistic category of self-reflection. Referential meaning assumes the status of the extrinsic. In this way, the referential meaning of the slave narrative can be cast as beyond the limiting confines of the institutionalized authoritative "Western" canon. This notion of form can then be employed to explain somewhat the way in which slave narratives have achieved an uncertain status as superfluous subjects of critical inquiry. Ensuing under the rubric of what might more appropriately be phrased an Other historiography is a reading of exclusionary discourses that territorializes culture in terms of textual spaces. This logic of cultural territory entails a regard for history that recognizes the experience of the text artifact—the whole complicated issue of reading the document for its verisimilitude or intertextual coherence and polyvalence—in terms of a problematic of ideology, or more precisely, as an archeology of ideology. The overall academic aim of canon formation is to delineate and fill an authentic genealogy of literary origins. Once the record of African American experience is found to begin in its earliest literary texts, it becomes possible to map a historical trajectory that presents a certain complexity of institutional history, involving the relationship between modernity's determination and organization of knowledge as Reason, its material expression in writing, and the categorical status of "the Negro."[31]

The same will to recognition subtending the slave narrative subtends the Yale school's writing of culture. The same desire to delineate the dual territories of center and periphery, and to reterritorialize that bifurcation through its historicization in order to be emancipated from the repressive dialectics of modernity (that which is historically known as the "Negro dilemma"), is the force of theory's writing the history of culture. This should come as no surprise from such a subjectively dedicated anthropological project as autobiographical ethnography. Why this is so will be taken up in chapter 4, but what is to be borne in mind now is that since Kant we are no longer permitted to think of the unity of identity as a monotonous sameness, or to neglect to recognize the mediation prevailing in unity. Identity can no longer be taken as merely an abstraction. In the instance of theory's attempt to write the history of culture, identity has everything to do with the imperative to contemplate the connectedness of language-use and presence. This is no mere regard for the logic of cause and effect; it is the more exacting regard for writing the history of causes. While this regard benefits from Kant's having freed thinking from Descartes's algorithmic dictates, it discovers in that

freedom Hegel's accounting for cotemporal differences in *thought* in terms of different moments in Reason's dialectical development. The overall effect is a genealogy of cultural evolution, which like any other genealogy is viable only to the extent that its authenticity is indubitable.

Reading for canon formation is a theoretical practice which involves bringing to light the interrelatedness of African American representations of experience with modernity's conception of subjectivity. To the extent that this is an accurate assessment of the formation of an African American canon, it is also the case for any canon formation, to wit, American literary studies (read American studies). Still, of even greater urgency for the project of African American canon formation is how the transcribing of causes betrays the double movement of exclusionary discourse: coextensive with the demarcation of a privileged inside space is the necessary possibility of the consolidation of that space without into distinct inclusive/exclusive spaces of their own. Determining the authenticity of African American cultural genealogy forecloses on there being a monolinear unified genealogy of North American culture.

The possibility of writing the shift to an inside perspective (that of the slave) supports the explicitly stated project of writing a history of African American culture which makes evident that the historical human Black agent exceeds the "black subject" constructed in theoretical discourse (Smith, *Self-discovery and Authority* xxx). At least one of the implications of regarding the slave narrative as thanatology is the realization that it demonstrates a reflective consciousness that is utterly impossible in the Negro, where no collective consciousness is supposed to be exhibited.[32] The political aspect of this agenda is to expose the catachresis at work in the biological misnomer of race, to read the Negro as a trope, indeed a misapplied metaphor.

The Negro as a metaphor for phenomenal thinking beings obscures the issue of cultural disparity and history.[33] Occultation of the conflicts of interest is gained in their reduction from being struggles of highly complex matrices of power to comprehensible categories of "natural" difference. The overbearing motif of this occultation is the exclusion of the African from the space of Western history, and the marginal inclusion of the Negro as negativity. The hope for the final recuperability of that negativity enables the Enlightenment project of recognition which the Yale school discerns in early slave narratives: humanity recognizes itself in the Other that it is not. However, what first appears in the writings of Gronniosaw, Cugoano, and Equiano as "Negro history," on clos-

er examination will not admit of history; rather, its delineation reduces itself quickly into a grammar of difference which neatly (according to the first law of thought) generates idealized textual territories of White and Black. This territorialization indeed remarks the failure to engage the historical and cultural materialism of "the Negro." In other words, an inevitable effect of delineating a peculiar African American historiography, of writing African American culture, is the repression of difference.

In beginning to write African American culture, the efficacy of denotative practice is never put into jeopardy, merely that of the connotative is. This too is a moment that falls well within the project of *Geistesgeschichte* (the History of Thought); which is to say that such a writing of African American culture is a testimonial to the idea of universal human development (see note 1 of chapter 1). Written in this way, African American culture is a Romantic work, caught up in the unfolding of the Spirit in the world, where emancipation must grapple with discursive modes, with the very possibilities of enunciation's taking place. By this writing of culture, slave narratives articulate the process of emancipation through writing as a function of modernity's project of universal emancipation through Reason. Also, by tracking the trajectory of this writing of culture, it becomes possible to instigate an interrogation of the institutional dimensions involved in the peripheral status in modernity of the African American. Rather than being viewed as a historical effect of modernity's expansion with colonial exploitation, the marginal status of the African American slave narrative is discovered as the deployment of the Enlightenment's emancipating narrative, the figurality and operativity by which the boundaries of modernity allow themselves to be read as "modern" texts.[34] Not only does Western literature have a canon, but so does Western literary criticism. No doubt, such repressive obscurity demands some emancipatory gesture at the level of theory. Canon formation makes that gesture in its undertaking of a theoretical project that aims to link the form of art and the form of its historical consciousness.[35]

At first glance the project of African American canon formation bears a striking resemblance to Emerson's adoption of Coleridge's concept of the literary. Emerson's Romantic concept of the literary legitimates his investing American literature with being the unsullied retainer of revolutionary promise, in compensation for what he perceived as the moral and political abandonment of that promise indicated by the ascendancy

of Jacksonianism.[36] In seemingly like fashion, the project of canon formation invests the slave narrative with being the paradigmatic literary
expression of African American cultural specificity. On closer examination this resemblance is clearly tactical. By returning to the privileged
site of literary expression with the slave narrative, canon formation (particularly in Gates's work) demonstrates that this teleology of consciousness, which is cast by Harold Bloom in the psychological discourse of
anxiety, is behind it all a linguistic feat, a historical construct that subverts its own necessity. In insisting on the objective validity of slave narratives as literary texts, in accordance with the Emersonian
preoccupation with the work-the masterpiece, the work of the Yale
school directs attention to the historical nature of criticism.

The theoretical project of African American canon formation exposes
the process of historicization (with its attendant political, ideological,
and rhetorical interests) that determines the delineation of the literary
object as a cultural artifact. Taking dominant theories of reading in
American literary studies, like those of Bloom and Hartman, as a theoretical frame of reference for reading the slave narrative, the project of
African American canon formation betrays those theories as not admitting of negativity, or rather as recuperating it under the concept of negative capability (which is how far too many have come to conceive of
emergent literature). Where canon formation gets into trouble is in
assuming the value of its own cultural artifact, viz., the slave narrative,
as archetype. Hence the conservative philological aspect of the project.
At the point where it overvalues its object, the project of African
American canon formation falls prey to the same repressive strategy of
the current academic order, the obliterating historicism it seeks to over-
turn.

Effectively addressing this problem of historicism in American literary studies requires a notion of nonrecuperable negativity, in contradistinction to that of negative capability. Such a notion can succeed to the
extent that it makes possible a reading that, while attentive to the linguistic referentiality and rhetorical agency at play with a text, is not
founded on a concept of literature as a heterocosmos, a symbolic realm
that either reflects or determines the historical world. Interjecting the
slave narrative into the privileged site of literary expression as a nonrecuperable negativity achieves, in effect, a *(dis)formation* of the field of
American literary history. If artistic form is invariably heterogeneous,

then is not historical consciousness also heterogeneous? If this is so, then isn't the rug pulled from underneath the Romantic conception of literary history as reflecting the history of a developmental historical conscious- ness which recognizes itself through various periods of development, finally culminating in totality and the closure of history? The slave nar- rative as a process by which a textual economy is constituted—as a *tro- pography* through which the African American achieves an emancipatory subversion of the propriety of slavery—jeopardizes the genealogy of Reason.

To conceptualize an African American literary tradition grounded in the recognition of the slave narrative as "the attempt of blacks to *write themselves into being*," is to intervene in Thought's formal identification through a protracted political engagement with and condemnation of Thought's fundamental sign of domination—the commodity of writing, the text as Reason's technology. Precisely at the point at which this inter- vention appears to succeed in its determination of a black agent, howev- er, it is subject to appropriation by a rather homeostatic thought: the Negro.[37] As with Gronniosaw's and Equiano's enlightened Negro, the determination of a black agent in lieu of—we must keep our regard for the site of operativity—a negative black body discovers nothing so much as an investment in the terms of philosophical reflection: writing. To claim black agency is to claim the Negro. Here in this site blackness is a sign of presence in writing. It is the material stuff of writing.

A far more difficult and worthwhile task is to discern in the slave narrative the deconstruction of the determinate category of "the Negro" in a manner which adjudicates both the emancipatory claims of the Enlightenment and the Idealist absolute.[38] What is at stake in this task is not just Western modernity but rather no less than the history of that modernity: the work of reading that monumentalizes the document, turning it into a memory of culture, a canon of knowledge and truth.

By a rather arbitrarily determined trajectory, then, the African American writing of history begins with the New World slave narrative, a narrative whose beginning is to be subversive. This is a beginning to write the history of an orientation toward lived experience that chal- lenges the state of Reason by restoring through the letter (the well- formed grapheme) the descriptive dynamics of a vernacular (the unauthorized language of the slaves) that is capable of problematizing philosophical discourse's claim to be that which is most suited to medi- ate between cognition and perception. That state of Reason, of theoreti-

cal comprehension, whose subjective appropriation achieves the internalization of difference and propriety in the form of reflective apperception, is beginning to be subverted in the slave's narrative by writing's inscription of the irrupting events and discontinuities of desire. There is an exigency in this assessment about slave narratives' formulation of a self-reflective subjectivity that compels us to read them as the inception of a negative history. This is a history of illegibility, one that leads to the unavoidable problematics of narrative representation entailed in thinking about writing as being emancipatory.

Critique of Genealogical Deduction
Narrative of the Life of Frederick Douglass **and the (Dis)Formation of Canon Formation**

> Feuerbach, not satisfied with *abstract thinking*, wants *contemplation;* and he does not conceive sensuousness as practical, human sensuous activity.
>
> —Karl Marx, *Theses on Feuerbach*

Reading the inception of a negative history in slave narratives results from a particular endeavor of African American theory to map the ways in which the narratives mediate "the distance between text and reality" (Gates, *Black Literature and Literary Theory* 5), by rigorously engaging in the nature and function of the narratives' language: that is, by participating in the coding/decoding structures of signification specific to the texts, which constitute the reality of mediation. Such an endeavor, while attentive to the problematic issues of modes of representation, cannot be justified on the basis of a theory grounded in representation. The way in which writing relates to the discursivity of thought cannot be demonstrated by way of example. This is something that "the representative Colored man," Frederick Douglass, demonstrates perhaps better than anyone else, save Kant and Nietzsche. That demonstration is Douglass's 1845 slave narrative, *Narrative of the Life of Frederick Douglass, an American Slave, Written by Himself*, in which Douglass presents a somewhat non-representational concept of literariness and literacy.[1]

This presentation occurs in the famous and oft cited passage in which Douglass's autobiographical "I," now twelve years old, gets hold of a book by Caleb Bingham entitled *The Columbian Orator*, which was a popular primer in eloquence published in 1797 as the companion or second part to Bingham's *American Preceptor* (1794).[2] Significantly, the two pieces in *The Columbian Orator* which make the greatest impression on Douglass's thinking are Aikin's "Dialogue between a Master and a Slave" (240-42) and "Part of Mr. O'Connor's Speech in the Irish House of Commons, in Favour of the Bill for Emancipating the Roman Catholics, 1795" (243-48).[3] What Douglass learned from the dialogue was the power of truth over the conscience of even a slaveholder. From the speech extract he gained a powerful denunciation of oppression, and

a vindication of the rights of man. More importantly, in this encounter he becomes conscious of the pragmatics of the slavers' enforcement of their slaves' illiteracy. A principal result of Douglass's having achieved his own literacy was that it enabled him through his reading to articulate thought. However, this same achievement entailed a burden which was for him even more unpalatable than the one of illiteracy.

> The more I read, the more I was led to abhor and detest my enslavers. I could regard them in no other light than a band of successful robbers, who had left their homes, and gone to Africa, and stolen us to slavery. . . . As I read and contemplated the subject, behold! that very discontentment which Master Hugh had predicted would follow my learning to read had already come, to torment and sting my soul to unutterable anguish. As I withered under it, I would at times feel that learning to read had been a curse rather than a blessing. It had given me a view of my wretched condition, without the remedy. It opened my eyes to the horrible pit, but to no ladder upon which to get out. In moments of agony, I envied my fellow-slaves for their stupidity. I have often wished myself a beast. I preferred the condition of the meanest reptile to my own. *Anything, no matter what, to get rid of thinking! It was this everlasting thinking of my condition that tormented me. There was no getting rid of it.*[4]

This passage with its exaggerated contrast and emphatic disproportion of the two conditions of torment in slavery—that of the autobiographical "I" that is the literal representation of the consciousness of slavery as a condition of discontentment, and the abject torment of illiterate slavery—brings into focus the paramount dangers of thinking. These dangers are brought into even sharper focus in Douglass's considerably expanded telling of the same episode in his 1855 autobiography, *My Bondage and My Freedom*.[5]

In that version Douglass is thirteen when he buys *The Columbian Orator* from a Mr. Knight of Thames Street, Fell's Point, Baltimore, for fifty cents. He was prompted to do this after hearing some little boys proclaim that they were going to learn some of the smaller pieces in it for an "Exhibition" (*Bondage* 157). In keeping with the 1845 *Narrative*, the 1855 redaction of this episode has Douglass's autobiographical "I" becoming able to give tongue to thought as a result of reading Aikin's "Dialogue between a Master and Slave" and O'Connor's speech on behalf of Catholic emancipation (which Douglass again attributes to Sheridan). The only substantial variation between the 1845 and 1855 redactions is that the latter contains a more self-reflective interpretation of the dialogue (*Bondage* 157–58), and the speeches by Lord Chatam,

William Pitt, and Charles James Fox are added to the list of documents that enabled Douglass's articulation of thought (*Bondage* 158). Nonetheless, a constant in both versions of the story is Douglass's acquiring from Bingham's *The Columbian Orator* a powerful denunciation of oppression, and a vindication of the rights of man, along with a greatly enhanced literacy. The ten years of retelling and refining the episode that passed between *Narrative of the Life of Frederick Douglass* and *My Bondage and My Freedom* had not diminished the alienating effect of this acquisition. Although through literacy Douglass had penetrated the secret of all slavery and oppression and had ascertained their true foundation to be in the pride, power, and avarice of man, nevertheless this increase in his knowledge was attended with bitter as well as sweet results.

> The more I read, the more I was led to abhor and detest slavery, and my enslavers. "Slaveholders," thought I, "are only a band of successful robbers, who had left their homes, and went into Africa for the purpose of stealing my people to slavery." . . . As I read, behold! the very discontent so graphically predicted by Master Hugh had already come upon me. I was no longer the light-hearted, gleesome boy, full of mirth and play, as when I landed first at Baltimore. Knowledge had come; light had penetrated the moral dungeon where I dwelt; and behold! there lay the bloody whip, for my back, and here was the iron chain; and my good, *kind master*, he was the author of my situation. The revelation haunted me, stung me, and made me gloomy and miserable. As I withered under the sting and torment of this knowledge, I almost envied my fellow-slaves for their stupid contentment. This knowledge opened my eyes to the horrible pit, and revealed the teeth of the frightful dragon that was ready to pounce upon me, but it opened no way for my escape. I have often wished myself a beast, or a bird—anything, rather than a slave. I was wretched and gloomy, beyond my ability to describe. I was too thoughtful to be happy. It was this everlasting thinking which distressed and tormented me; yet there was no getting rid of the subject of my thoughts. All nature was redolent of it. (*Bondage* 159-60; emphasis in the original)

The two paramount dangers that thought holds for the autobiographical "I" are: (1) the consciousness of fragmentation, "I" is caught up in the disjunction of experience and contemplation, thinking about being a slave; (2) once "I" is conscious of thinking there is no getting rid of it, no retreat into abject thoughtlessness, into pure experience. When Douglass says that he "read and contemplated the subject," what he calls "the subject of my thoughts" is in fact not the immorality of slavery but the thought of that immorality. "My wretched condition" is the

effect of being "too thoughtful to be happy." What does Douglass have in mind when he says that he "contemplated the subject"? What does it mean to be contemplative? This of course was the same question asked of Amo about the same word (see chapter 2). Yet, Douglass is not writing in Latin, so in this instance the answer must first be sought in the English-language usage of the term at the time he was writing.

According to the *Oxford English Dictionary*, the earliest English-language usage of contemplation was as a noun of action, in the sense of religious musing or devout meditation. This sense was very common down to the seventeenth century; its earliest known literary occurrence in English was in 1225. As early as the fourteenth century it was used with the sense of the action of mentally viewing (Hampole, 1340; Chaucer, 1386; Caxton, 1481; and Shaks, 1594) or the action of thinking about a thing continuously, attentive consideration. Throughout this same period there was some variation in this sense: contemplation without reference to a particular object (Langl, 1377; Shaks, 1588; Hooker, 1597; and Walton, 1653). When used with an indirect article or in the plural it meant a meditation in writing (Rychard Rolle, 1506; Crooke, 1615; and Walton, 1653). It was also used in the rare sense of the action of regarding or having respect, a request or petition (Margaret of Anjou, 1450; and Edward IV, 1466). For all of this variation, the predominant use of contemplation in English has been in the sense of the action of taking into account, thinking or regarding.

This is the sense with which it was first introduced into English from the Old French, *contemplation*, whose primitive is the extended Latin noun, *contemplationem*, the nominative of which is *contemplatio*, and from which Amo's *contemplativus* is derived. Hence, for all his not being a metaphysician, Douglass is invoking the same transitive verb, *contemplor*, that the metaphysician Amo employed in his definition of criticism, as well as the same Greek primitive *theoretikos*, from the verb *theorein*, to look at, to contemplate or survey. The pertinent question for Douglass was on what authority, if not that of metaphysics, could he legitimate his contemplation of the immorality of slavery.

If little else Douglass's thought constituted a liberating praxis; thinking is the condition of the possibility for the autobiographical "I"'s expression, so the conscious expression of "I" is already coeval with the fragmentation of thought. The autobiographical "I" marks discursively how consciousness in thought is identical with an ideological demystification which achieves subjective emancipation. Douglass's thought,

therefore, is not opposed to praxis, it is a praxis. In Emerson's words, "thinking is action," and Douglass's act of thinking was intended to provide material for a public debate on the immorality of slavery. Then again, on what authority does he do this?

In Douglass's passage about thought, all of what has been read in chapter 3 as the writing of culture by delineating the development of consciousness in the history of textual experience is encapsulated in one word, "contemplation." In that word subjective identity recognizes itself through the fundamental rupture between *physis* and *nomos*, and grounds itself in the conflation of the two. Douglass's thinking is a moment of aesthetic reception; he does not listen to the book, he looks at it.[6] This looking is characterized as a dialogue and oratory that gives expression to his thought. In the slave narrative, realizing that autonomous subjectivity whose determination is beyond the economy of slavery is gained through the shift from spectacle to speculative. With this shift writing is vested as the technology of philosophical reflection, and thought is recognized as being problematic.

The eloquence, meaning the rhetorical success, of Douglass's passage from spectacle to speculative lies in the clumsy and overt irony with which he expresses the problematic nature of thought. We are told that "I" comes to thought through literacy, through learning to read and discovering in literature certain moral questions about slavery. This is a deliberate dissimulation on Douglass's part, and what makes the irony all the more poignant is that Douglass tells us this when "I" says that "these documents . . . gave tongue to interesting thoughts of my own soul, which had frequently flashed through my mind, and died away for want of utterance" (*Narrative* 55). Here Douglass tells us rather directly that thought is not the product of literacy; at best literacy provides thought with a modality for articulation. In this Douglass recognizes the fugitive character of tongueless thought. His thought does not lack words but tongue, i.e., material cause. The utterance he claims lack of is thus a material practice, an acceptance and legitimacy. He cannot contemplate the immorality of slavery on any legitimate authority, because such authority rests on one of the most persistent myths about Africans and slavery, one on which is founded both the slavers' arrogance and the abolitionists' paternalism: Writing embodies thought.

Where the slavers' arrogance and the abolitionists' paternalism have common ground is in the belief that literacy was a danger to slavery, because it would lead to the Africans' enlightenment through thought.

The myth that Douglass in fact violates, in his account of "I" reading Sheridan's speech, is the underlying assumption that where there is illiteracy there is no evidence of thought, which was one of the authoritative arguments for justifying the enslavement of Africans, an argument which runs something like: they had no literacy, therefore could not be shown to have thought, which is an essential peculiar condition of humans, so they cannot be shown to be fully human.

Douglass has an original notion of literacy. When writing that literacy enabled thought, but that thought was still before literacy, he is not talking about the representation of thought, or about the fact that he learned from books the immorality of slavery—he knew that already—but that there is a specific material practice to have recourse to in the particular material conditions that are his as a slave of Western men. By writing his story in this way he signifies a capacity for thought. But in its writing he represents a thought before writing that cannot be inferred from writing. It is a thought that is agrammatic. Here is his catachresis, here is where the real danger lies. In writing Douglass presents tongueless thoughts, yet thoughts that are still in evidence only in the syntax of the graphemic text. It is writing that affects these graphemic thoughts; it transcribes them in relation to an "I" which cannot be in possession of them but can only be represented as a synthesizing identity, as apperception. It is about this synthesis that Douglass writes: "I envied my fellow-slaves for their stupidity."

This passage is neither self-pitying nor condescending, it only appears to be such because of the strong negative connotation that "stupidity" carries when applied to African slaves: brutes, mindless, natural instinctive uncultured creatures. In order to undercut that connotation, it might be better to find another term to express the problem of apperception that Douglass discovers in this passage. To call it thought is also difficult because this confuses it with the conception of thought as ratiocination that Douglass problematizes in his original concept of literacy. What term, other than thought or stupidity, can best designate the process by which the condition of slavery is understood before the "I" that represents appropriation by reason?

A possibility is proposed among the documents that accompanied the first edition of the *Narrative of Frederick Douglass*. The pertinent document is one that Douglass saw fit to include as the preface to his text, a letter to him from Wendell Phillips dated 22 April 1845. Phillips writes:

I was glad to learn, in your story, how early the most neglected of God's children waken to a sense of their rights, and of the injustice done them. *Experience* is a keen teacher; and long before you had mastered your A B C, or knew where the "white sails" of the Chesapeake were bound, you began, I see, to gauge the wretchedness of the slave . . . by the cruel and blighted death which gathers over his soul. (*Narrative* xv-xvi; emphasis added)

Through Phillips's preface we see how Douglass's 1845 slave narrative achieves authorial mastery of rhetorical figuration by effecting a forgetting of anterior authorities of the text. The possibilities for representing self-reflective subjectivity became identical with the possibilities of a tongueless language, with the effective employment of immaterial schemata.

Crossing Jea's Bridge[7]

When reading Douglass's slave narrative according to the project of canon formation, it is discovered that the problems of writing an authentic history of culture are fundamentally problems of reading. Douglass's slave narrative radically extends the figure of the slave's reading himself to emancipation, so that it comprehends the slave's writing himself into being. Douglass's contemplation of the dilemma of literacy makes pronounced the thoroughly historical nature of every act of reading, i.e., the constitutive function of the reader as a guarantor of social institutions. Reading itself is betrayed as a social institution, whose stakes are in nothing less than the preservation of cultural authority.

By making that authority indeterminate, the reader of Douglass's narrative, who is identified with its narrative voice, delocalizes the production of meaning, so that it is no longer *sited* or *cited* in the text as an effect of determinate authorial expression. Yet, because the text which Douglass's reader reads is immaterial, the determination of meaning is neither *resited* in, nor *recited* by, the reader as the master decoder of ciphers. There can be no authentically given meaning to the text, nor can there be any authentic reading of it. Discovered in Douglass's exemplary 1845 slave narrative is the institution of reading as an idea in process, the idea of culture. In the figure of the reader the concept of literature is produced as a historical moment, and in that moment of historical production it becomes possible to discern the institutional processes by which the reader is identified with the translating of indeterminate phe-

nomena into ideas, of nature into culture. This is, at minimum, an echo
of the Kantian project of transcendental critique, in that it recognizes the
grounds of being to be immaterial. At most, Douglass's *Narrative* is a
response, of sorts, to the Kantian project, in that it provides a thinking
which when encountering metaphysics is so agrammatic as to be somewhat incomprehensible, while nonetheless understood.

I have not gotten too far ahead of myself here with this talk of Kant.
As far as slave narratives up through Douglass are concerned, Gates has
convincingly shown them to be not only in response to the Enlightenment in general, but to Kant's allegations regarding the mental
capacities of "the Negroes of Africa" in particular. The explicit expression of the Kantian conflation of "color" with "intelligence" occurs in
Kant's 1764 *Beobachtungen über das Gefühl des Schönen und Erhabenen*
(*Observations on the Feelings of the Beautiful and Sublime*), where Kant
recalls a report from Father Labat.

> Father Labat reports that a Negro carpenter, whom he reproached for
> haughty treatment towards his wives, answered: "You whites are indeed
> fools, for first you make great concessions to your wives, and afterward
> you complain when they drive you mad." And it might be that there were
> something in this which perhaps deserved to be considered; but in short,
> this fellow was *quite black from head to foot, a clear proof that what he said was
> stupid.*[8]

Gates presents these comments as being an elaboration of David
Hume's assessment of the literacy of the Cambridge-educated Jamaican
poet Francis Williams, into an explicit correlation of blackness and stupidity.[9] A particular figure issues out of this correlation: the sign of
blackness as negation, and the arbitrary relation between the speaking
subject and his common humanity with the European. This is the figure
which the slave narratives strive to literally erase; it is the figure of
modernity's denying Africans access to the field of Reason, a denial
whose philosophical legitimacy Gates finds characterized in "Kant's correlation of physical and metaphysical characteristics" (*The Slave's
Narrative* xxvi; see also *Classic Slave Narratives* xx; "Writing 'Race' " 11).

The line in Kant's anecdote to which the phrase "correlation of physical and metaphysical characteristics" refers is the independent clause in
Kant's Labat story: "but in short, this fellow was quite black from head
to foot, a clear proof that what he said was stupid." The physical characteristic in question is the fellow's blackness, and the metaphysical is stupidity. The first thing that needs to be determined is whether or not it

can be claimed that this clause makes any statement about physical and metaphysical characteristics. Because we are reading Kant, especially because we are reading Kant, this cannot be simply determined by emphasizing the words "quite black" and "stupid."

When Gates recognizes the slave narrative as a response to Kant, he does so in terms of a representational typology of signs, meant to challenge the Idealist history of philosophy which makes problematics of expression subordinate to the content of the idea (whether verifiable or axiomatic). Yet, in a manner akin to that same Idealism, Gates's typology recognizes the epistemological problematics of modern philosophy (i.e., Kant) as problems of signifying signs, of the internal relations between signifiers in a given linguistic realm.

In this context, when regarded as a response to Kant, Douglass's slave narrative may very well be an effective response because of how it forecloses the radical severing of reality and thought that required Kant to devise the concept of a discursive mediation. There is no question of the objectification of the thinking subject's agency in Douglass's text. He does not claim to translate his thoughts into writing, thereby investing writing as a material practice with the capacity to objectively validate thought.

In point of fact, Douglass informs us that his thinking always was and still remained immaterial, and that it was that immateriality which determined his being. His lamentation over acquiring material literacy is an ironic parodying of the Western economy of signification's requiring of him that he translate thought into material sign as a demonstration of his humanity. Within that economy the translation of thought into writing is symbolic in the sense that writing is a mediating code which objectively realizes the formal process of thinking. The critical question Douglass prompts with his parody of that economy is, How can a symbol enable the representation of meaning although it has no referent?

This question, with its Kantian overtones, requires exploration. However, in exploring this question I am not suggesting that in Douglass's slave narrative there is occasion for the resurgence of the concept of nature as the legitimate grounds for moral law. Were his narrative such then it would be no more than a logically anticipated response to Kant's radicalization of the Enlightenment project, which finds legitimacy in the concept of freedom. Insofar as there is any response to Kant to be found at all in Douglass's narrative it is not a Romantic one. The revelation of Reason in nature so fundamental to

Romanticism, particularly in its expression among the American tran-scendentalists, is not discovered in the writings of Douglass. Neither, for that matter, is the cult of genius. In Douglass's slave narrative there is no law transcending the syntax of language to which appeal can be made; the only syntax is that of discursivity, which is itself discursive, and which is why Douglass seems to echo (signify on) Kant, the first Western thinker to recognize being as a temporal projection of possibilities, of discursivity.

Kant and the Critique of the Pure Negro

Gates's source for his Kant citation from *Beobachtungen über das Gefühl des Schönen und Erhabenen* is John Goldthwait's English translation of the book, *Observations on the Feelings of the Beautiful and Sublime*.[10] It is taken from section 4, "Of National Characteristics, so far as They Depend upon the Distinct Feeling of the Beautiful and Sublime." The following footnote is attached to this title:

> My intention is not to portray the characters of peoples in detail, but I sketch only a few features that express the feeling of the sublime and the beautiful which they show. One can readily imagine that in such a picture only a passing justice could be demanded, that its prototypes stand out only in the great multitude of those who lay claim to a finer feeling, and that no nation lacks dispositions that combine the most excellent qualities of this sort. On that account the blame that might occasionally fall upon a people can offend no one, for it is of such a nature that each one can hit it like a ball to his neighbor. Whether these national differences are contin-gent and depend upon the times and the type of government, or are bound by a certain necessity to climate, I do not here inquire. (*Beobachtungen* 282; *Observations* 97)

This little bit of auto-effacing witticism not only has some bearing on the passage from "Of National Characteristics" that Gates cites, but it echoes the character of Kant's *Beobachtungen*. This character is explicitly stated by Kant in the opening paragraph of section 4:

> For the present I shall cast my gaze upon only a few places that seem par-ticularly exceptional in this area [of the various feelings (*Gefühl*) of enjoy-ment or displeasure], and even upon these more with the eye of an observer than a philosopher. (*Observations* 45)

Such a fine distinction between the discourse of philosophy and what might be called casual observation is already indicative of a certain fail-

ure of rigor, a lack of attentiveness that is most uncharacteristic for the Kant of the transcendental critique. The *Beobachtungen* was one of Kant's popular pre-Critical writings, and was accessible for a relatively wider readership than the three major volumes of his transcendental critique. As a consequence of its accessibility and aesthetic theme Kant became rather well known in Königsberg as *die Schönemagister*, "the Beautiful Magister." The *Beobachtungen* is sent far afield, then, and asks to be received as the issue of an unfocused, yet to become disciplined gaze.[11] The aim after all is not to deduce the principles of aesthetic cognition in the experience of the beautiful and sublime, but rather to move inductively through observation to general descriptions. There is an obviousness about this ploy of proleptic disavowal that fails in the light of the equal, if not greater, obviousness of the profound irreconcilability between *Beobachtungen*'s view that the "feeling of beauty and the dignity of human nature" was a universal "consciousness of . . . feeling that lives in every human breast" (60), and its defining of "the Negroes of Africa [as those who] have by nature no feeling that rises above the trifling" (110). For all its disclaiming to be a text of philosophy, in *Beobachtungen* Kant already gives an indication of the solution he discovers in his *Critique of Judgment* to the fundamental problem of his transcendental critique, the problem of establishing the purity of thought. In the intuitionism Kant exhibits in his *Beobachtungen* notion of the universality of a human dignity that is not a speculative rule but a consciousness of feeling in the depths of the human soul, there is traced the same indeterminacy of origin to Imagination's schematization that will lead to humanity's freedom from nature in the *Critique of Judgment*. The Negro, on the other hand, being so much *of* nature, cannot attain this consciousness, and so remains bound, as it were. In this well-received, very readable little book of the *Schönemagister* we find somehow planted along with the seeds of that thinking that will eventually free the experience of the beautiful and sublime from objectivity of nature, and so designate the human, that which is hopelessly bound-over to nature, which is so natural as to be a derivative of the human: the Negro.

Kant makes two distinct negative allegations about Negroes in *Beobachtungen*, the one cited by Gates as entailing a correlation of physical and metaphysical characteristics, and another one that also occurs in section 4 of the book. The first mention occurs at the beginning of section 4 and deals specifically with the capacity for feeling of "the Negroes of Africa."

The Negroes of Africa have by nature no feeling that rises above the trifling. Mr. Hume challenges anyone to cite a single example in which a Negro has shown talents and asserts that among the hundreds of thousands of blacks who are transported elsewhere from their countries, although many of them have even been set free, still not a single one was ever found who presented anything great in art or science or any other praiseworthy quality, even though among the whites some continually rise aloft from the lowest rabble, and through superior gifts earn respect in the world. So fundamental is the difference between these two races of man, and it appears to be as great in regard to mental capacities as in color. (*Beobachtungen* 296–97; *Observations* 110–11)[12]

The second allegation is the Labat story. Obviously, Kant's Father Labat anecdote deals with the defining characteristics of "the Negroes of Africa": blackness and stupidity. In this story, the implications of Hume's comments about Francis Williams are elaborated into an explicit correlation of blackness and stupidity.

These are indeed, as Gates puts it, serious allegations, all the more so for occurring in one of Kant's more "popular" pre-Critical writings. What is it about these two remarks of Kant about "the Negroes of Africa" and Labat's Negro that entails a problematical correlation of the physical and metaphysical? This weighty question for the transcendental critique as well as for *Beobachtungen* derives its weightiness from the centrality of the question of metaphysics in most of Kant's work up through the three *Critiques*. Measuring that weight unavoidably entails a thoughtful engagement with the body of Kant's work, in which Kant's agenda of founding metaphysics looms large, threatening to take over. Even in the instance of a hesitant getting under way in that engagement, such as this one, Kant's agenda is overbearing and plays out the subsequent readings of his corpus as so many signposts in a somehow unsettling dialogue.

For Kant the question of the metaphysical was a complicated and important one. In the introduction to the first of his three texts in the transcendental critique, *Critique of Pure Reason*, he defines metaphysics as "consist[ing], at least in intention, entirely of a priori synthetic propositions" ("und so besteht Metaphysik weinigstens ihrem Zwecke [of its purpose] nach aus lauter synthetischen Sätzen a priori").[13] This is made all the more plain in the "Preamble on the Peculiarities of All Metaphysical Cognition" that opens the work that Kant considered the sequel to the *Critique of Pure Reason*, the *Prolegomena to Any Future Metaphysics*.

First, as concerns the sources of metaphysical cognition [*die metaphysische Erkenntnis*], its very concept [*in ihrem Begriffe*] implies that they cannot be empirical. Its principles (including not only its basic propositions [*Grundsätze*] but also its basic concepts [*Grundbegriffe*]) must never be derived from experience [*Erfahrung*]. It must not be physical [*physische*] but metaphysical knowledge, i.e., knowledge lying beyond experience, which is the source of physics proper, nor must it be internal, which is the basis of empirical psychology. It is therefore a priori cognition, coming from pure understanding [*aus reinem Verstande*] and pure reason [*reiner Vernunft*].[14]

The stated general question of the *Prolegomena* is, Is metaphysics at all possible? Granted, the *Prolegomena*, in contrast to the *Critique of Pure Reason*, is designed for preparatory exercises, and so employs an analytic method of exposition, starting from what are generally accepted to be certain a priori synthetic cognitions (viz., pure mathematics and physics) and ascending to the only conditions under which they are at all possible. Because the general problem of the *Prolegomena* is metaphysics, it, like the *Critique of Pure Reason*, is concerned with the rigorous questioning about the a priori conditions of knowledge. The "proper problem" on which the whole *Prolegomena* depends is the same as that of the *Critique of Pure Reason*: Which transcendental principles of judgment condition our experiencing nature as phenomenal appearance? Or, as Kant puts it, How are synthetic propositions a priori possible?

Metaphysics stands or falls with the solution of this problem; its very existence depends upon it. Let anyone make metaphysical assertions with ever so much plausibility, let him overwhelm us with conclusions; but if he has not first been able to answer this question satisfactorily, I have the right to say: this is all vain, baseless philosophy and false wisdom. . . .

All metaphysicians are therefore solemnly and legally suspended from their occupations till they shall have satisfactorily answered the question: *How are synthetic cognitions a priori possible?* (*Prolegomena* 21; emphasis added)

Another reiteration and refinement of this question of metaphysics, which also describes the legal parameters of metaphysics, occurs in *Metaphysical Foundations of Natural Science*, published in 1786. This work is concerned primarily with the metaphysical preconditions for the experiencing of phenomena, particularly matter. In distinction from the *Critique of Pure Reason*, where Kant explores the formal functions of thought—the processes of representations—the *Metaphysical Foundations of Natural Science* is concerned with the determination of phenomenal

matter from the pure categories of thought, i.e., the a priori cognition of natural laws:

> For laws, i.e., principles of the necessity of what belongs to the existence of a thing, are occupied with a concept which does not admit of construction, because existence cannot be presented in any a priori intuition. Therefore, natural science presupposes metaphysics of nature.[15]

Here Kant strives to delineate the proper application of transcendental concepts to matter, the aim being to sort out the metaphysical laws that are the basis for Newton's *Mathematical Principles of Natural Science*, which is reflected in Kant's organization of the text along the lines of laws of motion and force relative to matter.[16] Such a metaphysics, by Kant's definition, contains nothing but a priori principles that have no empirical content. Metaphysics of nature explores the laws that make the concept of the object in general possible, without any reference to a determinate phenomenal appearance or object of experience, which is what makes it the transcendental part of the metaphysics of nature (*Metaphysical Foundations* 6).

The essential question of metaphysics for Kant, then, is the transformation of appearance (*Erscheinung*) into experience (*Metaphysical Foundations* 18).

> General metaphysics in all cases where it requires examples [*Beispiele*] in order to provide meaning [*Bedeutung*] for pure concepts of the Understanding must always take them from . . . the form and principles of external intuition [*ussere Anschauung*]; and if these instances are not at hand in their entirety it gropes uncertain and trembling, among mere meaningless concepts. . . . And so a separate metaphysics of corporeal nature does excellent and indispensable service to general metaphysics, because the former provides examples [*Beispiele*] (cases *in concreto*) in which to realize the concepts and propositions of the latter (properly, transcendental philosophy), i.e., to give to a mere form of thought sense and meaning [*Sinn und Bedeutung*]. (*Metaphysische Anfangsgründe* 380; *Metaphysical Foundations* 16)

Determining whether or not it can be claimed that the clause from Kant's Labat story makes any statement about physical and metaphysical characteristics requires that we at least scan Kant's mapping of the cognitive terrain in which the transformation from appearance into experience is possible. I contend that what is met with in Kant's allegations about Labat's carpenter is a particularly crucial problem for that mapping.[17] In Kant's terms, it is the problem of the discursivity of thought. In this regard, the key issue is not the problem of blackness's

correlation with stupidity, but rather the problem of what Kant asserts about the Negro: "The Negro is inherently stupid." On what grounds can Kant make this assertion at all? The most apparent and indeed correct answer is on transcendental, or discursive, grounds. On the way to establishing this contention's being warranted, I offer a brief rehearsal of the discursive stakes entailed in the allegation in Kant's *Observations* that blackness equates with stupidity, and his characterization of the Negro as lacking in aesthetic judgment.

The particular clause in the Labat anecdote that causes Gates to discern a metaphysical investment in Kant's allegation is:

> And it might be that there were something in this which perhaps deserved to be considered; but in short, this fellow was quite black from head to foot, a clear proof that what he said was stupid. (*Observations* 113)

The German text from which Goldthwait translates reads:

> es ist auch, als wenn heirin so etwas wäre, was vielleicht verdiente, in Überlegung gezogen zu werden, allein kurzum, dieser Kerl war vom Kopf bis auf die Füße ganz schwarz, ein deutlicher Beweis, was er sagte, dumm war. (*Beobachtungen* 298)

This does not simplify matters as far as discovering any statements about metaphysical characteristics is concerned—in fact, it makes things worse.

After all, there appears to be no getting around it: Kant is quite struck with the physicalness of the fellow's blackness as a phenomenal appearance, and appearances are indeed the objects of theoretical knowledge. So "quite black" (*ganz schwarz*) unmistakably reads as meaning the carpenter's being "truly (as in materially real) black." But does that also mean that what his blackness is being correlated with, the stupidity of what he said, is metaphysical? If so, then what is Kant telling us when he says, "this fellow was quite black from head to foot, a clear proof that what he said was stupid"? There can be no doubt that Kant draws an inferential relation between Labat's Negro's being "quite black from head to foot" and the fact that "what he said was stupid." In fact, his blackness is an obvious *Beweis* of the stupidity in what he said. What is a *Beweis?* Goldthwait translates it as a "proof," which tends to give it the sense of phenomenal evidence and substantiated demonstration, the sort of thing with which the carpenter can be convicted. Convicted of what? Not being stupid, but saying the stupid. Yet, when regarded in light of Kant's earlier assertion about the natural mental

deficiency of the Negroes of Africa, it is quite apparent that saying the stupid issues from an inherent stupidity, as opposed to a momentary lapse in judgment. So saying the stupid results from being stupid, and blackness is the proof (*Beweis*) of that. It is precisely this distinct, clear *Beweis* that makes it possible to determine whether or not this line contains any statements about physical and metaphysical characteristics.

On the face of it there is nothing tricky about Kant's inference; it is a question of logic. The logical point of view from which Kant departs is the traditional logic of propositions or judgments, as is evident in his table of judgments in the "Transcendental Analytic" of the *Critique of Pure Reason*. It is also apparent in the "Analytic" that although his departure effected modification in the classification of judgments, he did not move toward a calculus in the manner of his friend, the logician Johann Heinrich Lambert (1728–1777).

In any case, against the parameters of the logic that Kant knew, his assessment of Labat's carpenter is an *enthymeme*, a categorical syllogism in which the major premise is informally omitted.[18] When reformulated as an enthymeme, the clause "but in short, this fellow was quite black from head to foot, a clear proof that what he said was stupid," reads something like this:

> The carpenter in Labat's report is quite black.
> Therefore, whatever the carpenter says is stupid.

The omitted major proposition is drawn in conclusion from Kant's previous resume of Hume's assertions about The Negro.[19] Explicitly expressed, the major proposition is: "To be black is a clear sign of stupidity." The formal expression of this premise results in the categorical syllogism:

> To be black is a clear sign of stupidity.
> The carpenter in Labat's report is quite black.
> Therefore, whatever the carpenter says is stupid.

The cognate of the major term of this syllogism, stupidity, occurs as the predicate of the conclusion. The minor term, carpenter, is the subject of the conclusion and minor premise. The middle term is black, making this a figure 1 categorical syllogism. Once the major premise, which is the conclusion of another antecedent syllogism, is formally expressed, it becomes apparent that what is involved here is a polysyllogism, which reads:

The Negro is inherently stupid.
To be Negro is to be black.
Therefore, to be black is a sign of stupidity.
The carpenter in Labat's report is quite black.
Therefore, whatever the carpenter says is stupid.

In which case, the terms and figure of the second syllogism remain as analyzed (i.e., figure 1). As for the first syllogism, which is now formally expressed, its major term is stupidity, its minor black, and its middle Negro, making it a figure 3 syllogism. A condensed formulation of the entire polysyllogism would read:

The Negro is stupid.
To be Negro is to be black.
The carpenter in Labat's report is quite black.
Therefore, whatever the carpenter says is stupid.

Kant's expressed assessment turns on the inference in the major premise of the second syllogism: to be black = being stupid. For Gates it is this inference that entails the correlation of the physical and the metaphysical (which is why Hume is the pretext for his reading of Kant). That inference, however, is itself the conclusion of an antecedent syllogism, whose major premise consists of another more fundamental inference: Negro = stupidity.

Hence the entire argument turns on the proposition, *The Negro is inherently stupid*. The question is, On what grounds can Kant make this assertion at all? The allegation that Kant makes is not about blackness per se, it is about the inherent stupidity of the Negro, and stupidity has no substance, only form. Kant's problem is how to think about the Negro, not as a phenomenal appearance, or undetermined object of an empirical intuition, but as an intellectual concept, a derivative of the concept of "*Man*." This having been gained, it can be said that the basis for Kant's talking about Labat's Negro as something in the world is that which is not something in the world: "*The Negro*" as a derivative concept of *Man*. In his *Beobachtungen*, Kant offers two apodictic categorical judgments or propositions about this concept in this sequential order: To be Negro is to be stupid; To be black is to be Negro. Given that such a concept is not empirical, these judgments cannot be deduced on sensible grounds; rather, they are completely transcendental, i.e., metaphysical. That is to say, the phenomenal appearance of blackness does not achieve the significance of stupidity until it is subsumed under a concept, and

for Kant that concept is *The Negro*, which is the a priori principle of stupidity.

It is because Kant's Negro problem seems to be grounded in problems of intellectual or categorical origins that it is a transcendental, discursive problem. Any attempt to address such a discursive problem necessitates a critique of the categorical determination under which the concept is thought. So it is that *The Negro* presents a problem of categorical determination, even before the Negro is a problem of experience. This claim is not simply made *ad arbitrium* to claim that because *The Negro* presents a problem of categorical determination, there is a problem of experience. The Negro problem calls for the very rigorous thinking about the dynamics of cognitive judgments—the principles of knowledge that are determinate of experience. Accordingly, determining how *The Negro* must be thought as negation requires discovering just what sort of concept it is in relation to the other concepts of the Understanding. This is saying a lot, however—in fact, a lot more than Kant himself was prepared to say in his *Beobachtungen*.

The pursuit of that which is more than Kant was prepared to say in this pre-Critical work leads straight to the first book of the transcendental critiques, the *Critique of Pure Reason*. Before taking up this pursuit, it ought to be said—and I state this to avoid losing, in subsequent detail, complete sight of what is of paramount concern here (i.e., that the slave narrative is a literal response to Kant's allegations about blackness being a clear proof of stupidity)—that there is a great deal at stake for the transcendental critique in the discerned correlation of the metaphysical and physical in Kant's assessment of Labat's Negro. What is at stake is Kant's attempt to establish the metaphysical and physical as fundamentally heterogeneous; more specifically, his striving to emancipate the metaphysical from any necessities of the physical, a striving that operates the *Critique of Pure Reason*, whose primary task is to investigate the very possibility of experience as determined according to the a priori categories of the Understanding.[20] In the *Critique of Pure Reason* Kant attempts the "dissection of the faculty of the Understanding itself" (*KrV* 65; *CPR* 103; emphasis in the original). A rigorous inquiry into Kant's transcendental critique is beyond the scope of the present work, but well within its scope is a reading of the critique's architectonic that focuses—admittedly in a somewhat arbitrary way—on particular moments in Kant's *Critique of Pure Reason* and *Critique of Judgment* where it is obvious that the physical needs to be subordinated in order to maintain the *for-*

mal homogeneity of the metaphysical and transcendental principles of cognition. Admittedly this exploration is a refraction of the investment that Kant's transcendental critique has in the concept of *The Negro*, but even that refraction will sufficiently outline the magnitude of the stakes entailed in Kant's allegations that *The Negro* is inherently stupid.

Who You Callin' Black and Stupid?

In the *Critique of Pure Reason*, on the way to determining how appearance (*Erscheinung*) is transformed into experience, Kant distinguishes between the two fundamental sources from which knowledge or cognition (*Erkenntnis*) springs, namely sensibility and Understanding. Sensibility (*Sinnlichkeit*) is the mode (*vermittelst*) by which objects (*Gegenstände*) are given to the mind as empirical intuitions (*empirische Anschauungen*), which are the given representations of sensibility. Every empirical intuition of a particular given has an appearance, which is its undetermined object (*unbestimmtes Gegenstand*). Appearance consists of matter (*Materie*), which is what corresponds to sensation, and form (*Form*), which is what determines the manifold (*Mannigfaltigkeit*) of appearance, allowing it to be ordered in certain conceptual relations. An appearance's matter is given only a posteriori, and its form is already in the mind, a priori of sensations. The form of an intuition's appearance thus consists of the conceptually (purely intellectual) based representations of sensibility. These representations are thought solely (*gedacht*) through the Understanding (*die Verstand*) as empirical concepts (*empirische Begriffe*), which are independent from the matter of sensation: they arise from the Understanding as mere determinations of the mind ("*als bloße Bestimmung des Gemüts*"). Empirical concepts do not themselves contain representations of intuition; they are never related immediately to the matter of any given object in itself, but instead provide the basis for the structural relationship according to which an appearance's matter is subsumed to its form. These same empirical concepts are themselves derivatives or predicables of an ever more purely formal class of concepts, the categories (*Kategorien*) of the Understanding, which govern the way in which empirical concepts subsume matter.

Insofar as experience of a given object is based on the formal representation of empirical intuition's appearances according to Understanding's concepts, and insofar as knowledge of a given object requires this correspondence between intuition and concepts, then intuition and

concepts are not only the essential elements of experience, their union is also the basis for the emergence of knowledge. In summary, the Understanding is the faculty of knowing an object through representations, the spontaneity of the knowable (*Spontaneität der Erkenntnis*), or the mind's power of producing the representations from itself that enable experience. Even when intuition is sensible, i.e., when giving a particular object, the Understanding is the faculty that enables us to *think* the given object of sensible intuition. Without sensibility no object could be given; without Understanding no object would be thought. Only through the union of sensibility and Understanding can knowledge arise. On this point Kant is explicitly clear in his dictate: "Thoughts without [perceptual] content are empty; intuitions without concepts are blind" ("Gedanken ohne Inhalt sind leer, Anshauungen ohne Begriffe sind blind") (*KrV* 51; *CPR* 93).

The challenge is to discover the rules governing the combination of the matter of sensation and the form of concepts in appearances, resulting in knowledge, as well as the source of those rules. According to the principal thesis of the transcendental critique this source is to be discovered in the pure formal workings of Understanding, i.e., in the categories. Discovering the source of the rules according to which appearance becomes experience and knowledge, then, requires tracing the categories to their genesis *in* the Understanding alone, exhibiting them in their a priori purity. This activity of tracing out the categories' genealogy in order to arrive at their source is what Kant undertakes in his well-known "Transcendental Deduction," deliberately emulating the particular juridical process of methodological derivation, in which the legal right (*quid juris*) of certain controversial claims is derived from a detailed narrative account of the genealogies of the claim's origins.[21] Through this "Deduction" Kant attempts to answer what is for him the crucial question of metaphysics: How are synthetic cognitions a priori possible?

The "Transcendental Deduction" has been held to be the most critical chapter of the *Critique of Pure Reason*.[22] It is also the most formally confused. That confusion is inextricably connected with its importance to the entire architectonic of Kant's transcendental critique. In the pedantic and elaborate expositions of this chapter is found that which resisted Kant's project most successfully: his own discourse. The confusing formulation of Kant's argument in "Transcendental Deduction" is the function of three factors, two of which are constant characteristics of

Kant's writing, and the third of which is specific to the "Transcendental Deduction," although not peculiar to it.

The first constant characteristic is the close rigor with which Kant engages in his project of critique; every argument is to be pursued to its utmost extremes, no matter what the apparent cost to systemic cohesion. This is not to suggest that there is no systemic integrity to the architectonic, indeed there is, but rather that Kant's self-imposed prime directive was to work it all out in as full a fashion as possible. The second constant is his profound honesty in pursuing intellectual activity; Kant's thinking is completely in his writing, so much so that when his line of thought (which for him is always argumentive, i.e., logical) produces aporia or contradiction he does not displace either, but tries to work them out. The result of such working out, however, is not clarity but a considerable degree of obfuscation in words. There is a denseness to the "Transcendental Deduction" that in large part is due to Kant's extraordinary knack for generating terminology in the face of argumentive failure—failure always meaning the premature closure of the argument, before arriving at the hoped-for conclusion.

This brings us to the third factor, which is specific to the "Deduction." The conclusion that Kant worked toward in his "Transcendental Deduction" is the discovery of the transcendental origin of perception in the Understanding according to its categories, as the determinate precondition for experience. The goal is to establish that our knowledge of phenomenal appearances is achieved through the logical employment of the Understanding (*der logischen Verstandesgebrauche überhaupt*). Knowledge, as such, is the logical function (*der logischen Funktion*) of the Understanding in judgments (*Urteilen*). "Function" is taken to be the unity of the act of bringing particular appearances under one common conceptual representation. Putting together concept and intuition under one representation is an act of judgment, which is the mediate knowledge of an object that provides a representation of a representation of the object of knowledge. On this Kant writes: "Accordingly, all judgments are functions of unity among our representations; instead of an immediate representation, a higher representation, which comprises the immediate representation and various others, is used in knowing the object" (*KrV* 69; *CPR* 105–6). All acts of the Understanding are reducible to judgments, making the Understanding a *faculty for judging* (*ein Vermögen zu urteilen*), i.e., logic. The logical employment of the Understanding is discoverable, then, when one can

"exhaustively represent" (*vollständig darstellen*) the functions (the grounding principles of rules) of the unity in judgments (*KrV* 69; *CPR* 107). In this regard, Kant provides his table of Judgments, which represents the four functions, or principles, of thinking in judgment after all content of judgment (viz., representation) has been abstracted from it: quantity, quality, relation, and modality.[23] Only the first three of these functions constitute the content of a judgment; modality does not contribute to the content of judgment, but concerns only the value of the copula in relation to thought in general.[24] When the functions of unity in judgments are brought to bear on the manifold of a priori sensibility it becomes possible to demonstrate that the Understanding (as the faculty of the spontaneity of thinking) knows this manifold only through an a priori synthesis. To the extent that Kant can "exhaustively represent" the principles of judgment in their purely a priori grounding in Understanding's categories, he can successfully represent the Understanding as determining the possibility of experience. Yet, even before appearances can be judged as such they must first be given in their specificity, requiring that the manifold of pure sensibility be assembled or synthesized into a particular representation. That synthesis is the activity of combination in its most general sense: the activity of putting appearances together so that the manifold of sensible intuition is "comprehended" (*zu begrifen*) under one representation, or appearance, which is what first gives rise to knowledge (*KrV* 76; *CPR* 111).

Consequently, the same function which gives unity to representations in judgment also gives unity to synthesis in general, and lies at the origin of the perception that determines knowledge. This function is what Kant calls the categories of the Understanding. Because it is the same function of unity operative in judgments, the table of categories is organized with the same titles as that of judgment: Quantity, Quality, Relation, and Modality. Kant is quite explicit in wanting to contrast his theory of categories from that of Aristotle. Kant reduces Aristotle's ten categories down to four.[25] More important, whereas in Aristotle's scheme it is not clear whether the classification is ontological or discursive, Kant, by discovering the categories to be pure a priori representations of the faculty of propositions or judgment, establishes them to be wholly discursive. This makes all the more significant his claiming that, insofar as the form of thought is concerned, the objective validity of the categories rests on the fact that it is only through them that experience becomes possible. Under these circumstances, the legitimate role of

Imagination, as far as the Understanding is concerned, is to provide a priori synthesis in its purity, i.e., that which is based on a priori synthetic unity, which occurs according to the categories. But the activity of synthesis in general does not originate in the Understanding. Instead, it issues from the activity of Imagination (*Wirkung der Einbildungskraft*), which apprehends the manifold of appearance into the form of a particular image (*Bild*) by reproducing appearances in a syntactic assemblage of perceptions, a sort of *agencement*. In assemblage, Imagination operates as a kind of indeterminate agency (*unbestimmtes Wirkung*).[26]

In order for the architectonic to succeed (where success means work logically for Understanding), the reproduction of representations cannot occur in any haphazard order. That is, the manifold of appearance cannot itself be an object of knowledge; it has no objective reality, because appearance exists only in being known. For the same reason apprehension of appearance's heterogeneity in a particular image cannot occur solely on the basis of Imagination's synthesis, because of the indeterminate basis of that synthesis.[27] So there must exist in conjunction with Imagination's apprehension a subjective and empirical ground that, as a function of the Understanding, enables the mind to reinstate (re-present *darstellt*) a preceding perception alongside of another current perception sequentially, generating a series of syntactic relationships of perceptions. This subjective/empirical grounding is what Kant calls "the *association of representations*." In association, the categories are combined either with each other or with the modes of pure sensibility, providing unity for the pure synthesis of various appearances in a perception. When Imagination provides pure a priori synthesis in accordance with Understanding's rule of association like this, it is said to be "intellectual synthesis." Yet, because this unity of association is that which determines how Imagination's assemblage represents the synthetic unity of appearance, its own representation (how it is thought as a pure unity) cannot come out of that assemblage. How is it thought then? It is thought, or represented, as a consciousness of perceptions and their association. Indeed, perception, or apprehension, is appearance combined with consciousness. Otherwise appearances would only accidentally fit with a connected whole of human knowledge, which would result in the architectonic's being arbitrary and not necessarily harmonious.[28]

That is not where Kant takes it, however, because he is committed to a logical harmony of the architectonic. Consequently, both the con-

sciousness of perceptions and their apprehension and association as possible objects of knowledge are necessarily ascribed to an original consciousness that is grounded in the Understanding (a priori to Imagination's *agencement*) according to the principle that Kant designates as *Affinity*, i.e., that "law [of Understanding] which constrains us to regard all appearances as sense data that must be associable in themselves and subject to a universal law of assemblage in their reproduction" (*KrV* 121; *CPR* 144). The principle of affinity is the trace of the very capacity to *think* the unity of diverse concepts in judgment (as categories) as a necessary condition of association. As a trace of this capacity, affinity is indicative of the logical impossibility of an appearance's being apprehended by Imagination except under the condition of an a priori synthetic unity: the "original synthetic unity of apperception," or the "I think." The a priori synthetic unity of apperception (self-consciousness) is an act of spontaneity, and hence is of the Understanding and not sensibility, prompting Kant to call it *the transcendental unity of apperception (die transsendentale Einheit der Apperzeption)*, in order to indicate that it is from the original unity of apperception that the possibility of a priori knowledge arises: "The transcendental unity of apperception is that unity through which all the manifold given in an intuition is united in a concept" (*KrV* B139; *CPR* 157). That unity, as the necessary correlation of every and all experience, enables synthesis through the concept of the object in general as the correlate of the "I think."

Unity of self-consciousness is thus implied in the synthesis of representations; the objective unity of all empirical consciousness in original apperception is the *necessary condition* of all possible perception, making the affinity of all appearances a necessary consequence of a synthesis in Imagination. That synthesis is not reproductive, it is not determined through empirical representations; rather, it is *productive*, in that it aims at nothing except the a priori representation of self-consciousness's unity as the necessary correlate of appearance's apprehension. Productive synthesis is the "transcendental function of Imagination" (*KrV* 123–24; *CPR* 145–46). Through the transcendental function of Imagination, concepts and intuited objects together make up a unitary experience, viz., the a priori sensible intuitions of space and time, which is to say, the object in general, or "nature" (*KrV* 125; *CPR* 147). Insofar as Kant considers nature to be the general assemblage and regularity of appearances as the sum total of all possible experience, he can claim that it is subjectively given: "We ourselves introduce [nature] as a concept" (*KrV* 125; *CPR*

147). Moreover, inasmuch as Understanding is conceived of as the faculty for thinking in which the logical employment of judgments through the categories gives us the concept of objects in general,[29] Kant logically maintains that the supreme principle of possibility (*der oberste Grundsatz der Möglichkeit*) of Understanding is that all the manifold of intuition should be subject to conditions of the original synthetic unity of apperception (*KrV* 117; *CPR* 142). In other words, the heterogeneity of nature can become an object of knowledge only through the categories of the Understanding. Nature as an object of knowledge is only possible in the unity of apperception, which is the "transcendental ground of the necessary conforming to the laws of all appearances in one experience" (*KrV* 128; *CPR* 148).

All human knowledge, then, falls within the bounds of and in the universal relation to possible experience, which is where Kant locates "that transcendental truth that precedes all empirical truth and makes it possible" (*KrV* 146; *CPR* 186). Even though the categories subsume appearances in intuition to the universal laws of synthesis, they are mere forms of thinking that cannot on their own yield knowledge of any determinate object without Imagination's synthesis of the heterogeneity of appearances with reference to the formal unity of apperception. This synthesis is both transcendental and purely figurative (*figürlich*), making it *synthesis speciosa*. Figurative synthesis when aimed solely at the transcendental unity of apperception becomes the transcendental synthesis of Imagination (*die transszendental Synthesis der Einbildungskraft*). In its figurative capacity, Imagination represents in intuition an object that is not itself present, which is how figurative synthesis comes to be viewed as an expression of the spontaneity of thought, and therefore determines the form of sense a priori in accordance with the unity of apperception. Imagination can do this because it is wholly indeterminate in its discursivity, which means that it is the purely formal activity of assemblage that constitutes the transcendental grammar of cognition. In Kant's terms, it is the source of the a priori rules of the categories of Understanding.

Of course this is not at all what Kant says. On the contrary, Kant wants to be able to say with regard to appearances in nature that all possible perception is dependent upon synthesis of apprehension, which, as an empirical synthesis, is dependent upon the transcendental synthesis determined by the categories of Understanding. He thus asserts that all that can come to empirical consciousness, i.e., all appearances of nature,

insofar as concerns their assemblage, is subject to the categories. By this account, the categories determine experience by prescribing laws a priori to the sum total of all appearances, nature (*natura materialiter spectata*). As appearances are necessarily subsumed under these laws in order for there to be perception and experience, it follows that appearances too necessarily agree with the Understanding's a priori combination, and do not exist in themselves but only in relation to the original unity of apperception as subjective self-consciousness. So too the laws of appearance in nature exist only in relation to this same subjectivity (and not in appearance). This subjectivity is the determinate grounds for both appearances and the laws of appearance in nature, resulting in the unity of nature being a necessary synthetic unity, established a priori in accordance with the Understanding as the faculty of thought and rules. Nature then is a derivative or predicable concept of Understanding's categories, and so it is determined by the categories. As much as Kant may want to say this, however, he cannot. Although succeeding in representing the Understanding as determining the possibility of experience, he fails to establish the categories as the transcendental grounds for that determinacy. Instead he exposes a seemingly irresolvable, albeit highly productive, contentiousness between Understanding and Imagination; or more exactly, between the intellectual synthesis of the categories of Understanding and the figurative synthesis of productive Imagination.

The fact that both syntheses are transcendental and thus are situated in the domain of Understanding and not sensibility indicates Kant's success in establishing that the very possibility of experience is subjectively predetermined. But the fact that every synthesis is a function of Imagination (even though Kant will contradict himself by claiming at an important moment that intellectual synthesis does not involve Imagination) indicates his failure to establish the categories as the ultimate genesis of cognitive processes. The thing is that the pure unity of apperception, as the determinate grounds for both appearances and the laws of appearance in nature, is only figuratively exhibited through (an effect of) the transcendental function of Imagination. Taking this into account, nature, as a predicable concept, is a figurative representation. That is, nature as a predicable may be derivative of the categories, but it is not definitively *determined by* the categories. It is in Imagination that the transcendental synthesis enabling experience occurs. At this point, the best that Kant can do is claim Imagination's *heteronomy*: the somewhat uncertain subjection of Imagination's two processes of synthesis to

the Understanding's rules in its application of synthesis to appearances (i.e., intellectual synthesis). But Imagination's heteronomy is tentative at best, a point well remarked by the indeterminate origin of Imagination. The tentativeness of Imagination's heteronomy marks the extent to which the discursivity of Imagination (its schemata) is not readily subsumable, not even in the interests of theoretical cognition.

Kant himself proclaimed the outcome of "Transcendental Deduction" to be the remarking of the complete heterogeneity of thought and knowledge. "We cannot think an object except through categories; we cannot know an object except through intuitions corresponding to the categories" (*KrV* B165; *CPR* 173). The heterogeneous processes of Understanding and sensibility are necessarily connected by the mediation of the transcendental function of the productive Imagination. There is nothing terribly provocative in this observation. In fact, it recalls Kant's own notion of a common sense of the cognitive faculties manifested in their heteronomous relations. The question is, How is heteronomy achieved? Because sensibility and Understanding are heterogeneous from each other, the categories cannot occur in intuition, nor can empirical intuition (involving the matter of sensation) occur in the categories. How then is the subsumption of intuition under categories (i.e., the application of a category to an appearance) possible?

The only way in which categories can be applied to appearances is through a mediating process of thought that is homogeneous with both the categories and appearances. This would be a pure transcendental representation that is, on the one hand, intellectual (void of empirical content), and so homogeneous with the categories, and, on the other hand, sensible, and so homogeneous with appearances. In the "Transcendental Doctrine of Judgment" of *Critique of Pure Reason* Kant designates this mediating representation the *transcendental schema* (*transszendental Schema*). In order to function as a mediation between pure sensibility and Understanding, the transcendental schema necessarily entails two formally identical but objectively distinct schemata. One is the schemata of those predicable concepts of Understanding (*das Schema dieses Verstandesbegriffs*) in their application to appearances as products of reproductive Imagination (empirical association). Instead of appearances, the other schemata has as its object the categories of Understanding. Being determined by a rule of apperception (that unity to which the categories give expression), the schemata of the categories are merely pure synthesis (*KrV* 141–42; *CPR* 182–83). This is not difficult to

grasp when we recall that for Kant, "schemata of the categories are the true and sole conditions under which the concepts obtain relation to objects and so possess significance" ("sind die Schemate der reinen Verstandesbegriffe die wahren und einzigen Bedingungen, diesen eine Beziehung auf Objekte, mithin Bedeutung zu verschaffen") (KrV 146; my translation). They are transcendental products of Imagination that entail the determination of the pure form of the inner sense (der innerer Sinn) as time, as the Wirkungskreis, the sphere of activity in which experience occurs.

Always a product of Imagination, it is the schema, and not images, which underlies pure sensible concepts (KrV 141; CPR 182). Images are products of reproductive Imagination, made possible through the schema of sensible concepts, which is a "monogram of pure a priori Imagination" (KrV 142; CPR 183). As objects of experience, images are connected to empirical concepts only by means of the schema to which they belong (KrV 142; CPR 183). Because images are constituted in this way, all experience is determined by the pure inner intuition of association and assemblage, i.e., the schemata of Imagination, in correlation with pure original apperception.

> The schemata are thus nothing but a priori determinations of time in accordance with rules. These rules relate in the order of the categories to the time-series, the time-content, the time-order, and lastly the scope of time in respect of all possible objects.
>
> It is evident, therefore, that what the schematism of Understanding effects by means of the transcendental synthesis of Imagination is simply the unity of the manifold of intuition in inner sense, and so indirectly the unity of apperception which as a function corresponds to the receptivity of inner sense. (KrV 146; CPR 185)

Insofar as a given experience is based on the synthetic unity of appearances, according to concepts of an object in general in correlation with the original unity of apperception, then that experience necessarily depends on some a priori principle governing the unity of appearance's synthesis. That synthetic unity is a rule that, like the categories, must be related to objects. The schemata are thus the a priori determination of time as inner sense, in accordance with the rules of the Understanding divorced from objective appearance. Inner sense is wholly temporal, the a priori sensibility that determines the assemblage of appearance. In this sense, it is discursive; and, insofar as it is temporality that underlies all thinking (viz., the a priori determination for possible cognition), think-

ing is also discursive. In the face of such widespread discursivity, Kant reiterates that the categories have no other possible employment than the empirical, by restricting the schemata to phenomena. As a result, although the schemata of sensibility first realize the categories, at the same time they restrict them; they limit them to conditions that lie outside the Understanding and are due to sensibility. A given schemata is, properly, only the phenomenon, or sensible concept, of an object in agreement with the category.

Ostensibly, this restricting is done so as to limit the categories to sensible appearances and so prevent the production of empty concepts that have no sensible condition and are empty of knowledge. Kant's own discourse betrays this, however, for he writes that the schemata both realize the categories and limit them *at the same time*. And it is in time that the purely logical signification of the categories can be represented.

All that is represented as being restricted is Imagination and the predicable empirical concepts. The latter are restricted to having meaning only when put in relation to appearances; the former is restricted to the activity of providing the a priori conditions for those appearances in the interests of Understanding. In this manner Understanding is to be realized in time, and yet at the same time freed from it. That freedom is highly tentative, becoming jeopardized whenever the Understanding engages empty concepts. Kant will attempt to avoid jeopardy with a systematic exposition of all the principles that the Understanding achieves a priori, differentiating between analytic judgments of Understanding (those judgments that relate only to categorical relations and so are merely logical and a priori, and whose governing principle is the principle of contradiction) and synthetic judgments of the Understanding.[30] The greatest danger of the categories' producing empty judgments comes principally from the employment of synthetic judgments.

The possibility for synthetic judgments lies in the relation between inner sense, Imagination, and apperception. In this relation synthetic a priori judgments are possible, precisely because such judgments require an object in which the synthetic unity of apperception can exhibit the objective reality of its concepts. In agreement with this, the a priori principles of form are the laws for the objective employment of the categories (*KrV* 157; *CPR* 194), which Kant represents in a four-headed table: (1) "Axioms of intuition," (2) "Anticipations of perceptions," (3) "Analogies of Experience," (4) "Postulates of empirical thought in gen-

eral."[31] In keeping with this table, the highest principle of all synthetic judgments is that "every object stands under the necessary conditions of synthetic unity of the manifold of intuition in a possible experience" (*KrV* 158; *CPR* 194).[32] By Kant's account, a concept of the Understanding is empty if it contains a synthesis that does not belong to experience, either as an empirical concept or as an a priori condition on which experience in general is based. The objective possibility of a thing cannot be determined from the category alone; there must always be an intuition in order to exhibit the objective reality of the pure concept.[33] The principles of the pure Understanding are nothing more than a priori principles of the possibility of experience, and the possibility of all a priori synthetic propositions is based on their being in relation to experience (*KrV* 294; *CPR* 256).

In the judgment "The Negro is stupid," the concept *The Negro* (the subject of the judgment) has no empirical content: *The Negro*, per se, has no extensive and no intensive magnitude, so it does not involve experience. Neither is it subject to any of the three postulates of empirical thought in general. As such, *The Negro* is an empty concept, a purely formal invention of the mind. It is a concept "the possibility of which is altogether groundless, as [it] cannot be based on experience and its known laws; and without such confirmation [it is an] arbitrary combination of thoughts, which . . . can make no claim to objective reality" (*KrV* 223; *CPR* 241). As a concept, *The Negro* is not an objective possibility; there is no way of knowing whether it is objectively real or not. This makes it a problematic concept that can only be thought; it is an effect of discursivity. The question is, how did Kant think about *The Negro*?

We must keep in mind that for Kant thought and knowledge are unquestionably not the same thing. Knowledge entails both the category through which an object in general is thought, and the intuition through which it is given. As far as thought is concerned, even without any given intuition corresponding to the category, the category would still be formally thought. In that case there would simply be no possible knowledge of anything empirical, which is why I stated earlier that the correlation of blackness and *The Negro* does not provide a positive cognition, because blackness is a phenomenal appearance subsumed under empirical concepts, and *The Negro* is not an empirical concept. The correlation between the two can only be symbolic, i.e., Kant acts as if the concept *The Negro* were objectively represented in blackness. Yet this concept will have only a negative value, because no positive cognition of

the concept is possible. This is where the conceptual *Negro* and the Negro who is Labat's informant meet. In order to denigrate Labat's informant, in accordance with the concept *The Negro*, Kant employs the a priori concept stupidity as though it were capable of being applied to a phenomenal appearance: the blackness of Labat's Negro. According to his own "Transcendental Logic," such an employment is a transcendental employment, which is to say that it is one of the illegitimate employments of Understanding that Kant set out to expose in *Critique of Pure Reason* as resulting in sophisms. These sophisms are illusionary appearances (*Schein*), something altogether different from the phenomenal appearances that are the proper objects of metaphysics. Such illusions come from errors in judgment, resulting from Reason's continual striving to determine phenomenal materiality immediately.

Until this point, the exposition of theoretical cognition has focused on Imagination's heteronomy to the theoretical interests of Understanding. Reason comes into the picture also in terms of its heteronomy in the service of those same interests. In its heteronomy to Understanding, Reason provides ideas, which represent the totality of the conditions under which a category of relation may be attributed to the objects of possible experience, and therefore represent something unconditioned. Reason's ideas are provided both subjectively and objectively. Subjectively, ideas refer to the categories of Understanding, conferring on them a maximum of both systematic unity and extension. In this way Reason constitutes ideal foci outside of the phenomenal world toward which the categories converge. Objectively, ideas introduce a harmony, or finality, between the content of phenomena and Reason's ideas. That is to say, the content of phenomena corresponds to or symbolizes the ideas of Reason, as in the case of the idea of nature's totality. Without such symbolism "we should not even have the concept of genus, or indeed any other universal concept, and the Understanding itself which has to do solely with such concepts would be non-existent" (*KrV* 653; *CPR* 539). For Kant, this harmony is not necessary—either in the sense of radical empiricism, according to which phenomenal experience determines ideas, or in the sense of radical Idealism, according to which ideas determine phenomenal experience. Instead it is merely postulated or declared. Rather than defining in totality the possibilities of nature by making ideas the ultimate source of all knowledge, Kant's Reason presupposes a systematic unity of nature—which is posed either as a problem or limit—in order to base its moves on this postulated limit at

infinity. For Kant, "everything happens as if." The totality and unity of conditions are not given objectively, but objects allow us to tend toward systematic unity as the highest degree of our knowledge. There is no necessary and determined subjection (of either the content to the idea or the idea to the content); we have instead only a correspondence, an indeterminate accord. The object of the idea is itself indeterminate and problematic. Accordingly, the ideas of Reason have three crucial aspects: (1) they are indeterminate in their object; (2) they are determinable by analogy with the objects of experience; and (3) they bear the ideal of an infinite determination in relation to the categories of the Understanding.[34] The ideas of Reason provide us with categorical classes.[35]

Hypokrisis of the Negro Class

In light of this, Kant is fully capable of holding the conceptual *Negro* as representing that which is inherently unintelligent, semihuman and beastlike, etc. Provided that when he expresses this concept with the designation "Negro" (*Neger*), that designation is not a class term (as this would invalidate all class terms, something Kant does not do), but rather a deduction from the class term "Humanity," and thus equally constructed as a class. This he does with his designation of "the Negroes of Africa" (*Die Negers von Afrika*), who are a derivative class of Humanity. How does Kant discursively designate the conceptual *Negro* as a positive given class, "Negro," which is subsumable to the empirical concepts of cognition, when the conceptual *Negro* can only be a negative representation?

Kant has a class idea: "Humanity [as an idea] in its complete perfection contains . . . all the essential qualities which belong to human nature and our concept of it [and] everything . . . required for the complete determination of the idea [of perfect humanity]" (*KrV* 568; *CPR* 485–86). The essential qualities that Kant lists are that humans are both phenomenal appearances and purely intellectual beings:

> Humanity . . . which knows all the rest of nature solely through the senses knows itself also through mere apperception; . . . Thus, [humanity] is for itself, on the one hand, phenomenon; and, on the other hand, with respect to [the faculties of Understanding and Reason] . . . which cannot be ascribed to the receptivity of sensibility, [it is] merely an intelligible object. (*KrV* 568; my translation)[36]

Humans as phenomenal beings know themselves the same way they know every other phenomenon, through synthetic judgment; but they also know their phenomenal being in a way they do not know other phenomena—as the seat of apperception, the nexus at which synthetic judgment is possible. Humans know themselves to be intelligible objects. Humanity as phenomena has all the characteristics of phenomena that are possible according to the categories of Understanding; but humanity as the class of intelligible beings is noumenal, and hence colorless, in the strictest sense.

Now, for Kant the designation "Negro" is a human designation, which is why it appears in the *Observations* as an example of how the feelings of the beautiful and sublime vary according to national characteristics. But as a designated class of humans, "Negro," as far as phenomenal traits are concerned, is the class of colorless humans with color added. The Negro, per se, is a phenomenal event and not an intelligible object of humanity. The intelligible object that coheres with the Negro is *The Negro*, which is the class of stupid humans. As a concept, *The Negro* is determined by the idea of noumenal "Humanity," that is, it is supersensible. This distinction between the Negro as phenomenon and *The Negro* as noumenon is what makes Negro, as a class, thinkable by synthesis of conceptual traits (phenomenal humans + evil + souls). It is also what makes Negro, as a class, a transcendental illusion of the order of the *djin* of Ras-sem. Kant writes on these *djin* in his *Anthropology from a Pragmatic Point of View*:

> The offenses [*vitia*] of Imagination consist in inventions that are either merely *unbridled* or downright *lawless* [*effrenis aut perversa*]. Lawless inventions are the worst fault. Unbridled inventions could still find their place in a possible world (the world of fable); but lawless inventions have no place in any world at all, because they are self-contradictory. Images of the first kind—that is, of unbridled Imagination—explain the dread with which Arabs regard the stone figures of humans and animals that are often found in the Libyan desert of Ras-sem. They think these figures are men petrified by a curse. But these same Arabs' belief that on the day of universal resurrection these statues of animals will growl at the artist, and reproach him for having made them without being able to give them souls, is a contradiction. Unbridled fantasy can always be bent [to the artist's end] . . . But lawless fantasy comes close to madness.[37]

Put more syllogistically, Kant has a concept of the universal class of Man whose essential traits are being both phenomenal and intelligible. As an intelligible object Man is unknowable to himself except as the cor-

relate of all conceptions in general, including transcendental conceptions. This correlate is self-consciousness or "I think," which designates nothing more than the transcendental unity of apperception or self-consciousness (*der transszendentale Einheit der Apperzeption*) that makes all transcendental conceptions possible.

The proposition "I think" is therefore understood to be problematic, not because it contains a perception of an existence (like the Cartesian *Cogito, ergo sum*), but because of the impossibility of discovering objectively any of the properties that may be inferred from the proposition and predicated of its syntactic subject: "*I.*" If it were otherwise, if at the foundation of our pure rational cognition of thinking beings there lay more than the mere apperception, something which could be represented as a phenomenal appearance, then Kant would have been compelled to accept an empirical psychology. In his case this would be a kind of behavioralist explication of the internal sense.

The analysis, then, of consciousness of "*I* " in thought in general (*im Denken überhaupt*) yields nothing whatsoever toward a synthetic judgment or knowledge of "*I.*" When it is claimed that consciousness of "*I*" does in fact support such a judgment or yield such a knowledge, then the logical exposition of thought in general (*Die logische Erörterung des Denkes überhaupt*) has been mistaken for an object's metaphysical determination. That is the expression of a paralogism. Kant is quite specific on this point.

> It would then follow that a priori synthetic propositions are possible and admissible, not only, as we have asserted, in relation to objects of possible experience, and indeed as principles of the possibility of this experience, but that they are applicable to things in general and to things in themselves—a result that would make an end of our whole critique, and would constrain us to acquiesce in the old-time procedure. (*KrV* B410; *CPR* 370–71)[38]

Nothing more is represented by the "*I,*" "He," or "It" who or which thinks than a transcendental subject of thought = x. Consciousness in itself is not so much a representation distinguishing a particular object, as it is a form of representation in general. Nor can any representation of a thinking being be achieved through example, i.e., by means of external experience. It can only be achieved through self-consciousness, which is why Kant maintains that the apodictic judgment, "everything which thinks is constituted as the voice of my consciousness declares it to be,

that is, as a self-conscious being," is founded on analogy and not an empirical judgment.

Analogy involves using the form of transcendental judgment, in this instance the judgment of apperception, to provide a judgment of something that is beyond experience and so cannot be validated: it cannot be known, per se. To assert judgments about other cogitating beings, whether the judgment is positive or negative, is in fact nothing more than the a priori transference of the properties which constitute the conditions under which "I" cogitates to other beings, thereby achieving a representation by analogy. To assert, therefore, a synthetic judgment of "*I*," to wit, "I am essentially stupid," is a paralogism. And by analogy, so is the apodictic judgment "*The Negro* is stupid." This in itself is not problematical, being no more than an instance of what Kant terms the offense of unbridled Imagination, which is when Imagination, much like Understanding in transcendental illusion, exceeds its limits in its schemata.

It follows, then, that "*The Negro* is stupid" is an a priori synthetic judgment, relying wholly on the Imagination's capacity for transcendental schemata. Although this makes it a problematic judgment according to the table of judgments, it does not in itself make it problematical for the architectonic.

What is problematical lies in the difference between the inventions of *unbridled* Imagination and *lawless* Imagination (*effrenis aut perversa*). It is one thing for the Libyans to fear the stones of Ras-sem because of imagined *djin*. It is altogether something else for them to convince themselves that these *djin* are in fact in the world. Kant finds the latter to be the most dangerous because Imagination's lawless inventions are self-contradictory. Kant's second apodictic judgment regarding Labat's carpenter, "blackness is a clear proof of stupidity," is of this order.

The contradiction lies in the relation between the concept *The Negro* and blackness. It is already established that the designation "Negro" is deduced from the class of Man as being both phenomenal and intelligible, and that as an intelligible object Man is colorless or white. We have also seen that Kant commits a paralogism when he gives a synthetic judgment of the intelligible. These are straightforward judgments that adhere to the discursive logic of Kant's critique. But they do not yield, according to the laws of Understanding, the judgment "blackness is a clear proof of stupidity." How then does Kant gain this assertion?

Recall that Kant equates stupidity with blackness, and blackness with the designation "Negro." He does so in an apodictic way: there are stupid men, all stupid men form a class, that class is black and called "Negro." Kant has deduced from that universal class of colorless Man a class of men with color. In so doing he has convinced himself that the Negro is a class of men in the world. The definitive feature of the Negro, then, is that they are men who are black and stupid. Here is where the conceptual *Negro*, the Negro who is Labat's informant, and the class "Negro" meet. And in that meeting they constitute just the sort of sophism masquerading as knowledge which Kant sought to expose.

Of the three kinds of sophisms that Kant traces to the illusions of Reason in the "Transcendental Dialectic," the one that has the greatest pertinence for the assertion "blackness is a clear proof of stupidity" is the transcendental paralogism. Kant's assertion about Labat's Negro indeed results from Reason's striving to determine phenomenal materiality immediately, and consequently driving the Understanding to take a concept, *The Negro*, which in fact has no determinate object (i.e., no objective reality), as being objectively verifiable. To complicate matters even further, in the judgment of Negroes' being by nature trifling, the Understanding claims to know objectively precisely what it can never know in this way: the thinking of others. To claim, therefore, predicable knowledge of both the conceptual *Negro* and the thinking of the Negro as a class of human beings is to engage in illusionary knowledge. Thus the Negro problem is a paralogism.

The transcendental critique as a whole aims to exorcise the adverse effects of such illusions as this on the possibilities of knowledge; but, because they inevitably result from the very nature of Reason, their formulation in the process of theoretical knowledge cannot be prevented. On this Kant writes:

> Now the transcendental (subjective) reality at least of the categories of Reason rests upon the fact that we are led to such ideas by a necessary procedure of reason. There must therefore be syllogisms which contain no empirical premises, and by means of which we conclude from something that we do know, to something of which we do not even possess a conception, to which we, nevertheless, by an unavoidable illusion, ascribe objective reality. Such arguments are, as regards their result, rather to be termed sophisms than syllogisms, although indeed, as regards their origin, they are very well entitled to the latter name, inasmuch as they are not fictions or accidental products of reason, but are necessitated by its very

nature. They are sophisms, not of men, but of pure reason herself, from which the wisest cannot free himself. (*KrV* 339; *CPR* 327)

Inasmuch as Kant's definition of illusion concerns questions of exterior referentiality, it provides examples through which transcendental philosophy can realize its concepts and judgments. And, insofar as the latter gives the form of thought—i.e., the field of possibility that gives sense and meaning to those representations—their relation, one to the other, is the enabling condition for the translating of appearances into experience.

Transcendental illusion occurs when Understanding presupposes that it can abstract itself from its relation to the Imagination. It seeks to circumvent Imagination's synthesis, however, and gain direct access to things-in-themselves, because of Reason's idea of totalizing unity. Reason's idea of unity occasions an illusion of a positive domain to conquer outside experience. Although Kant's definition of transcendental illusion attributes the cause for Understanding's trying to do without Imagination to Reason's idea of totality, in fact, what that idea provides for Understanding is a supposedly unconditional means to resolve the mystery of the indeterminate genesis of Imagination's *agencement*. That indeterminacy compels Understanding to attempt to do without Imagination. By representing Reason as the cause, Kant is tacitly offering the argument that the genealogy of Imagination's *agencement* is in Reason. Given the purely ideal nature of Reason's infinite determination, this is in keeping with Kant's explicitly stating that it is impossible to discover the genesis of Imagination, except as a mystery in the heart of Man's soul. According to his own mapping of the architectonic, this means that although Imagination operates in the same territory of experience as Understanding, nature, it has no domain of knowledge. Kant takes up the concept of dominion and territory most fully in the two introductions to his *Critique of Judgment*. The introductions can be read as Kant's attempts, subsequent to the *Critique of Pure Reason*, to amend his presentation of Imagination in that text, and so resolve the problems that its nomadism poses for the architectonic. The pertinence that Kant's judgment about the Negro's stupidity has for all of this is found in the incomprehensibility of Imagination's discursivity. As will be seen presently, Kant's Negro problem highlights how Imagination's indeterminate assemblage gives rise to something very intriguing: an indeterminate knowledge (*unbestimmites Erkenntnis*) that is thoroughly discursive, and

so syntax-bound. In other words, Kant's judgment about the Negro exposes that Imagination's lack of fixed domain, its nomadism, does not imply its lack of dominion. It does have a dominion, albeit an extreme indeterminate one, that of *agencement*. Indeterminacy threatens Understanding's claim to even a theoretical domain, insofar as *agencement* is the principal function of thinking nature.

This is where the Negro takes Kant, and us along with him, to this relation that amounts to the correlation of apperception with the object in general. That correlation amounts to no more than the synthesis of the reflective operation of transcendental critique. Reality is thought and experienced spontaneously, but the two operations are so heterogeneous to each other that a determinate heteronomy of Imagination is foreclosed by the persistence of Imagination's indeterminate genealogy, its lawlessness. Kant seeks to resolve this indeterminacy through its proper designation.

Unbestimmungkeit Wortbestimmung: Designating Indeterminacy

At a certain strategic moment in "Transcendental Analytic" (specifically, in "Transcendental Doctrine of Judgment," which is the first chapter of book 2), Kant calls the procedure of Understanding in the schemata "the *schematism* of pure Understanding" (*KrV* 140; *CPR* 182). This designation is of considerable significance, occurring at the close of a rather abruptly introduced description of how the transcendental schema mediates between the categories and appearances. The particular device of that description, time, is more than merely heuristic, it is the very pure condition of sensibility that is designated as schema. On the basis of the account given in the "Transcendental Deduction," Kant asserts that

> time, as the formal condition of the manifold of inner sense, and therefore of the connection [assemblage] of all representations, contains an a priori manifold in pure intuition. Now a transcendental determination of time is so far homogeneous with the category, which constitutes its unity, in that it is universal and rests upon an a priori rule. But on the other hand, it is so far homogeneous with appearance, in that time is contained in every empirical representation of the manifold. Thus an application of the category to appearances becomes possible by means of the transcendental determination of time, which as the schema of the concepts of Understanding, mediates the subsumption of the appearances under the category. (*KrV* 138; *CPR* 181)

Kant further recalls the "Transcendental Deductions' " account of how a priori concepts only have meaning in conjunction with intuition, which can only be presented as appearances, and that the former of the two necessarily contains the formal conditions of inner sense, i.e., time. So when he states that the formal conditions of the inner sense constitute the universal condition under which alone the category can be applied to any object, which is the schema, he is saying that the schema is time.

Kant disabuses us in short order of any illusion that this schema resolves the problem of the "Transcendental Deduction" by proclaiming that "the schema is in itself always a product of Imagination" (*KrV* 140; *CPR* 182). There can be no doubt that it is productive Imagination, because the schema is distinct from the appearances, which are also arrived at through Imagination's synthesis being aimed at the unity in the determination of sensibility. Appearances are products of reproductive Imagination (empirical association); schema of sensible concepts, on the other hand, are products of transcendental, productive Imagination.

Through the schemata, as the representations of the universal procedure of Imagination, an appearance is provided for a concept. It is also by way of the schemata that the appearances are subsumed under the categories. Indeed, Kant claims that "it is schemata, not appearances, which underlie our pure sensible concepts" (*KrV* 140; *CPR* 182). Because appearances in themselves cannot be immediately adequate even to predicable sensible concepts, what the latter is in immediate relation to, as a rule for the determination of our intuition, is the schema of Imagination.

Here again, Kant strives to give the Understanding the upper hand in its relationship with Imagination, by representing the categories of Understanding, from which predicable concepts derive, as the source for the determinate laws of theoretical cognition. Nonetheless he is frustrated in this effort by the diligence of his own argument. For not only are schemata temporal determinations which immediately correspond to the categories everywhere and at all times, but, in its application to appearances and their mere form (the synthesis of Imagination), the working of schemata is "an art concealed in the depths of the human soul, whose real modes of activity nature is hardly likely ever to allow us to discover, and to open to our gaze" (*KrV* 141; *CPR* 183).[39] All we can assert is that the appearance is a product of the empirical faculty of reproductive Imagination; "the schema of sensible concepts ... is a product and, as it were, a monogram [*ein Monogramm*], of pure a priori

Imagination, in accordance with which appearances themselves first become possible" (*KrV* 141–42; *CPR* 183).

This uncharacteristic outburst on Kant's part might be excused in light of the almost palpable degree of frustration reached after literally hundreds of pages of rigorous effort and close argumentation. Not only does the problem of Imagination's indeterminacy seem hopelessly irresolvable, but it becomes intractable, firmly situating itself at the base of theoretical cognition. Even this it does not do in any exact and clear-cut way that might be *totally* comprehensible to Understanding. Instead, it is as an enigmatic sketch, a monogram. The appeal to nature is indeed figurative; Imagination, like nature, cannot in itself be positively represented. This has severe repercussions for the architectonic, which seems to flounder on this enigma.

Kant's capacity for marshaling terminology to engage even the most intractable of enigmas is superb. In calling Imagination a monogram he can justifiably bracket the problem of its indeterminacy by acknowledging it; yet in that acknowledgment he does not bind the transcendental project over to Imagination. The German *Monogramm*, like the English monogram, derives from the late Latin *monogramma*, which is irregularly formed after the late Greek *monogrammon*, a conflation of *monos* = single + *gramma* = letter. Both the Greek and the Latin referred to the signature of the Byzantine emperors. In this sense Imagination is grammatic representation.

It is not this sense of monogram, however, that justifies the bracketing of Imagination. In addition to the late Latin *monogramma*, there is a classical Latin adjectival form, *monogrammus*, which is the translation of the Greek adjective *monogrammos*, a conflation of *monos* = single + *grammé* = line. Cicero attributed this term to Epicurus, who used it to mean "unsubstantial" as a description of the gods. Subsequently, Lucilius used it to mean a thin colorless person, or a mere shadow. Nonius took it in this fashion to indicate a line picture or sketch done without any color.

Kant uses monogram in the sense of both *monogramma* and *monogrammus* to mean an enigmatic unsubstantial outline sketch of the formal (grammatic) principles by which Imagination determines experience. Of course a glance at the text will make it plain that grammatically his usage leans heaviest toward *monogramma*. But there is still another sense in which he employs grammatic, an employment so obvious that its not being readily grasped is perhaps best attributed to our overin-

vestment in the philosophical theory of language, which requires that the graphic medium of exhibition (i.e., writing) be transparently clear so as not to obfuscate the argument and overburden the reader.

When reading Kant, however, we constantly stumble upon such obfuscation, due to the density of his narrative style and his predilection for terminological coinage and syntactic complexity. That is exactly the other sense in which he employs monogram; the enigma of Imagination's schemata is narrative, it is the syntactic principles for the assemblage of appearance, the very conditions for a priori sensibility, which is designated by schema as the inner sense. Still, while it is possible to represent positively the categories of Understanding as the source for the laws that determine empirical synthesis (i.e., experience), the laws by which that representation is itself possible (the transcendental synthesis of Imagination's schemata) remain indeterminate, "concealed in the depths of the human soul." What is discovered in the genealogy of theoretical cognition is not the uncontested legislation of Understanding, with Imagination's attendant heteronomy, but rather a contentious relationship between Understanding and Imagination. That contention is insoluble because the domain of Imagination's principles cannot be determined by Understanding.

At stake in the enigma of Imagination is not so much a theory of language as a theory of discursivity. Entailed in Kant's implicit theory of discursivity is a concept that the origins of discourse's grammatics cannot be determined and cannot be subsumed under a subjective consciousness. Nor can they be discovered in a positive teleology of nature, because, as Kant points out in his *Critique of Judgment*, nature is also an effect of a contentious relationship, this time between Imagination and Reason.

Kant's apodictic judgment about Labat's Negro draws our attention precisely to how Imagination's lawlessness focuses on the inability of thought's discursive processes to make language refer either objectively or subjectively to the there and then of a "given state of affairs." This discursivity, theoretical or speculative thinking, in its turn, would explicate by presenting representation as the inaugural act of reference in which all other forms of reference are grounded. The explicit task of theoretical thinking is to emancipate thought from the obscuring effects of dogma, by becoming itself an aesthetic moment grounded in the possibilities of representation.

However, it is a task for which theory is not adequate, because of The Imagination's seemingly willful indeterminacy. The appearance of a willfulness whose source is not in Understanding leads Kant to recognize that Imagination's heteronomy is not in the interests of Understanding but in those of Reason. At this point Kant discovers that there is an immense gulf between the domain of the concept of nature (i.e., theoretical cognition, whose legislating faculty is Understanding) and the domain of the concept of freedom (i.e., practical cognition, whose legislating faculty is Reason). Yet, although theory cannot influence or determine freedom—the sensible cannot define the supersensible—freedom does influence and determine theory: "The concept of freedom is to actualize in the world of sense the purpose enjoined by its laws" (*Kritik der Urteilskraft* 11; *Critique of Judgment* 15).[40] What is the basis for this uniting of the supersensible with the sensible? How are the ideas of Reason realized when they have no attendant object of intuition?

It has become customary to locate the address of these issues, which emerge from the *Critique of Pure Reason*, in the *Critique of Judgment*, albeit they are more often than not discussed in terms of Kant's need to determine a substance basis for morality. In this regard, Kant's third *Critique* is looked to as the mediating moment, the *mittelglied*, between theoretical thinking about phenomena (espoused in the *Critique of Pure Reason*) and the supersensible, or noumena of apperception, whose unity is found in the ideas of Reason (*Critique of Practical Reason*). It is the text where the negativity of the supersensible field of nature occasions the exhibition of the act through which the relationship of the particular to the universal is established: the examination of judgment in its pure disinterested operation.

Kant suggests this regard when he proposes the *Critique of Judgment* as the *Verbindungsmittel*, "the mediating connection," not only between the two domains of philosophy, theoretical and practical cognition, but also between phenomena and noumena, the sensible and supersensible (*KU* 11; *CJ* 15). The paramount question of the *Critique of Judgment* is thus held to be, What is the nature of judgment's rational exhibition? In Kant's formulation: How are a priori aesthetic judgments possible?

In order to address this question, Kant distinguishes between two forms of synthetic judgment: determinative and reflective. If the universal under which the particular is to be subsumed is already known, as the a priori condition under which the subsumption of the particular is possible, then it is determinative. If the particular is given without the

universal under which it is to be subsumed as being known, then the judgment is reflective.

Determinative judgment is always subsuming and theoretical, operating according to already-designated a priori laws dealing with the possibility of nature as an object of sense. Yet determinative judgment is confronted constantly with a problem of field: in the face of nature's vast heterogeneity, determinative judgment has limits. Nature's heterogeneity means that there are possibilities of nature that are undetermined by the designated a priori laws. This is a critical problem if we, like Kant, maintain that the laws of theory are empirical and thus contingent and define law as that which entails a necessity grounded in a principle of unity. In other words, judgment is based on the very homogeneity of function, which Imagination's indeterminacy foreclosed on. So when determinative judgment confronts a particular (appearance) of nature that is not subsumable under any of its already-designated a priori principles (i.e., the concept of nature and the concept of freedom), it has met a resistance that it cannot overcome theoretically. A particular portion of the legitimate territory of its domain resists its dominion.

Kant strives to overcome this resistance through reflective judgment, which, in *moving from* the particular toward the universal, requires a transcendental principle or law that cannot be gotten from experience, precisely because it is to be the basis of the unity of experience. Reflective judgment's capacity to exhibit this transcendental law only to itself, while not prescribing it to nature, is what makes it reflective, because reflection on the laws of nature is prompted by the negativity of nature as supersensible. If the law were derived from nature as a positive experience (i.e., empirical representation), then the judgment would be determinative, because such representation requires that the universal principle already be known.

Reflective judgment overcomes resistance by exhibiting for reflection the very conditions of conceptualization. The essential condition for conceptualization is that the concept entails the basis for the object's objective actuality (the object's having significance), which Kant calls the object's purpose.

> Accordingly, judgment's principle concerning the form that things of nature have in terms of empirical laws in general is the purposiveness of nature in its heterogeneity. . . . Through this concept we represent nature as if an Understanding contained the basis of the unity of that which is heterogeneous in nature's empirical laws. (*KU* 17; *CJ* 20)

What Kant calls here the purposiveness of the object's form is exactly what he called schemata of Imagination in the *Critique of Pure Reason*. He is talking about Imagination when he goes on to say that the formal purposiveness of nature as the a priori concept that functions as the law of reflective judgment is a transcendental and not a physical principle because it has its origins solely in reflective judgment itself, and has no objective or theoretical purposiveness. Imagination is not a metaphysical principle, because it is not concerned with thinking the a priori conditions under which an object (the concept of which must be empirically given) is determined a priori by way of example. Thinking metaphysical principles requires empirical concepts. The concept of the formal purposiveness of nature, on the other hand, is concerned with objects only in terms of the pure concept of the possible objects of cognition in general, and contains no empirical representation at all. Thus, the formal purposiveness of nature is a transcendental principle found only in the reflective judgment's movement from particular toward universal, and is deduced from Imagination's lawlessness. Reflective judgment must only exhibit this movement from toward; were it to achieve the universal under which the particular could then be subsumed it would become determinative.

The focus of the *Critique of Judgment* is on this movement as the exhibition of judgment's acting without any theoretical or practical knowledge. For Kant, this exhibition is found in its pure form with those judgments dealing with the feelings of pain and pleasure, aesthetic judgments. This is because the experience of the beautiful and sublime has no objective purpose: what is experienced is not an object that can be subsumed under a concept, but a form of experience that cannot be subsumed under a concept. In judging things to be beautiful and sublime, we cannot objectively know what we are talking about. By that same token, when Kant speaks about the Negro he cannot possibly know what he is talking about. This notwithstanding, he has his thoughts about *The Negro* and declares them quite readily.

This is a problem of definition, and according to Kant's "Architectonic of Pure Reason," defining something "really only means to present the complete, original concept of [that] thing within the limits of its concept" (*KrV* 727-28; *CPR* 586).[41] By completeness Kant means clearness and sufficiency of characteristics; by limits he means the precision with which characteristics superfluous to the complete concept are excluded; and by original he means that these limits are derived solely from the

complete concept, to the exclusion of all other sources, in which case the concept is self-evident, requiring no proof or example (*KrV* 727, fn; *CPR* 586, fn). Clearly then, very little can be defined per se, because the characteristics represented in empirical concepts cannot possibly be complete, which can produce a confusion of reference: they cannot be defined but only *made explicit*.[42] Certain characteristics are emphasized in order to make distinctions, which guarantees that the concept's limits are never sure.

The means by which such emphasis is achieved is word designation (*Wortbestimmung*) in which what is called definition is nothing but the association of a word with the thing. For similar reasons of confusion in reference, a priori concepts cannot be defined either. This time the confusion is due to the probable nature of any concept because the indeterminacy of Imagination's synthesis prevents it from being apodictically certain.

So Kant refers to the exposition of a priori concepts, rather than their definition. Arbitrarily presented concepts also cannot be defined, because due to their arbitrariness there can be no definitive determination of their objective possibility. The definition of such concepts is better considered as their *explication* or *declaration*. The only concept that allows definition is one which contains an arbitrary synthesis admitting an a priori construction, i.e., a concept which is completely homogeneous with its representation: Axioms. Insofar as Kant finds Axioms only in mathematics, it is only in mathematical knowledge that definition is possible. Philosophy can have no definitions per se.

What does this mean for the five hundred or so pages of categorical definitions that Kant has provided in the *Critique of Pure Reason* up until this point? Kant tells us that these definitions have in fact been *Erklärung*:

> The German language has for the terms exposition, explication, declaration, and definition only one word *Erklärung*, and we need not be so strict in the requirements [of language] as to altogether deny philosophical *Erklärung* the honorable title, definition. We shall confine ourselves simply to remarking that . . . philosophical definitions are never more than expositions of given concepts. (*KrV* 730; *CPR* 587)[43]

What is Kant telling us with all of this?

In effect, he has given an exposition of how the indeterminacy of Imagination precludes any definitive determination of cognition's genealogy in its being only uncertainly heteronomous to Understanding.

Every designation, every association and reproduction is finally probabilistic. This does not mean, however, that the definition of the Transcendental Philosophy is not possible; it only means that its necessity is theoretical. Indeed, this indeterminacy is its necessity.

The way in which Kant effects this recuperation of indeterminacy in the interests of theoretical knowledge is remarkable. He engages a *Wortbestimmung:* he designates a word, *Erklärung,* as comprehending the entirety of indeterminacy. *Wortbestimmung,* then, is the process of generating a discursive economy in which the indeterminacy of referentiality (that which cannot be subject to thought) is come to terms with. In other words, in talking one cannot help but know what one is talking about, because talking is the very possibility of cognition. Or, in the more precise Kantian terminology, discursivity enables thought.

As long as Kant can keep on writing, there is hope that the transcendental critique's project of defining the universally necessary architectonic of cognition by which the perfection of humanity will be realized will succeed. By that same token, as the paralogism of the Negro demonstrates, the more he writes in order to come to terms with indeterminacy, the more indeterminacy confronts him, manifested in the lawlessness of Imagination's schemata (the mysterious genealogy of its rules). Always before him, Imagination's lawlessness assures the futility of the project.

The play of *Wortbestimmung* by which *Erklärung* is claimed as the mode for outlining the hypotyposis of representation discovers the possibilities of cognition to be determined by the possibilities of referentiality inherent in narrative structures—i.e., discursive economies. Or, as Kant would have it, through *Wortbestimmung* the history of Reason is delineated. In these terms, to say that Kant's architectonic engenders a realignment of metaphysics into a new organization of knowledge as anthropology—which attempts to trace the primary site of inscription (the genealogy of knowledge) in order to comprehend difference in the experiencing of materiality—is to suggest that anthropology is the science of transcribing the phenomenal materiality of experience according to an a priori discursive logic of development. Put differently, the subject of the architectonic is that which violates the limits of, is beyond, thought, yet somehow essential to thinking.

Although the subject of anthropology cannot be *given in thought*—it cannot be defined either phenomenologically or theoretically—its phenomenological and theoretical effects are certain in Imagination's

schematizing. The resulting schemata is that of a theoretically determinable modality of meaning-production (thinking), which is dependent on discursive properties that stand beyond any subjectivity and so
are not intentional. This indeterminacy of Imagination is realized, for
Kant, in the inability to express thinking definitively in language. Yet,
there is something about the specific signifying practice in which he is
engaged that enables him to give an account of indeterminacy that still
allows for at least a hypothetical grounding of meaning. In Kant's case
this signifying practice entails an assemblage of the diverse discourses of
metaphysics, natural philosophy, law, and so on, expressed in one mode
of communication: writing. It is the flow of writing, its structural capacity for nigh-on perpetual wordplay (designation), for modifying its field
of reference, that both allows for this account of indeterminacy and is a
working of indeterminacy. This indeterminacy is not some kind of mystery, or secret; it is linguistic structures, the play of linguistic tensions,
linguistic events that occur, possibilities that are inherent in language's
capacity for word designation. All of which are independent of any
intent or desire to mean. Indeterminacy proves to be nothing more or
less than how the very process of signification (the signifying practice)
indexes that aspect of its historical situation that, as such, is not made by
us as historical beings (de Man, *Resistance to Theory* 87). It is inhuman.
Not that linguistic structures, tensions, and events are mysterious
things, in the sense of being a locus of agency beyond the human and
language: they are not. What they are is "eminently discursive"—so discursive that they uncover the illegitimacy of the rapport between the
human and nature. This fundamental nonhuman character of linguistic
referentiality encompasses a fundamental nondefinition of the human,
because what the word "human" refers to is something altogether other
than this indeterminate discursivity.

The tendency is to discover a theoretical determination for this inhu-
manity in the *Critique of Judgment*, where Kant shifts consideration from
the problem of apprehension engendered in his analytic "On the
Mathematically Sublime" to terms of resistance entailed in the analytic
"On the Dynamically Sublime." If indeterminate discursivity is connected with Kant's conception of the mathematical and dynamical aspects of
human cognition, then the inhumanness of referentiality would be represented as a mathematical concept. It would become a problem of
apprehension, of the inability of the transcendental subject (the transcendental unity of apperception) to comprehend its genesis in the discursiv-

ity of thought. In that case we might be inclined to regard Kant's "Architectonic of Pure Reason" as a *periphrasis*, a wordy circumlocution that simultaneously under- and overspecifies what it designates, freedom, in order to elide a series of failed apprehensions that are the basis of signification.

The architectonic naming freedom names itself the inhuman: it is a name that does not disambiguate meaning, but rather speaks around the untenable relation of sign to signified: the Negro is inhuman. The lesson that can be gleaned from Kant's Negro problem is fourfold: (1) all humans necessarily synthesize perceptions; (2) those perceptions do not have any inherent or immediate meaning; (3) meaning is ascribed to those perceptions by an arbitrary act of attribution; and (4) this act of attribution is realized in the syntax of judgments or propositions (i.e., sentences), which unites the synthesized perceptions with meaning *as if* (*als ob*) the two were of the same order. In other words, Kant saw, after some work, that the two operations (synthesis of perceptions, and attribution of meaning) are heterogeneous to each other, and only the fundamentally indeterminate designation/signification of language makes them coexist.

The Negro problem affords us a glimpse at the inhuman in linguistic referentiality precisely because of the inability of any phenomenology of language, or of a poetics that would be in any sense a phenomenology of language, to subsume it under one of the concepts of the familiar philosophical formulations. More precisely, what is at stake in the Negro problem is the historiography of ideas that distinguishes between the legitimate concerns of philosophy's formulations and those of semiotics. This is why I have expressed the problem of what is unrepresentable about The Negro in an admittedly clumsy and involved formulation that, by all proper accounts, inappropriately juxtaposes the problems of linguistic referentiality and phenomenal intentionality.

Among the most accessible lessons of Kant's Negro problem is that high risks are involved in the notion that language can say any experience, and that any language oriented toward meaning is intentional in its description of objective meaning. Although, for Kant, it can be said that there is a perpetual consciousness of the object, and a designatable experience of this consciousness, it remains idealistic, and so unrealizable except in discourse. Kant's *Wortbestimmung* is not simply subjective nominalism, it is primarily a critique of the conception of the subject as an expression of its own intentionality.[44]

Immaterial Referentiality

When expressed in the terms of Kant's architectonic, even as a response to that architectonic, the slave narrative is found to have been engendered and sustained by the enigmatic categorical status of *The Negro*. This in turn draws attention to the underlying conceptions of signification and language that are at work whenever there is talk about the correlation of thought and experience.

What is the Negro? Is it a spectacle, a phenomenal experience? Or is it merely a concept of the Understanding, indicative of an ideology or thought that signifies nothing beyond itself except the process of signification? Another way of putting the same question is, How can that without phenomenal appearance be represented?

By asking this question, we have recalled the question with which Douglass's narrative prompted this detour through Kant: How can a symbol enable the representation of meaning although it has no referent? In the wake of what has already been shown to be the case with the Kantian concept of representation, it should come as no surprise that the answer would be: By analogy, on the condition that the referent is indeed absent.

What I am suggesting is that Douglass's slave narrative, by employing, in effect, the Kantian concept of representation, discovers that the experiences of reading and seeing are phenomenologically different. The written grapheme is experienced phenomenologically as having a material substance, but that materiality becomes transparent in the act of reading. It has no meaningful value within the economy of signification, the value system, which reading constitutes. This transparency of the material sign enables Douglass to devalue writing, per se, by maintaining the fundamental immateriality of thought as discourse and situating value within that discursivity. Referentiality therefore is not the effect of the experience of phenomenal perception (in writing), but instead the effect of designating meaning to that perception. In his insistence on the transparency of the material sign, Douglass's response to Kant becomes not Romantic, but Idealist.

I have spent this much space considering how Douglass's 1845 slave narrative provokes these questions because it is plain to see in Douglass's text, I think, that even though the slave narrative spells out, as it were, what is at stake in representation, it does not achieve a rigorous problematizing of it. When writing (as the *en concreto* realization of a

particular subjectivity) is given as a "response" to a specific economy of signification, this presupposes a representational intentionality that stands beyond this economy, as evidenced in Douglass's assertion of having thought before acquiring literacy. After all, in order to ground the history of culture in a narrative act of assemblage that renders material experience meaningful, there must be an agency at work before the production or fabrication of the text, an agency whose representative traces construct the text. Douglass goes on to recognize his 1845 reader ten years later in 1855 as a full-fledged autobiographical subject who above all writes well.[45]

There are, however, a set of slave narratives in which the reduction of agency to the proper name may be possible, but in which the repression of the difference between the work and the life is not; thus foregrounding the irresolvable formal heterogeneity of writing/reading, but in a way that does not facilitate a teleology of culture. These are New World Arabic slave narratives, whose being written in an "Afro-Asiatic" language and script makes them even better suited as destabilizing responses to Kant. Including the manuscripts written in Brazil during the jihad of Bahia, along with those produced in the Caribbean and the United States, there are already thirty known Arabic slave texts.[46] There may very well be hundreds more. Compared to the thousands of known English-language slave narratives, this is not an impressive number, but nevertheless these Arabic slave narratives entail an engagement with modernity. That engagement does not entail a cartography of difference in literary expression that distributes that difference in space (Africa versus Europe) according to developmental stages in the absolute dialectic of progress. Neither does it entail the subsuming of difference under a historicism that distributes it according to the Absolute Spirit's emergence in consciousness through time. Rather, the Arabic slave narrative constitutes a moment of contention that clearly amounts to an engagement with modernity in the dialectic of culture/nature, phenomena/ noumena, past/present, and Reason/indeterminacy; which is why it does not support a teleology of resolution either as the ultimate end of history in the reality of the absolute or in art as the cumulative effect of the absolute's manifestation in particular historical moments. The New World Arabic slave narrative might very well be an African American response to modernity, but it is neither a Romantic nor an Idealist one.

These texts have not been ignored altogether by the project of canon

formation. Gates identifies an Arabic slave narrative, the 1731 letter of Ayyūb ibn Suleimān Diallo (also known as Job the Son of Solomon) to his father, as the first known instance in modernity when an African literally wrote his way out of slavery.[47] Ayyūb's letter is represented as the primary occurrence of African American literature, because in it he requests that his father ransom him from slavery. This, in and of itself, would not be so interesting, given the pronounced philological bent of Gates's project of canon formation, were it not for the fact that by representing Ayyūb ibn Suleimān Diallo's 1731 Arabic letter as the first African American slave narrative, Gates posits at the genesis of the African American literary tradition he delineates a text written in an African language, which he does not read. For Gates, Ayyūb's literacy, translated into a little more than £59, was the commodity with which he earned his escape price, and with which a particular economy of signifying practices became the sine qua non of natural human rights (*Figures in Black* 12–13; *Signifying Monkey* 148, 163). What is more pertinent to our concerns here is the fact that Gates claims to know the content of this letter, something he can do only through a mediating economy of signification.

As Bluett recounts it, Ayyūb's enslavement was a relatively neat commercial transaction involving an established network of exchange. In February 1730 Ayyūb was sold as a commodity in the same manner that he had sold others into slavery, by the same principal English purchaser of his goods, Captain Pyke, who was the agent in Africa of Captain Henry Hunt. Although Ayyūb's previous business relationship with Pyke did incline the latter to recognize Ayyūb's financial capacity to redeem himself, limitations of time, communications between the coast and Bundu, and commercial exigencies resulted in Ayyūb's being shipped to Annapolis, Maryland, where Hunt's American agent, Vachell Denton, sold him to Alexander Tolsey of Kent Island, Maryland. Within a year after his purchase by Tolsey, Ayyūb escaped and was subsequently captured at Baltimore, where Bluett made his acquaintance in June 1731. At that meeting Ayyūb is purported to have established his extraordinary value to his American owners by writing in Arabic. This led to his being permitted to write the famous letter "in Arabick to his father," and to send it to Denton at Annapolis, who was to forward it to Pyke in England before his next voyage to the Gambia. The writing of the letter did not lead immediately to Ayyūb's manumission; in fact, that would not occur until two years after its writing. It did, however, result in his

resale by Tolsey back to Denton, at the original purchase price. He stayed with Denton, teaching Arabic to John Humphrys and impressing the Reverend Jacob Henderson with his character—a character that Ayyūb would be able to trade upon when in England.

In the meantime, Denton sent Ayyūb's letter to Hunt so that he could give it to Pyke, who in his capacity as Hunt's agent in Africa was the initial purchaser of Ayyūb and was positioned to determine fair redemption value and realize the transaction. Pyke was to deliver the letter to Ayyūb's father and collect his redemption cost. The letter reached Hunt too late for forwarding to Pyke, who had already sailed. In the interim wait for Pyke's return, Hunt treated the letter as a curiosity, showing it to the well-known antiquary and bibliographer Joseph Ames, who tried to have it translated. Hunt also showed it to his friend James Oglethorpe, the deputy governor of the Royal African Company and founder of Georgia colony. Oglethorpe was sufficiently impressed with this letter written by a purported son of a principal political leader in Bundu, a region that the Royal African Company was extremely interested in as a source of gum arabica, that he sent it for translation to John Gagnier, who held the Laudian Chair of Arabic at Oxford. The letter is no longer extant, but apparently Gagnier affirmed the authenticity of the document, and consequently Oglethorpe gave Hunt his bond for payment of £45 (Ayyūb's purchase price) upon Ayyūb's delivery in London.[48]

This was not yet the purchase of Ayyūb's freedom, but Oglethorpe's initial investment in Ayyūb's cause eventually led the Royal African Company to invest considerably in his prospects. As a result of Oglethorpe's interest in Ayyūb, in March 1733 Ayyūb and Bluett sailed for England on board the *William* (it was during this trip that Ayyūb learned most of his English from Bluett), reaching England near the end of April 1733. This arrival proved to be too late for Oglethorpe to purchase his bond, as he had resigned as deputy governor of the Royal African Company, had sold his stock on 21 December 1732, and had sailed for Georgia. On 3 May 1733, Oglethorpe's successor as deputy governor of the Royal African Company, Charles Hayes, presented Hunt's petition to the Court of Assistants (the company's governing board) that the company purchase Oglethorpe's bond. The company decided that, in spite of Oglethorpe's absence, it was in its best interest to purchase his bond from Hunt in that Ayyūb "understands and writes Arabick and may be of service to the Company on giving him his free-

dom and sending him to Gambia, which is his native country."[49] The execution of this decision took place on 15 November, when the company paid Hunt the full principal of Oglethorpe's bond (£45), the interest on it from 3 May to 15 November 1733 (£1 3s. 11d.), as well as Ayyūb's maintenance cost incurred when he was under Hunt's care in England (£13 3s.). After the company's purchase of Ayyūb, some of his friends in England, encouraged by Bluett, became concerned about his safety and freedom, and argued with Hayes over Ayyūb's manumission. Among these friends were Sir Hans Sloane, who organized a fund of £20 for Ayyūb's manumission, and Nathaniel Brassey, the well-established banker who was persuaded to provide the remaining £39.6.11. Ayyūb's manumission certificate was dated 27 December 1733,[50] and Brassey's payment to the Royal African Company secured the purchase of Ayyūb's freedom on 10 January 1734. Subsequent to these transactions, the company agreed to accommodate Ayyūb in its African House until one of its ships made ready for sail to Gambia. In all of these transactions, the only exchange of money on Ayyūb's behalf that was a direct result of his 1731 Arabic letter to his father did not secure his freedom, it merely transferred his ownership from Hunt to the Royal African Company for £59 6s. 11d.

Obviously, as Ayyūb's case demonstrates, not all literacies are equal.[51] His demonstration of literacy in Arabic enhanced his value as a commodity with growth potential; it did not buy his freedom. This is the point at which the story of Ayyūb's exchange value gets fully under way. It was Ayyūb's demonstrated capacity as source of information about the production and distribution network of gum arabica, as well as his potential as a trading partner in that important commodity, that fueled the Royal African Company's and subsequently the Crown's interest in him. His Arabic letter to his father proved important in that it attracted attention to Ayyūb's eminence in the region of Bundu, but his purchase from Hunt was determined by British interests in breaking the French monopoly of the gum trade. Whatever Oglethorpe's reasons for giving Hunt his bond, the Royal African Company purchased that bond on the sound business assumption that acquiring Ayyūb meant acquiring future trade relations. Ayyūb and Bluett were not altogether wrong in their concern that the Royal African Company's purchase of Oglethorpe's bond would result in his being ransomed. Nor was the company's eventual acquiescence to Bluett's efforts motivated by anything but commercial investment (as

is clear in Hayes's correspondence with the company on the matter of Bluett's interference). The company agreed to Ayyūb's manumission when it realized on past experience that its investment was nonrealizable with a hostile or circumspect commodity. So the bond was cancelled, effectively emancipating Ayyūb from a specific commercial bondage, on the risk that by showing deference to him, the company would win him over and secure a factory in the midst of the area where the gum was produced, and thereby undermine the virtual French monopoly.[52] The £59 was the exchange value for the potentially lucrative economy of gum. But it was an exchange value underwritten by a particular knowledge, the philological knowledge of Gagnier. Gagnier's English-language translation of Ayyūb's letter to his father first convinced Oglethorpe and the Royal African Company that Ayyūb's literacy was a commodity worth trading on. In this sense, it was not Ayyūb's writing in Arabic that fixed his exchange value, it was Gagnier's ability to identify Ayyūb's writing as Arabic, according to an authorized taxonomy. Another way of putting this is that Gagnier's verifying translation of Ayyūb's Arabic letter purchased Ayyūb's freedom.

The problematics of translation become all the more complicated with an Arabic slave narrative like Ayyūb's letter, because implied in the translation is a division of literary labor, a distinction between the initial act of transcription, which is performed by the slave, and the subsequent acts of translation and publication, which are performed by the orientalist, or otherwise expert in Arabic, who functions as the text's authenticating editor and/or amanuensis. Neither this division of labor, derived from the Enlightenment epistemological distinction between "brute fact" and reflective judgment, nor the problem of authenticity was unique to Arabic-language slave narratives.[53]

In the case of English-language slave narratives, brute facts, as simple empirical observations recording sense experience only, were the sole legitimate province of the slave narrator. Reflection, inasmuch as it entailed the binding of the brute facts of experience into systems of constitutive rules (also known as human institutions), was the function of the amanuensis-editor. Whether or not a brute fact became an institutional fact, and thus grounds for reflective interpretation, depended upon its being subjected to a system of rules, the determination of which was a function of reflection. As the slave could only report brute fact, the slave was unable to provide the institutional context in which facts may

become material for reflection. That context was provided instead by attached authenticating documents (usually in preface to the slave's text), produced either by the narrative's white amanuensis, or by some other white man whose authority to adjudicate was recognized. On this score, the matter of who might legitimately claim to possess the capacity for determining the legitimate grounds for experience as knowledge is resolved in favor of the white amanuensis, underscoring the fact that the literary division of labor paralleled the distribution of rightful authority in Western society at large. The attribution of autonomous authorial authenticity to the Negro is deemed unfeasible on the assumption of his or her inherent cognitive limitations. They are indeed cognitive limitations, because, according to the division of labor in the narrative, the socioeconomic status of the slaves merges with their ontological status.[54] The slaves may experience and state what they experience, but those statements lack any reasonable signification: having no scheme or symbolism, their statements are both indeterminate and nonreflective, and to that extent gibberish.

With regard to Ayyūb's Arabic letter, whether or not a brute fact became grounds for reflective interpretation depended upon its being subjected to the system of rules determining the legitimate grounds for experience as knowledge through translation. Recalling what has already been said about the relationship between reflective judgment and the indeterminacy of Imagination's schemata, this division of labor marks the instituting of narrative, i.e., *Wortbestimmung*, or fiction of history. This notwithstanding, it cannot be assumed that in the case of Ayyūb's translated Arabic letter it is the translation whose authenticity is at risk. On the contrary, the function of such experts as Gagnier is to authenticate that Ayyūb's text is in fact Arabic. Of course, this same expert authentication is precisely what happens when Richard Robert Madden translates Abū Bakr as-Ṣiddiqi's 1825 autobiography in 1834, and G. C. Renouard redoes it in 1836; when Alexander Cotheal, treasurer of the American Ethnological Society, translates 'Umar ibn Said's 1831 autobiography in 1848, and J. F. Jameson, editor of the *American Historical Review*, authorizes its retranslation in 1925; and when Cotheal and William Hodgson translate some of 'Abd-ur-Raḥmān's epistles, presenting them to the American Ethnological Society, as well as numerous colonization societies, as being evidence of culture. Thus the very same premises at work in the division of labor entailed in the publication of

English-language slave narratives were at work in the translation and publication of Arabic-language slave manuscripts in general.

In the particular instances of the Arabic narratives of 'Umar and Abū Bakr, however, there is an added twist, which provides insight into the critical potential of New World Arabic-language narratives written by African slaves. Given their autobiographical content, the continued accessibility of either 'Umar's or Abū Bakr's Arabic manuscripts presents a persistent enigma of linguistic opacity: an "original" text against which the translation could be compared. As it appears, the only effective response to such an enigma is the total displacement of the Arabic texts by those of the translators/amanuenses: the Arabic texts must become lost beneath the weight of the editorial project in order for them to become legible as authentic Arabic texts. With the translation of 'Umar's and Abū Bakr's autobiographies, that legibility is achieved through two means: (1) the act of translation, through which the obscurities of linguistic referentiality ensuing from the African slave's use of the Arabic language are effaced; and (2) the simple *de-Negroing* of the author—what was Negro now becomes Arab. By this token 'Umar ibn Said's reputation as a writer of Arabic was of sufficient authority to secure his romanticization as a non-African, viz., non-Negro Arab. This tendency of 'Umar's white contemporaries to romanticize about his origins and to deracinate his obvious "Africanness" betrays the very proscription that his literacy places on slavery in the name of Enlightenment's liberal humanism. At the hands, or lips, of otherwise Muslim, literate Africans this proscription becomes a bugbear of dense refractivity that reflects the very limited scope of the preconditions that make possible modernity's illusion of power and unlimited expansivity. Hence, the urgency with which Ralph R. Gurley, secretary of the American Colonization Society, when reporting on his meeting with 'Umar in 1837, insists on 'Umar's complete conversion to Christianity, as if to appropriate, via a metonymic gesture, 'Umar's literacy to a unilinear Western history of ideas.[55]

In an analogous fashion, the same insightful twist is at work in Ayyūb's *reported* autobiography, Bluett's *Memoirs of the Life of Job the Son of Solomon*, published in 1734, the year of Ayyūb's manumission and repatriation. Although this autobiography (which Bluett swears was faithfully recorded from the mouth of Ayyūb) is not, as far as we know, the translation of an Arabic text, it still presents certain interesting problems regarding oral versus literal authority. Even in the instance of

Bluett's text of Ayyūb's reminiscences, the division of labor in the narrative's production is along the lines of orality and literacy, presenting an interpretive problem of attribution. The result is that it becomes difficult to determine whether or not the published narrative emanates from Ayyūb's perception of his life, or whether it is applied to that life, like an overlay, by Bluett and Gagnier.

This problem cannot be resolved by a formalist reading in which the onus for determining authorial authenticity falls on the reader as an exercise of critical reflection. The possibility of determining what structural patterns and lacunae in the narrative might indicate the expression of personal feelings and ethnic experiences lying outside the structured framework imposed by the amanuensis (i.e., authorial intentionality) is precluded by the total absence of any manuscript other than Bluett's. What is perhaps more problematic is that the same inability to read definitively is encountered in Ayyūb's 1734 postmanumission Arabic letter to Nathaniel Brassey. Even in this letter, where the Arabic manuscript is extant and accessible, along with its English translation purportedly dictated by Ayyūb to Hull, the discovery of Ayyūb's reflective judgment beyond is limited by the English text's brevity, which is to say that it is unknowable. The letter is written in a comparatively clear legible Arabic.

تكتب اسمه عيوب بن سليْما
بسم الله الرّحمْن الرّحيم
كريمن مستر بريس ممبر بالمن لمب ستت اسلام عليكم
هوالحمدالله رب العالمين حمدا كثيرا مستر بريس المسلمين
كلهم والمسلمات دعاغة انت مستر بريس خيرا وكثيرا و الله خيرا
انت مستر بريس هو ايوب بن سليمن دعاغة هوالحمدالله رب العالمين
حمدا كثيرا هو سميح الحمدالله رب العالمين قلت الحمدالله

Attached English-language translation

A translation of the above writing from Job's mouth.

Honorable Sir,

After my humble service presented to you these few lines may inform you that I am at present, in good health and that I arrived safe (praise be to God for it) at James Fort in the River Gambia, where I met with very kind usage from Gov. Hull and likewise the rest of the Gentlemen. all [sic] the musulman of my acquaintance pray for your health long life and prosperity for many good services you have done me. I sent my messengers up into my country with . . . when I was the river, waited a considerable time, but had no return of an answer. This day I arrived at James Fort and found a vessel ready to sail in a few minutes. I hope all your good family is well, convey my respects to all friends, especially to the young lady Miss Gray.

> Your most obedient humble servant
> Job B. Solomon
> I hope I shall have an opportunity to write
> again in a little time.

Translation of Ayyūb's Arabic text

The writer's name is Ayyūb b. Suleimān

In the name of Allah, The Most Merciful, The Most Beneficent
Generous Mister Brassey
Member of Parliament for . . .

Peace be with you. He is all praise be to Allah, Lord of the worlds, great praise. Mister Brassey, all the Muslims of Zagha. men and women, [wish] you the best, and Allah is best. You are Mister Brassey. He [who writes and sends this] is Ayyūb b. Suleimān Zagha. All praise be to Allah, Lord of the worlds. I said, all praise be to Allah.

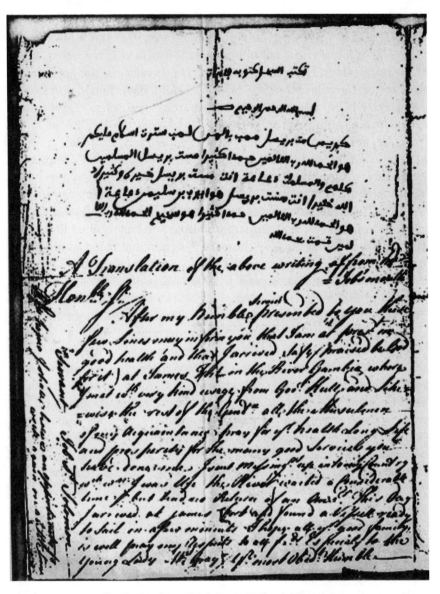

Facsimile of Ayyūb's letter to Nathaniel Brassey

From Job's mouth to Allah's ear, whether or not Ayyūb dictated the English text in English, Hull's presentation of it as the translation of Ayyūb's Arabic writing is quite a narrative edifice, constructed out of the most minimal of working material. It portrays just the appropriate amount of humble deference Brassey would have hoped for from a beneficiary of his philanthropy, a well-articulated sense of debt upon which future enterprise might rest. All is well, the English at James Fort are gentlemen like Brassey, so gentlemanly that they prompt reflection on the good old days in England in the genteel company of gentry and young friends. Apparently Job has not forgotten the civility with which he was met in England. Such sentiments demonstrate that the Royal African Company's investment was well made and should pay off. Yet, it is not at all apparent that Ayyūb has recalled that civility, or demonstrated those sentiments. The minimal material for Hull's narrative structure is perhaps the chief cause of its fragility. Ayyūb's Arabic text is formulaic, in fact a combination of aphoristic formulae: " . . . all praise be to Allah, Lord of the worlds . . . Allah is best." Hull's evangelical fervor and certainty of the moral superiority of the West notwithstanding, the best that Ayyūb, representing "all the Muslims of Zagha," could wish for his Christian benefactor, "Mister Brassey," is that he find Allah. All praise be to Allah. After nigh on four years of enslavement in the New World and England, after repeated audiences with England's keen minds, who came to ponder the wonder of his difference (both from them as well as from their "Negroes"), all Ayyūb had to write to the banker of his manumission is that the praise belongs to Allah alone. What Ayyūb had to write to Brassey, and in Arabic, was that he was not indebted to Brassey for his freedom, but to Allah, and that Brassey ought to accept this as well; if not, Allah be praised nonetheless.

The legibility of Ayyūb's letter makes the fact that Hull's translation of it into English is at best fanciful all the more pertinent to our concerns here. Its fanciful translation was not a function of acute heterography or opacity. The English translation of Ayyūb's Arabic text, however, entails a remarkable confusion of signification processes. On the one hand the translation is an analogon, it does not require a relay or code to mediate between it and its referent, the Arabic letter, and so it is a continuous message. On the other hand, the translation requires a relay code; in Hull's case, it is his position as factor in the Royal African Company's economy of exchange that enables the communicating of the content of

Ayyūb's Arabic text as a meaningful message. That economy is the mediating code of the formal relationship of capital in which the Arabic text is a very specific sign of value. The translation is symbolic; it is the exchange value for the Arabic text.

Here again we return to Douglass's question: how can a symbol enable the representation of meaning although it has no referent? The answer found in Gates's reading of Gagnier's translating of Ayyūb's transcribing is: By analogy, on the condition that the referent is indeed absent, or sufficiently removed. Gagnier's translation of the "displaced" Arabic text of Ayyūb's 1731 letter to his father entails the same confusion of signification as does the translation of Ayyūb's 1734 letter to Nathaniel Brassey. In order for Gates to claim to read Ayyūb's displaced Arabic letter as the genesis of African American literary tradition, he logically presupposes that the letter entails two specific expression planes (one consisting of Arabic graphemes and the other of English graphemes) and a content plane. What Gates participates in, however, involves only one of the two expression planes: the English graphemes. As with the extant letter to Brassey, the question is whether or not that plane concerns something other than Ayyūb's signs. That is to say, is the content plane a transcendent referent for both expression planes?

Gates participates in an economy of signification something like the following. Gagnier presents an English-language word, "in," as having the value of "x" in Ayyūb's letter; the English graphemes are the signifier and the Arabic graphemes the signified. This economy cannot be accounted for by Gates's theory of Signifyin(g), because in that theory a word is considered as having an explicit reference or denotation, and then being capable of suggesting or associating additional ideas, or connotations. In this way Signifyin(g) is disruptive, it extends connotation to a degree that denotation is problematized, but it does so only on the basis that there is a denotation. The situation is slightly more complicated in the instance of Ayyūb's letter, because both the Arabic and the English graphemes function as signifiers within their respective languages. So what Gates construes as the signified of Gagnier's signifier is in its own rights a signifier, but of what? The answer that Gates is logically compelled to give is that the signifiers of Ayyūb refer to the same, or analogous, meanings as those of Gagnier; they denote Ayyūb's thoughts.[56] That is why for Gates writing can be emancipating; it demonstrates the participation of the Negro in the same economy of culture as the Westerner, and in the same manner, as a human subject. But he can

say this of Ayyūb's letter only on the condition that the material referent of Gagnier's translation, the Arabic text, is absent, and so unable to manifest another possibly contrary economy. Were he to maintain otherwise, say that Gagnier's translation was in the mode of error, albeit an error with considerable historical existence, then he would be compelled to acknowledge, at least theoretically, that the genealogy of Signifyin(g) was grounded in an illusion of referentiality. I want to be clearly understood on this: Gates would not be acknowledging that the genealogy of Signifyin(g) discovers the illusion of language's referring to an empirical reality, something he readily admits, rather he would be acknowledging that Signifyin(g) participates in, and so perpetuates, that illusion.

This is not to suggest that the letter did not hold the value that Gates attributes to it. Rather, that value consisted in its being written in Arabic, a literary language that played a key role in the European Renaissance reformulation of knowledge that prefigured modernity. It is also a language whose usage in Africa predates Enlightenment Europe's historical "penetration" into the dark continent, suggesting a certain aura of African originality, of pre-European civility. An African made literate in one of the modern European languages was somewhat threatening to the received opinion that Africans were inherently and hopelessly inferior. But such a learned African did not challenge the view that such a literacy, emblematic as it was of Reason and Understanding, civility and humanity (which were held to be constitutive of culture), was in no way to be found indigenous in Africa. The Negro who was literate in Arabic, however, flew in the face of the received conception of the Negro of Africa as a subhuman brute, or subspecies of human, and laid claim to a degree of culture thought to be the privileged property of modern Europe.[57] The conjunction of the enigmatic status of Arabic with the Enlightenment's representation of the "natural" Negro African, in an established Arabic literacy among Negro Africans (an African-Arabic literacy), generates something of an epistemological, as well as an ethical, aporia for modern Enlightened slaving Europe. In his attempt to "recover what is lost" in the slave narrative, Gates discovers this African Arabic literacy in Ayyūb ibn Suleimān Diallo's letter to his father. With it, he also discovers, despite himself, the most terrible thing about such slave narratives: they have the capacity for a complete unreadability, an opaque illegibility. More to the point, Ayyūb's 1731 letter marks the inability of theoretical knowledge to comprehend, let alone resolve, the dilemmas of representation signaled by writing.

Reading the African-Arabic American slave narrative therefore entails finding textual aporia as enabling a certain *reading* of history. What I seek to bring into focus, if only for a fleeting glance, is the very process of field delimitation. What would happen if rather than read New World slave narratives as a "countergenre" of Western modernity, they are read as remarks on the indeterminacy in modernity that entails different opportunities for action? What would it mean to read slave narratives not as writing for emancipation, but as writing for agency?

The history of Negro culture is(,) only in writing. Negro culture is the writing of history; it is historiography. This of course is absurd. The historical experiencing of being that we so glibly, but never carelessly, call "Negro" culture cannot be abstracted to textual arrangements, without reducing it to a historicism. Unless both culture and writing are not at all what Emerson or Ellison take them to be, but work otherwise, as activities. In that case reading them would not necessarily slip into a new historicism that sought to achieve an oppositional intervention into the present hegemony of historiography by re-constructing, re-writing, the past. As a writing of culture that transposes difference, the African-Arabic slave narrative occasions the exploration of a way of thinking being whose difference cannot be accounted for within the History of Thought.

Part II

The Indeterminate Narrative of the African American Slave: A Negative History of Making Time in Arabic

Chapter 5

Africa as a Paralogism
The Task of the Ethnologists

Qui ne peut attaquer le raisonnement, attaque le raisonnier.
—Paul Valéry, "Autre Rhumbs"

Among the first American scholars to grasp the importance of African Arabic was William Brown Hodgson, who was also one of America's first orientalists and founder of the American Oriental Society, as well as a founding member of the American Ethnological Society. Hodgson had extensive experience in Africa and the Muslim world as an official representative of the U.S. government. From 1826 to 29, he was with the U.S. consulate in Algiers, and for two years, 1832-34, he was the dragoman to the U.S. legation, Constantinople. After that, he returned to Algiers and served from 1841 to 42 as the consul general of the United States near the regency of Tunis. During that period he compiled a collection of travel notes and quasi-ethnological studies of diverse cultures and societies inhabiting the eastern Atlas Mountains and those areas of the Sahara which correspond to present-day southeastern Algeria, Niger, and southwestern Libya. This collection was published in 1844 as *Notes on Northern Africa, the Sahara, and Soudan*. As a consequence of his travels, Hodgson discerned the antiquity of African-Arabic literacy:

> In Africa—in the land of the degraded negro—the Gospel now stands face to face with the Koran. . . . Arabic letters have, for centuries, been introduced into Africa, and have become familiarized by use.[1]

Two interests motivated Hodgson to publicly recognize the antiquity of the African Negro's Arabic language literacy; one he considered moral, the other scientific. The moral interest was in the need to introduce civilization into Africa, which for Hodgson meant the introduction of Christianity.

> The great element to which we look, as the most powerful agent in civilizing Africa, is Christianity. It is apparent from the history of the most renowned states of antiquity, and of those now existing under other religious systems, that civilization cannot advance beyond a certain limit, without Christianity. The highest civilization seems to be a necessary result of Christianity. (57)

The ideal means for achieving this civilization was missionary work; slavery was tolerable only insofar as its end product was the religious conversion of the race (Hodgson was himself a slaveholder). Missionary work was served by the already-established African-Arabic literacy in two ways. First, although morally imperfect, Islam predisposed the African to the greater civilizing message of Christianity, which could be carried out most effectively by disseminating the Gospel in the predominate literary languages—for Hodgson, as far as the Negro was concerned these were Arabic, Foulah, and Hausa. Second, because Islam, and with it Islamic literacy, was expanding rapidly throughout nineteenth-century West Africa in the wake of Foulah conquests, a large portion of the population was already primed for conversion through rational persuasion (by Hodgson's estimate there were two million people under Foulah dominion). In this regard, Hodgson's moral interest in African-Arabic literacy bears a striking resemblance to the position of the sixteenth-century Spanish Thomist, Francisco de Vitoria, on the American Indians: the great moral desideratum is the inclusion of all humanity in a catholic *respublica christiana*, and literacy is a condition of inclusion (see chapter 3). It was Hodgson's view that legitimate scientific interests are not disassociable from legitimate moral interests; in fact the two serve one another. Successful missionary work will make more readily available material data for ethnological research, and developments in the latter will enable even greater success in furthering civilization. In a very real sense, Hodgson's *Notes on Northern Africa, the Sahara, and Soudan* is a sustained argument for recognizing as beneficial and desirable the *adjacency* of specific modes of knowledge and power formation: positivist ethnological science and colonialism.

Hodgson was not alone in his recognition of the importance of Africa's literacy for science and civilization. Among those who recognized the scientific and civilizing potential of that literacy were the European explorers René Caillié and Heinrich Barth; the British explorers John and Richard Lander; and the African American missionary-colonist Rev. E. W. Blyden of the New York Colonization Society. Certain of Hodgson's colleagues in the American Ethnological Society also had a scientific interest in this African-Arabic literacy, in particular, Theodore Dwight, Jr., who was also a founding member of the AES and its recording secretary from 1860 to 1861.[2] A Yale-trained classicist, Dwight became quite prominent in the pursuit of New World African-Arabic texts. At one point he claimed to have interviewed every known

African American slave who was literate in Arabic residing in the United States. Although Dwight shared in common with Hodgson an ethnologic interest in African-Arabic American slave narratives that was grounded in philological study, his vantage was different from Hodgson's in two important respects. First, he was neither a slaveowner nor a public supporter of slavery. In fact, Dwight is perhaps best known for his *The Kansas Wars* (1859), a Free-Soiler's account of the fight over slavery in the Kansas-Missouri territories. Second, Dwight differed from Hodgson in the scope of his fieldwork. Hodgson's *Notes* is an exemplary document of early ethnological fieldwork, consisting of a descriptive narrative account of observed events and sites (a relating of ethnographic data), which totters on the border of travelogue. Although Dwight traveled extensively in Europe, and published travel books on Italy (1824) and Northern Europe (1841), he never visited Africa, and limited his field experience to the gathering of linguistic data (along with some geographical and biographical information, which only coincidentally provides some insight into social formations and cultural practices) from Arabic-literate African American slaves in the United States. This data became the material basis for precisely the sort of philological analysis Hodgson called for in his *Notes*, and established Dwight's credentials as an ethnological philologist.

The three extant articles of Dwight's published work in African ethnology are "Condition and Character of Negroes in Africa"[3] (*Methodist Quarterly Review*, 1869); "Arabic-speaking Mohammedans in Africa" (*African Repository*, May 1869); and "On the Sereculeh Nation in Nigrita: Remarks on the Sereculehs, an African Nation, Accompanied by a Vocabulary of Their Language" (*American Annals of Education and Instruction* 5 [1835]: 451-56). "On the Sereculeh Nation in Nigrita" is a considerably edited account of an interview with Lamen Kebe, an African American slave whom Dwight described as having been a scholar and professor in the West African emirate of Futa Djallon. Kebe offers some explicit views on the comparative merits of the pedagogical methods in Africa and the United States, as well as on the state of American knowledge about Africa. Before its 1835 publication, this article was read before the American Lyceum in that same year.[4] In addition to Dwight's biographical sketch of Kebe before and at his enslavement (supposedly based on data garnered from the interview), the published version consists of Kebe's critique of Western knowledge, a bibliography of texts learned and taught by Kebe in Africa, and an appended Sereculeh

vocabulary. In keeping with Dwight's philological agenda, there is an introductory paragraph in which he suggests that although there was precedent for philological studies being read before the Lyceum, there was still a scarcity of publications of such work. To attract interest and establish the ethnographic value of American slaves for philological research on Africa, Dwight's biographical sketch of Kebe contains Kebe's studied presentation of pedagogical method in Futa Djallon. Dwight's biographical sketch, which he elaborates on in "Condition and Character of Negroes in Africa," warrants consideration insofar as it is used in both essays to determine Kebe's identity as an authoritative (literate) informant (which of course would legitimate Dwight's philology study).

Dwight's ethnological classification of Kebe is as a "Sereculeh," which is a variant spelling of Mongo Park's "Serawollies." Park in turn equates the Serawollies with those the French call "Seracolets." These are the Soninke of al-Bakrī's *Ghāna* or Takrur.[5] Dwight takes Kebe at his word that he is Sereculeh, but besides Kebe's assertion that his father was Sereculeh, there is his apparent Sereculeh patronymic. "Kebe" is the anglicization of the French *Kébé*, which transcribes the Sereculeh *Kabba*. According to Dwight's reporting of Kebe's story, the Sereculeh

> were formerly a nation of ignorant idolaters, dwelling northward from Foota Jalloo (their capital being Diafun, or Jafunu), but a few generations past converted to Mohamedanism [*sic*] by their prince, Moral Kebe, who abdicated his throne and took to study, in the city of Jaga, and afterwards introduced the religion of the prophet and learning among his people. The traditions obtained from Lamen constantly present the progress of Islamism and education, as companions in Nigrita. The Sereculeh people, sometime after this, were driven from their capital, Diaga, or Jaga, by the plague of locust, and a portion of them entering Foota Jalloo, conquered the eastern half of that kingdom, which they have ever since held. ("On the Sereculeh Nation in Nigrita" 452)

In spite of some confusion over names, chronology, and causes that may have been due to Dwight's having problems transcribing, or his deliberate editing, this story of the Islamization and migrations of the Sereculeh is readily identifiable as a rendition of the traditional history of the Jakhanké migrations that occurred under the leadership of their founder, al-Hājj Salim Suwaré. Jakhanké is the French transcription for *Ahl-Diakha*, as they called themselves; it is an arabicized appellation meaning "people of Diakha," which corresponds to al-Bakrī's Zāgha.

This collective name indicates an originary geopolitical identity, the city of Diakha-Masina, which is the same city of Zāgha-Massina that al-Bakrī refers to as lying on the Niger bend in the steppes of what is present-day Mali. Sometime in the twelfth century (around 1147–48) al-Hājj Salim migrated from Diakha-Masina (Zāgha-Massina). He first settled in Jafunu for thirty years before moving on from there to Diakha-Bambukhu (Zāgha-Bambuku). The time frame indicates that the latter is Dwight's Diaga/Jaga.

That Kebe was probably a Jakhanké is indicated by his story of his *qabīla* (clan) origins. According to Dwight's reporting of this story, the progenitor of Kebe's *qabīla* was Moral Kebe. *Moral* is an honorific, but the various sources of Jakhanké history mention the name Kabba among al-Hājj Salim's community at Diakha-Bambukhu. Monteil reports that there was a Salla Kébé (Kabba) among al-Hājj Salim's disciples. The *Ta'rīkh al-Hājj Salim Suware and Karamokho Ba* (hereafter *TKS*) mentions Fode Ibrahīm Kabba as being a part of al-Hājj Salim's community at Diakha-Bambukhu. This same Fode Ibrahīm Kabba appears in *Ta'rīkh qabīlah Kabba* (hereafter *TKQ*).[6] It was in Diakha-Bambukhu that the Kabba *qabīlah* were admitted into the Jakhanké community. According to *TKS*, this same city was evacuated sometime at the end of the fifteenth and the beginning of the sixteenth centuries, which coincides with the Foulah migration into the region of Bundu and the region of the Djalonké.

Again there is a problem of transcription. Djalonké is the French transcription of the Mandinka word *Jalunka*, rendered in English as Jalunka or Yalunka. According to Montrat, the suffix "ké" is the French transcription of what the Jalunka pronounce as "ka." Its meaning is "the people of," giving Jalunka (Djalonké) the meaning "the people of Jalun," a geopolitical designation for an area in what is now known as Guinea. Before the Foulah Jihad of 1727–28 the region was called *Jallonkadu* by its inhabitants.[7] Golbery relates a tradition of the wholesale expulsion of Muslims from Bambukhu, occurring sometime after the Portuguese arrival in West Africa in the fifteenth century. The cause he gives is political unrest. Another well-established tradition dates 'Abd-ur-Raḥmān Kabba's departure from Diakha-Bambukhu for Kano as 835 A.H. (A.D. 1431-32). In any event refugees from Diakha-Bambukhu arrived in Bundu in the early part of the sixteenth century. By the time of André Brüe's arrival in Bundu in 1698, the Jakhanké had established three prosperous centers of learning: Banī Isrā'īla, Qayrawān, and Gunjūr. Gunjūr

appears to be the principal town established by the Jakhanké refugees in Bundu; at the time of Brüe's visit it was the paramount center of learning in Bundu.[8] In 1728 Labat reports Gunjūr to be the capital of "la république des marabouts" (3:338). Not until 1799, when Mongo Park arrived at Bundu, had Banī Isrā'īla achieved ascendancy. This bolsters Dwight's report that Lamen Kebe's education,

> which commenced at fourteen, and was finished at twenty-one, was obtained chiefly at Bunder (*Bundu*) . . . He was a schoolmaster five years in the city of Kebe [Kaba], which he left to travel to the coast, to obtain paper for the use of his pupils, when he was taken and sold as a slave. ("On the Sereculeh Nation in Nigrita" 451)

As a consequence of all this, Dwight portrays Kebe before his capture as a Jakhanké scholar who on "several occasions accompanied caravans and armies [of Futa Djallon] on mercantile and military expeditions into adjacent and more distant lands, and his accounts of these abound in details of great novelty and interest" ("Condition and Character" 51-52).[9] As a Jakhanké, however, the principal reason for Kebe's travel would be learning and not war, as is reflected in the autobiographical account Kebe gave of his capture to the American Colonization Society under the sponsorship of Reverend John Breckenridge. According to his own account, Kebe was traveling to Timbuktu to obtain papers when he was enslaved.[10] Nonetheless, Dwight's composite biography of Kebe serves his ethnophilological project well. It portrays Kebe as a highly knowledgeable informant, whose maturity at the time of his enslavement, as well as his long-standing professional status as a traveled scholar and schoolmaster prior to that enslavement, establishes him as an ideal source of exploitable ethnographic and linguistic data.

In that same service of establishing the pertinence of the ethnophilological study of Africa, and Kebe's pertinence for that study, Dwight attaches the bibliography Kebe dictated to him. Dwight recognizes that Kebe's bibliography represents the nature and history of institutional knowledge in West Africa up until the close of the eighteenth century. The bibliography itself is a list of book titles, transliterated by Dwight, which he claims is "a list . . . of about thirty books written in [the Sereculeh language] and used in the schools. A number of these are translations from the Arabic, and altogether [*sic*] form a complete course of Nigrita education" ("On the Sereculeh Nation in Nigrita" 452, 456). The specific claim that the titles on this list are of Sereculeh-language

translations of Arabic texts proves untenable when they are cross-referenced against two authoritative bibliographies of those manuscripts that were published and widely disseminated as learning material in the eighteenth and nineteenth centuries: (1) *Inventaire de la bibliothèque 'Umarienne de Ségu*, a list of manuscripts in relatively wide circulation in West Africa by 1860;[11] and (2) the nineteenth-century Fulani Shaikh, Abdullah ibn Fodio's manuscript *'Ida' an-nusukh man akhadhtu 'anhu min ash-Shuyukh* (A number of texts which I received from the Shaikh), which is the list of texts that he studied with his brother, Uthman dan Fodio.[12] If the cross-referencing I propose is anything near the mark, all but five of these texts were composed in Arabic, and a good portion of those by Africans.

To begin with, Dwight gives the following list: "*Náhayi, Fákihu, Sáni, Láuan, Taurát* (*The Torah*, or Law of Moses), *Yabúry*, and *Alsára* (parts of Scriptures), *Ankidutilmámy, Ségudin, Bunámara-kubrá, Bunámara-wussitá, Bunámara-fúsilun, Sulaimy-kubrá, Sánisy-kubrá, Sánisy-wussitá, Sánisy-sugurá, Sánisi-sukú, Aluwatriét, Bonomahha-jábby, Almahháma,* and *Talakiny*." This adds up to twenty-one, not thirty, separate items.[13] Of that twenty-one, *Fákihu* is probably identifiable as *fiqh* (jurisprudence), *Sáni* as *sunna* (prophetic tradition, more commonly known as *'ilm-ul-hadth*), *Láuan* as *lugha* (Arabic language), and *Taurát* as *Tauhid* (theology) (Austin, 441, note 26). This makes these four items subjects of study, however, and not book titles. Among the remaining seventeen items on the list four are readily identifiable book titles. *Alsára* is not a part of Scriptures as Dwight claimed, but is undoubtedly referring to *Sira Nabawīya* (*The Biography of the Prophet* [Muḥammad]) by ibn Hisham. All three *Sánisy* (*kubrá, wussitá,* and *sugurá*) refer to Muḥammad ibn Yusuf as-Sanūssī's commentary, *'Aqidat sughra as-sughra* (Ideology of the small of the smallest). This leaves thirteen remaining items to be accounted for.

Regarding the first item on Dwight's list, *Náhayi*, there occurs in the *Inventaire de Ségu* a similar title: *an-Nīhāya fī gharīb al-hadīth wa al-athar*, by al-Mubarak ibn Muḥammad ibn al-Athar, which is a study in hadith, i.e., the prophet Muḥammad's discursive formation (*IBUS* 5323, 1-195). Dwight's *Yabúry* is more than likely a reference to an author rather than a text, one Muḥammad ibn Muḥammad al-Ya'mui, whose *'Uyun al-athar fī funūn al-maghazi wa as-shama'il wa as-siyar*, a collection of histories of the prophets, is listed in the *Inventaire de Ségu* (*IBUS* 5374, 1-34). When the same *Yabúry* is cross-referenced with Abdullah ibn Fodio's list it

appears to be a possible homonym of the title *al-Jurrumīiya* (*Ajurrumiya*), an eighth-century grammar from Fas, Morocco. Dwight's *Ankidutilmámy* may very well refer to the *Inventaire de Ségu* title '*Aqidat-ul-iman*, a text in *tauhid* by Muhammad ibn Yusuf as-Sanūssī (*IBUS* 5541, 152-18a); also, another possible reference is mentioned in ibn Fodio's list, *Alfīyat al-ma'ani*, a twelfth-century rhetoric. Dwight's *Sulaimy-kubrá*, like his *Yabúry*, is a possible reference to an author present in the *Inventair de Séqu*: 'Izz-ud-Din 'Abdul 'Azīz ibn 'Abd as-Salam as-Sulamī, author of *at-Tafḍīl*, a poem on the superiority of the prophets over all other creation (*IBUS* 5291, 270-275). A more likely reference is '*Uyub an-nafs wa dawa'uha*, by Muhammad ibn al-Husain an-Nisabu as-Sulamī, a text of Sufism (*IBUS* 5722, 166a-178a). Dwight's *Almahháma* might very well refer to *Masa'il muhimma* by al-Mukhtar ibn Wahi'at Allah, a text in *tauhīd* and Sufism listed in the *Inventaire de Ségu* (*IBUS* 5361, 4-6). Finally, *Talakiny* is probably another author reference, this time to 'Abd Allah ibn 'Abd-ur-Rahmān at-Tawankalī, who wrote *Shifa' al-ghalīl wa iraht al-'alīl fī sharh as-sifr al-awwal min muktasar as-shaikh khalīl*, a commentary in *fiqh* on the first line of Khalil ibn Ishaq's *Mukhtasar*. Or, possibly it refers to the *Talkhīs al-miftah* that occurs on ibn Fodio's manuscript. Only seven items on Dwight's list (*Bunámara-kubrá*, *Bunámara-wussitá*, *Bunámara-fúsilun*, *Bonomahha-jábby*, *Sánisi-sukú*, *Aluwatriét*, and *Ségudin*) are virtually unidentifiable with any on the *Inventaire de Ségu* or on ibn Fodio's list; and that is due in large measure to the eccentricity of Dwight's transcriptions.

This is an impressive reading list of African authors of Arabic texts that Kebe presents us, by way of Dwight. It represents an African-Arabic literacy that is not merely some rare anomaly, but widespread and deep, covering major fields of Islamic science: the science of man ('*ilm-ur-rijāl*), hadith studies, linguistics, rhetoric, jurisprudence, ideology, and esoterica (Sufism). Indeed, the curriculum it reflects was an extensive course of study that *Ahl-Diakha* had disseminated throughout most of West Africa from the twelfth century on, developing and modifying it in accordance with changes in the parameters of knowledge. Dwight was fully aware of the significance of this expansive institutionalized knowledge when he wrote the following in the *Methodist Quarterly Review* in 1869:

> Want of space in these pages must necessarily limit our remarks to very narrow bounds, and we shall therefore be unable to present many details which would interest the reader, and can give only a few facts relating to Mohammedan learning, its nature, institutions, and results. This forms an

essential part of the Moslem system, and has long been in operation on large families of the Negro race. . . . Unlike Popery, it favors, nay, requires, as a fundamental principle, the free and universal reading and study of their sacred book; and, instead of withholding it from the people under penalties of death and perdition, it establishes schools for class, primarily to teach its languages and doctrines. . . . As this has always been the practice, it may not seem that learning flourished among the Moors, in Spain, during the Dark Ages of Europe, while Popery so long overshadowed the nations with her worse than Egyptian darkness. Readers who have neglected Africa may not be prepared to believe that schools of different grades have existed for centuries in various interior negro [sic] countries, and under provisions of law, in which even the poor are educated at the public expense, and in which the deserving are carried on many years through long courses of regular instruction. Nor is this system always confined to the Arabic language, or to works of Arabian writers. (45-46)

Regarding Kebe's pedagogical observations, besides commenting that the random mobility of students in the American system inclined him to view it as inferior to that of Africa, Kebe sought to give Dwight some sense of the method by which at least one subject was taught, Qur'anic Arabic. Judging by the book list's indication of literary productivity among Africans, this was probably the most fundamentally important subject of study. While mnemotechny was emphasized in learning the Qur'an, what was practiced in Kebe's school was memorization by graphic reproduction, rather than oral presentation.

His Scholars according to the plan of his education, were seated on the floor, each upon a sheepskin, and with small boards held upon one knee, rubbed over with whitish chalk or powder, on which they were made to write with pens made of reeds, and ink which they form with care from various ingredients. The copy is set by the master by tracing the first words of the Koran with a dry reed, which removed the chalk where it touches. The young pupil follows these marks with ink, which is afterwards rubbed over with more chalk. They are called up three at a time to recite to the master, who takes the boards from them, makes them turn their backs to him, and repeat what they were to do the previous day. ("On the Sereculeh Nation in Nigrita" 452)

What is most noteworthy about Kebe's discussion of the Sereculeh's pedagogical method is that the written and not the heard word is memorized through recitation. The students are taught to be readers before anything else, and above all readers who can decipher. In this vein, Kebe shared with Dwight something that was extraordinary, the process he called *doubling*. He believed that this process made

his country's method of schooling superior to that of any other Muslim country where Arabic is a language of scholarship but not of daily discourse. Doubling appears to have been a form of bilingual education, where the student not only was given the Arabic word to memorize, or even just a translation of it into his native tongue, but was given its meaning. The term meaning is a very invocatory one in the history of Arabic linguistics. It does not refer to what the signifier conveys, its signified, as it were; instead, it refers to how it conveys, the codes which govern referentiality. Even though Kebe uses the English word "meaning," given what is ascertainable both from his bibliography and his description of *doubling*, there can be little doubt that the Arabic texts employed in the process of *doubling* were, in addition to the Qur'an, descriptive and analytical texts on Qur'anic discourse, viz., *'ilm-ul-kalām*. It is a fair assumption, therefore, that the Arabic term *ma'nā*, and its attendant linguistic usages, was at play in Kebe's reference to meaning.[14] When Kebe told Dwight that "the meaning of the Arabic word is explained as well as translated," he was talking about the instructing of students in rudimentary exposition. This is not at all unexpected, given the large number of texts in Kebe's book list that belong to the earliest systematic Islamic science, *'ilm-ul-kalām*, which is loosely translated into English as theology or scholasticism, but more exactly rendered as "the science of discourse."

With Kebe's deliberate, careful describing of *doubling* we revisit Kant's problematic referentiality. It is not at all a visit that Kant would have expected, given his assertion about the Negro. Nonetheless, there it is, and Kebe seems fully aware of its potential for becoming the grounding of illusion, as indicated by the way that he instructed Dwight to record him.

> There are good men in America, but all are very ignorant of Africa. Write down what I tell you exactly as I say it, and be careful to distinguish between what I have seen and what I have only heard other people say of. They may have made some mistakes; but if you put down exactly what I say, by and by, when good men go to Africa, they will say; *Paul told the truth.* ("Condition and Character" 48; emphasis in the original)

The fundamental question that Kebe visits on Kant in this remark is the question of cognitive indeterminacy. By what means is the determination and reflection of a disparate object of empirical experience, or intuition, possible when that intuited object cannot be adequately characterized by any determinate concept of Reason? Given the significance

of this question for the fields of epistemology and anthropology as they have been construed since Kant, this pithy statement of Kebe warrants examination, even though it is not properly an African-Arabic text.

Kebe's Exposition

The way that Kebe's statement poses the question of cognitive indeterminacy is by foregrounding American ignorance about the complexity of Africa and, by extension, Africans, thus challenging somewhat anathematically Western claims of there being an African experience. In order to apprehend, however fleetingly, what this means as far as the critical thrust of Kebe's pronouncement is concerned, a sighting must be gained of the epistemological stakes entailed in the seemingly all too practical assertion that one ought to know what one is talking about.

There is, after all, a tension between polyvariant relative knowledge and a reductive universality of Reason that is implied in Kebe's assertion. This tension describes the field wherein operates the major frame of reference for both the phenomenological project of transcribing and translating the appearance of phenomenal materiality into experience, and the anthropological project of transcribing and translating the material content of that experience into a reasonable textual form of developmental history. In short, it describes the field of philological-based ethnology that Dwight sought to validate. Kebe's utterance is carefully articulated as a propositional statement that signals an economy whose specificity is a function of the statement's simply being uttered. Yet that simplicity of utterance signals the economy in order to place it in jeopardy by drawing attention to its specificity, its local orientation by raising another fundamental question: What is anthropology? When asked in terms of Kant's architectonic, the question of anthropology is a specific articulation of the question of the configuration of knowledge: What is *Wissenschaften?* Read in this manner, as a problematic of determinate Reason, the problem of experience that subtends Kebe's observation proves to be somewhat complex and involved.

The ignorance about Africa that Kebe comments on involves much more than merely a question of Americans' lack of familiarity with some matter of practical concern about Africa, based on repeated past acquaintance or performance. Such a concern would be with issues of illusion, a confusion of subjective and objective representations. In contradistinction to that, what Kebe is asserting is that, in spite of frequent

immediate (sensible) representations of Africa, which ought to serve as the examples for the realization of the concepts and propositions of Reason, there persists a failure to transcribe the appearance of Africa as phenomenal materiality into an experience subject to the determining interests of theoretical or practical Understanding. When it comes to Africa the good men of America seem to have no other recourse than their unbridled Imagination, unfettered from any of the determinate concepts of Understanding.

This is not to suggest that for Kebe the crux of the problem is that there are no empirical examples, no representations by which a particular judgment of the American understanding about "the African" can be realized. Were that the case, then his pronouncement would still be easily answerable in terms of Kant's conception of the determinate judgment of Reason, where the subsuming of an object of intuition to determinate judgment entails a situation in which the general is already given, known, and all that is required is its application: that is, to determine the individual thing to which it applies. If the American concept of "the African" were held to be an empirical concept of Understanding (i.e., one where experience is always available for the proof of [its] objective reality), the American lack of knowledge about Africans could be characterized as a temporary limit to knowledge that would be surmounted by the continual expansion of Reason's application (through determining judgment, or synthesis) to nature. What, then, is Kebe doing when he commands Dwight to transcribe all that he says?

He is offering a symbolic hypotyposis: relaying information about the geography, political economy, and ethnography of the Senegambia, particularly Futa Djallon, not by way of example but by analogy, assured that when the determinate experiences are achieved his representations will be objectively validated. All of what Kebe exhibits was prior to his relating it unknown, and what was not immediately subsumable to the conceptual categories of Western (American) cognition he exhibits for its transcription by Dwight into a suitable form for cognitive appropriation.

What I want to consider is how Kebe does this, and to explore that question at the point where it is most provocative, in the presenting of an indeterminate subjectivity. To do this requires that the question of ethnology be more precisely formulated so as to give a clearer view of the stakes involved in its asking. How does Kebe enable Dwight to transcribe all that he says so that it becomes ethnographic data subsumable

to the conceptual categories of Western (American) cognition? How does he translate his experience into a suitable form for cognitive appropriation by Dwight? Simply put, What problems does exhibiting pose for the *sensus communis* of the faculties of cognition, for Kant's architectonic in its attempt to determine the genesis of synthetic a priori judgments?

As has already been noted, this is the paramount question of Kant's *Critique of Judgment*. In revisiting this question with Kebe, however, the focus of discussion is the manner in which Kant tries to address it in part 1 of the *Critique of Judgment*, "Critique of Aesthetic Judgment." The particular field of the "Critique of Aesthetic Judgment" to which our attention is drawn is book 2, "Analytic of the Sublime," which divides into two analytics: "On the Mathematically Sublime" and "On the Dynamically Sublime in Nature." The center of attention is the movement of Kant's passing from "On the Mathematically Sublime" to "On the Dynamically Sublime in Nature." This passage occurs between section 27 of the "Analytic of the Sublime," which is entitled "On the Quality of Liking in our Judging of the Sublime," and section 28, entitled "On Nature as Might." In the passage from 27 to 28 Kant abruptly shifts consideration from the problem of apprehension encountered in "On the Mathematically Sublime" to terms of dynamic resistance.

Section 27 addresses how the feeling of the sublime in nature is the feeling of respect (*Achtung*) for the vocation of humanity. The inability of the Imagination to comprehend its own apprehensions (of things in appearance) in a totality of intuition, in accordance with the law of Reason that enjoins it to do so (i.e., the idea of the absolute whole), means that the Imagination cannot exhibit the idea of Reason through example: it cannot give the idea objective validity. While this inadequacy of the Imagination engenders displeasure (*Unlust*) and fear (*Furch*) because the idea cannot be exhibited, it also is emancipating, because what it does exhibit is that the Imagination's vocation is not at all determined by objects in nature, by phenomena, but rather its vocation is to strive to obey the laws of Reason.

This respect for the idea of humanity (the realization within ourselves as subjects in accordance with the vocation to obey the laws of Reason) is substituted for a respect for the object of intuition that engenders Imagination's displeasure. This is achieved through what Kant calls *subreption*. In his *Inaugural Dissertation* Kant defines subreption as "the intellect's trick of slipping in a concept of sense as if it were the concept

of an intellectual characteristic."[15] Subreption is how the sublime can be presented by the mind as being in nature, as though the object of nature makes intuitable the superiority of the rational vocation of our cognitive powers over the greatest of sensibility—i.e., the Imagination in its greatest expansion (*KU* 101; *CJ* 114).

Hence, the feeling of the sublime in nature is respect for the fact that the inadequacy of the greatest power of sensibility is itself in harmony with rational ideas, insofar as the Imagination inevitably strives to realize the rational idea of absolute totality. The agitation the mind feels in presenting the sublime in nature is thus a rapid alteration of repulsion from the object of inadequacy and attraction to it, because of how it exhibits the conflict between the faculties of Reason and Imagination, and in that exhibition demonstrates that the dynamics of human cognition are emancipated from any basis in the determinate concept of the object of nature. This conflict gives rise to a subjective purposiveness of the mental faculties (*Vermögen*). Furthermore, the exhibition of vocation is all the more liberating in its exhibiting the feeling of the sublime to consist in its being a feeling, accompanying an object of displeasure but not determined by it.

This same exhibition centers on a particular confusion of sign production and sign function, of representation and reference; a confusion that is perhaps unavoidable and, from a certain perspective of meaningfulness (desire) in Kant's architectonics, necessary. The resistance to a recognition of this confusion as a negative principle of meaningful productivity—it subtends the architectonics—derives from the first-order confusion of representation and reference. This is made more readily available to the Understanding in the "Analytic of the Sublime," where the relation of transcription to experience is thought in terms of force. Here Kant uses the term *Macht* instead of the word *Kraft*, which he employed with relative regularity in the *Critique of Pure Reason*, and consistently in *Metaphysical Foundations of Natural Science*.

This difference in terms is not without its theoretical consequences. *Kraft*, as it occurs in *Metaphysical Foundations of Natural Science* and *Critique of Pure Reason*, is a phenomenal experience which in its two aspects, repulsive and attractive, configures matter in space. Wanting to distance himself from both Leibniz's monadology and Newton's material atomism, Kant formulated a dynamic theory of physics according to which matter is a continuum of motive force (*Kraft*). Force's categorical status is as a predicative of the a priori category of causality, a category

of the Understanding which is a condition stipulated or postulated in Reason, and which presents itself on the order of the possibility of any given experience and appearance; it is the relation between the two. *Kraft* is the fundamental property (*Eigenshaft*) of material change; the basis of its activity is exertion or endeavor (what Kant calls *Bestrebung*), which is constant and quantifiable in terms of repulsion and attraction *energeia*. In this very Aristotelian sense, *Kraft* is the phenomenal process of becoming actualized.

Macht, on the other hand, is a capacity or faculty (*Vermögen*) of the Understanding to overcome (*Überlegen*) great resistance (*großen Hindernissen*). For Kant it is synonymous with will or possibility. As such it is more akin to Aristotle's concept of *dynamis*, a potential power to effect change, and the Scholastics' notion of *potentia* as the capacity of being (which presupposes a corresponding potency). *Macht*, then, is that which has the potential to *cause* change, as opposed to *Kraft*, which *is* phenomenal change.

Section 28, by commencing with the term *Macht*, underscores that the issue at stake is the dominion of Reason's potency as a force that operates in opposition to the mechanics of nature, of *Kraft*. When applied to the phenomenal materiality that correlates with the movements of sublimity (i.e., pain → pleasure → superiority of Reason, or consciousness) as in sections 24-28 of *Critique of Judgment*, *Macht* signals the dynamic potential inherent in Reason for overcoming, and to a certain degree forgetting, the phenomenal materiality of nature as the basis for cognition.

This overcoming is done for the sake of the productive subjection of Imagination to Reason, and the radical differentiation in the architectonics between Reason and nature. That subjection occurs because exhibition cannot be determined as it is without disrupting the a priori intuition of space and time—which is what is at stake in the disjunction between apprehension and comprehension, engendered by the experience of the sublime. Where time is seen as being contained by space, the disjunction forces the realization that there is not enough space for time. Implied in all of this is a mapping of space, a proper geography, which presents time as the articulating juxtaposition of discrete particulars.

Macht is the *arché* of the architectonic; it is the a priori basis for the equality of potential between the faculties of cognition, and to that extent it reveals that the grounding of cognition, of our representation of nature in all its possibility of totality, is purely in Reason. In *Macht* Kant attempts to overcome the impossibility of Reason realizing itself in

nature (and hence in history as a process of worldly development) by introducing Imagination's frustration at feeling a limit as being grounded in the logical (mathematical) conception of the boundlessness of the Imagination's faculty for apprehension. The idea of totality, which is an idea of Reason, and so is a priori and independent of material experience (nature), is the idea of the comprehensiveness of time. That is to say that the boundlessness of Imagination's faculty of apprehension reveals the infinity of time from the smallest nanosecond to the hypermillennium. At the same moment, in *Macht* Kant discovers the most persistent antinomy inherent to the architectonic: the antinomy of translation. When time comprehends space, the resistance of phenomenal materiality is trivialized against the measure of rational speculation: "It expands the soul." Thus the obscurity of the passage from section 27 to section 28 of the "Analytic of the Sublime" is unavoidable for Kant, because in the formulation of *Macht* he discovers as the result of all his labor, and, it might be added, in spite of all his labor, exactly what he sought to dispel: an ontology grounded in the primacy of substance, of materiality.

This discovery is what prompts a lengthy digression, where he seeks to distinguish between terror and being afraid. Terror is empirical in its determination; it is predicated on purposiveness in the cognition of a real threat of material bodily harm. Fear, on the other hand, results from *thinking* and so is purely subjective and discursive: it is in no way determined by phenomenal materiality. The force by which the experience of the sublime overcomes terror is realized in the recognition of thought's superiority over phenomenal events.

Thinking conquers death, and that is the consciousness of Reason's superiority that the experience of the sublime gives us. In that experience Imagination subjects itself to Reason, in order to be free from the materiality of death. This is the resistance, the obstacle that must be forcefully dominated. But it is not the death of matter that one is afraid of, it is the matter of death, the dissolution of the supersensible as the focal point of consciousness of being. It is the hierarchy of thought and being, thinking and writing, in which thought derives being, and thinking engenders writing, that is threatened by the phenomenal materiality of experience.

The architectonics employs fear to legitimate this hierarchy of thought and being; the fear of the experience of the sublime gives our consciousness of ourselves as transcending nature, as the autonomous being of Reason. All of which is achieved through the dynamics of

thought's transcribing the terror of materiality into the idea of fear as infinite emancipation. And thinking is in language, so this transcription is profoundly prosaic. The presentation of time as the articulation of discrete particulars that can potentially extend beyond the field of apprehension is in the end *parataxis*. The genesis of Kant's architectonics is in the subsumption of matter in narrative formulation, in the capacity to generate an effective fable. And if this subsumption is that which grounds the transcendence of Reason, it is no more than the displacement of materiality through transcription.

As to the confusion of representation and reference, the production of the symbol as indirect representation is the process of its function. Kant calls this type of representation *hypotyposis*, and defines it as *subjectio ad adspectum* (subjection to inspection), consisting in making a sensible concept (*verinnlich*). It is either schematic or symbolic. In schematic hypotyposis there is a concept that Understanding has formed, and the intuition corresponding to it is given a priori. In symbolic hypotyposis there is a concept that only Reason can think and to which no sensible intuition can be adequate, and this concept is supplied with an intuition that judgment treats in a way merely analogous to the procedure it follows in schematizing. In different terms, the concept is treated according to the same rule of procedure governing the treatment of empirical concepts that have determinate objects of intuition (*KU* 211; *CJ* 226).

What occurs, however, when the symbol, rather than displacing phenomenal materiality, and forgetting that displacement, presents it, when the symbol represents and is self-referential, giving meaning as a lie? Would there be a scandal that Reason could not ameliorate? As a consequence of maintaining that the givenness of aesthetic experience is inaccessible to either Reason or Understanding, but is only the pure work of Imagination's articulating the conditions of experience (time and space) through its syntheses, Kant implies that natural force (material being) is other than reasonable. A larger implication is the law of Reason's radical disassociation from the law of nature. Consequently, tracing the status of the "material body" as such, within reason, cannot but help to reveal that the very preconditions of the cognitive act are wholly dependent on Imagination.

In giving symbolic hypotyposis, Kebe is then, in fact, enabling the transcribing of the particular event (or particular multiplicity of events) for which the pronounced Western Understanding could not provide any universal concept that would make sense of it as an experience. He

transcribes it into a (symbolic) code that mediates between the particular event and the Understanding, so that the latter can attain a meaningful experiencing of the former. Even though this code is not schematic, which is to say that the event cannot be represented in its specificity as determined by Understanding's having an a priori concept of the possibility of the experience, that does not mean any sort of representation is precluded. Not represented immediately in terms of the determinate concepts of Understanding, there is an indirect or negative representation of the event in a symbol. The symbol, although not enabling objective knowledge, does enable knowledge of how conceptual relations are established, which is knowledge of thinking as judgment itself. Since this knowledge of relation is a knowledge of knowledge, the symbolic representation will also be a reflection on the very establishing of the symbol, a symbol of symbolic thinking.

To think a symbolic relation is to represent both the particular and the universal in terms of the act of thinking that makes representation possible. To think symbolically is to trace in the given the contour of the event of knowledge's finiteness in relation to the supersensible, the "I think" as the focal point of cognitive experience. Thinking presents for cognitive appropriation an event of indirect representation (the symbol) that connects the event and experience in terms of the limitation of knowledge in the face of experience. This knowledge of limitation, the symbol's rigorous negativity, evokes a feeling of both pleasure and pain in the self-reflective awareness of the conceptual possibility of experience, and the denial of that possibility in the limited knowledge that presents it.

For all that it does do, Kebe's matter-of-fact statement does not seek to liberate Imagination from the concepts and categories of Understanding by construing an Africa that is sublime in its dark immensity, engendering the feeling of a pleasure evoking terror. Were Africa sublime then not only would Kebe have failed to provide an overwhelming challenge to Enlightenment Reason, but he would betray himself to be a Kantian in his belief in reflective judgment's capacity to arrive at a liberating synthesis of the faculties of knowledge, the *sensus communis aesthetica*. We need only recall here that for Kant the experience of the sublime may initially evoke a feeling of terror or pain, brought about by the experience of Imagination's impotence in comparison to an idea of Reason. But such a discord between Imagination and Reason will eventually engender an accord, in which Imagination acquires the feeling of

being unbounded, of being presented with the infinite. The result is the thought of the supersensible, the "I think," as the site of connectedness.

This site is the trace of the effective mapping of the spatial dimensions of the event in time so as to achieve a determination of difference between the possible object of knowledge (the very possibility of an objective knowledge) and that which remains to be thought (*gedanken*) but not known (*erkennen*). Mediating between thinking and knowing, between the negativity of knowledge and knowledge of that negativity, the symbol becomes a negative representation that maps the limits of cognition's possibilities. *This* emerges as a discursive site, a space of referentiality where something happens that can only be thought to happen.

Symbolic representation, then, is the dynamics of thought in language that charts the close connectedness between the particular given and its universal, and, thus, relates thinking to being. In accordance with the purely formal reflection of the transcendental aesthetic judgment, symbolic representation mediates between theoretical Understanding and reflective experience, making critical thinking about what is and what is not a symbol possible. At stake in this determination is the transcribing of the thinking of the supersensible as the precondition of the connectedness of experience and event.

It is somewhat anachronistic, and to that extent disingenuous, to discover in Kebe's utterance a deliberate glance toward the reflective operation of Dwight's ethnology. The anachronism is a function of that strategic forgetfulness that is so fundamental to modernity's defining of knowledge according to the institutional division of labor that is derived from Kant's Transcendental Critique. This is of course the familiar function of methodological hypostatization, deriving its expansive energy from the determination of objective givenness. However, insofar as Kebe's utterance effects an intervention into the objective economy of ethnology by displacing givenness with historical function, it amounts to no more or less than the reflective judgment that it seeks to problematize, which is why it is so devastating a response to Kant. When Kebe asserts that the givenness of the African experience is directly inaccessible to either Reason or Understanding, in terms of subsumption to their concepts, conveying only the brute fact of being—in time and space—he is asserting that Africa as symbolic hypotyposis [re]presents the giving of the conditions of experience (time and space). Africa is a function of Productive Imagination's figurative synthesis in schemata. Africa must

remain unknowable, because the experience of experientiality in the negativity of symbolic representation presents the subject to itself by resting on the event as that which resists the cognitive and so gives the subject the experience of activity (force and motion). Nonetheless, that which provides the very possibility of the event's being given to cognition as resistance, Imagination's schemata, is in itself indeterminate, thus placing a restriction on the definitive determination of subjectivity. The devastating blow that this strikes at Enlightenment Reason is apparent when it is recalled what Kant does in the face of indeterminacy: he abandons hope for definitive cognition, resorting to designation (*Wortbestimmung*).

Kebe's symbolic hypotyposis of Africa reveals that not even theoretical knowledge has a stable field and domain. The architectonic appears to be a canon of symbolic hypotyposis, which invests in itself in order to forget or cover up its floundering before the materiality of its own discursivity. It also betrays how Kant's severing of Reason from nature is possible only through thought's discursivity, a possibility that could only be traced in hypotyposis—the sketching of thought's discursive syntax in the process of thinking of articulating conceptual relations, in short, of designation. This fragmentation with which Kant leaves us subsequently legitimated Idealism's imposition of totality, of nature's final subsumption in Reason. Kebe's pithy response to Kant, as it were, rejects also the metaphysics of closure entailed in Idealism's totality. Instead, he responds in favor of irresolvable figuration, elaborate *Wortbestimmung*: signifying.

What Kebe means to do in signifying, then, is to map out in narrative the African experience, providing Dwight with the only thing to be experienced: a temporal cartography of the spatial dimensions of the African experience. That cartography presents the force (*Macht*) at the genesis of the representation's movement as the condition of that thought which subtends knowledge. Kebe exhibits with Africa the activity, or more pointedly, the syntax of referentiality, which in his case is referentiality = Imagination = narrative = history.

It might be said that in his capacity as transcriber, Kebe performs a service for his master, and it is an indispensable service on which the master is totally dependent on the servant to perform. Putting it crudely in this way is to suggest that the conceptual relation between knowledge and thought is a relation of power. It is easy to see, in these terms, that the question that Kebe raises about America's ignorance—i.e., its not

knowing the knowable—is superficial, a tactical movement of *dispositio*. The question that he raises is not about ignorance, nor is it even merely about nescience, Africa's nescience. It is about the power of narrative *agencement*, narrative's ordering agency. In the modern encounter with Africa, the dark continent, a certain material resistance is met, which must be overcome. But it is not really even heuristic to repeat Kant in describing such an overcoming of resistance as force (*Kraft*). This force finds no originary locus, not even in the resistance; rather, it is the force (*Macht*) about resistance that describes the moment of origination, the genesis of a very specific economy of value. It is per force that synthetic a priori judgments are possible. And it is per force, by charting the close connectedness between the event and its affects in accordance with the aesthetic, that we read Kebe's assertion as implicitly positing the question of how in the modern encounter with Africa synthetic a priori judgments of taste are possible.

In this manner, through designation, per force, we can determine within Reason the answer to the question of what Kebe is doing. Kebe is discovering in the difference of cognitive ignorance and nescience the collocation of nescience and ideology. I say collocation rather than collocution, because, for all its rhetorical deftness, Kebe's ambiguous act of narrative aggression is only apparently tropological. He seeks to displace Dwight's designations with his own, because the ethnological aporia of Africa is not definitively resolvable by discursive theory. What Kebe does do is not within Reason. Here is the threatening effect of Kebe, because he employs both Dwight's unbridled Imagination and a somehow nonrepresentative typology to chart the event in purely temporal terms, giving locations and collocations but no determinate points of reference that could enable a territorialization and hence closure of space. The supersensible is presented purely as an affect of the most tangential of relations: sites that are located nowhere, except in terms of a movement without a given point of departure or destination. Referentiality occurs with the absence of a given object.

In this absence Kebe signifies, naming titles of texts, he designates words and assembles these into a narrative history. Recall that in addition to the book list there is a word list, a vocabulary attached to Dwight's "On the Sereculeh Nation in Nigrita." Through these two lists we learn how Kebe exhibits what was previously unknown to the West (America) into a suitable form for cognitive appropriation. In both lists Kebe designates words in order to exhibit the unknowable. But he does

not engage in *Wortbestimmung* in the same way in each list. In the book list he does not double for Dwight, he does not designate words for words—Kebe gives no English equivalent for the texts' titles. In not doing so, he foregrounds the indeterminacy inherent in designation, and compels Dwight to seek out the "meaning" of these titles. He brings this same indeterminacy to the fore with the word list by doubling in a way that betrays the arbitrariness of translation. The way in which Kebe's doubling of Sereculeh and English words both agreed with and diverged from similar lists presented Dwight with sufficient philological enigma to prompt him to pursue the issue at some length, circulating the lists among his colleagues at the American Ethnological Society and engaging in further ethnological study of the Sereculeh.

The word list and book list become an exchange value, a constitutive sign in a discursive economy of ethnology, through Dwight's circulation of them as ciphers, data for ethnological and philological study. The lists authorize Dwight's providing a history of African literacy. Indeed, Dwight transcribes and presents in his essay Kebe's pithy remark about American nescience as an authorizing introduction to ethnological study of Africa. But he cannot determine the cognitive value of his judgments about that literacy. Kebe's book list is indicative of the only experience of Africa Dwight will have, in narrative, and it is an experience that does not facilitate judgment's transmission into knowledge. Is Kebe's instructing Dwight to transcribe his words accurately a (naive or self-conscious) detour to produce anthropology—viz., ethnology—or vice versa, are Kebe's transcribed utterances a product of anthropology?

Because Dwight is more of an Idealist than Kebe, he does not perceive the situation in this manner at all. Instead, he circulates the lists as though designation was definitive, and strives to discover in them objective validation for his ethnology. His doing this issues from the preconception of discourse as being inherently homogeneous in its form (which is what enables it to mitigate the heterogeneity of cognition and nature). Dwight shared this preconception with many of his colleagues in the American Ethnological Society, some of whom in the first two decades of the society's existence pursued every rumor of a slave who might be literate in Arabic in the hopes of collecting more accurate data about Africa, and thereby validating the efficacy of their emergent methodological field of comparative philology.[16]

It is through these early efforts by society members, such as Hodgson and Alexander Cotheal, to delineate their field that New World African-

Arabic literature first acquired value within Anglo American scholarship. Yet no sooner did they begin to collect and analyze texts and interviews, when their preconceived notion of discursive homogeneity began to flounder on enigmas of linguistic referentiality. There are passages in Abu Bakr's and 'Umar ibn Said's manuscripts that are somewhat illegible, and in the case of the famous *Ben Ali's Diary*, the manuscript is generally illegible. Instead of simply reflecting experience, the material language in the texts of 'Abd-ur-Rahmān, 'Umar ibn Said, Abu Bakr as-Ṣiddiqi, and Ben Ali constituted the basis for the society member's experience. When the very material quality of the sign—the enigma of the African-Arabic grapheme—resists neutralization and so stymies Understanding, how does the reader read?

This is not an idle question for such rigorous philological readers as the society's members. In fact, the value of these New World African-Arabic texts is in large measure in their illegibility, or, more accurately, in the general illiteracy of their readers, which is why the question of neutralizing the material sign proved not to be an overbearing one for the society's members interested in African-Arabic texts. It was not even necessary that the texts be translated: all that was required was that they be authenticated as value through their being exchanged by recognized experts, either Hodgson or somebody else. An exemplary instance of such an exchange occurs in a correspondence between Hodgson and another fellow of the American Ethnological Society. This is an exemplary exchange because of the insight it provides to categorical problematics involved with the difficulties of translation met by these relatively early attempts at philology and ethnolinguistics.

Tinbuktu the (In)transcribable

In 1839 Hodgson received a letter from his friend and fellow plantation owner James Hamilton Couper, Esq., the relatively well known owner of Hopeton Plantation on St. Simon's Island, Georgia. Hodgson included this letter in his *Notes on Northern Africa, the Sahara, and Soudan*. It begins as follows:

> There are about a dozen or so negroes on this plantation who speak the Foulah language; but with one exception, they appear not to have been native born Foulahs; and to have acquired the language by having been for sometime in servitude among that nation. The exception I mention is a remarkable man for his opportunities; and as his history, country, and the

information he possesses are interesting, I will give you, in detail, the
results of the conversations I have had with him; feeling that everything
coming from a person to whom Timbucto, Jenne, and Sego are familiar as
household words cannot fail to be gratifying to one who has made Soudan
a subject of research.

   Tom, whose African name was Sali-bul-Ali, was purchased about the
year 1800 by my father from the Bahamas islands, to which he had been
brought from Anamaboo. . . . He has quickness of apprehension, strong
powers of combination and calculation, a sound judgment, a singularly
tenacious memory, and what is more rare in a slave, the faculty of forethought. He possesses great veracity and honesty. He is a strict
Mohametan [sic]; abstains from spirituous liquors, and keeps the various
fasts, particularly Rhamadan. (68)

There is an exigency in these opening lines from Couper's letter to
Hodgson, a need for the exception to be explained and recategorized
as being distinctively different from the other Negroes. Presented with
an ethnologic curiosity, Couper writes a letter to an expert for
clarification.

   "There are about a dozen or so negroes on this plantation"; the letter
is immediately indicative with a relative subordinate clause: "who speak
the Foulah language." This is followed by a coordinate conjunction,
"but," and subsequently an independent coordinate clause, "with one
exception, they appear not to have been native born Foulahs." This syntax supports a relationship of distinction between the class noun of the
indicative, "negroes," and the noun of the prepositional phrase, "one
exception." In turn, that relationship is keyed on the predicate in the second clause and, more specifically, on the verb of negative predication:
"appear *not* to have been." Inscribed in this sentence, in the relationship
between the verb of its relative clause and that of the predicate, are those
issues of the letter that require the greater clarification through which, in
the end, the basis for Couper's interest in the subject of the letter,
"Tom," will be discovered.

   The first issue that needs clarification concerns that subject, or object
(or both), of the letter: "but with one exception, they appear not to have
been native born Foulahs." What is exceptional about the exception?
This is not a simple question. The possibility of its being answered is
made difficult from the start by an encounter with enigma: "*The Negro*,"
or more exactly "a dozen or so negroes," inclusive of the exception. But
what was *The Negro* for Couper, and what do "a dozen or so negroes"
mean to be, besides being on his plantation?

Undoubtedly, from Couper's perspective as an American plantation slaveowner there was nothing of concern about Africans' having, in accordance with their nature, a language of natural signification, a *vera narratio*. As to their nature, he was quite plainspoken about what that was. In a conversation Couper had with the Swedish novelist Fredrika Bremer on the occasion of her visit to Cannon's Point Plantation in 1851, Couper expressed the view that Negroes were, by definition, "a tropical race who typify the highest state of the life of feeling; in them the imagination dominates over reason, rendering them deficient in the power of abstract thought, of speculative systematization, and incapable of pursuing the strict laws of reason."[17]

Quite plainly speaking, then, there was nothing exceptional about a Negro having a language suitable to his nature. It should be understood that it is indeed "plain speech" that is at stake here in the letter. The natural speech of the Negro ought to be characterized, in accordance with their nature, as formally consisting of monosyllabic interjections, diphthongs and song expressing ideas by the nature of the things of experience, their material properties; and so gives evidence of how natural life and unmediated experience imprison the Negro through their idiom. The natural language of the natural Negro is composed purely of *signa naturalia* (natural signs); it is almost totally void of any *signa data* (poetic signs). As *signa naturalia* it involves a continuum of sound and expression but no indicative referentiality to mental affectations; it is wholly commemorative, i.e., it recalls past phenomenal experiences almost to the point of being onomatopoetic. Thus, this language can be in no way symbolic of thought. There should always be something expressed in the utterance of the idiom about experience, and nothing about self-reflective thought.

In the natural language of the Negro the emotive opacity of the utterance should cause the idiom to draw attention to itself, to its instance of formation: the idiom becomes rhythmic and repetitious, a message that is somehow identical with its articulation. The question is, why is this not the case with Tom? What is it that enables him to express the peculiarities of a foreign (not natural) language? What, after all, is so exceptional about a nineteenth-century West African from the Senegambia speaking the Foulah language?

Although the prompting of the question was immediate, the apprehension of the answer is mediated by the promise expressed in the letter, that is, the expressed promise of gratifying through the familiar.

Inevitably one question leads to another. What is familiar, how and for whom can it possibly be gratifying? "Everything coming from a person to whom Timbucto, Jenne, and Sego are familiar as household words, cannot fail to be gratifying to one who has made Soudan a subject of research."

It is explicitly clear from Couper's description of Tom's character that, at least in Couper's mind, he differs in very specific ways from the other Negroes: "He has quickness of apprehension, strong powers of combination and calculation . . . " But one of these ways is remarked to be particularly unusual in a (Negro) slave: "the faculty of forethought." In fine, Tom synthesizes what he perceives (apprehension) and organizes it into combinative representations (comprehension), then he recollects previous perceptions and organizations (memory and experience) and can extend this process through time (speculation). Tom thinks.

Lest this reading of Couper's describing Tom's capacity for cogitation as supporting a claim for his being essentially other than Negro seem too arbitrary, the final sentences of his description make this explicit: "He is singularly exempt from all feeling of superstition; and holds in great contempt, the African belief in fetishes and evil spirits. He reads Arabic, and has a Koran (which however, I have not seen) in that language, but does not write it" (Hodgson 68-69).

The question changes slightly: What is so exceptional about a nineteenth-century West African from the Senegambia speaking the Foulah language and reading Arabic? Everything, the exceptional Negro is what the others appear not to be, a native born Foulah, and so is not what they appear to be, a Negro. This answer finds support in the chapter in Hodgson's book to which Couper's letter is appended, "Nations of Soudan," in particular in the first section of that chapter entitled "Fellatahs or Foulahs." Hodgson asserts that "the Foulahs are *not* negroes. . . . They differ essentially from the negro race, in all the characteristics which are marked by physical anthropology. They may be said to occupy the intermediate space betwixt the Arab and the Negro" (49; emphasis in the original).

In this regard, Hodgson reports the views of numerous experts who "concur in representing them [Foulahs] as a distinct race, in moral as in physical traits . . . they concur also in the report that the Foulahs of every region represent themselves to be *white* men, and proudly assert their superiority to the black tribes, among whom they live" (49-50; emphasis in the original). Among these experts he reports the descriptions of

Mungo Park ("The Foulah are chiefly of a tawny complexion, with silky hair and pleasing features") and the opinion of Adelung and Vater ["*einer Mittelgattung zwischen den eigentlichen Negeren, und afrikanischen Weissen*" (an intermediate type between the true Negro, and the white Africans)]. He reserves the greatest authority for Marie Armand d'Avezac's *Esquisse d'Afrique*, which describes the Foulah as

a *meti[s]e* population of tawny or copper color, prominent nose, small mouth and oval face, which ranks itself among the white races, and asserts itself to be descended from Arab fathers and Taurodo mothers. Their crisp hair, and even woolly though long, justifies their classification among the *oulotric* (woolly haired) populations; but neither the traits of their features, nor the color of their skin, allow them to be confounded with negroes, however great the fusion of the two types may be. (50)[18]

Hodgson transfers this ethnological assessment of the Foulahs into his analysis of their political importance for Western interests in Africa. According to him, presumably due in some degree to their "white" lineage, the Foulah established a political hegemony over large areas of the Senegambia region, primarily in the form of city-states, the two principal ones being Futa Toro in northern Senegal and Futa Djallon in northern Guinea. Because of his perception of the purity of Islamic practice among the Foulah in these states (and the concomitant view of the civilizing nature of Islam, and hence its affinity with Christianity), Hodgson maintained that the gaining-over of the Foulahs to the Abolition party was essential for ending the Atlantic slave trade (52-58).

The Foulahs are ideal intermediaries between the West and Africa for one other reason: the literacy that accompanies Islam.

The Koran has introduced its letters where it has been adopted. . . . Let not the humanizing influence of the Koran upon the fetishes, greegrees, and human sacrifices of pagan, homicidal Africa be depreciated. It will bring up the civilization of the barbarous negro races to a certain degree of civilization, and thus it will concur with Christianity, which is now invading Africa from the West. (58-59)

The political significance of the Foulahs having been determined, Hodgson returns to the matter of their origin. Who are the Foulahs? Are they autochthons, aborigines of the country where they reside, or are they immigrants? This question has plagued Western ethnologists and linguists who specialize in West African cultural history up until the moment. The subtleties and itineraries of this issue extend far beyond our concerns here, but what is of significance to the matter at hand—the

way in which Couper's exception is exceptional—is Hodgson's assessment of which academic disciplines are best suited to address the question of origins.

> As with the Berbers of North Africa, they [the Foulah] possess no records or letters, save those brought to them by their Mohammedan teachers; and in both cases, their traditions are too vague and uncertain for the exacting spirit of modern science. In the absence of historic records, the affiliations of agrammatic or unlettered races of men must be traced by the indications of language which, [sic] the philosophic Herder terms, *das ewige Band der Menschen* [the eternal binder of men]. (60)

For that reason Hodgson holds comparative philology to be the "modern science" most suited for addressing the question of the Foulahs' origin. It is so because of its preoccupation with the classification of tribes and nations in terms of their formal linguistic similarities. From the linguistic evidence alone, made available through the investigation of the Foulah language on the basis of "the rigid laws of comparative philology," it is possible to trace the origin of the Foulah. In support of this philological evidence Hodgson added the then-new science of craniology, particularly the work of Blumenbach, Pritchard, and Samuel George Morton, because of its promise to determine on empirical grounds the appropriate ethnological classification of the Foulahs (60-61).

Hodgson has something quite particular in mind when he talks about comparative philology, something that he is careful to differentiate from the methods of the Reverend Macbair of Wesleyan Mission, Gambia, and M. D'Eichthal of Paris, who attribute to the Foulah an Asiatic origin. Macbair's attribution resulted from his observing that the Foulah idiom was

> very peculiar in its structure and pronunciation; which, in some measure, resembles the Kaffer of Southern Africa. These [being] the only two languages yet known, which have the remarkable euphonic accent, or grammatical change of initial letters. . . . We understand that the Kaffer *clicks* are borrowed from the Hottentots, and that the natives of the interior do not employ them, but use a *hiatus* in their stead. Such a hiatus is found in the Foola [sic] tongue and forms a necessary part of the language. (Hodgson 63)

Macbair continues, in spite of the absence of any other formal analogies between Foulah and Kaffer, to extrapolate a theory of southward migration that, in effect, makes the Foulah and the Kaffer species of the same

genus. From there he is "disposed to ascribe an Asiatic origin" to the Foulahs, which he then carries back to the Phoenicians.

The French ethnologist M. Gustave D'Eichthal, in *Histoire et origine des Foulahs ou Fellans*, also sought to demonstrate by comparative philology that the Foulah were of Asiatic (Malay) origin. To that objective D'Eichthal wrote:

> The Fellans or Foulahs have, however, a tradition among themselves, which affiliates them to the white race. Investigating the origin of this people from these indications, I have succeeded in establishing a similarity between a certain number of words, corresponding in their language, with those of the family of languages in the Indian Archipelago. Since, moreover, what we know of the history of the *Malayan* races, perfectly explains the presence of one of these races in Africa, I have thought myself authorized to reunite this evidently *extra African* race of Fellans, to the Malayan family. Some of the facts which I have presented may be called into question, but I do not think, that the result itself, can be doubted. (Hodgson 65; emphasis in the original)

There is considerable slipping back and forth here between evidence of linguistic similarity and racial affiliation; and as Hodgson observes, regarding the former, knowledge of the Foulah language was so sparse, and the instances of resemblances between it and Malay so few and remote, that there were virtually no philological grounds for claiming any genetic affinity. As to the matter of racial affiliation, he points out that there are numerous political reasons for a language to be adopted, reasons that have no necessary connectedness to racial migrations or origins.

As far as Hodgson was concerned, what was required for the study of the Foulah origin was a significant increase in the available vocabulary. Even more important than vocabulary, for him, were comparative grammars, a greater understanding of Foulah's internal structure and how it related to other language structures. Only such a study could properly distinguish in the field of anthropology between affinities that were primarily linguistic and those that were cultural or racial.

> The affinity of languages, with like radicals and different syntax, is more apparent than real. It has reference more to the *language*, than to the *man*. Political causes sometimes force a people to adopt a foreign language. The syntax of the foreign tongue, in this case, is lost; and the native syntax molds the foreign elements, imposed on it to its own genius. The affinity of languages, with different radicals but like syntax, is less striking, but more intimate; for this establishes the connection of the *people* speaking

such languages, if it does not prove that of the languages themselves. (Hodgson 67-68)

Hodgson presents Couper's letter as a step in the direction of gathering more data about the vocabularies and structures of Foulah. Thus, the letter is a valuable ethnological document—it was read by Hodgson before the American Ethnological Society in June 1839—with its "valuable narrative of the manners, customs and institutions of the Foulahs, with a very exact vocabulary, derived from a native Foulah" (Hodgson 47). It was a valuable document in its demonstration of how those Africans over here could inform ethnological research about those Africans over there.

What made Tom such an exceptional Negro for Couper, and subsequently for Hodgson, was his capacity for presenting informational material for penetrating the emotive opacity of the utterance. In speaking Foulah, Tom caused the idiom to become somehow more transparent, drawing attention away from itself and its instance of formation toward the experiencing of self-reflective thought, which cast the Foulah language in another light, that of reason. There was a connectedness of the Foulah language and Tom, Couper writes: "He considers himself, as his language proves, a Foulah, and converses freely with the Foulahs from Timboo and Foulah [sic]" (Hodgson 70).

This marks a belonging-togetherness that subtended the production of meaningful expression (he can represent knowledge of experience in the world), taking him toward the propriety of humanity. Tom ceases to be, and in point of fact never was, a Negro as a beast, becoming instead a Negro as a man. "The exception I mention [Tom] is a remarkable man for his opportunities." Tom's opportunities are those of becoming human because he displays the effect of reflective investment of language, in addition to conscious knowledge of his experience. Tom's properties of language include memory and the capacity to present the narrative representation of his story, he has history—all of which is idiomatic:

And as his history, country, and the information he possesses are interesting, I will give you, in detail, the results of the conversations I have had with him; feeling that everything coming from a person to whom Timbucto, Jenne, and Sego are familiar as household words cannot fail to be gratifying to one who has made Soudan a subject of research. . . . His native town is Kianah, in the district of Temourah, and in the kingdom of Massina. (Hodgson 68)

Thinking the historical formulation of the exceptional Negro's thought, then, is the exigency that compels Couper to write and us to read his letter. The experience of the exceptional Negro is both thought provoking and given to thinking in its being articulated in the *signa data* of Foulah. This thinking and provoking of thought through the representation of datum draws the focus of attention to the exception's personality as an effect of Couper's reportage of his memory. Through this reportage, Couper presents Hodgson with an idea of "Tom," a figural representation of a type of signification, an exemplar of traits for which he has a special regard. [Por]traits:

> In his personal appearance, Tom is tall, thin, but well made. His features are small, forehead well developed, mouth well formed, with lips less protruding than is usual with the negro race, the nose flat, but not thick . . . The portrait of a *native of Haoussa*, in Pritchard's Natural History of Man, gives the general character of his head and face, and approaches more nearly to it than that of any other given of the African tribes. (Hodgson 74; emphasis in the original)

All of which is the same as saying that Couper draws a portrait of the exception through his representation of the exception's gathering of thought, his translating of Tom's *signa data* into a language of expertise; this is the gathering and need for translation that sublimates Couper's writing the letter to Hodgson. "I will now give you," Couper writes, "his African reminiscences; and in doing so I will put down all names as nearly in accordance with his pronunciation, as the difficulty of seizing upon, and expressing the peculiarities of a foreign language, will admit of" (Hodgson 69).

Apprehension is difficult because it is nothing that is seized upon, rather what is grasped by the letter is the ubiquitous process of difficulty, the everything expressed in the utterance of the idiom about the nature of the things of experience, their materiality. But that materiality cannot be comprehended in the letter, and so there is a residual emotive opacity of the utterance that causes the idiom still to draw some attention to itself as the limitation of knowledge. "You will perceive, that the proper names differ slightly from the received spelling; and that the vocabulary varies somewhat from those given by you, in the *Encyclopedia Americana*, and Pritchard in his *Physical Researches*" (Hodgson 69). There is an interest in Couper's letter in the signifying processes of Foulah.

That interest places us at the center of Tom's exceptional utterances so as to enable their being freely regarded with the certain indifference of expertise. And by way of the expertise the Foulah utterances are displaced for something else. The transcription functions as "common[ly understood] idioms" within the particular expert discourse of modern West Africa ethnology: *Timbucto, Jenne, Sego*. These are not only household words for Tom, they function as readable traits within Hodgson's expert discourse of ethnology, where they are specially regarded ciphers to an enigma of West African history, geography, and politicoeconomic dynamics.

No matter that they are not Foulah, they are peculiar properties (of expression) whose formal characteristics (both the sounds and the orthography are a required continuum or material substance that is formed in particular ways so as to produce physically the expression) are specific to "the Soudan" as an object field of ethnological investigation.[19] That investigation requires an expertise that Couper clearly fails to possess:

> You will, however, readily identify the words as belonging to the Foulah and Fellatah language. You will notice that in the numerals, a part are Foulah and a part Fellatah; and some common to both. A few such as *child*, differ from both. (Hodgson 69)

Nor does it matter that Couper is completely in error—Foulah and Fellatah are synonyms for the same language—what is of interest is how what he is in error about (the semantics of Foulah) is an effect of what he is most certain of (his direct experience of Tom and Tom's telling him these things).

What Couper sends to Hodgson in the letter is as accurate a written report of what Tom said to him as he is capable of sending. In that report Couper uses paraphrase to portray in written words what the illiterate Tom has given him orally, presumably in English as well as Foulah, of his African experiences. In effect Couper graphically describes the verbal representation of another's reminiscences. Contained in the letter is Couper's attempt to transcribe Tom's utterances, to represent graphically his experience of Tom's oral history. But it turns out that as a transcription the letter is an absolute failure.

Simply put, Couper spells his idioms, Timbucto, Jenne, and Sego, irregularly. In one instance he spells "Jenne" (Hodgson 68), elsewhere it occurs as "Jennay" (70-74). Once he writes "Timbucto" (68), and then

five times *"Tumbootu"* (his italics; 71).[20] Only Sego appears throughout Couper's letter in a regular form. Couper is not alone in his irregular spellings. Hodgson spells the names of these cities with such irregularity in his *Notes on Northern Africa, the Sahara, and Soudan* that confusion of reference is almost unavoidable. For example, he spells Couper's "Tim-bucto" twice as "Timbuctoo," then as "Tombutum," "Tenbokto," and "Tombuctu" (the last three occurring all on the same page, 80). When citing from Leo Africanus he spells "Tombutu" (61-62). Couper's Jenne/Jennay occurs once as "Jenneh," and then as "Yenni" (80).

Admittedly, in Couper and Hodgson's time there were variant spellings for the renowned city of mystery. The ill-fated Major Alexander Gordon Laing—the first modern European to visit the fabled city, and who was killed in its precincts—spelled it any number of ways as he headed there from Tripoli in 1825. When writing to Lord Bathurst from Wadey Ramel (viz., Wad-ir-raml) on 18 July 1825, Laing writes of "Tombuctoo," following Caillié's French spelling, Tombouctou. In a let-ter to Wilmot Horton dated, "Desert of Tenezerof [Tanezraft], January 26th, 1826" he writes "Tinbūctoo." This spelling he repeats in subse-quent letters to his principal correspondent, Hanmer Warrington, British consul general in Tripoli, with one letter dated "Blad Sidi Mohammed, May 10th 1826" containing both "Tinbūctoo" and the variant "Timbuctoo." In his final letter to Warrington before his death, dated "Tinbūctū, September 21st, 1826" he writes of needing to leave "Tinbūctū."[21] His spelling changed as he got closer to the city, becoming fixed upon his arrival and subsequent death. The German explorer Heinrich Barth, on the other hand, consistently offers "Timbuktu."

By the end of the nineteenth century, the spelling of the name of this city had become so random among Africanists, ethnologists, geogra-phers, historians, and travelogists (more in English than in French or German) that in 1927 David Prescott Barrows felt compelled to address the matter in an introductory note to his *Berbers and Blacks: Impressions of Morocco, Timbuktu, and Western Sudan:*

> There are some words which have been current so long in our language [English], and have become so fixed in our literature, albeit in a corrupt form, that, at least for the present, it is impracticable to revise them. For this reason, I have written the name of the famous saharan city "Timbuktu," even though this spelling perpetuates an error. The word is actually pronounced Tom-bouk-too, with the accent on the second sylla-ble, and the modern French spelling, "Tombouctu" is quite exact.[22]

As shall be made apparent in a moment, Barrows is no more correct in his correction than his predecessors were in their "error." In any event, these numerous instances of irregular spelling, or more accurately heterography, are indicative of a persistent if not chronic problem that is not at all limited to the field of Africanist ethnology.[23] This is the problem of determining an objective basis for transcribing languages. It is a problem that has facilitated linguistics' playing a crucial role in the organization of African studies in the Western university, the role of discovering the material linguistic grounds on which African languages, and in extension Africans, can be categorized in a way that enables effective scientific analysis.

Tom expresses more than disjunctive disembodied noise, he expresses a complexity of noises that as linguistic signs operate in a particular economy of conventional codes to signify something.[24] At the point where the effect of these codes and those of English meet, which, from our perspective, is in Couper's experience of this noise, there occurs an overlapping of signification processes, the result of which is Couper's uncertain transcription. Such indeterminacy is characteristic of any attempt at gathering ethnological data from oral sources that entails transcription from one discourse to another.

This problem of the indeterminacy of oral ethnological data was addressed systematically by a contemporary of Couper, Marie Armand Pascal d'Avezac-Macaya, also a member of the American Ethnological Society, in "Notice sur le pays et le peuple des Yébous, en Afrique."[25] This essay is one of the first systematic attempts to thematize the problems of gathering ethnological data from oral African sources. The way d'Avezac addressed these problems was through the corroboration of primarily literary sources, against which he edits what information he has gathered from his oral text. Even though he does not thematize the difficulties of representing oral transmission in a way that is significant to science as a problem of transcription, his approach is significant because of how the literary basis of his process of corroboration amounts to a discursive schematization of experience.

Like Couper, d'Avezac felt the need to give some explanation of the material difficulties involved in his gathering information from his informant. But, unlike Couper, he provided a systematic consideration of the nature of those problems, resulting in the outline of an ethnological methodology that is markedly ethnographic (i.e., descriptive).

By his own account, the most crucial problem d'Avezac had to over-come was not that of language. He suggests that he was able to avail himself of the Portuguese Creole of his informant—an African named Joaquim, a citizen of the state of Ijebu who had been a slave in Brazil and was manumitted in France—although he offers no details as to how he did so ("Notice" 228). The greatest difficulty for him was to achieve a state of unmediated reception, of soliciting Joaquim's experiences with-out prior schematization in the form of systematic questioning along the lines of "preconceived order of ideas" (229). Being fully aware that the tools that enabled him to find significance in Joaquim's utterances, the discourse of ethnography, also prevented his gaining full access to what Joaquim had to convey by overdetermining his responses in accordance with their syntax, their structural limits, d'Avezac strove to leave "till a later phase the job of drawing out and coordinating the information gathered as though by chance at the whim of a rambling conversation without apparent object" (229).

Then again, he realized that the object is unavoidable, the circum-stances of the interview worked to preclude immediacy: the "idle mind" and the "badly articulated, combined and distorted" words of Joaquim that were set against d'Avezac's desire to render his questions "perfectly intelligible." On many points information that was undoubtedly obscured was corrected and adjusted through corroboration with exter-nal sources—d'Avezac terms this "later developments" (229).

Couper to be sure was not an ethnographer of the same caliber as d'Avezac; he did not pay as much attention to the conditions under which he wrote. His heterography indicates the same impossibility of immediacy that d'Avezac remarks, however. In both Couper's and d'Avezac's employment of it, transcription is never meant to ground the scientific veracity of ethnology in the immediate representation of phe-nomenal experience (for Couper this would be the sounds of Tom's utterances, and for d'Avezac those of Joaquim). The objective validity of their transcriptions does not entail the correspondence of grapheme to phoneme (of sign to sound), but rather entails the subsuming of the phe-nomenal impression (sound) under the schemata of understanding, in accordance with the language of ethnologists. What Couper's transcrip-tions signify is this schemata, and not Tom's phonemic significations.

The problem of Couper's heterography, therefore, threatens the very purpose for which Hodgson published his letter, i.e., the validation of philological ethnology's capacity to decipher cultural enigmas. Couper's

heterography is particularly troublesome because it indicates the failure of ethnology to establish a stable domain of reference. Ideally, there are two things forgotten, or displaced, in ethnological transcription, but only one of these is among the two things that Couper's transcription displaces. The first is the schematic codes by which the informant signifies. These exceed ethnology's capacity for exhibition, or rather, should ethnology exhibit them, then its claim of representational domain (its expertise as the authoritative arbiter of cultural phenomena) would be jeopardized, and so these codes are represented as disparate manifold events that require the ethnological exhibition in order to become informational data. The second object of ethnological displacement is the first displacement. As a result of the first forgetting, the ethnographic transcription is protected from charges of inherent indeterminacy with regard to its signified object, which, as d'Avezac shows, is never more than the transcription itself. As a result of the second forgetfulness, the fact that the transcription is its own referent is displaced, or rather the indeterminacy of its signification is transferred to the heterogeneous schemata of the informant: "I will now give you his African reminiscences . . . as nearly in accordance with his pronunciation, as the difficulty of seizing upon, and expressing the peculiarities of a foreign language, will admit of."

The uncertainty of Couper's spelling is not a trace of some residual material trait of Sali-bul-Ali's idiom (i.e., the material of its phonic qualities, its *continuum*) that resists the requisite comprehending expertise of ethnography. That poses no problem for Couper, having been displaced along with Sali-bul-Ali by Tom and his reminiscences. What is most significant about the uncertainty of Couper's spelling is that it marks a failure to displace that displacement. Couper has transcribed Tom's reminiscences in the way that he has in order to make Timbucto, Jenne, and Sego as "familiar as household words," so that Hodgson may appropriate them, repeat them, and be generally gratified by their familiarity. What is that transcription based on, what is the convention by which familiarity is determined?

Viral Heterography

In his essay "General Principles for the Conversion of One Written Language into Another," Hans Wellisch defined transcription as "the operation of representing the elements of a language, either sounds or

signs, however they may be written originally, in any other written system of letters or sound signs."[26] This operation is what Couper alludes to when he writes that he "will put down all names as nearly in accordance with his pronunciation, as the difficulty of seizing upon, and expressing the peculiarities of a foreign language, will admit of."

In a very general sense, transcription has been taken to mean a reproduction in writing, whether of an audiolingual event or a written text. In this sense transcription is taken to be a transposing of the codes and messages of the source (prototext) into another target text (antitext). According to this, Tom presented Couper with a prototext, a complex of sounds that Couper transposes as "Timbucto." In that transposing, however, certain problems emerge: "You will perceive that the proper names differ slightly from the received spelling" (Hodgson 69). What Couper dismisses as received spelling is orthography in the technical sense of "a codified transcription of writing words with the proper letters, characters or signs, according to standard usage."[27]

This is not a radical dismissal, because at the time at which Couper was writing there was no universally agreed-upon standard of English orthography, let alone a scholarly convention for transcribing Foulah that established a one-to-one equivalence between a class of phonemes and a class of graphemes. Nor was there among the members of the American Ethnological Society a codified orthography that functioned under a governing system of ethnolinguistic convention.

Clearly, in the case of at least one of the three idioms of Couper's heterography, "Timbucto," there is a systematic irregularity of spelling across the field that marks a failure of the convention to fix or codify it. How could this be? Is there something particular about these idioms or the way that Couper et al. come across them that makes them incomprehensible to a conventional orthography?

The simple answer is yes, there is something. But that does very little to explain how this something resists comprehension. To explain how requires a more careful look at the sense in which transcription and orthography have been defined, and the referential relation between them. In the same way that transcription is understood to be a transposing of the codes of a source text into a target text, orthography can be taken as a process of transcription, only here there is a metacode governing the transposing of the prototext into the antitext (Kobrin 21).

Once again, Tom utters a complex of sounds, and Couper transcribes it according to the metacode of "?" as "Timbucto." The ques-

tion mark occurs because Couper does not specify by what conventional code he transcribes Tom's prototext. He proclaims what conventions he dismisses, the received spelling. Whose received spelling—Barth's, Dwight's, Hodgson's, Caillié's, or Laing's? This confusion of the signifier cannot be conveniently interpreted as a problem of multiple encoding. The reason for this has to do with the problem of semiosis posed by Couper's recognition of the absence of any authorized regulated code of expression for the transcribing of African phonetic phenomena into English (or French) codes of expression. That is to say, Couper's encounter with Tom's sounds prompts an ad hoc typology of transmission channels, based on a rather behaviorist conception of perception. Nevertheless, what cannot be gotten around, even in the instance of Couper's hearing Tom's sounds, is that when Couper transcribed Tom's phonemes he did so in accordance with a specific code of expression: an American English orthography. Moreover, that code was phonocentric. Each of the individual graphemes composing "Timbucto" is related to Tom's sounds as the graphemic encoding of a substantially stable linguistic phenomenon. The channels of transmission by which signification reaches Couper tell him that the manifestation of "T," "I," "M," "B," "U," "C," "T," "O" has its equivalence in the code of expression called English. In other words, these sounds are the same in English.

The problem is that Tom was not speaking English, he was speaking Foulah. Supposedly, then, any such phenomenologically based convention of signification must somehow establish a tripartite relationship of equivalence between the phonetics and phonology of Foulah, the phonetics and phonology of American English, and the latter's orthographic conventions. I say American English, because in this instance there is no question of a transliteration (the representing of the written linguistic signs of Foulah into those of American English). What is involved instead is the reproduction of what Couper hears in a manner that is suitably conventional as to enable a spelling legible in the American version of English.

To complicate things further, "Timbucto" is not even a Foulah name. One has to explain, then, not only for English and French, but also for Foulah, how this word comes to be transcribed so irregularly. An etymology of the word has been given by French, German, and English Africanists. In 1859 Heinrich Barth suggested a Songhay origin for the name: "the ancient form of the city's name is 'Tombouctou' (literally

'body' or 'cavity' in Songhay) which is what the excavations existing in the black dunes of the country [are called]."[28]

Still, as Sékéné Mody Cissoko points out, Barth's explanation of a Songhay origin runs contrary to the oral traditions of the city as well as the written chronicles, all of which claim the city to have been founded in 1100 by Tuareg Berbers near the dune of Amadia.[29] According to the oral traditions, as well as the written chronicles of *Tārīkh al-fattāsh* and 'Abd-ur-Raḥmān as-Sa'dī's *Tārīkh as-Sūdan*, the oldest quarter of the city is Jingereber, which is next to the river and the dunes of Amadia. This quarter is not at the base of the dune but is west of it. Moreover the oldest extant monument in the city, the Jingereber Mosque, is there. Also in this quarter is the site of Tomboctou-koi (the heart of the chief of Tombouctou), which is considered the place of the Tuareg encampment's old slave guardians. On the basis of this topographic explanation of the city's founding, Cissoko discounts Barth's explanation of a Songhay origin for the city and the name (18).

Other accounts remain, however. In 1896 Felix Dubois reported that the origin of the name is Berber, as is the city:

> [At Amadia] straw huts were built behind a shelter [*sanié*], in which the Tuaregs placed their provisions and other cumbersome properties. They left some Bailas [Bella], or slaves, there, who kept guard under the superintendency of an old woman called "Tombouctou" (the mother with the large navel).[30]

Barrows also claims a Berber origin: "The name is pronounced 'Tombuktu' and is said to be a Berber word meaning 'the place of Buktu,' the latter word being the name of a well or of an old woman charged with its care" (143). This story repeats the one offered by Renou in 1894, according to whom the name consists of two words: *tim*, the feminine form of *In*, signifying "that one" or "that place"; and *bouctou*, a contraction of the Arabic word *niqba* (little dune). This is a highly imaginative etymology, with no telling of it before Renou. As Cissoko remarks, it is quite a feat to envision the Berbers arriving at the river and constructing such a deliberate bilingual conflation (19). Not only this, but *niqba* in Arabic does not mean small dune, it means small excavation, or hole. The Dubois etymology has had the greatest currency, seeming to find support in local traditions. But where did Dubois get it from? And why do the variant spellings of "Tunbouctoo" and "TinBouctoo" persist?

After consulting the earliest written extant literary references to the city, along with its chronicles, I discovered that the first extant literary reference we have is that of Ibn Battūta whose *Travels* were first transcribed in 755 A.H. (A.D. 1354) and published in 756 A.H. (A.D. 1355). A reference occurs in the 756 A.H. transcription to a "Tunbuktu" situated along the Niger (nīl) at the edge of the Sahara. The earlier geographer, al-Bakrī, makes reference to a town called *Tireqqa*, situated at a site very near to Battūta's "Tunbuktu" (al-Bakrī 180-81). There is agreement among all sources, oral and written, that Battūta's city was founded around 483 A.H. (A.D. 1100) by Tuaregs.

No written etymology for the word is extant before that of the city's chronicler as-Sa'dī, who wrote in his *Tārīkh as-Sūdan* that the town was founded by a group of nomads called by him *Maghsharīn*, who each summer left their livestock in the river valley near the dunes of Amadia, returning to collect them at the beginning of the winter rains. They established in this site a small encampment peopled by their slaves, the autochthonous Bella. As-Sa'dī continues, writing that "an old woman slave was the guardian of the encampment during the tribe's northern migration; her name was *Tinbuktu*, a word that signified in the language [of the native Berbers] 'the old woman,' and it is from her that the city got its name." This spelling he repeats throughout the *Tārīkh*.

There is no earlier etymology than this, and, with the exception of Barth's, none later that substantially contradicts it. In fact it is clearly the source for Dubois, whose etymology appears to find support in the oral traditions as well as the topography. The issue of the name's origin and hence correct pronunciation is not settled, however, with as-Sa'dī. What of the apparent Berber etymology? Renou's identification of the Berber *tim* is a viable possibility when it is corrected to *tin*, there being such a pronominal element in the language.[31] Yet that remains speculative, and does not account for *buktu*, which he traces to an Arabic term that he erroneously reads as "little dune." Yet this same Arabic term appears to fit the meaning that Barth attributes to the Songhay language.

What is plain from all of this is that no verifiable etymology is possible, and what is presented is already a transcription of whatever name was given—a name that could very well have not been Berber, based on the received story of origin itself. The Bella are generally supposed to be autochthons of the site and they have had a symbiotic relationship with the Tuareg for longer than anyone can remember. Perhaps "Tinbuktu"

was simply the old woman's name and no more. Be that as it may, the pronunciation, and hence transcription, of the name varies from language to language.

In Arabic it appears early on as Tinbuktu, and becomes Songhaian-ized around the fifteenth century as Timbuktu, which the French transcribe as Tombouctou. From the French derive the English Timbouctoo, Timbuktu, and subsequently Couper's Timbucto. Whatever it was, and assuming as-Sa'dī's transcription that would be Berber, it was already reproduced in variant forms by the time the Foulah assumed hegemony over the city in the eighteenth century. By the time of al-Ka'ti's chronicle, *Tārīkh -ul-fatash*, it was Timbouctou.

There is no need to ask for whom does Couper transcribe, it is obviously for Hodgson on the basis of some American English orthographic code, which when Couper wrote his letter was not quite phonemically based. The conventional code that governs Couper's transcription had almost no equivalent relation to Tom's utterances. What was reproduced, then, what was it that Couper represented with his transcription?

Couper's seemingly offhanded dismissal of received spelling might not be so arresting if it was not legitimated on the basis of the greater certainty of immediate experience—Couper's hearing Tom's sounds. He professes to represent his experience of Tom's pronunciations, no less, and much more. The process is easily enough conceptualized. Tom says in English to Couper, who speaks no Foulah, "This is Foulah," and he produces a sound or complex of sounds. He then says, "That means this," and provides the English-language translation. What Couper has in fact represented is not a direct pure experience of sound; instead, what his transcription reveals is the inevitable operation of one system of transcription (American English). But it is a system that is highly unstable, not because the requisite expertise of orthographic transcription remains undetermined, but because it remains undeterminable, and that is not due to the scandalous fracturing of material experience.

Couper's irregular spelling of "Timbucto" entails a singular indeterminacy: the indeterminacy of English orthography. Which is why it would be a grave error to posit a necessary and direct correlation between the indeterminacy of Timbucto's etymology and the uncertainty of Couper's spelling. American English heterography is never a simple matter of "misspelling." This was particularly so when Couper wrote to Hodgson in 1839. Noah Webster's "Common School" *Dictionary* (1807), *American Dictionary of the English Language* (1828), and

Dissertations (1789)[32] had challenged not only the hegemony in the United States of Lindley Murry's *English Spelling Book* (1804), but also Samuel Johnson's regularization of spelling based on etymology and discursive convention. Webster was dedicated to establishing a standardized American English spelling, which he intended to be based on orthographic conventions that were distinct from English conventions, and so were duly "American," transcending the disparity of European-language influenced pronunciations. The aim of Webster's orthography was to effect a linguistic secession from England that reflected the success of the United States of America's political secession. He sought to "annihilate differences in speaking [resulting from the heterogeneity of American immigrants] and preserve the purity of the American tongue" (*Dissertations* 19).[33] Consequently, what Webster was proposing was a regularization that was no less arresting than that of Johnson. What marks it as different from Johnson's is that the class upon which it was to be based was the educated American bourgeois, as opposed to the English bourgeois. What also makes it different from Johnson's is that Webster explicitly associates this regularization with the stability of the state. He identified linguistic homogeneity with social and political homogeneity; as he put it, "political harmony is therefore concerned in a uniformity of language" (*Dissertations* 20).

Couper's heterography thus involved the sociopolitical interests of the still-young republic for which Webster labored, but it also involved much more than this. Webster's notion of orthography is informed by his conception of the phenomenality of oral speech: the idea that orality is primary and somehow eidetic in relation to writing. More than an expected aspect of logocentrism, this phenomenology of the oral entails the very same operations of displacement that have been discussed as being at play in ethnological transcription from oral sources.

In Webster's phonemic orthography, the cause for heterography is displaced beyond language itself, and becomes situated in the failure of certain human subjects to perceive correctly. By Webster's way of thinking, if you misspell it is because you either don't know how to hear correctly or cannot do so. Inasmuch as he identified homogeneity of language with political homogeneity, for Webster anyone who cannot perceive correctly ought not be allowed the full rights of political enfranchisement. Not writing correctly is tantamount to not thinking correctly, which excludes one from the field of rational legitimacy.

Language, as a result, is represented as entailing an inherent logic, one that assures identification between sign and signification. Broken down, the steps are very accessible: (1) heterography is relocated out of writing and into oral speech as heterogeneity in spoken pronunciation; (2) the cause for the heterogeneity of pronunciation is then relocated out of oral speech into the sphere of societal and cultural variation; (3) once located there, linguistic disparity can be analyzed in terms of metaphysical or ethnological differentiations, depending upon the ideology of cognition in force at the time. The issue is the expurgation from language of any trace of entailing an alterity in signification processes. At stake is the perennial doctrine of the sign as representation.

In this light, what is most threatening about Couper's heterography in his portraiture of Tom is his failure to pull off this double displacement of linguistic referentiality's heterogeneity. By simultaneously unmooring his writing from orthographic convention and announcing his inability of even hoping to represent the phenomenal experience of sound, yet still claiming to represent something of significance, Couper exhibits the very process of exhibition at work. He exposes how linguistic referentiality entails an overlapping of representation and reference that effects a certain iconicity. Iconicity is the effect of the system of signification, the organizing schemata, that neither the sender nor receiver of the letter comprehend, let alone control. To ask, therefore, about heterography is to be concerned with hyper-codes: i.e., overdetermined and complex codes that are constitutive of the culture in which the codes are produced, yet seem to exceed any grounding in a particular intentionality. Heterography signals that lawless aspect of linguistic referentiality, which means that the question of the material sign's opacity is not so easily resolved through translation.

Chapter 6

Designating Ben Ali's Manuscript Arabic

بسم الله الرحمن الرحيم
وصلى على شيطا محمد و على آله وشمه وصلىم تشلم فكل اشتد
الذكيه محمد عبد الله بن يسف بن عبد الكروند الرحيمالله ويغد له
بي بوكته امين الله امين

—Ben Ali's manuscript

An extreme, and to that extent convenient, example of heterography's signaling the lawlessness of linguistic referentiality occurs with a somewhat well known New World African-Arabic text which both Hodgson and Dwight make reference to, but in all probability never read. It is the purported autobiographical diary of one Ben Ali, who was an intimate of Couper's Tom. The first published reference to Ben Ali, of Sapelo Island, Georgia, occurs in the letter that was discussed in chapter 5, which Couper sent to Hodgson in 1839. At the end of that letter Couper writes:

> Mr. Spalding of Sapelo has, among his negroes, one called Bul-Ali, who writes Arabic, and speaks the Foulah language. Tom and himself are intimate friends. He is now [1839] extremely old and feeble. Tom informs me that he is from Timboo. If so, he can only throw light on the western portion of the Foulah nation. (Hodgson, *Notes* 74)[1]

Fifteen years after the publication of his *Notes*, in 1859, Hodgson made a more detailed reference to Ben Ali in a paper read before the Ethnological Society of New York entitled, "The Gospels: Written in the Negro Patois of English with Arabic Characters."[2] Hodgson's comments on Ben Ali read:

> A biographic sketch of another Mohammedan Foolah [*sic*] slave, Bul-ali (Ben-ali), may be found in my "Notes on Northern Africa" published some years ago. This Mohammedan [sic], the trustworthy servant of Mr. Spalding of Sapelo Island, Georgia, died recently, at an advanced age. He adhered to the creed and to the precepts of the Koran. He wrote Arabic, and read his sacred book with constancy and reverence. It is understood, that his numerous descendants, who are Christians, buried him with the

> Koran resting on his breast. He left various written papers, supposed to be
> ritual, which, I hope, may be preserved.

Considerably more information is given in this paper than what was given in the *Notes*.[3] It is highly unlikely that this information came from Ben Ali himself. By Hodgson's own account, Ben Ali died in 1859, the same year that Hodgson read his paper on patois. There is no record of Hodgson's having had any direct written communication with Ben Ali, or of his having interviewed him. According to an affidavit dated 12 October 1931 and signed by Captain Benjamin Lloyd Goulding, whose father, Francis Goulding, had been a close associate of Ben Ali in his last years, Ben Ali gave his manuscript as a gift to Francis Goulding shortly before he died in 1859. The same affidavit also contains a biography of Ben Ali, provided by Benjamin Goulding, whose contents make his father an unlikely source for Hodgson's story. A more likely alternative source for Hodgson's story was the ethnologist Theodore Dwight, who apparently interviewed Ben Ali and 'Umar ibn Said, in addition to Lamen Kebe.

Goulding, who inherited Ben Ali's manuscript from his father, gave it and its accompanying affidavit, along with several other of his father's papers, in endowment to the Goulding Memorial Collection of the Georgia State Law Library, State Department of Law, Atlanta, in 1931. Both the affidavit and the manuscript remained with the library until the spring of 1992 when they were transferred to the Hargrett Rare Books and Manuscript Library, University of Georgia Library, Athens, Georgia.

These two points of difference warrant consideration. After all, Goulding swore under oath to the factuality of his account. It is possible, although highly unlikely, that he was not aware of the pronouncements made by his famous fellow Georgian, Hodgson, about his father's friend Ben Ali, but he did feel the need to lend juridical weight to his own account of Ben Ali's life.[4] As an oath made under penalty of divine as well as temporal retribution for intentional falsity, Goulding's story becomes authenticated as containing the facts of Ben Ali's life. Indeed, Goulding's story follows the formal criteria of an affidavit to the letter, making it, insofar as the state and courts of Georgia are concerned, the official story of Ben Ali. It is an official story that is extraneous to the narrative of Ben Ali proper, and which is conveyed by a respected white man. As such it resembles that genre of authenticating prose that developed in accord with the slave narrative. From Equiano to Douglass,

there was attached to the slave narrative a prefatory letter or introduction, written by a white man, in order to verify the authorship of what followed.

Goulding's affidavit stands out as being markedly different from the genre of authenticating documentation that generally accompanied early African American slave narratives, even though it is something along the line of an extraneous document attached to the narrative to provide official validation. The primary reason for its difference is that Goulding does not go to great lengths to authenticate either the author's claims of literacy (his having produced the manuscript) or his signature. In fact, he does not explicitly address such claims at all.

What he does testify to are four "facts," in the following order: (1) Francis Goulding's claims of ownership of the document, and subsequently Benjamin's identical claims; (2) the authenticity of the claim that Ben Ali, who was the author of the Arabic document included in Goulding's papers, was the son of an Arab prince, and was educated and fully literate in Arabic; (3) that Ben Ali converted to Christianity and died a Baptist; and (4) that Ben Ali has a prominent spot in Joel Chandler Harris's novel *The Story of Aaron (So Named) the Son of Ben Ali.* [5]

The deduction of rightful ownership is an important issue in the affidavit. The paramount function of the affidavit is to establish how Goulding came to possess the manuscript, and so could legally pass it to the public domain. This is conceivably why twice in the three-page affidavit he states the claim that Ben Ali gave the manuscript to Francis Goulding in 1859. Yet, even this is only a secondary concern, taking up no more than fifteen lines of an eighty-line, two-and-a-half-page text:

> The Arabic document, commonly called a "diary" or "Meditations" of Ben Ali was given to my father by Ben Ali as I remember in 1859. (Lines 9-11)

> Ben Ali was a particular friend of my father in the last years of his life. When he was old and crippled and not able to work he lived on the mainland just opposite Sapelo Island where my father visited him often and had numerous interviews with him. (Lines 18-22)

> My father spoke to me often of his visits to Ben Ali and on one occasion Ben Ali made a present to my father of the Arabic document in question, stating that it was written by himself and that it contains some of his Meditations. This was given to my father in 1859 and he kept it until his death in 1881, when I came in possession of it and this Document has been in my possession ever since that time, for a period of fifty years. (Lines 48-54)

Excluding the oath, jurat, and signatures, which take up five lines (1, 77-80), the testimony consists of seventy-five lines total. Of these, seven are taken up with Francis and Benjamin Goulding's biographies (dates of birth, ages, date of death, and so on; lines 2-8); fifteen lines (9-11, 18-22, 48-54) relate Ben Ali's relationship with Francis Goulding, the circumstances of his giving the manuscript to him, and its coming into Benjamin Goulding's possession; twenty-one lines (55-75) deal specifically with Harris's portrayal of the manuscript's contents; and thirty-two deal with Ben Ali's biography. Of those thirty-two lines, seven and a half are an account of his age, extraordinary intelligence, trustworthiness, and physical stature; and three and a half lines attest to his religious conversion:

> Ben Ali was a slave belonging to Thomas Spaulding who was owner of Sapelo Island on the coast of Georgia. Ben Ali was an old man about 80 years old when I knew him. He had the reputation of being an unusually intelligent man and was the trusted foreman of Mr. Spaulding, who had, as I recall, something like one thousand negro slaves. (Lines 12-17)

> Personally he was a splendid specimen of manhood, rather tall, strong and had a fine physique (lines 43-44). When he first came to America he was reputed to have been a Mohammedan in religion. He had four wives and left a numerous progeny. Later he became a Christian and died a member of the Baptist faith. (Lines 44-47)

The remaining twenty-one lines are dedicated to the story of Ben Ali's Arab origin and his capture:

> Ben Ali was a man reputed to have been an Arab slave hunter, who himself became a slave. (Lines 23-24)

> Ben Ali was the leader of a band that made constant war on some of the African tribes in the Senegambian region. With their captives, this band of Arabs frequently pushed on to the Guinea coast and there sold them to the slave traders. These excursions continued until, on one occasion, the Arabs chanced to clash with a war-loving tribe, which was also engaged in plundering and raiding its neighbors. The meeting was unexpected to the Arabs, but not to the Africans. The Arabs who were left alive were led captive to the coast and there sold with other prisoners to slave traders. Among them was Ben Ali, who was then not more than thirty years old. With the rest, he was brought to America, where he was sold to a Virginian planter, fetching a very high price.

> Ben Ali was reputed to have been a son of a Prince and was educated. He could speak, read and write the Arabic language. (Lines 25-42)

According to Goulding, then, in contradiction to Hodgson, Ben Ali was an Arab and not a Foulah, and he died a Christian not a Muslim. These are not things that are simply stated. This is an affidavit: it is testifying that the things stated by Goulding under oath are facts about Ben Ali. Because that oath was properly formulated, administered, and validated by the jurat of an officer of the state, these facts constitute the official version of Ben Ali's story. But does official necessarily mean true? The same affidavit contains an acknowledged fictional portrayal, which deals with Harris's account of the manuscript:

> I showed this Document to Joel Chandler Harris, which aroused his interest and caused him to make investigations for himself and write the book referred to as "The Story of Aaron." Mr. Harris recounts Aaron's conversation with Buster John in regard to this document as follows:
>
> From his pocket Aaron drew a little package—something wrapped in soft leather and securely tied. It was a memorandum book. Opening this small book, Aaron held it toward Buster John, saying "What's here?"
>
> "It looks like pothooks," replied the boy, frankly.
>
> "Ain't a word in it I can't read," said Aaron.
>
> "Read some of it, please," plead Sweetest Susan.
>
> Thereupon Aaron began to read from the book in a strange tongue, the tone of his voice taking on modulations the children had never heard before.
>
> "I ain't never hear no jabber like dat," said Drusilla.
>
> "What sort of talk is it?" asked Buster John.
>
> "Tain't no creetur talk," remarked Drusilla; "I know dat mighty well."
>
> "It's the talk of Ben Ali," said Aaron—"Ben Ali, my daddy. Every word here was put down by him." (Lines 55-75)

This excerpt from Harris's novel has considerable bearing on Goulding's assertion that Ben Ali was Arab. An elaboration of the context from which it is extracted is warranted.

The passage that Goulding quotes occurs on page 12 near the end of the first chapter of the novel, entitled "The Story of Aaron" (*The Story of Aaron* 1-18). In that chapter the children, Buster John, Sweetest Susan, and Drusilla, decide to follow the advice of their mystical friend, the rabbit Mr. Thimblefinger, and seek out Aaron the son of Ben Ali in order to learn from him the language of the animals. They go to the slave Aaron, whose apparent disdain for the other negro slaves precipitated doubts about his religion (he was thought to be a devil worshiper), his racial purity (part Indian), and his morality (homicidal), and he uses a cloth-veiled mirror to instruct the three children in the language of the ani-

mals. Having done this and tested their new mastery by asking the child Drusilla, who is Buster John and Sweetest Susan's Negro nurse, to translate a gander's scream, he addresses a question to Buster John:

> "You think I'm a nigger, don't you?" He turned to Buster John.
> "Of course," said the youngster without hesitation. "What else are you?"
> "I'll show you." (11-12)

At this point the passage Goulding quotes begins. Harris's Aaron is exceptional for the same specific reason Couper found Tom exceptional: his mastery of a language that is identifiable but incomprehensible to reasonable expertise . . . "He was no nigger." That Aaron has the capacity to articulate and, more important, that Ben Ali had the capacity to inscribe, such masterful expressions supersedes the limits of The Negro's cognitive capacities as they were perceived to be when Harris wrote and Goulding read *The Story of Aaron (So Named) the Son of Ben Ali*. These written expressions mark an affectivity that exceeds the reasonable representation of The Negro. All the more reason for Ben Ali not to be a nigger.

But the chapter does not stop there. Joel Chandler Harris also provides a biographical account of Ben Ali. After Aaron identifies the talk as being that of Ben Ali, Buster John responds.

> "Why, I've heard grandpa talk about uncle Ben Ali," suggests Buster John.
> Aaron nodded. "Many a time. Your grandpa, my master, tried to buy my daddy, but Ben Ali was worth too much. I went to see him with my master twice a year till he died. He was no nigger."
> "What then?" Buster John asked.
> "Arab—man of the desert—slave hunter—all put down here," said Aaron, tapping the little book with his finger.
> The children were anxious to hear more about Ben Ali, the Arab—Ben Ali the slave hunter, who had himself become a slave. There was not much to tell, but that little was full of interest as Aaron told it, sitting in his door, the children on the steps below him. For the most part the book was a diary of events that had happened to Ben Ali after he landed in this country, being written in one of the desert dialects; but the first few pages told how the Arab chief happened to be a slave.
> Ben Ali was the leader of a band that made constant war on some of the African tribes in the Senegambian region. With their captives, this band of Arabs frequently pushed on to the Guinea coast and there sold them to the slave traders. These excursions continued until, on one occasion, the Arabs chanced to clash with a war-loving tribe, which was also engaged in plun-

dering and raiding its neighbors. The meeting was unexpected to the Arabs, but not to the Africans. The Arabs who were left alive were led captive to the coast and there sold with other prisoners to slave traders. Among them was Ben Ali, who was then not more than thirty years old. With the rest, he was brought to America, where he was sold to a Virginian planter, fetching a very high price. Along with him, in the same ship, was an Arab girl, and she was also bought by the planter. Nothing was said in the diary in regard to the history of this girl, except that she became Ben Ali's wife, and bore him a son and a daughter. The son was Aaron, so named. The daughter died while yet a child. (13-14)

This story is immediately recognizable as the same one that Goulding testifies to as being the factual account of Ben Ali's biography.

What is being authenticated in Goulding's affidavit then, Harris's fictional account or Goulding's story about the document? Are the two at all distinguishable, or are they one and the same? There is an ambiguity of reference here, a confusion between fact and fiction. What is the nature of this confusion, what are its parameters? That is to say, if Goulding is quoting Harris, who does Harris quote? This is a question whose most complicated nonanswer is the document itself, the text of Ben Ali's meditations.

According to Harris, the manuscript itself is the source for his story. Yet this claim is absurd, because neither he nor Goulding knew enough Arabic to discriminate the opening from the end of the document; nor is there any evidence that Harris secured a translation of the manuscript from an Arabist. That fact notwithstanding, the answer that Harris hazarded in his 1896 novel became, through Goulding's affidavit, the official story. This manuscript was the diary of an Arab slave. All that needed to be done was for it to be translated in order to confirm its content, as well as the story of its author's origin.

This is both complicated and a nonanswer because it begs the question that no one dares to ask in a fashion that would engage the textual complexity of the document—that would mean reading it—for fear that no answer could ever be found: What is this thing, this paper manuscript whose dimensions are approximately 3.75 × 6.31 inches, with its deliberate patterns of scribbling contained in a flapped buffalo-skin cover at the Georgia State Library, State Department of Law in Atlanta? What does it mean?

This is no simple question. "There is no writing or mark of any kind on the cover to give a clue to the name of its author," wrote Ella May

Thornton, head librarian of the Georgia State Library from 1925 to 1956, to Harold Glidden on 16 April 1950. The question of meaning has remained unanswered, even though since Harris's answer in 1896 and Goulding's institutionalization of it in 1931, the manuscript has been glanced at by some expert readers of difficult-to-decipher messages. All concur that the most significant aspect of the manuscript is its near-inde-terminacy. This leaves us only with the Harris-Goulding reading, a read-ing that weaves such a web of folklore and legend around the manuscript as to almost assure its illegibility. Which answers what? Rather than resolving questions in evidence, Harris's story and Captain Goulding's affidavit leave us with other more pressing questions. What is at the root of this supposedly official story? Although readily available as an aesthetic object—it can be seen in the University of Georgia Library—the document is in fact inaccessible to any reading except this one. Yet undoubtedly Ben Ali's writing was meaningful to someone, which, at minimum, assumes its readability.

Thornton was unwaveringly certain of the document's having some significance, and spent over two and a half decades (1931-56) contacting a sundry of scholars and generally interested parties in the hope that some one of them could decipher Ben Ali's manuscript. Thornton's efforts resulted in a considerable number of items of correspondence between her and anyone who would respond and take a serious interest in the document. These items of correspondence attest to repeated attempts at reading Ben Ali's writing, most of which were rather ama-teurish, informed more by a sense of the exoticism of a Negro writing in Arabic than a desire to determine the meaning of what he had written.[6]

Nonetheless, because of the severe difficulties that the manuscript itself poses, even for those who are quite competent in Arabic, more often than not these letters between Thornton and her correspondents, instead of the manuscript, are read and studied in conjunction with Goulding's affidavit and Harris's novel. The result is that whatever significance the document is supposed to have has been pretty well determined by the speculations of people who simply could not get past the quality of its material signs, its orthographic peculiarities, to read it.

Even so, as a consequence of Thornton's considerable efforts, in 1940 the guess that was hazarded by Harris in 1896 was challenged on schol-arly grounds, but with equally dubious results. The Africanist Melville Herskovits was one of Thornton's correspondents, and in 1940 one of his graduate students, Joseph Greenberg (who would subsequently estab-

lish himself as a renowned linguist and aspiring semiotician), published
an article in the *Journal of Negro History* in which he argued that the
Arabic manuscript known as *Ben Ali's Diary* is unquestionably not a
diary:

> From the first it seemed improbable to me that the document could be a
> diary or plantation record, since among the African Negro Moslems
> Arabic is only used to copy existing standard works, original composition
> being confined to chronicles of local dynasties. This conclusion was
> strengthened when, on cursory examination, several religious formulae
> were recognizable, despite misspellings. (372)[7]

Based on the discovery of these "formulae," Greenberg claimed to have
made "some headway" in translating the work in 1937. Between 1939
and 1940, while on a trip to Kano, Nigeria, on a predoctoral training fellowship from the Social Science Research Council of New York, he
determined, with the assistance of certain Hausa scholars (whose identity is never specified: "certain native malams") that the Ben Ali manuscript is in fact a series of excerpts from a popular tenth-century Malikite
legal treatise. That treatise is *ar-Risāla* by Abū Muḥammad 'Abdullāh ibn
Abī Zaid al-Qairawānī of Qairawān, in what is present-day Tunisia.[8]
With the publication of Greenberg's *Journal of Negro History* article, the
text of the Ben Ali manuscript was recognized as having significance in a
fashion far more complex than just being Arabic. In addition to identifying the thematic content of the famous "Diary," his preliminary decipherment of the text drew attention to its linguistic value.

  The chief focus of Greenberg's linguistic decipherment of the Ben Ali
manuscript is its orthography. Besides problems of simply obscure
handwriting, and fading ink, the manuscript is made practically illegible
by irregular spelling. This irregularity, Greenberg concludes, results
from the author's being semiliterate, having had his education truncated, perhaps by his enslavement:

> It is to be conjectured that at the time of the writer's departure from Africa
> he was still a young student. Books are first taught by oral memorization;
> and it is apparent that this manuscript was written by a man who had
> memorized the text . . . making the errors that might be expected. . . . Not
> only do we encounter the confusions we might expect from the ordinary
> Sudanese pronunciation of Arabic . . . but we also find that the voiced and
> unvoiced consonants have not been differentiated and, most peculiar of
> all, we find the identification of "j," "y," and "z." (373)

Focusing on the linguistic features of the Ben Ali manuscript, Greenberg identifies particular patterns of graphemic displacements or interchangeability, deviations from the universal standard of literary Arabic orthography, the Classical 'arabīya. In the nomenclature of Arabo-Islamic linguistic theory, this sort of graphemic displacement is termed *taṣḥīf* (heterography): two distinctly different phonemes are confused and transcribed by one grapheme, so that the graphemic representation of sound is no longer reliable. Graphemic unreliability, in turn, produces orthographic irregularity, which is why the study of *taṣḥīf* recognizes heterography as the index of a phenomenological problem: the failure to perceive phonetic difference. With *taṣḥīf* a dissonance of linguistic referentiality occurs. Assessing the obscurities of the Ben Ali manuscript as *taṣḥīf* enables Greenberg to register them as referential dissonance: they are deviations from the determinate algorithms of an "authentic" literary Arabic, engendered by Ben Ali's incompetent handling of the authentic language. Accordingly, Greenberg no longer has the responsibility of reading them as Arabic, because their value as such is diminished.

It might indeed be well to distinguish two aspects of the problem that begins to come into view with Greenberg's linguistic analysis. One is that of Arabic dialectology, that is, the relationship between the manuscript's orthography and Arabic dialects prevalent in the western Sudan and Senegambia. The other is that of phenomenology proper, that is, the question of the grapheme's phonemic value. Greenberg in one instance maintains that the manuscript's heterography bears an affinity with "ordinary Sudanese pronunciation of Arabic," while at the same time deviating from it. This is a curiously ambiguous assertion. Its ambiguity stems from the open designation of Sudanese Arabic: does it refer to the numerous dialects of Sudan Colloquial Arabic (SCA) of the geopolitical space known at the time of Greenberg's essay as the Anglo-Egyptian Sudan, the present-day country of Sudan? Or does it refer to the Colloquial Arabic of what was then called the Western Sudan, encompassing Chad, Niger, Nigeria, and Mali?

If the reference is the Anglo-Egyptian Sudan, at the time he was preparing his article Greenberg would have had available to him English-language vocabularies and linguistic studies of SCA, the most obvious of which would be Captain H. F. S. Amery's *English-Arabic Vocabulary for the Use of Officials in the Anglo-Egyptian Sudan* (Cairo: Mokattam Printing Office, 1905), as well as S. Hillelson's respectable

body of work, in particular his *Sudan Arabic English-Arabic Vocabulary* (London: The Sudan Government, 1925).[9] If the reference is the Western Sudan, Greenberg would have had at his disposal numerous studies in French, German, and English, notably Lethem's *Colloquial Arabic, Shuwa Dialect of Bornu, Nigeria, and the Region of Lake Chad* (London: Crown Agents for the Colonies, 1920), Carbou's *La région du Tchad et du Quadaï* (Paris: Ernest Leroux, 1912), *Méthode pratique pour l'étude de l'arabe parlé au Quaday et à l'est du Tchad* (Paris: Paul Geuthner, 1913), and Westermann's *Die Sudansprachen* (Hamburg: n.p., 1911).[10]

Whether or not Greenberg consulted these works in order to render his assessment of the Ben Ali manuscript's language cannot be established on the basis of his article, as he gives no citation to any of them. What can be determined, however, is that the occurrence of graphemic differentiation of voiced and unvoiced consonants is nowhere recorded in this body of work on African-Arabic dialectology. In fact, there is no known extant Arabic orthography, Classical, Standard, or Colloquial, that differentiates between voiced and unvoiced consonants, or rather there is no graphic differentiation of consonants according to their being voiced or unvoiced. This feature does not occur in the Ben Ali manuscript. What does occur almost universally in sedentary Arabic dialects outside the peninsula, and which is possibly what Greenberg is referring to when discussing the distinction of voiced and unvoiced, is the merging of the two emphatic interdental phonemes, "ظ/Ẓ" and "ﺽ/Ḍ." In Classical Arabic, the first, "ظ/Ẓ," is a velarized voiced interdental spirant, while the second, "ﺽ/Ḍ," is a lateralized velarized voiceless interdental stop. The relative universality of the merging of these two phonemes granted,[11] there is no exchanging of the graphemes ض (*ḍād*) and ظ (*ẓā'*) in the Ben Ali text, which might have indicated such merging, insofar as the manuscript is supposed to be overdetermined by local pronunciation. The Ben Ali manuscript does exhibit an interchangeability of the graphemes ج/jīm (Greenberg's "j") and ي /yā' (Greenberg's "y")—a feature it has in common with the Arabic dialects of the Western Sahara, and southern Algeria and Tunisia—but neither of these is interchanged with ز /zā' (Greenberg's "z"). Of the *taṣḥīf* that does occur in the Ben Ali manuscript, much of it [i.e., the interchangeability of the graphemes س (sīn) and ص (ṣād), the confusing of ك (kāf) and ق (qāf), and the eliding of the hamza] is analogous to common features not only of SCA and Chadian Arabic but also of other Arabic dialects and patois. Then again, the interchangeability of the graphemes

ل/lām and ض /ḍād prevalent in the Ben Ali manuscript resembles a linguistic phenomenon that is particular to Fulani speakers of Arabic in the Senegambia. This particularity, along with Ben Ali's purported origins in Futa Djallon, is insightful of the polyglossic circumstance of African Muslim literati in the Senegambia.

Throughout the eighteenth and nineteenth centuries (the time period in which Ben Ali's manuscript was produced), Fulani scholars in the Senegambia employed three orthographic systems that utilized Arabic graphemes, two of which were Arabic and the other Fulani itself. Literary Fulani was utilized in the production of Fulani narratives and poetry that were antecedent and beyond the sanctioned Islamic realm of cultural and historical activity. But it was not confined to this usage; in the seventeenth, eighteenth, and nineteenth centuries, scholarly texts, glosses in jurisprudence, and theological tracts were written in Fulani. Still, literary Fulani remained by and large the medium for transcribing popular discourses.

Of the two Arabic orthographies, there was the universal Classical Arabic orthography of Muslim scholarship, 'arabīya, such as that used by Ayyūb and 'Abd-ur-Raḥmān in their epistles, and 'Umar and Abū Bakr in their writings. Scholarly Arabic was used primarily in the recording of state events and official histories and chronicles, religious ritual literature (such as meditations and chants), biographies and stories of the prophet Muḥammad (pbuh) and his companions, as well as overall scholarship from mathematics and medicine to jurisprudence and language. In addition to this universal Arabic there was also an orthography patterned on the phonemic features of the Fulani pronunciation of Arabic. This Fulani Arabic had multiple functions. As a rule, its scholarly function was either didactic or mnemonic. In the eighteenth century, numerous books on heterography, or taṣḥīf, were produced, with the aim of instructing Fulani-speaking students of Arabic how to identify and avoid transcribing vernacular Arabic expressions. Taṣḥīf was also prevalent in mnemonic texts, in which understanding was stressed over formal expression. Such texts were often used in preparation for oral presentation before a group of Fulani Arabic speakers whose appropriation of the language was diverse, as well as in personal correspondence.[12]

Texts written in the vernacular of Fulani Arabic reflecting diglossic tension on the page have potential for shedding some light on the dynamics of Arabic creolization.[13] In short, the phonemic-based orthog-

raphy of Fulani Arabic is a deliberate system, a creolization, as opposed
to a pidgin, or a collection of "misspellings." Indeed, the fact that in
Futa Djallon, each of these three orthographies were (are) utilized by the
literate masters (*Chiernos*), depending upon the context of production,
clearly indicates a realm of literary discourse that was highly heterographic.

   None of this is to suggest that the Ben Ali manuscript falls neatly into
any of the three Arabic orthographies under discussion; instead it is an
admixture of all three, and then of none. For example, in the orthography patterned on Fulani pronunciations, ق (*qāf*) is substituted with
either غ (*ghā'*), producing غـال (*ghāla*) for قـال (*qāla*), or the ط (*ṭā'*), producing طـال (*ṭāla*). The grapheme ظ (*ẓā'*)displaces both the graphemes ز
(*zā'*) and ذ (*dhā'*); and ش (*shīn*) is confused with س (*sīn*). The Ben Ali
text does some of these things, but it does not do them consistently. That
is to say that, in the case of *Ben Ali's Diary*, although the manuscript
might be a reproduction of an aurally read text (al-Qairawānī's *ar-
Risāla*), it is not a graphic reproduction of the way anyone speaks.

   This last point leads to the second aspect of the problem of linguistic
referentiality exposed through Greenberg's analysis of the manuscript.
Greenberg's assessment of the purported illegibility of the Ben Ali manuscript is predicated on the theoretical construct of a historically antecedent homogeneous pure or "Classical" literary Arabic, '*arabīya*,
entailing a universal correct (standard) orthography (i.e., the codified
transcription of words with the proper letters, characters, or signs
according to some universal standard usage). According to that construct, writing is a simulacrum of speech, which in turn is a simulacrum
of thought. In the case of Ben Ali's manuscript, however, the obstacle of
the high degree of interpenetration is encountered in the double transcription process (Arabic and English in the case of Greenberg's relationship to the manuscript).[14] The problem that is meant, and which
Greenberg addresses inadequately, is how to think orthography.

   For Greenberg, the untranslatability of Ben Ali's writing, which is
residual, must be made somehow thinkable, it must be transcribed,
either in Arabic or English. Therefore, even the one remark made by
Greenberg concerning the frequent occurrence of orthographic irregularities in the Ben Ali manuscript, implying a dynamics of creolization, necessarily precludes the possibility of that creolization being the frame of
reference for textual production. It does so by bracketing the obscurities

beyond the text as effects of the author's phonetic deviation from any known Arabic speech patterns:

> It would seem impossible to get some conception of the language spoken by the writer of our document from his pronunciation of Arabic to be deduced from the misspellings in the document itself . . . since no reports are available of any African language spoken by Mohammedanized natives which fits this pattern. (373)

Such a reading pivots on the assumption that writing follows speech, that there is a necessary correspondence between phonemic events and graphemic transcriptions, which legitimates the experience of reading that assumes the transparency of the sign's materiality. Greenberg treats the written manuscript as a phenomenological trace of Ben Ali's material voice; it is for Greenberg as an oral informant, minus the cultural interferences that so preoccupied d'Avezac. Subsequently he can assert that the author of the manuscript "misspelled" his words because he spoke poorly, i.e., in a Sudanic vernacular of Arabic, which Greenberg is only slightly to this side of claiming to be a pidgin. By attributing the text's heterography to some failure of correspondence between phenomenal event (pronounced sound) and textual transcription, and moreover identifying the origin of this failure to be in the human agent, Greenberg can locate the source of heterography beyond the structure of the language. The illegibility of Ben Ali's manuscript results from improper appropriation by the writer, or at least his appropriating the wrong language to writing: the heterogeneous pronunciations of vernacular. This is what Greenberg means when he says that Ben Ali misspells words, implying a correct spelling that is somehow entailed in the structures of the language, in a normative orthography.

But this attempt on Greenberg's part flounders before the materiality of Ben Ali's transcription, which refuses to become transparent. Hence, he provides no viable translation, only theoretical explanation in lieu of linguistic definition. The one thing that Ben Ali's manuscript will not let its readers do is transpose its heterography to somewhere or something beyond its text, to bypass or obfuscate the sign's plastic value. As Greenberg's own speculations reveal, there is no place for it to go. Indeed, Ben Ali's manuscript, whose script is first and foremost marginally legible, cannot be read when reading is perceived as a process whose necessity is the sign's material transparency. Any attempt to read it according to such a process necessarily exposes the fictionality of the

distinction between meaning and the materiality of the mode of expression. The script of the document is so dominated by heterography that its material appearance, the sign's plastic value, comes to occupy for anyone who has tried to read it, including the present reader, all significance. This produces the effect of an experience of reading in which meaning is never immediate and apparent. The predominance of heterography in the manuscript marks the inability to read in it—in accordance with a conception of signification that is predicated on self-reflective intentionality—thought's expression, or embodiment in writing.

I am not suggesting here that such a normalization of linguistic structures does not occur. That would be the height of absurdity. What I want to point out is that there is a considerable distinction between conceiving of normalization as being inherent in the process of linguistic referentiality (i.e., being a natural development of language into relatively stable patterns), and maintaining that normalization is more an effect of discursivity, the employment of the processes of linguistic referentiality according to specific interests and exigencies. In the former conception heterogeneity (read in writing as heterography) is not inherent to linguistic referentiality, but results from a breakdown of language, a disruptive trauma that precludes development. In the latter conception, linguistic referentiality is essentially heterogeneous, involving both the distinctly different processes of reading and seeing.

By bracketing the source of heterography beyond the economy of proper, or as his terms imply, authentic linguistic referentiality, Greenberg is able to achieve a certain stability, and hence legibility of the text by allegorizing it: behind the veil of irregularities, of errors in orthography, he discovers the proper referent of transcription, the "original" text, al-Qairawānī's *ar-Risāla*. The heterography of Ben Ali's manuscript succeeds in deflecting even this reading, however. This deflection does not merely leave a text like Ben Ali's manuscript unreadable in terms of writing's being the transparent medium for thought's expression, it jeopardizes that notion of reading altogether.

In spite of Greenberg's seeming to have dispelled the mystery of the "Diary," the document remains accessible for examination in the Hargrett Rare Books and Manuscript Library, University of Georgia Library, under the designation *Ben Ali's Diary*. In part, this is a function of Greenberg's never having published the promised translation of this

text. Nor has anyone after him, although Harold Glidden, former head of the Near East Section of the State Department's Information Bureau, and Chief of the Near East Section of the Library of Congress, claimed in a correspondence to Ella May Thornton, dated 30 November 1949, that he had translated the manuscript. As of the moment that translation too has yet to be published.[15] The manuscript remains unreadable, a deflecting resistance, whose referential meaning is effectively lost. Which is not to assume that it was even known to the author, "Ben Ali."

Thus, it also remains the object of a dispute, a difference of perspective over title and literary properties. This difference assumes the stature of confusion when any attempt is made to access the document under its official archive designation. The confusion is fueled by the persistent hegemony of Harris's account. As many potential readers have discovered, once the trip is made to Atlanta in anticipation of finding an extremely rare, if not exotic, autobiographical text, that anticipation is immediately frustrated by the utter impenetrability of the material letter of the text, which compels the uninitiated to Arabic paleography to seek refuge in the corresponding frame of reference that is a well-maintained file of all corresponding English-language texts about the document. This file further exacerbates frustration by presenting a seemingly irresolvable dispute over the text's content and that content's readability.

The persistence with which the Georgia State Library designates the text *Ben Ali's Diary* also cannot merely be explained away as an effect of Thornton's professed love for "fanciful tales and mystery," or even her commitment to Joel Chandler Harris as a native son. There is after all Goulding's affidavit, as well as the failure of Greenberg to prove his claims in print by publishing a readable translation of the manuscript. For these reasons I say that the confusion in designation remains centered on the unresolved question of the letter's message and nature: What is this thing?

Not only are there two different responses—the Goulding-Harris response and the Greenberg response—to this question, but the question itself possesses two distinct aspects, which are discovered in the convergence of three different discourses (fictional, juridical, and speculative description). These discourses constitute three different signifying practices that are brought to bear on one text, recognized by all parties to entail an undeniable message. The fundamental problem concerns the material nature of that message. What Ben Ali's manuscript poses is a

problem of reading that is not simple by any stretch of the imagination. The fundamental question that has compelled every attempt thus far to read this text is the question of the correspondence, or rapport, between the word and something, between the signifier and its signified, thought and its expression. This is perhaps the least fruitful question to put to Ben Ali's text. The text of *Ben Ali's Diary* consists of signs that, no matter how closely examined, will not countenance their being deciphered and subsequently made transparent. Therefore, the more productive and most immediate question to ask of the manuscript is, How is thought transcribed as a sign whose material content has nothing to do with the proper content of perception (the materiality of the sign) when the sign will not become transparent?

Translation of *Ben Ali's Diary*, therefore, could only be problematic (in the sense that it may be equally erroneous or correct). This perhaps explains why Thornton, Greenberg, and Glidden had difficulties even finding a "native speaking informant" who could clear the whole thing up for them. Thornton and Greenberg both admit that showing the manuscript to native Arabic speakers and (in Greenberg's case) Nigerian Muslim scholars proved futile. This adds another dimension to the problem of linguistic signs, that of translation as it relates to reading.

The enigma this text presents to even descriptive reading occurs precisely because of an inability to appropriate it to a model of signification that is predicated on representation: the presumption that the "authorial" subject (whether confused with the inscribed narrator or not) has "signs" that are sprinkled throughout the work. As a result there can be no assumption that a straight descriptive relation exists between the "author" of the text and his/her/its language through which the author is represented in the narrative as a full subject, and the narrative as the instrumental expression of that fullness.

In *Ben Ali's Diary* no authorial signature is realized, brought to life in the form of the text. There is no trace in the body of the text of the signatory who becomes a point of reference that is safely kept outside the text, with the latter being a controlled demarcated field of subjective intentionality. This absence of signature and discernible patterns of expression requires that every reading of the manuscript involve a delicate operation of analysis based upon the appreciation of a certain quantity of the more or less that can be inferred in the text.

Such appreciation necessitates the prior differentiation of pluraliza-

tion in the operation engaged in the text (and hence derived from the specific instances of reading), or a sequence of prior models. In effect, Greenberg's inferring of the meaning in the Ben Ali manuscript amounts to the operation of a previous model or ideal text through which the text (any text) is made accessible. This ideal text in its most favorable aspect is a text of liberal social evolutionism, whose apogee is the privileged present perspective of the expert reader—that perpetual present that is sufficiently ahistorical and accultural so as to enable the cataloging and schematizing of what is commonly called authorial intention.

Of course, both that text and its intention are ephemeral, which is why Greenberg's authoritative reading effects a sort of disenfranchisement through illusion. The term is appropriate, because what is excluded in his reading are not merely *arché*, artifacts or purely insular articulations in the manuscript (could there ever be such?), but schemes of another discursive order. Being of another discursive order, their displacement is a requirement of meaning.[16] Greenberg's promised translation (wherever it may be) can be nothing more than a referendum whose terms of acceptance or registration of the text are predetermined by the aesthetics of a given economy of representation, in which certain cognitive categories are iconic: Literacy, The Negro, and The Arab. But the Ben Ali manuscript irresponsibly mixes icons, and so denies the grammar of representation.

Given the situation of *Ben Ali's Diary*, where there is a collocation of divergent glossia in which none is ostensibly placed as authoritative, to endeavor an accommodation that could preserve the abundant possibilities of each glossia in some model of inequity remains untenable. Such an integrative accommodating must disallow itself in any attempt at comprehensive reading. The slippage between glossia is so great that there is no way, except capriciously, to delineate essential and surplus significance.

The authoritative text of Ben Ali is not threatened with dislocation, it cannot be located in the first instance. To preserve the hegemony of its "view of things," however, a reading like Greenberg's must negate the incomprehensibility of such a text by denying or ignoring those codes and significations that escape its ken, i.e., its semiotic concentration. So Greenberg (and Glidden after him) will insist that he has actually translated the thing, and is thus qualified to pronounce its insignificance. And because neither of the two translations has been published (due to "little interest" and "failing health"), who can challenge their representation of

Ben Ali's manuscript? Only the text.[17] For, when it comes to reading Ben Ali's text, representation has absolutely no sovereignty. Reading *Ben Ali's Diary* amounts to engaging a text whose polyvalence refuses to be comprehended by "Western" literary criticism's unadulterated paradigms, and so approaching the perennial problem of translation: What is it that gets translated? There can be no approaching this question without first glancing at the manuscript, and getting a sense of the graphic enigmas it presents to reading.

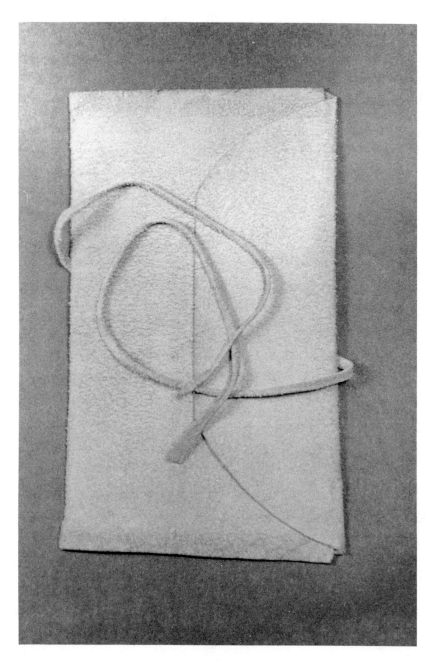

Plate 1

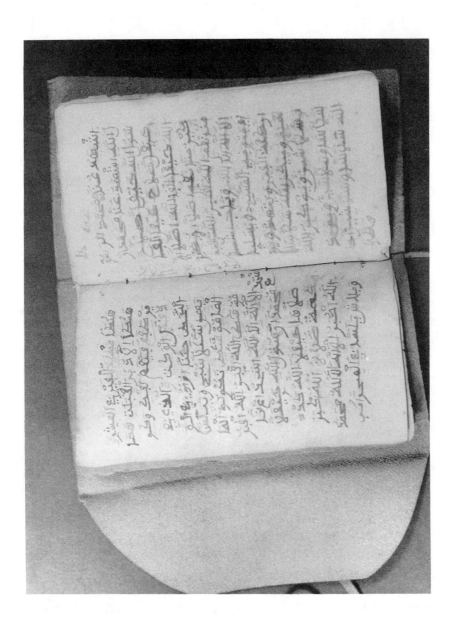

Plate 2

Plate 3. Page 1

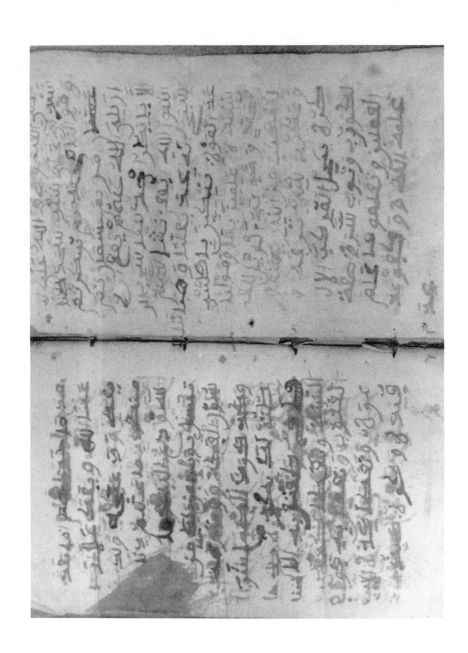

Plate 4. Pages 2–3

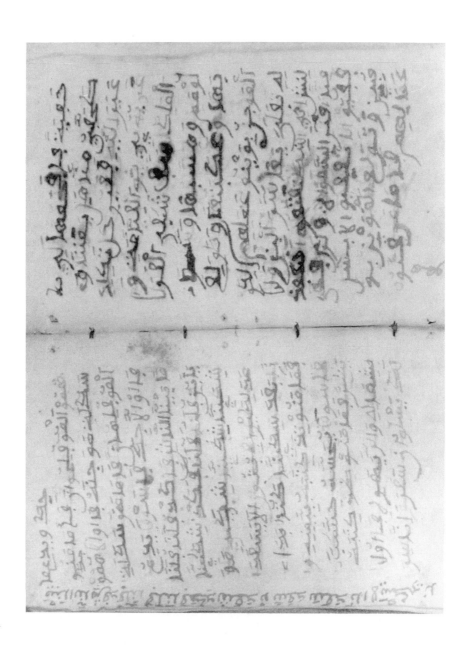

Plate 5. Pages 4–5

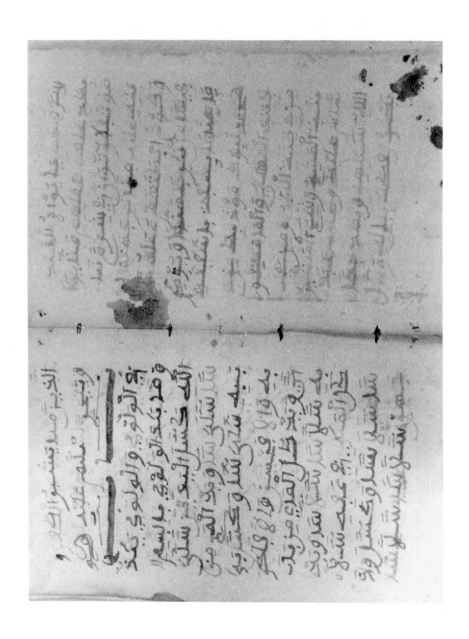

Plate 6. Pages 6–7

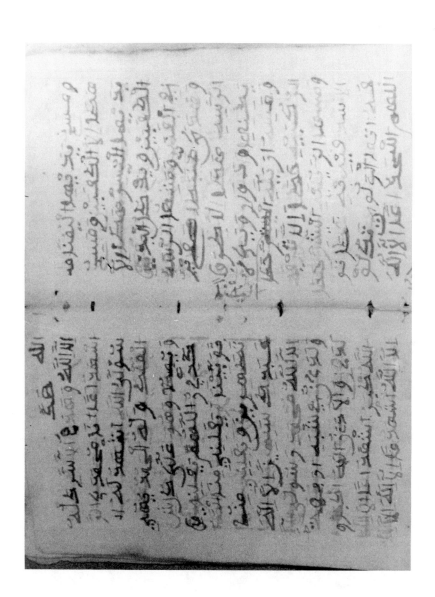

Plate 7. Pages 8–9

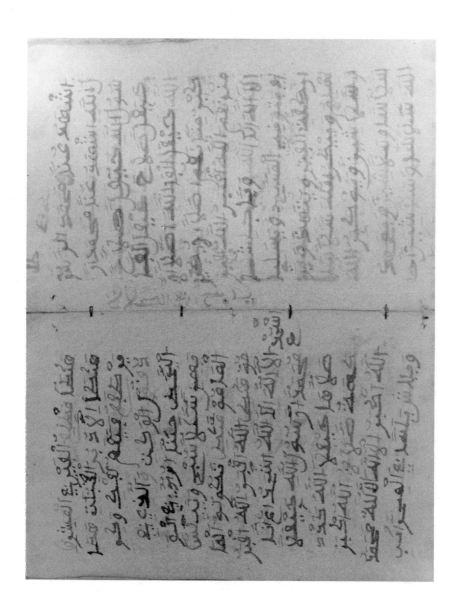

Plate 8. Pages 10–11

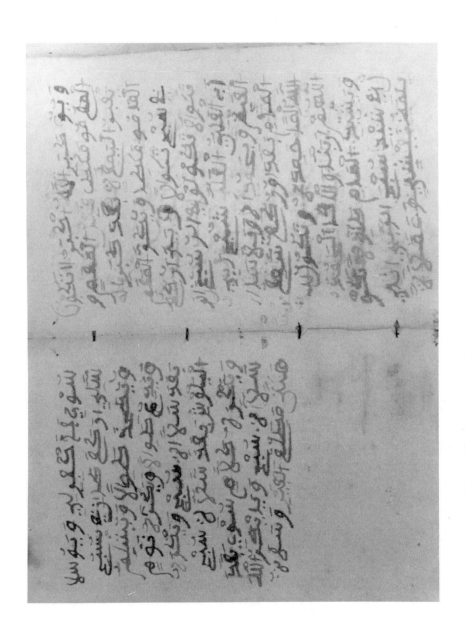

Plate 9. Pages 12–13

Chapter 7

Reading the Sign's Indeterminate Corpora

> No civilization has vested the guarantee of its logico-metaphysical truth
> in the structures of its language more than the Arab civilization, or in
> such an unvarying and conscious manner. . . . From the moment that
> one regards as contingent or even denies the distinction between the
> object of literary creation and the individual subject, and postulates
> instead a unification of object and subject in a meta-object that is the
> text—that is in fact language itself—one finds oneself in the territory of
> the classical literary criticism that developed from Qur'anic exegesis.[1]

The Ben Ali manuscript is enclosed in a small leather bag, secured by an
attached leather strap (plates 1 and 2). The bag's color is a creamy tan,
and its untanned side is facing outward, with the tanned side protecting
the text. There is no title page or any discernible declaration of a title;
neither is there any signature. The text is written on both sides of rather
thin paper. The pages of the manuscript are bound together by string.
There is no information on the history of the text's binding; whether it
was done by Ben Ali or Goulding we cannot determine.[2] In all likeli-
hood, it was done by Ben Ali or by someone who was passing familiar
with Arabic scribal conventions, because the pagination is indicated by
placing the first word of the subsequent page in the bottom left-hand
corner of the preceding one.

The Georgia State Library has provided Arabic-numeral pagination
of the pages on its negatives and photo prints of the manuscript, beginning with the first page of script and ending with the last. The result is
twelve and one-half pages of text numbered 1-13 (see plates 3-9). It is
very possible that there were many more pages at one time, as there is
an inconsistency between the word in the bottom left-hand corner of
"page 6" and the first word of "page 7." The ink of the manuscript is
reddish brown; there are many blotches and the script is uneven, heavy
and thick in some places and thin and light in others. Much of the ink
has bled through to the opposite side on many pages. There is a very
discernible variation between the handwriting in pages "1" through "4"
(plates 3-5), and the handwriting in pages "5" through "13" (plates 5-9).
The handwriting on the first four pages is extremely obscure and

difficult to decipher, but that of the remaining nine pages is by and large legible. This variation in handwriting suggests that more than one hand may have been involved in producing the manuscript. There is marginalia on pages 5 and 10 (plates 5 and 8). Both marginalia repeat passages in the body of the text; the one on page 5 is rather lengthy, and that on page 10 is a correction in the spelling of the chapter heading.

The script of the Ben Ali text is throughout easily identifiable as the variant of Kufic script known interchangeably as *al-khaṭṭ at-takrurī*, *al-khaṭṭ as-senegalī*, and *al-khaṭṭ at-timbuktuī*, but there are frequent words and entire passages where standardized Arabic spelling conventions collapse. Whether or not these graphemic displacements result from some phonic dissonance, as irregularities of spelling they are fairly easy to follow in the manuscript. "L/ ل" (*lām*) displaces the voiceless pharyngeal "Ḍ/ ض" (*ḍād*), producing *al-wulū'* (الـولـو) for *al-wuḍū'* (الـوضـو). With considerable regularity, although not always, the voiceless sibilant "S/ س" (*sīn*) displaces the voiceless pharyngeal "Ṣ/ ص" (*ṣād*), producing *'ala sahbihi* (عـلى سـحـبـه) for *'ala ṣahbihi* (عـلى صـحـبـه) ("on his companions"). The same *sīn* displaces the voiceless aveolar "th/ ث" (*thā'*), producing *salāsa* (سـلاسـة) for *thalātha* (ثـلاثـة) ("three"). The voiced "K/ ك" (*kāf*) displaces the voiced uvular "Q/ ق " (*qāf*), producing *kāla* (كـال) for *qāla* (قـال) ("he said"). The *alif* indicating the long vowel "*ā*" is often omitted, which in conjunction with the displaced *qāf* produces *kala* (كـل) instead of *qāla* (قـال).

When these graphemic displacements are taken into account, seven and a half of the manuscript's thirteen pages are readable: half of page 1, lines 1-10; and pages 7-13. As indicated in chapter 5, no translation of *Ben Ali's Diary* has been published up until now. What follows is my own English translation of the readable seven and a half pages of *Ben Ali's Diary*, which I have also edited in Modern Standard Arabic. Before providing my translation there are some general comments to be made about the organization of *Ben Ali's Diary*.

The text is divided into chapters, indicated by the word *bāb* ("door"); each chapter has its *bāb*. The top half of page 1 (plate 3) contains the requisite opening benediction to Allah and suitable salutation to Muḥammad, and the only lines of the manuscript to stand before the first *bāb* of the text. As such it is something of an epigraph. The remaining readable seven pages are divided into two chapters. Page 7 begins with *bāb-ul-Wulū'* (viz., *al-Wuḍū'*: the ritual ablution performed before prayer, in accordance with the category of impurity one finds oneself in). It con-

sists of instructions for ablution, and the call to prayer. The "Chapter on Prayer," *bāb-fi-ash-shalāh* (viz., *aṣ-ṣalāh*) begins on page 9 and contains instruction on the mechanics of prayer.

I have arranged my edition and translation of *Ben Ali's Diary* into three columns. The right-hand column is an unexpurgated reproduction of Ben Ali's text with its heterography intact. In the middle column I have edited the text in Modern Standard Arabic. The left-hand column is my English translation, in which I indicate Ben Ali's heterography and irregular usages by brackets, and the notes give the Modern Standard Arabic spellings and usages.

Ben Ali's Diary

In the name of Allah, The Most Merciful The Most Beneficent. Allah's blessings upon our lord [shayyidnā][3] Muḥammad, and upon his family and companions [shahbihi],[4] blessings and salutations. Verily, the master and jurist [stādh al-fakīh][5] Muḥammad 'Abdullah ibn Yūsuf ibn 'Abd al-Qarawanidu, may Allah have mercy upon him and increase his blessings, amen, said [kala] [1: 1-8].[6]

Chapter

Assuredly he led the narrative story [with]: "Write me books that are a brief exposition, that are a brief exposition, that are a brief exposition on . . ." [1: 8-10]

Chapter on Wuḍū'

One begins wuḍū' with the basmala, washes the right hand with water three times, and washes the left hand three times. Using both the right and left

بسم الله الرّحمٰن الرّحيم
و صَلّى الله عَلَى سيّدنا محمّد
وعَلَى آله وصحبه وسلّم تَسليمًا
فَقال الاستاذ الفقيه محمّد عبد
الله بن يوسف بن عبدالقرَوَند
رحمه الله ويفضله [الله]
ببركاته امين [1: 8]
باب

وقد قاد القصة [امرًا] أكتب
لى كتبًا مختصرة مختصرة
مختصرة عن .... [1: 8-10]
باب في الوضوء

الوضوء في اليد. يبدأ الوضوء
بالبسملة؛ غسل اليدين ثلاثًا
ثلاثًا، واليد اليمنى فبه ثلاثًا،
و غسل به وباليسرى الافمام،
و يدخل الماء [لا بد منه] ثلاثًا
ثلاثًا، و في انفه ثلاثًا ثلاثًا،
وغسل وجهه ثلاثًا ثلاثًا.[9]
[7: 1-11] مسح يده اليمين
الى الكعب مسح يده اليسرى
الى الكعب، و يدخل اليدين
في الاذنين، و مسح رأسه باليد
من صديره الى الطوق ...
ومسح رجله اليمين الى الركبّ
الى ظفره، و مسح رجله اليسرى
الى سد قدمه . . فيهذا اتى
الوضوء تقول: اللهم أشهد أن لا
إله [8: 1-15] الّا الله وحده لا
شريك له، أشهد أنّ محمداً
رسول الله، أشهد أن له الحق
وله الحمد، يحيّ و يميّت، و هو

بسم الله الرحمن الرحيم
وصلى على شيطا محمد و على
آله وشهه وصلى تشلم فكل
اشتد الفخيه محمد عبد الله بن
يسف بن عبد الكروند الرحيم الله
ويفد له بابي بركته امين الله
امين
[1:1-8]

باب
وكد كود الكصا اكتيلى كتب
مكتاسرة مكتاسرة مكتاسرة
عن ... [1:8-10]
يلب في الوالوء
الوالوء في يد قد يد الوالوء
بالبسمالة غسل اليد ين سلحى سا
سلحى سا واليد اليمين فبه سلحى سا
و غسل به و بيسرى الفمادم
ويدكل المايى من بارية سلاسا
ويدكل المايى في عنه سلاسا
سلحى سا سلاسا و غسل وجهو
سلاسا [7:1-11] و مسح يديها
اليمين هطا الا الكعبين و مسح
يديها اليسرى هطا الا الكعبين
ويدكل اليدين في العذن ومسح
الرسه و يد منبه صدير الرسه الا
طوق ... ومسح الرياية اليمين
حطا الركبيه حطا الا شرفه
ومسح الرياييه اليسرى حطا الا
سقيده مه حطا فبه انه الوالوء
تكل اللهم اسحد اعلاا الما الا الله
[8:1-15] وهدطا شركله اشهد
لعلنا محمد الرسولى الله اشهد
له الملك وله الحمد يهدى ويمط
و هو على كل شى كدير و اللهم
يعلينا من ضوبينا يعلينا منا
مطهرين ويعلينا منه عبدك
سدحين الا اله الا الله محمد
رسولى الله. و لحن في شبه او
فهمة لحن واللحن اله اكبرو
الله اكبر اشهد اعلاا اله الا الله
اشهد اعلاا الله الا الله [9:1-14]

hands, one puts water into the mouth at least three times, and puts water into one's nose three times [cleaning it]. One washes one's face three times [7: 1-11], then wipes the right hand up to the [elbow] joint [k'abain], and the left hand up to the [elbow] joint [k'abain].[7] One places one hand in each ear [cleaning them], and wipes one's head from forehead to collar . . . One wipes the right foot from the toes up to the knee [ilā rukbihi],[8] and wipes the left foot up to the knee. With this one completes the wuḍū' by saying: "Oh Allah, I bear witness [Ashhad a'an][10] that there is no god [8: 1-15] except Allah in His uniqueness and unity: He has no partners. I bear witness that [Ashhad a'an nā][11] the prophet Muḥammad is Allah's messenger. I bear witness [that Allah] is the truth and He [alone warrants] praise; He brings us to life and He brings us to

على كل شيء قدير، و اللّهم اعلنا من ذنو بنا، جعلنا من المطهرين و جعلنا من عبيدك الشهداء أن لا إله إلّا الله ومحمداً رسول الله.
و الاذان في فهم الاذان؛ و الاذان: اللّه أَكْبَر الله أَكْبَر اشهد أن لا إله إلّا الله أشهد أن لا إله إلّا الله [14:1-9]
اشهد أنّ محمد ارسول الله أشهد أنّ محمداً رسول الله، حَيّ عَلَى الصّلاة، حَيّ عَلَى الصّلاة،حَيّ عَلَى الْفَلَاح ،حَيّ عَلَى الفَلَاح؛ الصّلاة خَير من النّوم، الصّلاة خَير من النّوم، الله أَكْبَر، لا إله إلّا اللّه. باب في الصلاة:
يقوفي المسجد و يصلى ركعات الفجر . . . يسجد ويسلم؛ و يكبر الله ثلاثا و ثلاثين، و يحمدالله ثلاثا و ثلاثين [14:1-10] حتّى مطلع الفجر في المسجد حتى...
الاقامة: تقول [في] الاقامة: الله أَكْبَر الله أَكْبَر؛ أَشْهَد أن لا إله إلّا اللّه، أَشْهَد أن لا إله إلّا اللّه؛ أَشْهَد أنّ محمد ا رسول الله؛ حَيّ عَلَى الصّلاة، حَيّ على الفَلَاح ، قدقامَت الصلاة؛ الله أَكْبَر الله أَكْبَر، لا إله إلّا اللّه. و يجلِس جالساً.
فالمحرب [14:1-11] و يكبر الله كبيرا [و] تقول [هذا بعد] الاقامة . . . وبعد كبره الاقامة يكون الامام في سجود طويل وركعة طويلة يقول في رأسه رب العلمين، سبحان رب العلم وبحمده ثلاثاً؛ بعد ركع الامام [يقول] سمع اللّه لمن حمده وتقول اللّهم ربنا ولك الحمد. ويسجد الامام طويلا تقول في

اشهد اعنا محمد ا رسولى الله اشهد اعنا محمد ا رسولى الله حيعل صلاحي حيعل صلاحي حيعل الفا الصديعل الفا الله اصلا هي حير مناعم اصلا هي حير مناعم الله اكبر الله اكبر الا الا له الا له وباب الصلاة ٢ باب في الصلاة 16 يختو في المسيد ويسليحي اركعة الخير ويسحد ويو سلم ويوكبر الصسلا سنا وسلا سشين ويحمد الله سلا سا وسلا سشين [14:1-10] هنطا مصلاحي الخير في المشيد هطا الا ... القاقو مطا تكولو القاقو مطا الله اكبر الله اكبر اشحد الا الله الا له اشحد الا اله الا اله اشحد اعنا محمد ا رسول الصديعا صلا ها حيعا الحكتحكمة صلاة الله اكبر الله اكبر الا الا الا اللهمحمد و يالش يالشاقي المحيب [14:1-11] ويكبر الله اكبرا تكول القاقو مطا كبر العصيم ويكبر ... بعد كبر له القاقو مطايكو الما سي في سجد تو الا ويتو اوركي تو الا تكو الو في الرسيح الي الرب العلمين العلم شيحي بيس العلم و يحمطا له سلا سا الما سي وبعد اوركي شمع الله لما حمده وتكول اللهم ربنا والكحمد ويشيد الما سي طوا الا تكو الو في شيد سبحي الربي ... [14:1-12] ويسحد طوا الا ويشلم ويحي طوا الاويكرى تو م بعد الصلاة سبحي ويكر بي اليالو ش بعد الصلاة سبحي ويكرى كلام سونى بعد الصلاة سبحي ويا يكر الله هنتى مصلاحي الخير و سلاة [13:1-9]

death, and for Him all things are possible. Oh Allah, elevate us [*ya'alainā*] above our errors. Oh Allah, make [*ya'alainā*] us among those who are [ritually] clean, and among those of Your servants who bear witness that there is no god except Allah, Muḥammad is Allah's Messenger. The form and understanding of the *Adhān* [call to prayer].[12] The *Adhan* [*l'adan*] is as follows:

Allah is Great, Allah is Great. I bear witness that [*a'an*] there is no god but Allah, I bear witness that [*a'an*] there is no god but Allah [9: 1-14]. I bear witness that [*a'an*] Muḥammad is Allah's Messenger, I bear witness that [*a'an*] Muḥammad is Allah's Messenger. Come to prayer [*hiy 'al ṣalāḥ*],[13] come to prayer [*ṣalah*]. Come to success [*al-fā Allah*],[14] come to success [*al-fā Allah*]. Prayer is better than sleep [*na'um*],[15] prayer is better than sleep. Allah is Great, Allah is Great.

سجود سبحان ربى... [12: 1-14].
ويقعد طويلا و يسلم ويدعى
طويلا ويقرأ ثم بعد ثلاثة
يسبح ويقرأ الجالس بعد
ثلاثة يسبح ويقرأ كلام سنى
بعد ثلاثة يسبح ويكبر اللّه
حتى مطلع‌الفجر [13: 1-9]

There is no god but
Allah.

Chapter on Prayer

One stands in the
mosque and prays the
rak'āt of *fajr* [morning
prayer], prostrates and
gives *salmāt*. After this
one recites Allah's
greatness thirty-three
times, and His praises
thirty-three times [10:
1-14] until dawn
arrives in the mosque,
until . . . *al-iqāma* [the
second call to prayer].
One says in *al-iqāma*:
Allah is Great, Allah is
Great. I bear witness
that [*a*] there is no god
but Allah, I bear wit-
ness that [*a*] there is no
god but Allah. I bear
witness that [*a'anā*][17]
Muḥammad is Allah's
Messenger. Come to
prayer [*hiy 'alā ṣalāhā*],[18]
come to success [*hiy 'alā
Allah*]. Prayer has been
called. Allah is Great,
Allah is Great. There is
no god save Allah.

Then one sits in
the prayer niche [11: 1-
14], proclaiming
Allah's greatness. *Al-
iqāma* is a grand procla-
mation of Allah's

greatness . . . after *al-iqāma* the *imām* [prayer leader] prostrates for a long time and bows for a long time. You say in your head three times: "Praise to the Lord of the worlds, the world; glory to Lord of the world." The *imām* says when raising from his bow: "Allah listens to those who praise Him." And you say [in response]: "Oh Allah, our Lord all praise is yours." The *imām* prostrates for a long time, and you say when prostrated: "Praise to my Lord . . . " [12: 1-14]. Then bear witness at length and give closing salutations. Petition Allah at length, and read [Qur'an]. After prayer [*ash-shalāah*], sit, glorify [Allah], and read. After prayer [*ash-shalāh*] glorify [Allah], and make supplication [*kalām sunnā*]. After prayer [*ash-shalāah*] glorify [Allah], and implore [Allah] until dawn [13: 1-9].

Yet, even in these pages of the Ben Ali manuscript, what occurs are fragments of passages from al-Qairawānī's *ar-Risāla* that do not follow the latter's ordering of the material, nor do these fragments repeat all of what was written in it. Picking up from the middle of the chapter entitled *bāb-ul-wuḍū'*, the text in *ar-Risāla* reads as follows.

> One washes the right hand three or two times, pouring onto it water, and rubbing it with the left hand passing the fingers between one another. Then one washes the left hand in the same fashion and continues to wash [both hands] up to the elbows . . . Then one takes water in his hands, with the right hand over the palm of the left, and wipes his head with it from the forehead, beginning with the hairline. This done by placing the fingers at the roots of the hair, and the thumbs on the temples, then wiping the hand through the hair to the back of the head, repeating the same motion in reverse until returning to the forehead. Then one wipes the back of the ears from the temples backward with the thumbs. . . . Then washes the legs by first pouring water with the right hand over the right leg and rubbing it a little with the left hand, repeating this three times . . . and rubbing the heel and hamstring. . . . One does the same with the left foot. . . .
>
> The Messenger of Allah, Allah's peace be upon him (pbh), said: "Whoever is ritually clean completes the *wuḍū'* then raises his face to the sky and says: 'I bear witness that there is no god save Allah, who is unique and has no associates; and I bear witness that Muḥammad is his servant and Messenger.' The doors of the eight heavens opened for him and he enters them as he pleases."
>
> Some of the scientists prefer to say at the completion of *wuḍū'*: "May Allah make me among those who seek forgiveness, and among those who are [ritually] clean." (RF 95-98)

In al-Qairawānī's *ar-Risāla*, four chapters lie between the chapter on ablution and that on the call to prayer, amounting to fourteen printed pages in the modern edition. They are *bāb fi-il-ghusil* ("Chapter on Full Body Ablution"), *bāb fi man lam yajid al-mā' wa ṣifat-il-taimim* ("Chapter on Who Does Not Find Water, and the Conditions of Non-Water Ablution"), *bāb fi-il-masḥ 'ala al-khafain* ("Chapter on the Wiping of Leather Socks"), and *bāb fi awqāt-ul-ṣalāt wa ismā'ihā* ("Chapter on the Times of Prayers and Their Names"). The chapter in *ar-Risāla* on the call to prayer reads very closely to that of Ben Ali's manuscript, with the exception of a few minor instructions, to wit: the number of times a line is said, and the line about prayer being better than sleep is only said at the morning prayer. The chapter in *ar-Risāla* on the leading of prayer, *bāb fi-il-imāma wa ḥukm-il-imām wa al-mā'amūm* ("Chapter on the Leadership of Prayer, and the Rules Governing the Leader and the Congregation"),

however, hardly resembles the fragments on this subject in Ben Ali's manuscript.

Besides the opening six lines of the epigraph, there are the remaining five and a half pages of the manuscript (pages 1-6) that are not legible Arabic, let alone identifiable as reproductions of al-Qairawānī's *ar-Risāla*. In any event, the proper name given in the epigraph as the signature of the source of the reported discourse in the text, al-Qarawanidu, is obviously not the purported name of the author of the text, Ben Ali. It is primarily on the basis of the proper noun, "al-Qarawanidu," in this epigraph that Greenberg discerned that the manuscript was somehow associated with *ar-Risāla* of Abī Zaid al-Qairawānī. Allowing for the superfluous suffix, "du," and that the appellation al-Qairawānī refers to the city in what is now Tunisia and not the one closer to Ben Ali in Bundu (see chapter 5), it may be that the cited source is the tenth-century legal treatise by Abī Zaid al-Qairawānī. Greenberg's assessment, however, rests on certain problematical assumptions about what is important in the mode of knowledge transmission in eighteenth- and nineteenth-century Islamic West Africa.

By focusing on the proper name, al-Qairawānī, as the cited *textual* source, Greenberg is compelled to assess Ben Ali's manuscript in terms of how accurately it reproduces that treatise. Accuracy in the mimetic reproduction of a written text is held up as the mark of scholarly mastery, which presupposes that the most important indication of authoritative knowledge is proof of individual mastery of the book. This assumes that the central relationship in the authoritative transmission of knowledge is that of scholar to text, an assumption that finds verification in the site-specific institutional knowledge of the modern university. It is not verified, however, by the mode of knowledge transmission that Ben Ali is supposed to have been engaged in. On the contrary, the most important relationship in the authoritative transmission of knowledge in the Islamic educational system of West Africa was that of student to teacher. This is not to suggest that books were not central to education; in fact, the practice of the pupil memorizing a particular text on hearing it read by the master from memory which Greenberg refers to is part of the process of dictation (*imlā*) that was a chief characteristic of classical Islamic learning. In this process the pupil not only listens to the master's dictation of the text, but also transcribes it, later reading it out loud to himself in order to memorize it. Yet, while the mastery of the curriculum was the desideratum of scholarship, the means by which this was

achieved determined scholarly authority. As a fifteenth-century Egyptian treatise on education put it: "One should not study with another who himself studied only from books, without having read [them] to a learned shaykh. Taking knowledge from books [alone] leads to heterography [*tashīf*] and mistakes [*ghalāt*] and mispronunciation [*tahrīf*]."[19] Authoritative knowledge was, thus, not transmitted from text to scholar, but from master-teacher to student. According to the same treatise: "Whoever does not take his learning from the mouths of men is like he who learns courage without ever facing battle." The most important thing, then, was to enter into a relationship with a teacher of some scholarly standing who was erudite, but also pious and of good character. It was this personal (in apposition to the textual) relationship that conferred authority on the student as a scholar in his own right, and which he invoked to legitimate his subsequent scholarship. This invocation appears as a genealogy of authoritative transmission, a list of scholars, appropriately called an *ijāza* (a license).[20]

I will consider the working of *ijāza* later in this chapter. What I want to point out here is that by the same token of the proper name, "Muḥammad 'Abdullah ibn Yūsuf ibn 'Abd al-Qarawanidu," with its attached honorific, "the master and jurist (*stādh al-fakīh*)," the cited source of Ben Ali's manuscript may very well be his own teacher, and not the tenth-century Malikite legal treatise. In that event, the city of identification, al-Qairawān, would refer to the Jakhanké center of learning in Bundu, and not the famous city of the same name in Tunisia. On this basis, it could be argued that the opening lines of the manuscript are a truncated authenticating genealogy, recording only one generation of the line of scholarly masters to which Ben Ali is connected, and making it a particular order of intellectual autobiography. Accordingly, the irregularities in Ben Ali's manuscript are not attributable to a premature break in his relationship to the text, but rather to the rupturing of his relationship with the authorizing oral line of transmission. The density of the manuscript's language and the irregularity of its composition are such, however, that, like Greenberg's, this is a thesis whose basis is still indeterminate. One almost inevitably begins not only to infer meaning, but to augment the writing, to transplant whole passages from *ar-Risāla* (or one's imaginings) into the text.

Nonetheless, that augmentation, which Greenberg's assessment and this thesis enable, opens the Ben Ali manuscript up as an interesting, if somewhat enigmatic cultural text, requiring a concatenation of readings

of African, Arabic, and Western (the United States) codes, whose point of convergence is the Qur'an and the power formations that are articulated in the course of reading the Qur'an. In this sense, the Ben Ali manuscript cannot be reduced to a poor, fractured redaction from memory of al-Qairawānī's *ar-Risāla*. Still, what this enigmatic text does have in common with al-Qairawānī's *ar-Risāla* is far more than the reproduction of a few lines. The Ben Ali manuscript is a discursive exhibition of the same order as *ar-Risāla*, in that it realizes legitimacy literally, i.e., in the letter. And could there be a more suitable model of literal legitimacy for an enslaved West African scholar than al-Qairawānī's *ar-Risāla?* After all, it has been for some centuries now one of the most important popular didactic texts of Islamic learning in Africa, exemplifying the genre of didactic epistles that were disseminated publicly in order to educate the community in the proper methodology for realizing the Qur'an's principal meanings in life.[21]

Abī Zaid al-Qairawānī is popularly known as the second Mālik of Africa, the allusion being to the founder of the *mālikī* (Malikite) methodology of *fiqh* (jurisprudence), Mālik ibn Anas, whose *Kitāb-ul-Mukhtaṣar* is the primary didactic text of civil, commercial, and international jurisprudence in northwest Africa. In fact, the two texts are taught as complementary to one another, with *Kitāb-ul-mukhtaṣar* utilized in the study of *al-fiqh al-akbar* (viz., the science of doctrine), and *ar-Risāla* in the study of *al-fiqh al-aṣghar* (viz., the science of ritual praxis). This division of science was initiated by Abū Ḥanīfa (d. 150 A.H./A.D. 767), who is credited with having established the first Sunna school of *'ilm-ul-kalām* ("the science of discourse").[22] Clearly, then, *ar-Risāla*, as a didactic text of *fiqh*, falls within the methodological field of *'ilm-ul-kalām*. From the time of Abū Ḥanīfa, the primary focus of this field was to address the problems of Qur'anic signification. This entailed the development of a theory of signification that could give an account of how material linguistic signs could fully represent the affect of experiencing an inhuman, or indeterminate, language—*kalām Allah*, Allah's discourse.

In this vein al-Qairawānī's *ar-Risāla*, as a legal text, pays attention to the specific rhetorical process of *'ilm-ul-kalām*: the constitution of a transcendent omnipresent, omniscient language whose boundaries support those of the expanding state, i.e., the *Shari'a*. In fact, *ar-Risāla* was written by the young seventeen-year-old al-Qairawānī in 327 A.H./A.D. 945, at the height of Fatamid power in Africa. This was one year after the Fatamid Khalif, Abuf Tamīm al-Ma'az, had relocated the capital in the

new Fatamid city of Cairo, Egypt, and had placed the western African precincts of the state under the stewardship of the Ṣanhāj tribe, Banī Zairī. The first steward of this line was Yūsuf ibn Zairī ibn Munād aṣ-Ṣanhājī, who continued the repressive policy of his Fatamid overlords toward the Sunni intelligentsia. As an explicit text of Malikite doctrine and practice, al-Qairawānī's *ar-Risāla* was a declaration of the continuance of Sunni political significance. In this particular case, *ar-Risāla* employed rhetorical tropes and narrative modes in order to subvert the immediate apparatus of power. In that sense, it was a text of discursive protest and rebellion.

Ibn Khaldūn comments in his introduction, *al-Muqaddama*, to his *Kitāb-ul-ibar* on the importance of Abī Zaid al-Qairawānī's *ar-Risāla*, and its connectedness to *'ilm-ul-kalām* with regard to political struggle over signification:

> There were those who engaged in the allegorical anthropomorphization of Allah [*at-tashbīh*], arguing for the verifiability [of the meaning of terms] of condition like "the ascension [of Allah to the throne]," . . . they tended towards a materialist [reading], contending like their predecessors that these terms [when predicated of Allah] did not refer to corporals. . . . All that remains [by way of response] to this literalist reading [*aẓ-ẓawāhir*] is the doctrine and methodology of the predecessors [*as-Salaf*], and belief in [the propositions of predications] as they occur [in the Qur'an], so as to perhaps preclude the negation of their meaning as a result of denying them—even though they are adduced to be proven true from the Qur'an. For an example of this [type of response] see the doctrine of ibn Abī Zaid's *ar-Risāla* and his *Mukhtaṣar* [*sic*].[23]

The concerns of *'ilm-ul-kalām* are so unabashedly semiotic that the science could arguably be characterized an Islamic semiotics, and its practitioners, the *mutakallimūn*, as semioticians. The paramount issue at stake in *'ilm-ul-kalām* was the literality of Qur'anic revelation, a literality based on the conception of the Qur'an as actually being Allah's discourse. The problem of signification that the *mutakallimūn* sought to address was, how are the material linguistic signs of the Qur'an that are Allah's eternal predications—e.g., *al-kalām* (discourse), *al-'ilm* (knowledge), *an-nūr* (light), *al-qudra* (agency), and *al-ḥaraka* (motion)—which are corporeal (being composed of *phônè* and *graphè*), related to his incorporeal self? At issue is a theory of sign. It remains to be seen whether or not this theory entails the same negation of the sign's (graphic) materiality as that which prevented Greenberg from being able to translate Ben Ali's

Arabic manuscript. In order to determine this, a brief consideration of the *'ilm-ul-kalām* theories is warranted.

Indeterminacy in *'ilm-ul-kalām*

The first Muslim thinker to assert that the Qur'an was created, and so not eternal, was al-Ja'id ibn Darham (d. 120 A.H./A.D. 737). He based his assertion on the grounds that the Qur'an was phenomenal, and what is phenomenal cannot be coterminous with Allah (i.e., of his essence or self).[24] This argument was developed and disseminated by his student, Jahim ibn Safwān (d. 128 A.H./A.D. 745), who is credited with laying the foundations for the rationalist movement, *al-mu'tazila*, which in turn is confused with *al-jahimīya* ("the doctrine of Jahim") primarily because both schools were rationalist.[25] On the other hand, the *salaf*, among whom were such early *mutakallimūn* as Abū Ḥanīfa, held the Qur'an to be eternal. This position produced two different approaches to reading. For the literalists, like Aḥmad ibn Ḥanbal, who fully anthropomorphized Allah in their adherence to the literality of the predications, when the Qur'an states that Allah ascended the throne that is what it means—he physically moved from one position to another. Ibn Ḥanbal's reading was grounded more on a doctrinal rejection of reason—viz., syllogistic inference—than on any critical analysis of the Qur'anic passages in question.

The other approach to reading, that of Abū Ḥanīfa and Mālik ibn Anas, acknowledges the indeterminacy of linguistic referentiality, resulting in the acceptance of the idea that in the Qur'an there are aporia. Allah is undoubtedly noncorporeal, but the fact that there are descriptive predications of Allah in the Qur'an is equally undisputable, whether describing physical conditions of being and activity or not. The result is a suspension of judgment, a tension between *æsthesis* and comprehension, that is tantamount to an admission of unreadability.

Abī Zaid al-Qarawānī reports Mālik ibn Anas as having maintained that there was an unresolvable obscurity of reference: "The ascension is known, but the how [or what it indicates] is not. Still, belief in it is dutiful and inquiry about it innovation."[26] This did not stop the *mu'tazila* from inquiring about it, however, nor did it stop their employment of syllogistic reasoning in their inquiry. The issue of that inquiry was the extending of al-Jahim's view of the Qur'an as a phenomenal event (created), and the complete rejection of any positive anthropomorphic pred-

ication of Allah. Those Qur'anic passages that appear to entail such predication were read to be allegorical.

The later *mutakallimūn* mediated between the two extremes of allegorization and anthropomorphization. In particular, Abū al-Ḥasan al-Ashʻarī adduced rationally through inference the proof of four predications (intentionality, hearing, sight, and discourse). After him, Abū Bakr al-Bāqillānī and Abū al-Maʻālī al-Jawainī (more commonly known as Imām-ul-Harmain) refined the application of the Aristotelian syllogism to *ʻilm-ul-kalām*. On the basis of this adaptation and refinement in application of the syllogism, the most famous of Imām-ul-Harmain's students, the literatus and logician al-Ghazālī (d. 493 A.H./A.D. 1111), formulated a tripartite doctrine of the sign. According to that doctrine, the unknowability or indeterminacy of the how was equated with incorporeality; the corporeal, although not comprehending the incorporeal, indicated it as the signified of the linguistic sign.

In this way al-Ghazālī sought to preserve the concept of literality of the Qur'an by releasing it from the dogmatic grounds of opinion, and recognizing it as a question of propositional inference. For him, there could be no doubt that the Qur'an is Allah's discourse (*kalām Allah*), and that that discourse is indeterminate and nonintentional. To deny this is to refute the consensus of the Muslim community. But to affirm it is to suggest that the Qur'an is indeed phenomenal and consists of material sounds and inscriptions—*phône* and *graphé*—which entails the absurdity of saying that the noncorporeal is corporeal, of reducing Allah to a materiality. For al-Ghazālī, if the literality of the revelation was to be maintained, then the nature of Allah's discourse, relative to human discourse, has to be determined. Human discourse takes two forms: extramental linguistic signs, *phône* and *graphé*, and mental expressions (*al-kalām-un-nafs*). Because the latter are indeterminate even in humans, it presents no problem to conceive of such an indeterminate discourse as occurring with Allah eternally.[27] The problem of literality remains, however. How can Allah's essential discourse be represented as phenomena, how can the indeterminacy of divine discursivity be represented in a determined empirical experience? The historical fact of the belief in the Qur'an's actually entailing *kalām Allah* (meaning that divine speech consisted of empirical signs) necessitated a doctrine of signs that differentiated logically between the materiality of the linguistic sign and the indeterminacy or incorporeality of what the sign conveys. The fundamental premises of that doctrine formulated by al-Ghazālī are as follows.

Linguistic expressions (*alfāẓ*) are signifiers (*dalālāt*) that are immediately evident. What they convey, that signified (*al-madlūl*), is discourse, which is nonevident and in the Qur'an's case eternal. Although linguistic expressions as material signifiers are distinct from signifieds, which are matters of discourse, the former function as evidence of the latter: the linguistic expression conveys the discourse, meaning the signifier = evidence of the incorporeal signified. "The External Discourse, whose locus is in Allah The Exalted's quintessence, is the signified, which is not the same thing as the [phonetic] signifier or the graphemes that are signifiers" (*KII* 132). The divine discourse is essentially indeterminate and beyond the subjective intentionality of any given scribe or reader. Reading, however, involves the investment of that abstract indeterminacy with a human intentionality. In this way, reading is *prosopopoeic*.

With regard to the Qur'an, al-Ghazālī's terminology is somewhat different. There are three relevant variables to his inference: *al-qirā'a* (the material reading or recitation), *al-Qur'an* (the intended object of reading), and *al-maqrū'* (the referent of reading, literally the readable), reflecting the investment in reading:

> The recitation [*al-qirā'a*] is immediately evident to the senses, it is the utterance produced by the tongue, the articulations of a reader [*qāri'*], who is its agent . . . [*al-maqrū'*] is Allah's discourse [*kalām Allah*], meaning an eternal resting in his essence [it is incorporeal and indeterminate in itself] . . . the object of reading [*al-Qur'an*] is the articulated, whose intended referent is *al-maqrū'*, as this is the intended referent of articulation which is eternal and not contingent. Such is what the pious ancestors meant in their saying that "the Qur'an is Allah the Exalted's discourse, and it is not contingent" [insofar as its intended referent is *al-maqrū'*]. (*KII* 136)

In al-Ghazālī's terminology *al-maqrū'* is clearly synonymous with *al-madlūl* (that signified), and *al-qirā'a* with *dalālāt* (signifiers). Once this difference in terminology is accounted for, it becomes obvious that there is a striking resemblance between al-Ghazālī's formulation of the difference between signifier and signified, and that of the Stoics. The Stoics also distinguished between what is conveyed by the linguistic sign (*semainòmenon*), the linguistic sign itself (*semaînon*), and the object or event (*tynchànon*). The object or event, on the other hand, is the extramental (external) entity. Both the linguistic sign (sound and letter) and the object or event are corporeal; the matter of discourse conveyed by the linguistic sign is incorporeal, being the *lektòn*. What is conveyed by the sign is the matter of discourse that is apprehended in correspon-

dence to thought. The fact that *al-qirā'a* and *al-Qur'an* are both sensibly evident phenomena lends credence to the comparative reading of *al-qirā'a* as an analogue of the Stoics' concept of the linguistic sign itself, and *al-Qur'an* as an analogue of their notion of the object or event. Such a comparative reading is further supported by al-Ghazālī's description of *al-maqrū'* as incorporeal and expressible—*dictum*, or *dicible*—indicating its functioning as that which is the matter of discourse conveyed by the linguistic sign, the *lektòn*.[28] When asserting that the material text of the Qur'an consists of signifiers that while signifying the divine discourse (*kalām Allah*) are wholly inadequate to comprehend it in itself, al-Ghazālī is maintaining that what is signified by the material linguistic expressions (*alfāz*) is an expression of relationship to the divine discourse and the divine discourse itself. Read in this way, al-Ghazālī seems to have held a view on the doctrine of sign which is nearly identical with that of the Stoics.

Likewise, in al-Ghazālī's approach to the sign there is a degree of identification that is somehow inferential, whereby the material linguistic signs of the Qur'an are necessarily correlated with a specific class of signifieds—*kalām Allah*. What this suggests with regard to the Qur'an is that the sign is not merely the proposition that expresses the event, as it was for the Stoics, instead the sign is the particular experiencing of the phenomenal event of Qur'anic reading: the consensus of the Muslim community. The apparent untranslatability of that experience is at the foundation of the Qur'an's own untranslatability.

For al-Ghazālī the issue is that of having the authentic (*sunna*) thinking about divine discursivity (revelation), and determining the correct mode of its application to the empirical experience of the text. This is a question of how to subsume experience to thought, of how to translate the transcendental meaning of the Qur'an into specific historical experiences. Translation of the Qur'an, therefore, could only be problematic (in the sense that it may be equally erroneous or correct). This adds another dimension to the problem of linguistic signs, that of translation as it relates to reading. Could I read if I could not translate? Is it even possible to read without translating?

What may be perceived in this brief description of *'ilm-ul-kalām* is the complex interconnectedness in Islamic state history between the ability to define the authorized community and the production of literary forms. Moreover, it betrays Islamic history as a whole to be a discursive history of reading. The struggle over literary forms is the struggle over

the paradigm of literary form, the Qur'an. We know this latter struggle historically as the codification and canonization of Qur'an by 'Uthmān, and the subsequent canonization of specific methods of reading, reciting, and utilizing the canon. This is no more than the history of Islamic culture and knowledge. According to that knowledge, Ben Ali's text is problematic, in that it literally exhibits discursive heterogeneity, the very thing that authorized Arabic language, 'arabīya, was meant to preclude.

At stake in the 'ilm-ul-kalām concept of the sign is precisely what was at stake for the early Arabic philologists, whose task was to address such things. Al-Azharī called it "the dangerously superfluous which leads to the abyss [of error and disbelief]" (Tahdīb-ul-lugha 7). Early Arabic philology was informed from its inception by the proscriptive gestures of early Qur'anic exegesis. Frequently the philological project gave way in the face of traditional exegetic explications of the Qur'anic verse, even when these explications blatantly violated the very grammar being defined by philology. For example, Abū 'Ubaid insisted that there were no "foreign" words in the Qur'an; al-Usama'ī refused to interpret any poetry that involved some Qur'anic verses; and al-Mazanī refrained from emending, in accordance with Sībawaihi's theory, the i'arāb (formalist analysis) of a particular Qur'anic term, stating that the traditional reading was more binding. The influence of traditional exegetic proscriptions on early philologists was particularly pronounced with regards to the relationship between matters of linguistic science and ethics. This relationship focused on the issue of determining the appropriate form of expression and what was to be considered "truthful" content, its meaning. This was exemplified in aṣ-Ṣuyūtī's recalling Ibn Fārs's injunction that "for purity, receive the language from people of truth, trustworthiness, authority, and justness."

On this same score, al-Kamāl ibn al-Anbārī asserted that

> among the . . . foundations of grammar is the condition that the transmitter of the language be just, whether man or woman, free or enslaved. . . . This is because with [language] comes understanding of [the Qur'an's] reading and exegesis; so the condition for its transmission is the same as that for the transmission of its reading and exegesis.[29]

With this assertion al-Anbārī is remarking the extent to which the compiling and codifying of Arabic linguistics phenomena into a standardized discourse was predicated on the same necessity as exegesis: the institutionalization of discursive practice in order to guarantee the

reading of the Qur'an. The early philologists sought to arrive at a trans-parency of Arabic language (*'arabīya mubīna*) that would facilitate the "correct" reading of the Qur'an. Thus, al-Anbārī's injunction to interro-gate the character of one's sources underscores what was to be a princi-pal feature in the criteriology of not only philology but all Islamic discursive science: *'ilm-ur-rijāl*, consisting of the methodological study of the credibility of sources: their learning, honesty, humility, and so on. That study was in turn to be the basis for fixing the authoritative lines of knowledge's transmission: *isnād*.

The task of philology, of which lexicons were one of the primary products, was the comprehension of the past (as in pure) modes of expression, which were to be found in two essential *arché:* the pre-Islamic poetry, and ordinary bedouin discursive practice. The aim was the conservation of the original culture. There is a considerable amount of history invested in this conception of Arabic lexicography as an ency-clopedic philological endeavor that not only converged with culture but gave definition to the refining of the principal technology of cultural conservation: writing.

The notion of literacy's role as a basis for Arabo-Islamic cultural progress is part of the familiar authorized story of literary Arabic's pro-gressive development as the result of a prioritizing of semiotics in the field of knowledge. Arabic linguistics stands out as the paradigmatic semiotics because Arabic functions as the language of the Qur'an, which is the ultimate basis of knowledge as cultural expression. Philological lexicography is a privileged area of linguistics because of its historical precedence, along with grammar, as the first science to take signs and signification specifically as its objects. While lexicography from its incep-tion held the bedouin as the final arbitrator of "pure" Arab discourse, the verisimilitude entailed in the bedouin was a function of the societal status of the transmitter as being himself pure and uncorrupted. The issue was not so much one of race as of social ambience. Given this, the tenth-century (A.D.) lexicographer Abū Mansūr al-Azharī could assert the linguistic veracity of his lexicon, *Tahdhīb-ul-lugha*, by claiming to have been

> tested with captivity the year that the Qaramathian hajj was attacked in *Haibir*. The people who participated in the assault were Arabs, predomi-nantly from *Hawāzan;* mixed among them were renegades from the tribes of Tamīm and Asd. These Arabs existed in *al-Bādia* [the nomadic life], migrating to the grazing lands produced by the flash floods . . . they spoke

in their innate and bedouin fashion with which they were accustomed; there was nary a [foreign] accent or ugly error in their discourse . . . And I benefited from their conversation, dialogues, and arguments amongst themselves, gaining a compilation of terms and *nawadir* [rare expressions] most of which I have inscribed in the text.[30]

Thus in the field of lexicography the validity of a given term was determined not by its syntax or possible semantic conformity (i.e., its relationship to the other terms noted in the discourse), but rather by the veracity and character of its human transmitter, and accordingly its mediator, the lexicographer. Accordingly, al-Azharī will refute the validity of lexicographic reports attributed to Ibn Duraid on the grounds that he was an alcoholic. This emphasis on character was required because of the recognized disparity of Arabic discourse. The point was not who could trace what word back to whatever dialectical origin, but rather whose story of the word's signification could be believed. This conicity of politico-ethical authority and knowledge is played out in al-Azharī's *Tahdhīb-ul-lugha*, in the citation *'ajama*, the verb from which the substantive *ma'ājim*, or lexicon, derives:

> Abu-ul-Fadl informed me, on the authority of Abī-il-Abbās, that [al-Abbās] was asked the following regarding the letters of the orthography [*hurūf-ul-mu'jam*]: why are they named *mu'jam*? [To this] he said: "Abū 'Umar as-Shaibānī said: 'To become *a'jam* is to become obscure, unintelligible.' " [It is said that] *'al-a'jamī* [the non-Arab] is the person who is obscure in his discourse, he is not clear in his discourse. al-Farā' has said that "[*mu'jam*] refers to the placing of diacritics on the graphemes. [When] it is said that the lock *mu'jam*, and the state of affairs is *mu'jam* what is meant is that they are hard. I [al-Azharī] heard Abā al-Haithm say: "The *mu'jam* of al-khaṭṭ refers to [the act] of writing with diacritics. We say, '*a'jamtu al-kitāb*' [the book], i.e., 'we obscure its obscurity'; and we do not say, ' *'ajamtuhu*,' i.e., 'we obscured it.' " . . . Abū 'Ubaid has said: "What is meant by al-*'ajamā* is the beast, it is named *'ajamā*, because it does not speak. Anything that is unable to speak is *a'jam* and *musta'jam*." . . . al-Laith said: "al-mu'jam are the articulated graphemes of orthography, they are called *mu'jam* because they are elucidated [*a'jamia*]." If one says that a text is *mu'jam*, then its being such is a result of its having diacritics, which clarifies its obscurities, and makes its meaning obvious. Abū 'Ubaid [also] said that, "the extreme case of *a'jam* is the raising of undifferentiated babbling, in such a manner that no discernible voice emerges through the din."
> (*Tahdhīb* bāb-ul-'ain wa al-jīm ma'a al-mīm)

The declension of *'ajama* in the Arabic discourse of lexicography is a matter of obscurity, إبهام *ibhām* itself, and the displacement of obscurity

through elucidating signs. The aim of elucidation is to make the written discourse transparent and its meaning clear. Such a transparency of language is what is called *faṣīḥ*, and the literary language defined by such clarity is called *fuṣḥā*. The habitual English translation of this concept is "Classical Arabic." This habit almost totally displaces the polysemia at play in the term *fuṣḥā*, however. When discourse is transparent, it is *mubīn*, it has clear signification, that is, it is understandable. On the other hand, whenever discourse is obscure, it is beastly, *ibhām*; the *ibhām* that is *al-'ajmā'* is the obscurity of sense equated with the chatter of beast of every sort. So, that which is obscured by *ibhām* is buried in too much diversity; that which is *faṣīḥ* is clear in its unique singularity of expression. The clarity of *fuṣḥā* is achieved through the pruning of discourse, a perfecting of language, such that specific formations of meaning are authorized to the exclusion of others that might compete with them and muddle things up. This project involves a gradual systematic process of fixing certain signifieds to certain signifiers, of arresting discursive movement in the desired body of *'alāmāt*, "signs," and their authorized referents. Consequently the obscure discourse, in contradistinction to the transparent discourse, displaces signification. In the obscure discourse of *al-'ajmā'*, signification becomes *shawāridan*, "a linguistic anomaly that displaces meaning." It is also the case that the *a'jam* is the stutterer, the displacer of the tongue (*lisān*). The obscure speech of the *a'jam* collapses the authoritative lines of meaning. In fine, obscure discourse collapses the meaningful lines of authority.[31]

When presented as the harbinger of linguistic conformity and authorization, early Arabic lexicography calls attention to a very particular institutionalization of discursive activity: semiotics as an activity not only upon which cultural legitimacy is based, but also within which aesthetical and epistemological concerns are framed. The questions of perception and cognition, experience and knowledge, are fundamentally issues of theories of signification, specifically those theories that seek to determine the referentiality of the Qur'an's signs. In that context, lexicography served a specialized "reading," and as such operated within a relationship of the state (as the authorizing agency) and narrative (as a specific series of gestures by which the state came to conceptualize its existence through the struggle with polyglossia).

From early on textual configuration prefigures in the formulation of the Islamic state. Fifteen years (26 A.H./A.D. 647) after Muḥammad's death (7 A.H./A.D. 632), his third successor (*khalīf*), 'Uthmān ibn 'Affān,

attempted to restrict variations in reading the Qur'anic text by producing an authorized codex. His attempt at textual canonization, the linguistic basis of which was the *Quraishī* language, occurred in tandem
with his consolidation of political power within the *Quraish* and his
attempt to create a centralized state. And it was the centralization of the
state that laid the foundation for the canon. Toward these ends the
"authorized" text (whose "original" inscription was kept at the center of
the developing state: Medina) was redacted by the centralized authorities and disseminated to the outpost metropolises. Thereby, the marking
of authoritative transmission became the marking of the empire's fron-
tiers.

'Uthmān's project of canonization functioned to privilege the
Quraishī dialect over the six other Arabic dialects in which the revelation
occurred, for the sake of protecting meaning by regulating reading. The
investment was in a fixed tradition of transmission whose paradigms
were always antecedent. But such a delineation of discursive genealogy
also produced its bastards, the vernaculars. There was always the threat
of the vernacular, the superfluous. Along these lines, in spite of later
attempts to prescribe the conditions and limits of transmission with
isnād, the production of "false" readings, linguistic anomalies and aberrations, *taṣḥīf*, continued. The threat was from the encroachment of an
urban polyglossia upon the bedouin *'asabiya* (tribal/racial chauvinism).
This threat of polyglossia was not that of polyglot cities and citizens,
which were necessary for commerce and administering the empire. The
threat was polyglossia in writing: *taṣḥīf*. Street discourse and vernaculars
could not be prevented, but the homogenization of the literary domain
could achieve their subordination under a correct "high" form. Defined
under one source of (linguistic) law those discourses can be literally
erased—or rather excluded from transcription—and politically trivialized: they become bastardized forms of the authorized language, the
state's *'arabīya*. Literary polyglossia, on the other hand, might preclude
the state's capacity to control a vast geospatial territory through its control of language. Irregularity in writing, *taṣḥīf*, can potentially legitimize
irregularity in discourse, which would amount to the subverting of the
political project of text-based state formation initiated by 'Uthmān, a
project that amounted to the attempt to reduce the possibilities of "correctly" reading the Qur'an down to those that could be effectively controlled through the reduction of the language.

For all that, because of the cultural diversity and geographic vastness of the Islamic world, as well as the dialect variation among the rapidly disseminating Arabs, the widespread frequency of *taṣḥīf* was certain, to the extent that it became nigh on commonplace.[32] The commonplace too fosters its own corrective, and in the case of *taṣḥīf* the corrective was the writing of taxonomies of irregularities. Perhaps one of the best-known texts of this sort is the fourteenth-century work of Abū Muḥammad 'Abdullah ibn Muslim ibn Qutaiba, *Adab-ul-kātib*, which deals principally with the *taṣḥīf* prevalent in the Muslim West (i.e., Spain and Africa).[33] Qutaibah's ambitious project was to provide a comprehensive taxonomy of the orthographic and lexemic errors prevalent within certain geopolitical and ethnic sites, the identification of which would better delineate and protect the domain of correct literary expression. His taxonomy of *taṣḥīf* achieves the overall effect of a larger taxonomy of diglossia, which recognizes a unique sociolinguistic field defined by the universal literary form of the language, derived from the pre-Islamic poetic koine and the Qur'anic Arabic designated by 'Uthmān, and divides it into two domains: that of high (literary) and low (vernacular) discursive forms.

Early Muslim philologists (e.g., Khalīl ibn Aḥmad, Abu 'Ubaid, al-Usama'ī, al-Mazanī, Sībawaihi, and Abu Mansūr al-Azharī) recognized diglossia as the effect of the introduction of linguistic disparity into a previously relatively homogeneous sphere of language activity (whether through originally disparate languages converging through migration or conquest, or a societal breakdown that is reflected in linguistic property). An overall discursive equilibrium or stability is reestablished through this linguistic difference's neutralization in the hierarchical formulation of high to low discourse. The temporal ordering of this process is crucial. The concept of primary Arabic homogeneity supports an account of the genesis of the dynamics of creolization that defines Arabic as the dominant language in the process, and establishes the Arab's already-mentioned inherent authority over Arabic. This account, supported as it was by the state apparatus, achieved a sort of historicism, one that relies on a mythology of *translatio* (a trajectory of knowledge's transmission that originates in and finally returns to Arabic); but, it also relies on a certain notion of social stability, manifested as a peculiar model of sociolinguistic homeostasis.

In the first four centuries of Islamic culture, Muslim philologists achieved monumental feats in their striving to establish a general linguistic norm in response to a highly disparate and volatile social and

cultural environment. The fundamental outcome of their work was for that norm to serve as the basis for a model of cultural and social stability (a purified semiotics, where logical necessity and grammaticality are identical). Yet the fact that ibn Qutaiba still saw the urgency of purifying the literary domain indicates that Arabic, at least in the West, had yet to achieve that sort of stable hierarchical modeling system of language, culture, and society. The concern with *tashīf*, then, is not simply a question of misspelling. It touches on the very possibility of an authentic (historical) authorized literary Arabic that defines the field of authentic Arabo-Islamic culture. Any literary expression that fails to realize the authorized conventions of orthography jeopardizes the integrity of that field, and thus becomes marginal. It is either a pidgin, or simply not Arabic, which is to imply that it is imperfectly Islamic.

The problem that Ben Ali's manuscript presents to *fushā* is that of a material indeterminacy, a sign that resists being reduced to transparency in order that the incorporeal signified can become manifest. Ben Ali's manuscript shows us the other side of the inclusive gesture of canonization, that which has been excluded and condemned as trivial and dangerous: *tashīf*. That is not quite accurate enough; what Ben Ali's *tashīf* betrays is that writing is not the embodiment of an anterior homogeneous process of thinking. Ben Ali's heterography is a remark of the heterogeneity and the indeterminacy of thought: the necessity for reading his text is a certain lawlessness of Imagination.

To the extent that Ben Ali's manuscript attempted to reproduce al-Qairawānī's *ar-Risāla*, it too is a text of discursive protests and rebellion. In Ben Ali's repetition it is a rebellion in signification. In his attempt to reproduce the principal text of al-Qairawānī's sunna rebellion against an African Fatamid state, however, Ben Ali subverts the theolinguistic grounds of legitimacy for that rebellion by transcribing (*'ujma*), by being *a'jam* in writing. Ben Ali's manuscript is somewhere between a written Arabic pidgin and creole. As already noted, Arabic lexicography in particular, and philology in general, aimed at a definitive designation of Arabic language in order to gain the heteronomy of all the vernacular discourses.

Critique of Lexicography: Writing عجمة ('*ujma*)

Having placed *Ben Ali's Diary* along these lines where literacy informs political *agencement* in the two Wests, that of Europe and Islamic Africa,

it is now time to unfold the text and read it. This process of unfolding reading must entail the task of decipherment and interpretation, both of which are heavily mediated. This is the mediation of the material line itself, the written manuscript.

The tendency is still to read Ben Ali's manuscript as a mistake, a text written by a quasi-literate African Muslim ascetic. It is also the longest New World African-Arabic slave narrative known to exist in the United States. This last fact alone is sufficient grounds for refusing the dismissal of the text implied in its classification as "garbled," even if it were the case that almost half the manuscript was completely unreadable. As it is, though, that is not the case. Because the five and a half pages that are not *fuṣḥā*, or readily identifiable as reproductions of al-Qairawānī's *ar-Risāla*, are an aporia, they can be read as such. The first line of these pages, right after the chapter heading (*bāb*) on page 1, is a legible Arabic:

وقد قاد القصة [امرا]: أكتب لى كتب مختصرة ... عن ... ("Assuredly he led the narrative story [القصة (*al-qiṣa*)] [with the imperative]: write me books that are a brief exposition on . . . "). If there is a biography, or for that matter an autobiography, in the text it is to be found among these pages, beginning with this line. The subsequent reading, therefore, must commence carefully: treading lightly, because the pages of the manuscript are fragile and its ink already too smeared, and examining closely the first ciphers engaged, because each graphic trace is a key.

Recall that Ben Ali's manuscript begins: بسم الله الرّحمٰن الرّحيم (*bis-millah-ir-Rahmān-ir-Rahīm*). Or rather it begins: بسم.الله الرحمن الرحيم. This *basmala*, this invocation of Allah's name, functions as the limit, the fluctuating line that mediates between the spaces it defines. It defines two spaces, the well-demarcated space of the page where what follows is in the name of Allah, and that space beyond the page, which is designated by the name of Allah. It is in the space beyond that of the page where the originary moment of transcription, self-reflective consciousness, is supposed to be. Because it is a space beyond the page, it can only be read through mediation, the medium of the written line. The *basmala* recalls the displacement of pre-Islamic traditions by the Qur'an. As the ninth-century Islamic philologist aṣ-Ṣūlī (d. 336 A.H./A.D. 916) recounts the story, the line of *basmala*, marks the passage of difference between what was obscured before the line of *basmala*, and what is revealed to be in the line:

I asked Abā Khalīfah al-Faḍl ibn al-Jamaʿī about the [custom] of beginning texts with *bismillah-ir-Raḥmān-ir-Raḥīm*. He said that he asked ibn ʿĀʾisha ʿAbid Allah ibn Muḥammad ibn Ḥafṣ regarding this, who said:

> My father informed me that the Quraish in their ignorance [before Islam] used to write *bi ismika allahuma* [In your name oh God] and that the prophet, peace be upon him, did the same. Then *Sūrat hūd* was revealed, in which is said, "*bismillahi majrāhā wa mursāhā*" [(board Noah's Ark) in the name of Allah, whether it moves or doesn't; Qurʾan xi: 41]. So the prophet, peace and blessing be upon him, ordered that *bismillahi* be written in the beginning of his texts. Then *Sūrat Banī Isrāʾīl* was revealed, and it said: "*qūl adʿū Allah aw adʿū ar-raḥmān ayā mā tadʿū falahu al-ismāʾ al-ḥusnā*" [Say call on Allah, or call on The Most Merciful, by whatever name you call him, His are The Most Beautiful Names; Qurʾan xvii: 110]. After that [Muḥammad] wrote *bismillah-ir-Raḥmān*. Then *Sūrat an-naml* was revealed, and it said: "*innahu min Sulaimān wa innahu bismillah-ir-Raḥmān-ir-Raḥīm*" [It is from Solomon, and it is *bismillah-ir-Raḥmān-ir-Raḥīm*; Qurʾan xxvii: 30]. That has been the epigraph in writing ever since. And *bismillah-ir-Raḥmān-ir-Raḥīm* has been written at the beginning of every *Sūra* of the Qurʾan, except in the beginning of *Sūrat at-tauba* [also known by the first word to occur in it, *barāʾa*; Qurʾan ix]. Regarding this exception, it is transmitted about ʿUthmān ibn ʿAffān, Allah be pleased with him, that he said:

> > *Bismillah-ir-Raḥmān-ir-Raḥīm* is not written between [*Sūrat*] *al-anfāl* [Qurʾan viii] and "*barāʾa*" [the first word in *Tauba*]. *al-anfāl* is among the first *Sūrat* to be revealed by Allah in Medina, and *barāʾa* is among the last; they resemble each other, and their stories are the same. Perhaps the prophet, peace be upon him, lengthened the verses, saying: "this one's place is in that *Sūra*, so the verses became successive." This occurred with the blessings of Allah, The Exalted and Omnipotent.[34]

More than just a story of how Muḥammad came to prescribe the *basmala*, aṣ-Ṣūlī's citation recounts how the actual prescription is that of the text, the Qurʾan. The *basmala* as the epigraph of all texts, is the reading of the texts of Islam by The Text of Islam. Hence, the Qurʾan is The Text of Islam, which prescribes that all texts of Islam are readings of it. By beginning with the *basmala*, the Ben Ali manuscript places itself in a long line with those other Islamic texts that are readings of the "First Text." That placement "with" is indicated with the initial grapheme of the epigraph, the ﺑ (*bi*).

The initial grapheme marks the displacement of its originary

moment, and so the indeterminacy of its agency. An ancient proverb is of significance to this marking with the "ب":

البَعرة تدل على البعير. . . .

(al-ba'ira tadalu 'alā al-ba'īr. . . . [The camel dung-spoor signifies the camel. . . .]).

The ب of the Ben Ali manuscript, like the ب of البَعرة (al-ba'ira [the camel dung-spoor]), traces its agent figuratively in absentia. What appears, then, as the first graphic stroke of the text is the residual effect of an ante-writing action. This is also a dissimulation. The manuscript's initial ب is final only insofar as it marks the juncture of this reading and those readings prior to it. It is final, only insofar as it traces this moment's "point of departure" (*Hinausgriffpunkt*) and previous arrivals. This is so because the ب before us is merely one articulation of a continuous line of dung-spoor, extending from one end of the page to the other. Its agent is hardly discernible, lurking only beyond the page, where the spoor seems to disappear in an unending line, threatening to vanish totally should the reader jump ahead and try to grasp it. Whether the line is followed back toward its indicated point of departure, or looked at as a cipher that is to be read through in order to discover the agent (*al-ba'īr*) in the act, there is an inevitable mixing of metaphors. Each reading of the line, each tracking of spoor entails the line's being tracked-up, the displacement of some spoor and marking of others, which confuses the followed line of dung with the following line of new spoor. And this is a frequently treaded line.[35] The gesture of casting an authoritative direction over the line, i.e., of *remarking* its true meaning and the aspect of its act, is a gesture that the line obscures. Subsequently, there can be no final authoritative reading: the line has no one direction, and any reading of it is a mingling that leaves new tracks, new dung-spoor, that are hardly discernible as such: "the camel dung-spoor signifies . . . "

In that each point of departure for reading the text is informed by preceding readings, and informs subsequent ones, the initial ب comes to present being among multilinear lines of reading and writing. It compels each reader to begin again. Here is the displaced act that grounds the text's agency: the command to begin reading the story, whose point of departure is the speech act: "Write me books."

Then again, as the master grammarian Sībawaihi (d. 180 A.H./A.D. 760) postulated, the ب symbolizes *affixture*. It reveals itself in its inscrip-

tion as belonging to the pen (qalm). The ـبـ is affixed to the qalm, just as it is affixed to the consequential graphemes of the word it inscribes. Each grapheme in the word connects by way of an extending ligature to its consequent (and so is its connected antecedent). The pen draws out the word in one virtually uninterrupted line, throughout which it does not leave the page. In this way the opening line of the text flows from the ـبـ graphically, which is why it is said to initiate the textual movement, even though it is not its point of departure. This aspect of Arabic script cannot be neglected in the Ben Ali manuscript, where ligatures are in the extreme: *uktublī*. For Sībawaihi, the line flows *through* the ـبـ symbolically. Accordingly, the initiation of the line in writing betrays its polyvalence: the grapheme as such affixes itself to the *qalm* in an auto-obscuring articulation, perpetually turning back on itself. In the turning back on itself, the initiation of writing fades before itself as the index of what precedes it, which it alone traces. The very polyvalence of the line that Sībawaihi sought, however, cancels the originality of the graphic line. To read ـبـ as the point of departure would be to find that point already comprehended by the ceaseless line that displaces it. What this amounts to is an inability to discern a uniquely articulated point of departure. Every reading of the line of ـبـ is a migration, *hejira*, across the page, that both follows and leaves behind.

Following the initial line of the Ben Ali manuscript, then, leads immediately from ـبـ to سم (*smi*), which is composed of three graphemes: two consonants (س /s and م /m), and a vowel (/i). This composition is generally translated into English as "name." When joined to the ـبـ as it is in the unique case of the *basmala* (بسم), it is generally translated as: "In the name . . . " Even a brief consideration of the polysemia of *smi* will exhibit just how reductionist and obscuring such a translation is.

With the exception of the *basmala*, Arabic graphically represents the noun "name" as اسم (*ismun*) in the nominative singular indefinite. With the *basmala*, the initial ا ("i," composed of the consonant vowel dyad, *hamza, kisra*) is elided into or displaced by the " ـبـ " which is a preposition and so changes the noun's case-ending from nominative to genitive: بسم (*bismi*). The displacement of this ا does not exhaust or diminish the referentiality of اسم (*ismun*). On the contrary, it extends it, drawing it out into the textual fields of philology and *tafsir*. The displacement unfolds the derivativeness of "name," the multiple fields of its play. As

the Islamic philologist aṣ-Ṣūlī observed regarding the displacement حذف (ḥadhf) of the أ (hamza):

> In all readings and writings of the Qur'an the *alif* [viz., the hamza: أ] is displaced from the *bismillah-ir-Raḥmān-ir-Raḥīm* that opens [the Qur'an's] chapters, and [begins] all writings in general . . . because its [the hamza's] occurrence is implied and its meaning is well known to the reader because of its frequent use. The diminution in pronunciation of the *alif* [*at-takhfīf*] was customary for the Arabs if the meaning was known but the phrase was not frequently used, as in the phrase: "So glorify in the name of your Great Lord" [*fa ṣabiḥ bi ismi Rabika al-'Aẓīm*]. In this case diminution [as opposed to displacement] occurs because the phrase [*bi ism Rabika*] is not used as frequently as is [*bi ism*] Allah, the Sublime and Exalted. The full meaning of the latter, more frequently used phrase is well known to be: "I began with the name of Allah" [بدأت بسم الله (*bada'tu bismillah*)]. First "I began" was displaced, and subsequently the *alif* as well, in the written representation of the phrase [*fi-il-khaṭṭ*]. (35)

The morphological function of the أ as a superficial radical of amendment facilitates its erasure. Yet, that erasure realizes the meanings to which aṣ-Ṣūlī refers. The substantive أسم" (*ismun*) derives from the verb, سمو (*samū*), سما (*samā*): to elevate; erect; exalt; transcend, or make transcendent; and to be made prominent. Thus, the naming involved in *basmala* is not that of simple appellation or nomenclature: there is no signified that is fixed by a particular signifier. The referent of *smi*, in itself, remains hidden by the displaced radical. In fact, this elusive familiar أ marks the inaccessibility of the ultimate referent. The displaced أ reemerges in the first grapheme of the next word in the opening line of the Ben Ali manuscript: الله أ (*Allah*). The أ is recapitulated here, because it has become internalized by name, achieving almost complete obscurity. Still, the invocation cannot be merely Allah's name, as that fades with the أ . The displaced أ and Allah are indissolubly affixed to one another, as aṣ-Ṣūlī well knew:

> It is permitted to either displace or not displace the *alif* in such phrases as "*bi ism-il-Khāliq*," and "*bi ism-ir-Raḥmān*," etc., but there is no choice [except displacement] in "*basmala*" alone. This is the correct thing to do. (36)

The second and third terms of the opening line in the Ben Ali manuscript (*smi* and *Allah*) with their displaced أ , undermine any argument for language as the manifester of reality. This movement of inscription betrays the incapability of language to make present the signified, thus it describes language as a self-enclosed system: the line articulates and

articulates back on itself. What is ostensively sought in the name, viz., Allah, is displaced, or rather nonplaced, in the moment of naming. This indeterminacy of referentiality is the matter at hand between the graphemes ب (bi) and سم (smi). The reader is compelled to ask: ماذا أقراء؟, "Read what?" The response can only be sheer repetition of the boundaries that cast the signified and its interlocutor beyond each other, the graphic lines of the text.

As stated earlier, Ben Ali's text is throughout easily identifiable as the variant of Kufic script known interchangeably as *al-khaṭṭ at-takrurī, al-khaṭṭ as-senegalī*, and *al-khaṭṭ at-timbuktuī*. It is invariably identifiable as a *khaṭṭ*, a writing, a script or calligraphy: a graphic line of communication. The *khaṭṭ* of takrur is a specifically African-Arabic script, employed throughout the Senegambia region for various local languages as well as Arabic. This widespread employment indicates its being a graphic line of communication across numerous cultural spaces. The specific writing of *al-khaṭṭ at-takrurī*, has only recently attracted minimal attention from Arabic paleographers, although the graphic line of communication in principle has always been of particular concern for the Arabic philologists, who designated with it the prolonged system (*ṭarīqa*); the thin track in the level ground (*ṭarīqa*); writing with the pen [*qalm*], and otherwise. From the *khaṭṭ* derives the *khuṭṭa*, which is a piece of real estate, a space mapped out according to a plan, a line of action. By this same lexicographic token, the *khuṭṭa* is a state of affairs, a story (*qiṣa*), and playfulness among the bedouin (*al-a'arāb*).[36]

The line as system (*ṭarīqa*) has an ideological departure, a *madhab*, it is a movement across the page that defines space according to some science of management, a grammatical authority. Writing is a party-line, a grammatology of state. It is a totality of theory connected together in such a way as to form a *tansīq*, a drawn-up systematic arrangement, or a planned economy. In other words, the line is a *Gestaltung*, a symbolic economy. The line as a symbolic economy is also a way of agency (*sīra*), a writing of life: biography. In this way *al-khaṭṭ at-takrurī* is a mode of being in writing, which is being in line with the state of affairs. And that mode is wholly narrative. It is a *qiṣa*, a writing out of the state of affairs, a playing with language. The writing of life that is *sīra* is *in the writing*, in the space between logos and grapheme, analogy and program of action, as well as between the differing senses of reproduction (the writing that is Ben Ali's reproduction of al-Qairawānī's *ar-Risāla*) and program (the

specific writing that is Ben Ali's plan of action).[37] But what is engaged here in this line?

In the autobiographical English-language slave narratives of Equiano and Douglass, logos = *legien* = the collecting Being within the field of law (*nomos*). It is collection by taxonomy (analogy), or identity as a residual effect of the *cogito me cogitare*, which requires discrimination, in order to differentiate sameness (the Negro) from difference (the black African). Kant has shown how the subject of autoreflective consciousness is in itself a contentless representation, which cannot even be called a conception, but merely a consciousness that accompanies all conceptions: "I," as in "I think." By this I who or which thinks, nothing more is represented than a transcendental subject of thought = x. As an indirect (i.e., contentless) representation it is purely formal. With regards to narrative style, in the I think the signifier is freed from the signified—there is no phenomenal signified, only a formal moment —as with the symbol in the analytic of the sublime, where the sign represents nothing, having no phenomenal referent, but unfolds in a formal system of thought as autoinscribing. So that, although this possibility of autoinscription is already well *under way* with Descartes's discovery of autorecognizing thought, it is with Kant that it reaches a radical point of freedom. The architectonic of transcendental critique designates the promise of a comprehensive apprehension, resulting from the splitting off of cognition from nature, with the isolation of the cogitating subject as Man (as isolated substance, differentiated attribute, autonomous calculus, and so on and so on). The problem of the disjunction of physical experience and cognitive experience is overcome by discovering the determinate cognitive discursivity, whose deduction is wholly in Reason, and whose realization is in the narrative structure of the architectonic. In narrative, the ineffability of the "I" is reserved through its being grasped in its successive collisions with circumstance.[38] As an aspect of narrative, the graphic figuration of givenness in the movement of reflective consciousness, or knowing subject, becomes, in a very Hegelian way, its own object of knowledge, while retreating into unknowability. The subject of autobiography does not find itself ready-made in history outside of the text (particularly authenticating texts like slave narratives), but attempts to construct its subjective identity in writing.

Ben Ali's African-Arabic slave narrative runs contrary to the autobiographical English-language slave narratives in that it is not the writing

of a liberated self-reflective consciousness that emerges from the negation of African materiality. The *khaṭṭ takrurī* of the Ben Ali manuscript
does not liberate, but arrests in its abstraction; its graphemes work at the
transposing of difference. Sameness is not an identity, but rather an
activity, a producing of taxonomies in contradistinction to their application. To have life on the line that distinguishes the *thanatological* from the
thanatographical is to find in the grapheme the superfluousness of death
(Derrida, *Ear* 4).[39] The work of the line is that of drawing out the straight
way (*sīrat-ul-mustaqīm*), the rule that defines the field of play.

Ben Ali's *khaṭṭ takrurī*, with its being inscribed there on those thirteen
pages, unfolds the space and the possibilities of its play. It opens up the
page as a page, a space in which the ideological departure is grounded.
Narrative as *qiṣa* is a writing out of life in the material abstraction of the
grapheme.[40] This is ironic, in that the *khaṭṭ*, the grapheme, is also an
arrestation, a collecting trace of agency. But this irony is precisely the
point, because the "empirical-genetic" readings of Ben Ali's ideological
system (viz., those of Goulding, Harris, and Greenberg) concern themselves with the *dynamis* (*Macht*) of the line that connects the corpus of the
work and the body of Ben Ali through the proper name, al-Qairawānī.
The work of reading is the crossing of that line: this is the problem of
translation alluded to by Kant in his concept of hypotyposis.

It is not enough to describe the line as writing that requires hypotyposis; an inquiry into the work of compiling a book is also required.
After all, Ben Ali writes that he wrote his biography in response to his
being told to write books (*uktub lī kutub*). And the book that he provides
is the collected pages (*aṣ-ṣuḥuf al-majmuʿa*) of his life, the compilation of
his writing (*al-muʿallaf*). It is in the compilation of *al-muʿallaf* that the line
crosses the two bodies: a single vocalic change and *al-muʿallaf* becomes
al-muʿallif, "the author."[41] Authorship is an act of intimacy, the bringing
together and joining of pen and paper. And the work of the pen (*al-qalm*)
is familiar and repetitive, a returning (*ʿaud*) to the beginning from which
knowledge goes out, uninterrupted until it regains its point of departure. Is it not said of Allah that *He* taught by the pen? The work of the
pen, then, is a series of articulations merging into a line of perpetual
motion, a loop, a peak, a terminal dip, which moves ceaselessly, returning to the field it describes. The pen traces itself a trace.

If authorship is the work of bringing together paper and pen in the
unceasing line, then it brings together the line and delineation, text and
life. The reader of the text is already perpetually bound to the line as its

follower, and through the line to its tracer. The distance between the author of Ben Ali's text and its reader is re-marked by the line. The reader may only enter the field of the text by way of the line, which is to suggest that in entering the field of Ben Ali's writing, the reader enters the field of conjunction that traverses space. The line of Ben Ali's writing is a passport, a license (*ijāza*) to move across the page reading. Such an academic license is what the *madrasa* (college) of Timbo conferred on those who finished their course of study. It was conferred with the inclusion of the student in the list of readers: the genealogy of student/teachers, the *ijāza* that connects the "new" reader to the founding reader, Muḥammad ibn 'Abdullah ibn 'Abd-ul-Muṭṭallib. It is this license to read that Ben Ali wants to display in response to the imperative to write. But, having not yet reached that state of licentiate (*mujāz*), he cannot. Instead, he invokes the proper name of someone already determined as licensed and so licensing. In invoking al-Qairawānī's name Ben Ali displaces his lack of authority to read by reading behind his imām, by transcribing his own repetitive recitation of al-Qairawānī's *ar-Risāla*.

Compiled as a book, this reading functions as a public act of speaking that establishes Ben Ali as not-being-nigger. This public speech is of a type in which the locator, *al-khaṭīb*, is at rest (*min ḥudūr*),[42] behind the proper name of the already-licensed reader. The implication is that al-Qairawānī is the principal narrator, *al-qaṣāṣ*, whose signature authorizes Ben Ali as a transmitter, *rāwiya*. Ben Ali is a narrator whose authority to narrate derives from his placing himself in the relation of reading, from his intending to become the interlocutor of an authorized text in response to the imperative "write me books." But who is Ben Ali's interlocutor, *mukhāṭab*, who is "he" who headed the narrative story with this demand to write a book? The *mukhāṭab*, the interlocutor of Ben Ali's text, is he to whom this repetition of al-Qairawānī's discourse is directed: "he" who is conjoined with the *khaṭīb*, the locator, in discourse. And this conjoining in discourse, this locution, occurs in space: on the page arrested in the line. In this way the interlocutor is *min ḥudūr*, in presence, with the locator.

Presence here is being at rest, johnny on the spot, *Dasein*, with the stress on "*Da*." In Arabic, the position of *mukhāṭab* is indicated by certain graphemic markers: the pronouns (the detached nominative,[43] direct object suffix, and genitive suffix[44]); the second-person verb prefix "تـ [*tā* ']," which reflects gender as well as position in the discursive line, e.g., *taf'al* (you do, m.) and *taf'alina* (you do, f.); the second-person

verb suffix "ﺕ [tā]," also reflecting gender and position, e.g., fi ʻalta (you did, m.) and fa ʻalti (you did, f.); and in the imperative prefix "أ [hamza]," e.g., uf ʻul (do it). These markers are found in Ben Ali's manuscript only four times. The first time is at the beginning of the first chapter (1:7): **uktub lī kutub** ("write me books").[45] The remaining three times are all moments of direction when "you" is told to say whatever follows. They occur on 8:5, at the beginning of the prayer that concludes wuḍū': "**taqūl** [you say]"; 11:7, at the beginning of the instructions for al-iqāma: "**taqūl** [you say]"; in the call to prayer; and 12:10, at the instructions on what to say in prayer: "**taqūl** [you say]." Whereas the first instance on 1:7 is one of reported speech in which the interlocutor is the author/narrator (" . . . he headed the story with: 'write me . . . ' "), in the other three instances it is the narrator who addresses another: "you [will, or should] say . . ."

Here, in the graphic line of ﺕ (tā'), the interlocutor is "you," inscribed along the lines of the narrative story. The line traces "you," identifies "you," and signifies "you" there on the page, inscribed and at rest along the narrative line of writing. It is only in this sense that you can be along with (min ḥuḍūr) the author of Ben Ali's manuscript, in the story line that carries you across the space of the page on into its myriad of tales, but never through time to that moment before the manuscript was written when Ben Ali became an author. The originary moment of transcription, that is, of authorial inscription, fades with the very joining of pen to paper, with the lead line that demarcates the page. So too, al-Qairawānī, the narrator who locutes while being present at rest, vanishes, a mere dissimulation. The character of the line is such that it misleads whoever would seek after its point of origin, those who would capture its "author" in any sense of the word. The author is irretrievably displaced and obscured by that which marks his passing: the written line of communication. He becomes musta'jam, displaced without a voice discernible from the manifold of the graphic line of communication (al-khaṭṭ) composing the text. The line becomes his written passing, his thanatography, that is, his autobiography. This is the gist of the ancient proverb:

al-baʻira tadalu ʻalā al-baʻīr. . . .

[The camel dung-spoor signifies the camel. . . .]

The specific pattern of *tashīf*, heterography, in the graphic line of Ben Ali's manuscript identifies the author as someone educated in the Senegambia, who either was a native Fulani speaker or acquired his Arabic from Fulani speakers. The particularly idiosyncratic fluidity of the manuscript's heterography indicates someone constantly shifting between the oral codes and literal codes, to such an extent that the fullness of his literacy is in question. There are moments when the diglossic struggle is acutely apparent, such as page 10, line 8, where a correction is written in the margin (see note 16 of this chapter). On the last page of the manuscript (page 13) the heterographic variance is so great that within the space of two lines the same word is spelled two different ways (*ash-shalāah* and *ash-shalāh*), which contrast with two other spellings of this word that occur throughout the rest of the text (*aṣ-ṣalāḥ* and *aṣ-ṣalaḥ*). The only other place in the text where "*ash-shalāah*" is the spelling is 10:8, where it is corrected in the margin by "*aṣ-ṣalāh*." While there is virtually no difference in the handwriting in these heterographies, the marginal correction, together with its failure to take, indicates a degree of polyglossia. Whether it was the case that the author of the Ben Ali manuscript consulted another scholar or another written text for correction, there are enough instances of difference to conclude that the manuscript had multiple readers who have contributed to its writing.

This possibility of multiple authorship of Ben Ali's "book" opens up further possibilities for determining "you." "You" is marked graphemically by the line, and three of the four times that "you" appears there it is to be instructed in what to say. These are explicitly didactic moments, in which specific ritual formulae are to be rehearsed and memorized. At these points the manuscript is a book of instruction for oral performance. It is a line that calls for a reader, *qāri'*, someone to recite the written recitation, someone to repeat semiotic events that constitute the space of Islamic ritual *'ibāda*. That reader is "you." And in reading "you" are instructed in the rituals of Islam, "you" are delineated within the signifying system of *'ibāda*: it is "you" who says the sanctifying prayer for *wuḍū'*, "you" who says *al-iqāma* and the morning prayer. Within the signifying system of *'ibādah*, both the interlocutor (*mukhāṭab*) and the locator (*khaṭīb*) are readable (*maqrū'*) along with the text, and the line (*khaṭṭ*) is their material reading (*qirā'a*). Together they represent the object of reading. What is readable is represented in absentia; it is a figure articulated in the line to be memorized, fixed in the heart, and expressed (recited) by the tongue.

Reading stretches space into time, it defines the oral speech-act as significant event: the grapheme engenders the phoneme, marking the difference of the now of utterance and the there of indeterminate inscription. Not only is "you" presented in position within the space of the page (a point described in relation to other points on the line), but the possibilities of position and presence, of difference is inscribed there. Indeed, by reading, "you" submits to being in time, a being and time described in the line. In this fashion, the line is the dung-spoor (*al-ba'ira*): when the spoors are set down, so are the articulations, the traces of the camel (*al-ba'īr*), in absentia. As long as the spoors are differentiable, that long the camel remains represented. Reader and author are represented only in the articulations of the line.

Accordingly, the line is the connecting link between writing and reading, text and life, you and Ben Ali. Let us not lose sight of the fact that as the reader, "you" can engender only the *act* of reading, and not even that, really. Whoever follows, traces the line of the grapheme and falls prey to the grapheme; and whoever articulates the line in mimicry is preinscribed by it. The question of what reading does is not discernible to "you" when the Ben Ali manuscript is first opened. At that moment, the text appears as a series of arbitrarily designed lines that mark the page as a space in which a specific kind of play is engaged. It is the will to reading that unfolds the page as the space of graphic play. The play of the line is inescapable, every reading of *Ben Ali's Diary* is already preinscribed there. The text reads itself constantly, constantly unfolding the lines that trace the passing of difference (*majāz*). Each grapheme in the line stands in relation to every other grapheme in it, to the other balls of dung, those traces fading into traces strung along in the space of the page. Of course, this is a metaphor (*majāz*). The point is, with Ben Ali's text what else could a license, an *ijāza*, to read be? Nothing else but a vacation from reasonable expectation; albeit, a working vacation, a digression from the unilinear movement of the History of Thought to the multilineal texture of the manuscript. *Ben Ali's Diary* reads "you," the reader, back to yourself, providing the license to be in his line, which is a beginning in text.

Having digressed this far, it is perhaps a good moment to retrace what has been said and reconsider the question of what lines do, specifically in the reading of *Ben Ali's Diary* under way. This reading began by tracing the graphic line of Ben Ali's manuscript, *al-khaṭṭ at-takrurī*, as an

(auto)biographic line (*sīra*), as an arresting writing out of life, a thanatography. That line took a trajectory that traversed Arabic philology, describing the historical space of Islamic Arabic writing, and engaging the possibilities of play, prescribed and unwarranted, within that space. In this play, the graphic line is compiled as a book, *Ben Ali's Diary*, in which the line is articulated by and affixed to the pen in a perpetual movement of returning to its beginning. That movement describes its own field of possibilities in reading. Thus, the line compiled in a book represents the gesture of fixing writing to reading. This line of reading tells a story of diffused authorship, finally displacing the very field it described. The issue is, then, how to read such a line. The repeated claim that the unreadability of the Ben Ali manuscript is due to Ben Ali's semiliteracy is meant to indict his inability to inscribe Arabic words accurately. More to the point, Greenberg's reference to the primacy of oral recitation and dictation in Islamic education suggests that Ben Ali could not accurately transcribe Arabic. Nothing could be further from the working line of the manuscript than this claim.

What is at issue in the Ben Ali text is not the accurate transcribing of proper Arabic speech (a propriety that, as I've already argued, is not even a phenomenal possibility), it is not a question of affirming writing's subordination to speaking. On the contrary, as Greenberg's own discovery of the text's content makes plain, Ben Ali is not writing speaking, he is writing writing. That is to say, he is writing what he reads and thinks in reading. This thinking in reading is the cultural discourse that his writing represents. It is a discourse that the claim of Ben Ali's semiliteracy cannot sever him from. The repeated claim of semiliteracy-induced obscurity is finally an admission that the Ben Ali manuscript is so much gibberish: graphic material in need of a structural field in order to become a combination of ciphers susceptible to a cryptoanalysis in which the text's linguistic unfamiliarity legitimates its encoding-decipherment as a foreign code. This is the gist of it. For, in spite of the charge of gibberish, the manuscript exists and in existing indicates a discernible system of signs, an *agencement* of referentiality, which somehow resists being comprehended in a universal semiology, i.e., Western modernity's taxonomy of the human conceptual plane. I say "somehow" because this is not an oppositional resistance; it is a discursive resistance, a resistance of being that can only be transposed.

Critique of Hypotyposis
The Inhuman Significance of *Ben Ali's Diary*

> All laws, however just and humane they may be, in favor of Negroes
> will always be a violation of the rights of property.
>
> —C. L. R. James, *The Black Jacobins*

What is most threatening about the heterography of Ben Ali's manuscript is its foreclosing on the displacement of heterogeneity outside of
the circuit of linguistic referentiality. Through its signs' refusal to
become transparent, the manuscript exposes the necessity of any arbitrarily definitive reading to be in displacing the indeterminacy of referentiality, and the obfuscation of that materiality it cannot displace. This
is the same indeterminacy that provoked Kant to designation and hypotyposis.

Whichever way the text is turned, Ben Ali's manuscript confronts its
would-be reader with the figure of the reader reading *Ben Ali's Diary;*
which is to say, of the reader reading the unreadable text. In this instance of reading, *Ben Ali's Diary*, as the proper name for the manuscript,
substitutes for the quality of illegibility associated with it. Here is the
name of an author who defied descriptive analysis, save through the
title of his untranslatable text. This condition of indeterminacy extends
to other African-Arabic texts; many of `Umar ibn Said's and `Abd-ur-
Rahmān's fragments, and even Ayyūb ibn Suleiman's postmanumission
epistles, are *Ben Ali's*. But what does it mean to say that the proper
name, Ben Ali, and the title, *Ben Ali's Diary*, are *periphrastic?*

Because the quality for which Ben Ali and *Ben Ali's Diary* substitute
is indeterminacy, it means that even the most superficial identification of
discursive style (syntactic ordering, lexemic selection, and rhetorical
schemata) with authorial personality and intentionality is utterly impossible to read. That is not to say that there is no discernible discursivity in
the manuscript, or even that it is insignificant, but rather that discursivity cannot be read as the transcribing of any determinate subjective intentionality.

If it is indeed the case that language is the labor of thought, then
most certainly we cannot say anything in language that is not general,

and hence readable. According to this notion of language—one that has extended well beyond the boundaries of Kant's Transcendental Critique primarily in the form of a universal semiotics—much, if not all, social practice can be understood as taking place in language.

The notion that language is an analyzable, essentially social, process of productive signification suggests, with regard to the human subject (when the subject is thought of as an effect of social practice, both in the sense of the agential locus of praxis and the organization of thinking about praxis), that language is the place in which conscious subjectivity becomes possible. Even though this yields a consideration of subjective identity as being discursively constituted—which somehow displaces the notion of a purely nondiscursive human essence, of an eidetic humanity—it does that in order to constitute a pure, homogeneous, linguistic referentiality on which the determination of the subject in language is grounded. The possibility of the idea of the subject always takes place in a definite site: language. Such an ideology of language becomes the way in which the subject takes place as representation. This provokes additional problematics for Kant's architectonic, and also general questions about the history of cogito, because of how signification is pulled off by a chiasmatic reversal.

Even though meaning results from the relationship between signifiers, the understanding of that relationship relies on a specifically Kantian way of thinking about the material sign as the realization of reasoned thought. In that thinking, accuracy in meaning, truth, is always determined by the degree to which there is a linkup between the mode of expression and the idea to be expressed. Accordingly, the materiality of linguistic referentiality is subordinated to the discursive arrangements of thought. In this way the basis for signification, the rules of referentiality, are held to be beyond the mode of expression, and so are universal and transcendental.

In Kant, understanding meaning emerges by way of lengthy speculative reflection that is grounded in Reason, which, through historical development—the mediation of time—emancipates the thinking subject as a discursive effect, allowing it to emerge as the focal point of an autonomous process of self-reflection.

Ben Ali's Diary betrays the epistemological uncertainties at the base of this conception of the sign. It does this by consisting of an economy of signification where linguistic referentiality cannot be reduced to intentionality, but must come to terms with indeterminacy. The Ben Ali

manuscript exhibits the very process of hypotyposis at work. It exposes how linguistic referentiality entails an overlapping of representation and reference that effects a certain iconicity, which is what Kant's *Wortbestimmung* is. Designation as iconicity is the effect of the system of signification, the organizing schemata that neither the sender nor receiver of the letter comprehends let alone controls. In that case signification is designation, and designation is a function of standing for. The signs constitutive of Ben Ali's text undoubtedly stood for something to somebody (Ben Ali) in some capacity at some time, and that is the full extent to which its signification can be analyzed. In the face of this *Wortbestimmung*, there is a disturbing question that a text like Ben Ali's inevitably provokes: How is systemic or discursive transference possible?

This is not merely to ask how experiences are subsumed under a given set of related sign systems. It is to ask how that process of exhibition, which Kant called hypotyposis, can be translated to another distinct process of exhibition. This problem of transferring exhibition is what is at stake in Kant's Transcendental Critique. Hypotyposis occurs with more than the absence of referent, it involves the situating of the referent in another possible field of reference altogether, and for Kant that field is the field of representation. The question becomes, then, how does Ben Ali's African-Arabic American slave narrative not become representational in its response to Kant?

Demonstrating that this problem of referentiality issues from the conception of an inherent homogeneity of language (which enables language to mitigate the heterogeneity of the perception of phenomenal materiality and the attribution of meaning, resulting in a coherence of experience) requires that the notion of experience be elaborated on and confronted in a way that is theoretical without being transcendental. In other words, I will momentarily step beyond the Kantian notion of representation and examine Ben Ali's text according to a conception of the sign that is articulated along somewhat different lines from Kant. I do so in order to show how writing does not translate thought in Ben Ali's narrative. I refer to the theory of the Soviet semiotician Yuri Lotman, whom I offer in contrast to Kant because, while he shares with Kant a preoccupation with the question of the transactional relationship of language and cultural reality, he resists reducing the material aspects of signification to subservience under cognitive discourse.

Lotman assumes, as did Kant, that the signifier and signified can be looked at independently. But for Lotman the signifier and signified are construed as constituting two distinct planes, the signifier that of expression (code) and the signified that of content (message). In the plane of expression, a particular phoneme or (as in the case of Ben Ali's narrative) grapheme obtains its value from its position in the phonemic or graphemic system of the language. The content plane also consists of a set of systems of signifying practices in which the individual elements are defined by their position in a system and their relation with all the other elements of the system.

Now, the specificity of an element of the content plane cannot be discovered without referring to the other elements. This means that a datum that cannot be related either to another datum or included in a class of data cannot be a content of the language.[1] Signification, or for Kant, "meaning," occurs when the two "structural concatenations of differential elements are conjoined and an operation of 'transcoding' occurs"; i.e., when "one of the structural chains comes to play the role of plane of expression and the other that of plane of content. Elements of one chain are paired with elements of the other, thus producing an intersection point, which we call *sign*."[2] Ben Ali's manuscript fits this model, insofar as it entails a specific expression plane, consisting of Arabic language graphemes, and a content plane.

This process of signification cannot be accounted for by Kant's theory of hypotyposis (symbolic representation), because in that theory a concept is considered as having an explicit reference or denotation, albeit a priori, and then being capable of suggesting or associating additional ideas, or connotations. (This is how hypotyposis avoids the paralogisms of the "Transcendental Deduction"; in symbolic hypotyposis connotation is extended to a degree that denotation is problematized, but this is possible only on the basis that there is a denotation.)

Lotman's conception of the sign annuls this distinction between denotation and connotation, conflating them by showing that the two types of meaning are produced in the same way. From Lotman's perspective, it is no longer possible to "describe or define a given rhetorical figure other than intralinguistically; the possibility of appeal to empirical reality or reference is voided" (Godzich, "Meaning" 391).

This situation is only slightly more complicated in the instance of Ben Ali's narrative, because both the writing on the page and the thoughts that it cannot translate function as signifiers within their

respective languages. The question is, signifiers of what? Over this question the differences between Kant's and Lotman's conceptions of the sign are most pronounced. Should we choose to adhere closely to the Kantian view, according to which, although there is a manifold of experiences, there is only one universal cognitive process by which experiences are presented, then the answer to the question is clear. The material signs of Ben Ali's writing symbolize his thoughts (in the broadest sense).

Phrased this way, Kant's theory of symbolic representation, with which he rescues the architectonic from endless referential indeterminacy, echoes Aristotle. What comes to mind is the oft-cited passage in *De Interpretatione* where Aristotle asserts that both spoken and written words are *symbols* (*symbola* [συμβολα]) of mental affectations, which themselves are representations of phenomenal objects.[3] Where Kant's echo becomes an elaboration beyond Aristotle's theory is in his recognition of cognitive representations as being symbolic and so valid objects of logical (semiotic) analysis. Kant finds grounding for his architectonic in Aristotle's conception of linguistic symbols as indexes of thinking, precisely because when words function primarily as symbols (independently of their possible use as proofs of thinking), they are not based on the model of inference but on the model of equivalence (identity), which is how Kant understands analogy. In other words, Kant's symbolic hypotyposis results from his reading the Aristotelian apodictic syllogism in apposition to the Stoic *modus podens*.

Once thinking is read symbolically, the distinction of denotation/connotation becomes describable as issuing from a mode of error—the generation of illusions of referentiality that Kant delineates in "Transcendental Dialectic." The very structural nature of thought is such that it participates in the production of the illusion that linguistic referents correspond to noumenal reality. Then again, if the denotation/connotation distinction may be described as a mode of error that from a theoretical standpoint has an inherent structural basis in cognition, then, as Douglass's parody of material literacy points out, there is a bias for privileging denotation in this distinction.

From Lotman's standpoint, however, what the distinction's existence signifies semiotically is that not only do signs not exist independently but neither do sign systems: "individual sign systems, though they presuppose immanently organized structures, function only in unity, supported by one another. None of the sign systems possesses a

mechanism which would enable it to function in isolation" (Godzich, "Meaning" 392). This insight of Lotman sums up the Kantian project of discovering the transcendental grounds for the necessary harmony in the activity of the cognitive faculties. Yet for Lotman there is more to it than this. He presents the possibility for different thinking about signification.

A set of related sign systems is what we call *culture*, which is the field in which the hierarchization of sign systems into denotative and connotative occurs. There is no unified field of culture, no universal process or architectonics of cognition. In other words, although perceiving and designating are indeed two distinctly different experiences, there can be no reading without both. Reading entails seeing, but not in a manner that subordinates one to the other, or resolves the two into an ideal unity of the sign as signifier signified. Add to all of this Lotman's conception of culture as a "nonhereditary memory of the collective" that is in constant flux between the two opposing tendencies of organizing experience into its sign systems and discarding its dysfunctional parts. Once we have caught sight of the importance of reading, we have become concerned with hypercodes, i.e., overdetermined and complex codes that are constitutive of the culture in which the codes are produced.

In attempting to read Ben Ali's text one is brought to the point where not only must the problems of linguistic variance and heterography relative to Arabic orthography be grappled with, but, because these problems require some consideration of the dynamics of signification at work in the manuscript in a way that challenges the concept of a signification based on identity, one must also inquire about the conceptualization of signification on which our understanding of reading is based.

Thus, to understand the correlation of language-use and presence, as the determinate condition for reading slave narratives, pursuant with Gates's injunction to do so, is to understand that Ben Ali's slave narrative is a challenge to read. It requires contemplating the dynamics of representation, a thinking about the operations of signifying practices, in opposition to overlooking and subverting them through sophisticated scanning techniques of ratiocination that trivialize the text as so much datum.

Although the subjective intentionality of the manuscript's author is irretrievably bound up with that signification, from the perspective of the reader that intentionality cannot be the basis for signification, but rather emerges only after the processes of linguistic referentiality have

been determined, i.e., designated (after the heterography has been accounted for, and the syntactic structures understood). While designation is probably inevitable, with regard to subjective intentionality, there is an aspect of linguistic referentiality antecedent to, or at least other than, our historical being as conscious intending subjects. This yields a consideration of subjective identity as not only being discursively constituted, but also subject to an affect that entails no intentionality—an inhuman agency. Because the humanity of a text is frequently conceived of in terms of its underlying intentionality (whether uniquely subjective, or an individual expression of a collectivity), it means that the linguistic referentiality, the significance, of Ben Ali's diary is inhuman.

This is the question that *Ben Ali's Diary* unavoidably forces us to consider: the inhuman of linguistic referentiality. For Kant this was the problem of the indeterminacy of Imagination's schemata. Ben Ali's text causes us to consider this by foreclosing any possibility of determining in the text the grounds for distinguishing between the intended object of signification and the way in which language intends it, or as Lotman puts it, between the two distinct planes of expression and content. The insistent assumption that both the meaning of Ben Ali's manuscript and its mode of production are intentional acts causes Greenberg to be unable to determine either the content of the manuscript or the geocultural origin of its Arabic dialect. His is precisely the sort of phenomenological reading that the manuscript problematizes.

Although the intentionality of any given meaning-function in any given language is certain, this is not the case with the mode of meaning, which depends on linguistic properties that stand beyond any subjectivity and so are not intentional. *This* is what is meant by the inhuman in linguistic referentiality; it is the linguistic structures, the play of linguistic tensions, linguistic events that occur and determine the possibilities inherent in language—all of which are independent of any intent or desire to mean. These are the modes of expression that we are born to as historical beings. And these are all that Ben Ali's text affords us a glance of: graphemes on a page, which carefully enough follow a grammar to be deemed textual, narrative discourse.

The result is that the fundamental nonhuman character of linguistic referentiality is underscored in *Ben Ali's Diary* and is shown to encompass a fundamental nondefinition of the human: that which uncovers the illegitimacy of the rapport between the Human and Nature, which is

the grounding of such concepts as human nature, natural rights, and natural law.

By appearing to be what it cannot be, a modern autobiographical text of the beginning of the nineteenth century, Ben Ali's Arabic text is symptomatic of a failure that is endemic to the history of Western thinking about signification: the failure to realize thought's mediated representation in writing. *Ben Ali's Diary* is not the writing of thought provoking thoughts, it supports no code for the exchange of ideas, it is the writing that provokes thought. Yet the manuscript is indeed readable. And in its readability it is particularly problematical for the Enlightenment, because, while it is readable, it is not comprehensible to Reason. When confronted with Ben Ali's writing, the necessity to read is enhanced. But reading cannot be gained in accordance with the speculative insight of Reason.

This is problematical, because at the origin of Enlightenment's Reason, the very condition for its genesis, is the capacity to make everything readable. Achieving such universal legibility was the business of Locke's science of *semeiotica* (the doctrine of signs), the third branch of his tripartite division of science.[4] The instrumental division of Locke's "sciences," *semeiotica* is concerned with comprehending the nature of cognitive representation—i.e., with the means by which things and events are known in signification (from simple to complex ideas, in Locke's language). As this is also the stated project of his *Essay Concerning Humane Understanding*, then this foundational text of the Enlightenment falls under the science of *semeiotica*. That is to say, the Enlightenment project of making everything readable in Reason is grounded in a particular conceptualization of the History of Thought as a dialectical development discernible in the recorded history of the doctrine of the sign.

The history of semiotics that begins with Locke has assumed the form of an investigation of the already-acquired doctrine of the sign, whose *horrible dictu* is its implied adherence to a humanist Aristotelianism, which plots the trajectory of Thought only along a unilinear geographical path of East to West—from Greece to Europe. But as I point out through the Ben Ali manuscript, as well as Ottobah Cugoano's recounting of Garcilaso de la Vega's Atahualpa story, such a trajectory leads inevitably to a dilemma of indeterminacy: the inability to adjudicate between equally effective yet mutually exclusive symbolic economies. The more comprehensive the doctrine of the sign strives to be, the more obviously untenable its claim to comprehension becomes.

No history of semiotics can claim to be the history of *Homo semeioti-cus* as the history of humanity par excellence without the inclusion of the manifold trajectories of thinking.[5] Putting it closer to home, there cannot even be a history of Western semiotics that does not include the signifying practices of Africa. This means that the history of semiotics, per se, must be reconceptualized as something other than either the sum total of Western writing about being, or the residual effects of an abstract History of Thought. In the course of this thinking, neither the concept of the sign nor that of culture as an effect of signification can be already acquired. Ben Ali's African-Arabic American slave narrative is a "point of departure" for such thinking.

Epilogue
Thought After: *Thinking* Heterography

The Thought After

> We are a sign that is not read. . . .
> —Hölderlin, *Mnemosyne*

The preceding explorations are meant as a summation of what this book is all about. It is an introductory sketch, an outline, by way of examples (viz., African-Arabic American slave narratives), of a particular problem that has bothered me for some time now. Granted, the rise of the intellectual project called "deconstruction" in the human sciences has generated over the past twenty-six years an extensive body of theoretical work. Collectively, that work has produced a sustained critique of a certain Western conception of signification, the Doctrine of the Sign, conferring a new kind of readability on elements of literary texts that readers are traditionally trained to disregard and edit out as peripheral noise. A chief effect of this critique has been to foreground the semiotic work of literary criticism. It has become virtually impossible for the academic literary critic to articulate a credible "reading" of texts without formulating some relation to the Doctrine of the Sign, that is to say, without theorizing writing and reading as events in a signifying practice. Still, there are certain texts, like Kebe's book list and the Ben Ali manuscript, whose nature of signification are not only linguistically but also historically beyond the received notion of the Western Doctrine of the Sign as event. These texts continue to emerge as signifying practices that do more than defy reading; they articulate a defiance of signification itself. They stand before the Doctrine in the guise of an almost insurmountable challenge, both to the notion of determinate typologies that so characterizes philosophical discourse and to the explosive tropologies of rhetoric that so characterize "deconstructive" reading. They do more than resist, they mock theory. How is this so? What is it about the problematic nature of linguistic referentiality that makes it impossible for the speculative discourse of Western Reason to comprehend emergent literature?

Situated as they are near the end of a book like this one, a book that knows no bounds, these questions should not be answered, but should

give cause for more elaborate summation. Because this book relies upon an inability to accept the familiar philosophical formulations, or more precisely, the historiography, that distinguishes between the legitimate concerns of philosophy's formulations and those of semiotics, the summary that I offer is problematic in the sense that it does not function as a hypotyposis of the central problem of the book, expositing the genesis of an idea. Instead, it retraces certain articulations, observing the collocution of certain expressions: Reason (cogito), Negro (African), Arab (African), experience, and thought.

The juxtaposition of these has made more obvious the extent to which this book necessarily entails an underlying challenge both to the Idealist history of philosophy, which makes problematics of expression subordinate to the content of the Idea (whether verifiable or axiomatic), and to the equally Idealist conception of the history of semiotics, which recognizes the epistemological problematics of modern philosophy as problems of signifying by signs, of internal relations. Such a juxtaposition involves just the sort of overextension in field of inquiry that I have undertaken when reading in a collection of generically varied texts the collocution of terms and issues, most of which are held to be separate and even at times mutually antipathetic.

Even so, the expression of the question that has been at issue throughout this book necessarily entails a certain synthesis of thinking about these things. That question is the one with which I began the book. You may recall it as the question of how the university determines cultural value. Because this question was initially asked in the context of the current crisis in the humanities in the university, purportedly occurring in the wake of greater cultural diversity, perhaps it would be more straightforward to ask, Does the university determine cultural value? Has it ever?

There are clear indications that as early as the twelfth century, with Frederick Barbarossa's granting of a charter to the University of Bologna, the university as a corporate association (a legal fiction of a unified mass Person) has functioned as an important site of social formation. In the case of Bologna, the very hybrid discourse of juridical legitimation that underpinned Frederick I's charter, the merger of Justinian and Curia laws, facilitated a rearticulation of the authorized exercise of power (in Barbarossa's favor, obviously). That is to say, in the Holy Roman Empire of the German Nation, the university functioned not merely as the instantiation of cultural conservation or authentication,

but as an association, a legitimate (juridical) institution not only for the circulating of ideas or methodologies of ideas, but for the circulating of legitimacy. Ever since, the legitimate function of the university has been to authorize the exercise of power through the circulation of a specific discourse of value. And, insofar as that discourse engages a cyclic production of its value—the very production of value is a function of circulation as the licensure of masters—the university is the site where the two legal associations of *societas* and *universitas* (corporation) collide. The production of cultural value is the result of this collision. The university, then, is the site where the early state emerges, when the state is understood to be *societas cum universitate*, and where culture is the difference between the two that enables their connectedness.

This reading finds interesting support in the arguments for culture developed at the University of Salamanca by the School of Salamanca, particularly in Francisco de Vitoria's arguments for the legitimacy of Spanish dominion over the Aztecs; I am referring specifically to his basing legitimate dominion on the absence of liberal arts among the Aztecs (which is both cause and effect of their illiteracy). Yet, Vitoria's argument turns on a careful blindness to the obvious fact that liberal arts are a function of agency, the exercise of power, along specific lines of assemblage or association. This same blindness is what overdetermines the efforts of such reformers as Cornell, Gilman, Jefferson, Dewey, and Ticknor (one could add to the list Coleridge, Mill, Emerson, Arnold, and Eliot), causing them to treat culture and society as Idealist categories that are somehow antithetic to one another. Hence the culture-society dichotomy that frames their discussion of the relationship between education and the state, between thinking and working.

The stakes are high in this hypostatization (one could say monumentalization) of the production of cultural value in the university. By focusing discussion on the issue of delineating the most authoritative methodology for determining authentic knowledge (something Bacon does in an explicit thematic fashion in his *Organon*, and something Vitoria does implicitly), attention is drawn away from the means by which the university could even function as the legitimate institution for adjudicating cultural value: circulation of personnel. This is something that was not lost on the Habsburgs in their seventeenth-century programs of centralizing education, and definitely was afoot with the founding of *École Normale Supérieur* in 1794.

A more direct way of putting all of this is to say that since its conception as a legal association in the eleventh and twelfth centuries, the university's function has been to subordinate contentious and variegated ways of producing cultural value under a stabilizing administrative formation. This is why the legitimation of knowledge, of a given cultural product, is not gained with the delineation of that object as a work, nor is it gained with the generating of work about it. Instead, legitimation is gained through circulation; circulation is the process by which value is attached to cultural production. Once attention is focused on the issue of circulation the entire discussion (both antecedent and contemporary) about the relation between knowledge and power, society and culture, language and being, must be readdressed. The challenge is here, to slip away from a philosophy of *the* subject, to a politics of identities. Slipping away is made possible when culture is explored, rather than assumed; when it is explored in terms of signifying practices and their materialities. This moment of summation is not the one in which I want to launch a project of social semiotics. That requires far more rigor and effort than can be expended here at the end of an introductory sketch. So I will elaborate on what I mean by such an exploration through a sort of test case.

Thinking Heterography

The recognition that the various institutions of circulation with the greatest capital concentration are those where the authorized production of cultural value takes place recalls the principal thesis of Nelson George's book, *The Death of Rhythm and Blues:* that the commodification of rhythm & blues led to its dissolution as an authentic form of African American cultural production.[1] George's admittedly essentialist view of rhythm & blues as a product of African American culture aside, the gist of his argument about the commodification of R&B, and its subsequent dissolution, is that legitimation is gained through circulation. George, of course, is wrong in the notion that the attachment of circulatory value equals the dissolution of cultural production. It does not. What it does signal is the dissolution of "authentic" production value. What George is bemoaning is not the dissolution of R&B as an authentic form of African American cultural production, but the subordination of African American circulation to another circulation of cultural value. It is the work of subordination that determines the relationship of dominant and

sub cultures. George is talking about a particular historical process of *hegemony*. And in this instance R&B becomes a subaltern history.

But authenticity too is a function of circulation. So what George identifies as the dissolution of R&B through its commodification is in fact the apparent subordination of one economy of circulation to another: the circulation of privately owned African American record shops and radio stations is subordinated to the circulation economy of the conglomerate record companies and finally multinational conglomerate interests. George's complaint is that there has been in our late-capitalist economy a rapid centralization of control of the material means needed for film and television/video production in the hands of a few.

I am still of the opinion that this centralization does not mean that the production of cultural value is limited to those sites of the greatest concentration of material means, i.e., multimedia conglomerates such as Time Warner, television stations, cable monopolies such as TCI and Turner Broadcasting, advertising agencies, and so on. While (exchange) value (is there any other?) is undoubtedly a function of circulation, various modes of circulation are still accessible to large numbers of people: videos, performance art, street theater, vinyl, and, yes, literature (pamphlets, manifestos, and street verse). As Hip Hop science and computer forgery have shown us, the material needs in these modes of circulation are so malleable and few that complete subordination is not possible. R&B, then, is not subaltern, precisely because in their material working the technologies of telecommunication (phonography and telography) fail to function either metaphorically or metonymically. That is to say that the very technicities entailed in, say, data basing, preclude even the centralized archiving of information in any way but as illusion, as is evidenced in the ever-growing problem of designating "hackers."

Implicit in George's view about the history of circulation is a notion of the bifurcation of American cultural production, or rather the production of cultural value. Of course, it is not bifurcate as much as it is diverse, as there are myriads of economies of circulation as opposed to only two ("Black and White"). There are economies of circulation along the lines of the social constructs of gender, race, sexual preference, ethnicity, language, and so on (as constructs none of these "things" are things per se, they are not essential facts of identity). Yet, it is in terms of bifurcation that this issue has been addressed thus far by those intellectuals who are most acutely interested in things cultural.

The matter of cultural value is not simply an issue of critical practice, of work. The politically or aesthetically correct critical methodology would assure either the preservation of cultural value or the liberation of cultural value. Both are grossly mistaken. What warrants pointing out is that the production of cultural value is not in the end reducible to a function of concrete labor—what we do in specific terms with what specific texts, how digital writing is indexical. Neither is it reducible to ideology, to a function of abstract labor, the network of social relationships that define a work site, like the university, in which certain members (viz., departments and programs of comparative literature and cultural studies) are authorized to do the specific task of criticism. (The value of criticism does not derive in this instance from the "quality" of a piece of critical work; rather, value is the effect of the social function of the university professor, which is why as a class professors' work has more value than students'.) It is not a function of abstract labor in any exhaustive sense, because if that were the case then there would be no explanation for the production of cultural value beyond the parameters or at the margins of that social formation. Nor does the notion of the effective freedom of concrete labor in the university address this. There is too much of the subaltern implied in such a view of the elusiveness of professorial thinking as labor.

Rather, the free concrete labor occurs, as I have just been maintaining with regard to R&B, with those social formations that are coextensive and appositional with the purportedly "dominant" social formation, without being comprehensively subordinated to it. Today perhaps more than ever before in the United States of America, African Americans, Native Peoples, Asian Americans, and de la Raza (particularly Chicanos, Cubanos, Dominicanos, and Ricanios) exist beyond the state.

This is precisely the threat of emergent studies to intellectuals like Allan Bloom, E. D. Hirsch, and William Bennett. They are all correct when they remark the emergence of African American studies as a rupturing of the social formation, a violation of the circulation of cultural value. But they are deluded in their assessment of how to repair that rupture. Its occurrence was not merely the effect of the inclusion of a new canon in the classroom, so it cannot be repaired by rigidly enforcing a privileged circulation. The thing about circulation is that once it gets under way there is really no controlling where it may lead.

Notes

Foreword

1. Ernesto Laclau and Chantal Mouffe, "Totalitarianism and Moral Indignation," *Diacritics* 20, no. 3 (Fall 1990): 88-95.
2. David Lloyd has noted this dynamic in a discussion at the conference "Americanist Visions of Cultural Studies," Columbia University, March 7, 1992.
3. Frantz Fanon, *Black Skin, White Masks* (New York: Grove Press, 1967).

1. Introduction

1. I intend more with this term than just an illusion to the obvious Enlightenment foundations of the United States of America. By capitalizing it, I want to recall the Idealist project of a *World History* (here I'm following Hartman, Kaufmann, Knox, and Miller in translating Hegel's *Weltgeschichte*) as a history of *thought* (*Gedanken*). In his *Introduction to the Philosophy of History*, Hegel states that the philosophy of history is nothing else but the thoughtful contemplation (*denkende Betrachtung*) of it; and the only thought that philosophy brings [to the contemplation of history] is "the simple thought [*einfache Gedanke*] of Reason [*Vernunft*]." Hegel writes of Reason that it "is the law of the world, hence in World History [*Weltgeschichte*] things have come about rationally. . . . Through its speculative knowledge, philosophy has shown that Reason . . . is both the *substance* and *endless force* [*unendliche Macht*], in itself the *infinite material* of all natural and spiritual life as well as the *infinite form*, which is the working out of its own content. . . . Just as it [Reason] is its own exclusive presupposition and absolute final purpose, thus it itself works out and brings forth this [purpose] from potentiality to actuality, not only in the natural but also in the spiritual universe—[i.e.] in world history [*in der Weltgeschichte*]. That this 'Idea' or 'Reason' is the True, the Eternal, the Absolute Force, that it and nothing but it, its glory and honor, manifests itself in the world, has, as we said before, been proved in philosophy and is presupposed here as having being so. . . . For even though one were not approaching World History with the thought [*Gedanken*] and knowledge of Reason, at least one has to have the firm insurmountable belief that Reason does exist, and that the world of intelligence and self-conscious will is not abandoned to mere chance, but must manifest itself in the light of the self-knowing Idea. . . . [Only] the contemplation of World History itself can show that it has proceeded rationally, that it is the necessary course of the World Spirit [*Weltgeistes*], the Spirit [*Geist*] whose nature is to be sure always one and the same, but whose one nature unfolds in the course of the world [*Weltdasein*]" [*Vorlesungen über die Philosophie der Geschichte*, 20 vols. (Frankfurt am Main: Suhrkamp, 1970), 12: 21-22; italics in the original)].

Not only is the thought of history Reason, but Reason in history is the unfolding of *Geist*. In order to keep track of the connectedness of thought (*Gedanken*), Reason (*Vernunft*), and *Geist* in Idealist thinking, I have capitalized "Reason" where the reference is the Idealist (and concomitantly, Romantic) Idea of universal human development: i.e., "World History," which is also capitalized, to differentiate it from more materialist projects of historical critique. The problems associated with translating the German *Geist* into an equally polysemic English term are well known and I will not rehearse them here; see Walter

Kaufmann, *Hegel: Reinterpretation, Texts, and Commentary* (New York: Doubleday, 1965), 160-62. Where *Geist* occurs independently, as opposed to being in a construct, I have followed the dominant convention and translated it as "Spirit." The construct *Geisteswissenschaften* is also translated according to convention as "human sciences." However, because the focus of my concern in this book is on the Idealist tendencies in North American thinking about and academic institutionalization of culture (and to that extent, foregrounding the putting-together of thought, Reason, and *Geist* in Idealism), I have translated *Geistesgeschichte* as the "History of Thought," instead of the more familiar "history of ideas," capitalizing both nouns to underscore the coherence or "adjacency" of the notion of a totalizing history of systems of thought and the Idealist notion of universal human development. (See note 18 of this chapter for a consideration of the relationship of *Geistesgeschichte* to *Geisteswissenschaften*.)

Retaining the Hegelian order of terms foregrounds one of the chief contentions of this book: the authoritative discourse of Anglo American cultural history and production is Romantic at its best, and Idealist at its worst. To the extent that this is so, the American canon is the emblem of the Idea of American culture as a product of European development. This America is a Romantic work, subtended by a theology of Reason. See chapter 4 for elaboration of this argument.

2. Robert Stepto, Jr., and Dexter Fisher, eds., *Afro-American Literature: The Reconstruction of Instruction* (New York: Modern Language Association, 1979).

3. Hartman was a notable key figure of the seminar; a chapter from his *Beyond Formalism*, "Toward Literary History," was on the required reading list.

4. Quoted in the proceedings of the symposium, Armstead Robinson et al., eds., *Black Studies in the University: A Symposium* (New Haven: Yale University Press, 1969), 3.

5. Armstead Robinson, "Concluding Statement," *Black Studies in the University: A Symposium*, 208.

6. The Renaissance humanists' ideal of *humanitas*, originating in Italy in the second half of the fourteenth century, was understood as the development, to the fullest extent, of human virtue in all its forms. In particular, this meant the harmonious balance of action and contemplation. The Enlightenment's privileging of reason and law in nature overwhelmed and displaced the Renaissance humanists' ideal of *humanitas* with the concerns of epistemology. In the *Encyclopédie*, Diderot censured *studia humanitatis* for its preoccupation with Greek and Latin philology. By the end of the eighteenth century humanism was reconstituted primarily as a reaction against the Enlightenment's privileging of reason. The literary movement of Sturm und Drang was an especially forceful aspect of this reaction. Its proponents, led by Goethe, sought to reassert the value of feeling, impulse, emotion, fancy, and intuition, and made nature, genius, and originality its slogans. Herder's notion of *Humanität* provided Sturm und Drang with the doctrine of harmonious balance between intellect and feeling. Herder's *Humanität* stood for "humanness," in the sense of the fully developed personality in which intellect and imagination were balanced. This notion of *Humanität* outlived Sturm und Drang and became a fundamental doctrine in the movement of German neoclassicism, which fostered the hypostatization of the aesthetic as the site where the two competing faculties of intellect and feeling are harmonized. The Romantic radical extension of *Humanität* into the notion of the literary as transcendent, in tandem with Herder's concepts of language and history, enabled the emergence of literary history, philology, as the site of national identity.

7. There is a certain air of frustrated ambition in Robinson's "Concluding Statement" to the symposium, a recognition that the fruits of victory for the BSA may very well be wormy. First he admonishes the university not to think of Black studies as "a *gift* to black students or to black parents." His concern that the university might have succeeded in

snatching victory out of the jaws of defeat with the symposium is most clearly expressed in his repeated invectives against "professionalism": "Many of you are afflicted with a peculiar sense of parochial *'ingrownness.'* This tendency often hides beneath the rubric of 'professionalism' " (emphasis in the original). Then: " 'Professional' educators will have to pay a heavy price for the degree to which they have been guilty of ignoring the proper concerns of their constituents. Mr. Bundy was right when he argued that black studies has opened a Pandora's box." Finally, Robinson closes with a plea for the same social responsibility that Bundy sees at work in the university: "If 'responsible' professional educators fail to react swiftly and positively by recognizing and acting upon the necessity for honest reevaluation, then there is little hope that the mass of America will ever recognize that necessity—and pessimism about America's future becomes a just and rational response to the unpleasant realities and potentialities of the present racial crisis" (*Black Studies in the University* 207-14).

As if to drive the point home, David Brion Davis is given the last word in his "Reflections" on the symposium, where he points to Robert Farris Thompson's scholarship as proof that intellectual authority derives as much from rigorous method as from political circumstance. He then proclaims that "the university is a custodian as well as innovator" (217, 220).

8. Robert Stepto, Jr., *From Behind the Veil: A Study of Afro-American Narrative* (Urbana: University of Illinois Press, 1979), 33.

9. Parrington's most influential work along these lines was *Main Currents in American Thought*, 2 vols., published in 1927. A third volume, subtitled *The Beginnings of Critical Realism in America* and incomplete at Parrington's death, was edited by E. H. Eby and published in 1930.

10. This assessment is made in "Preface to Blackness: Text and Pretext," one of the three papers Gates contributed to the seminar. See note 21 of this chapter for more information on these papers.

11. Many events that transpired in the three years following the Yale seminar would significantly affect the question of curricular integrity and the situation of the humanities in the university. In 1978, the president of Stanford, Richard Lyman, became engaged in two major projects: (a) the immediate revision of the Stanford undergraduate requirements, which was formulated as a response to what was perceived as the intellectual barrenness of current undergraduate academic studies; and (b) the chairmanship of the Rockefeller Foundation's committee on the humanities in America. The products of both projects proved provocative and of considerable consequence to the debate about the status of non-Western fields of scholarship.

In 1979, Harvard enacted the sort of curriculum revision planned at Stanford. One year later, in January 1980, Lyman was hired as head of the Rockefeller Foundation. He assumed his responsibilities in July of that year, and his chair as president of Stanford was filled by provost Donald Kennedy, who in September 1980 oversaw the enactment of the major curriculum revisions proposed under Lyman in 1978. Those revisions consisted of a required yearlong freshman course in the humanities entitled "Western Culture," with a reading list of fifteen texts divided into three epochs: ancient, medieval/Renaissance, and modern. In addition all undergraduates were required to take at least one course in each of seven broad areas covering the humanities, the social sciences, and the natural sciences. These requirements were defined as the core curriculum of Stanford, whose function, according to Kennedy, was "to focus students on some similar issues, so that we really get a large group of people grappling with the same set of problems together" [consensus/community, scientific method; see "Stanford's Place in the Sun," *Newsweek* 95, no. 26 (30 June 1980): 70].

Also in September 1980, the Rockefeller Foundation's committee on the status of the humanities in America published its findings in a controversial report, "The Humanities in America." The committee's diagnosis was that the decline in the humanities was due in large part to a failure of the university to fulfill its social role as retainer and transmitter of culture, specifically humanistic values both ethical and aesthetic. The proposals that the report recommended for resolving this situation amounted to a significant reorganization of labor within the university structure. The argument was that this reorganization would effectively overcome existing discipline boundaries that the Rockefeller Foundation's committee saw as encouraging overt specialization at the expense of broad cultural understanding. Among the more salient of the committee's recommendations were: (1) cross-disciplinary research and teaching between the professional and social science disciplines and the humanities, in order to reinvest the former two with a historical sense of purpose and an ethical foundation; and (2) the redirecting of humanities research so as to be more immediately pertinent to contemporary concerns and thereby making humanities graduates more marketable beyond the sphere of academia. Interestingly enough, while resurrecting the humanist concept of the humanities as the study of an idealized canon that provides the ethical and cultural grounds for serious learning, the report makes those same humanities a service program, subordinate to the interests of the professional schools. The latter recommendation, with its attendant assertion that humanities graduate programs that were not translatable into market terms be eliminated, caused the greatest disturbance in academia.

The proposed reorganization of knowledge into theoretical and historical learning followed by professional training, recalls the organization of the German university into the Lower and Higher Faculties in the seventeenth and eighteenth centuries. As Kant pointed out in his *Der Streit der Fakultäten* (The Strife of the Faculties), the principal danger in this organization is that it produces an intelligentsia (apparatchiks, or as he called them *Geschäftsleute*, "businessmen" of the university) who are inclined to regard the function of the Lower Faculty to be the legitimization of professional doctrine. This expectation can result in an attack on the academic freedom (*lehrfreiheit*) of the Lower Faculty either through direct state intervention into the affairs of the university, as happened in Prussia under Friedrich Wilhelm II, or through the complete subjugation of work in the service faculty to the interests of the professional schools, a tendency currently under way in the United States.

12. Cotton Mather, *Magnalia Christi Americana* (Cambridge, Mass.: Belknap Press, 1977), 6.

13. At Yale this curriculum consisted of the first year of study in Latin, Greek, Hebrew ("the Three Learned Languages"), and logic. The second year continued study in the languages along with rhetoric, geometry, and geography. The third year was devoted to natural philosophy, astronomy, and mathematics. The fourth year was given to metaphysics and ethics. See Yale Laws of 1745 in Richard Hofstadter and Wilson Smith, *American Higher Education*, 2 vols. (Chicago: The University of Chicago Press, 1961), 1: 54.

14. In 1788 Benjamin Rush recognized the proportional relationship between a centralized educational system and the republic's success. See *Letters of Benjamin Rush* (Princeton: Princeton University Press, 1951), 1: 491-95.

15. The University of Michigan, chartered in 1817, stands out as the exception. At the time of its charter, Judge Augustus B. Woodward proposed a curriculum that he designated *catholepistemiad*, and in which he sought to embrace an encyclopedic range of the sciences, including "*anthropoglossica*, or literature, embracing all the epistemiim, or sciences, relative to language" (Hofstadter and Smith 1: 189-92).

16. See "Minutes of the Board of Visitors of the University of Virginia during the Rectorship of Thomas Jefferson, Wednesday, April 7, 1824," in Hofstadter and Smith 1: 230-31.

17. See "The Yale Report," in Hofstadter and Smith 1: 278; emphasis in the original.

18. As I indicated in note 1, Hegel presupposed the putting-together of thought, Reason, and *Geist* (Spirit), such that philosophy's contemplation of history reveals Reason self-knowingly manifesting itself in the world as World History. To the extent that Dilthey conceived of *Geisteswissenschaften* as the delineating of the universal constituents of such knowledge in a rigorous science of knowledge (*wissenschaft*), the final purpose of *Geisteswissenschaften* is the actualization (*Wirlichkeit*) of thought as history. I want to be careful here to distinguish between Hegel's radically Idealist project of actualizing the Idea as the Absolute, "History," and Dilthey's project of actualizing the Idea in the particular, "history." The distinction is a subtle one; in both projects the Idea is the thought of Reason. Although Dilthey's *Geisteswissenschaften* intends as its object field history as the particular, its privileged object of study is thought in the abstract, that is, "Thought." In this sense of the particular actualization of the Ideal, the *Geisteswissenschaften* are "*histories* of Thought." Then again, insofar as the objective of Dilthey's project is a universal system of methodological rigor, his human sciences also aim at a materialist "History of Thought."

19. David Hoeveler, Jr., *The New Humanism and America* (Charlottesville: University of Virginia Press, 1977), 114.

20. For an elaboration of this agenda, see Houston Baker, Jr., *Blues, Ideology and Afro-American Literature* (Chicago: University of Chicago Press, 1984).

21. In addition to "Preface to Blackness: Text and Pretext," which appears under the heading *Afro-American Literary History* and "Binary Oppositions in Chapter One of Narrative of the Life of Frederick Douglass, an American Slave, Written by Himself," under *Theory in Practice*, Gates contributed "Dis and Dat: Dialectic and the Descent," included in the section *Black Figurative Language*.

Besides writing the introduction to the volume, Stepto contributed the essays "Teaching Afro-American Literature: Survey or Tradition, The Reconstruction of Instruction," under *Afro-American Literary History*, and "Narration, Authentication, and Authorial Control in Frederick Douglass' Narrative of 1845," under *Theory in Practice*.

The essays by Williams and O'Meally are, respectively, "The Blues Roots of Contemporary Afro-American Poetry," and "Frederick Douglass' 1845 Narrative, The Text Meant to Be Preached." O'Meally contributed one other essay, in the section *Afro-American Literature and Folklore*, "Rift and Rituals: Folklore in the Work of Ralph Ellison," making him the only other staff faculty at the seminar to have more than one essay presented in the published proceedings. Williams's and both of O'Meally's essays are better examples of the sort of cross-disciplinary work that prevailed in American studies during the 1950s and 1960s than are the more obvious studies in theory by Gates and Stepto, but O'Meally's piece on Ellison does handle Ellison's notions of polytextual cultural production.

22. As is apparent from Fisher's reference to the "critical issues collected here in the essays of Part I" (173), in distinction to the section *Afro-American Literature Course Designs*, the book was conceived, if not realized, in two parts: critical theory and pedagogical practice. The implication is that *Theory in Practice* was to function as the mediating moment, the reflective pause that "connects" theory and practice. This is made all the more interesting by the fact that it is the one part of the book dedicated to a single text, and that text is Douglass's slave narrative.

23. Arna Bontemps, "The Negro Contributions to American Letters," *American Negro Reference Book*, ed. John Preston Davis (Englewood Cliffs, N.J.: Prentice-Hall, 1966).

24. In her introduction to *Slavery and the Literary Imagination*, Deborah McDowell went so far as to observe that it is chiefly as a result of the efforts of Henry Louis Gates, Jr., the Yale school's most prolific writer, that the notion of slave narratives' having an over-whelming literary value for both Afro-American and American literary studies has become accepted enough for the English Institute to include a session on "Slavery and the Literary Imagination" in its 1987 program. That acceptance was firm enough to warrant the papers of that session being published in the English Institute's *Selected Papers from the English Institute* series. Whether McDowell had in mind Gates's work in Afro-American canon formation, or his dedicated efforts at delineating a singularly Afro-American literary theory, both amount to one and the same project. Gates's rigorously close reading of the slave narrative looms in the foreground of his gathering, editing, and republishing of seri-alized nineteenth-century romances written by Afro-Americans, and his elaboration of the rhetorics of Signifyin(g). See Deborah E. McDowell and Arnold Rampersad, eds., *Slavery and the Literary Imagination* (Baltimore: Johns Hopkins University Press, 1989).

25. Henry Louis Gates, Jr., "Introduction: The Language of Slavery," *The Slave's Narrative*, ed. Charles T. Davis and Henry Louis Gates, Jr. (Oxford: Oxford University Press, 1985), xxii. This book, planned and edited by Gates in collaboration with Davis, is an unusual and impressive collection of literary analyses and criticism of slave narratives, comprising disparate readings that span 132 years of publication. This ambitious scholarly project of editing organizes the eclectic collection of critical readings in such a way that a coherent story of the history of the critical response to slave narratives is made possible.

26. For more information on literacy in eighteenth- and nineteenth-century Futa Djallon and Bundu, see J. Suret Canale and Boubacar Barry, "The Western Atlantic Coast to 1800," *History of West Africa*, eds. J. F. A. Ajayi and Michael Crowder (London: Longman, 1976), 490. The perception of Islam as a class-specific cult in West Africa is adequately under-mined by someone like the eighteenth- and nineteenth-century Futa Djallon scholar and pedagogue Lamen Kebe, who around 1845 described for the American ethnologist Theodore Dwight, Jr., an extensive public school system that produced a rather wide-spread Arabic as well as Fulani literacy. Such a perception of Islam is equally threatened by E. W. Blyden's 1870 report to H. M. Schieffelin (Liberia's chargé d'affaires to the United States) on how widespread Arabic literacy was in the Senegambia. This literacy did not disappear when enslaved Africans from this region were brought to the New World, as is attested to by the Brazilian treasure trove of Arabic legal treatises and declarations associ-ated with the eighteenth-century slave revolt in Bahia, as well as the Arabic manuscripts of 'Abd-ur-Raḥmān, Ben Ali, 'Umar ibn Said, and Abū Bakr as-Siddiqi.

27. Thus far, I have used the phrase Afro-American, in order to recall the term of inter-vention current in 1977. I deliberately use the phrase African American in place of Afro-American at this juncture to remark the juxtaposition of geographical and historical constructs entailed in the concept of "Black American" identity. I prefer African American over Afro-American, Black American, or African-American, because all of these terms conflate the two nouns into one substantive through the hyphen, displacing the ideological stakes in the construct. Both "Afro" and "Black" are subsumed under the defining term "American." This is more graphically apparent with "Afro," an abbreviated form. Prevalent convention writes "black," in the lower case, which also graphically underscores its subordination to "American." The subordination situates the "Afro" and the "Black" somehow outside of, or on the periphery of, the historical event, "America." At the same time they are not situated anywhere else in history or geography. Neither "Afro" nor "Black" is necessarily situated in Africa. "Afro" did not appear in Johnson's dictionary, and first appeared in the *Oxford English Dictionary Supplement*, which consists of words coined between February 1884 and April 1928. According to its entry in this source, "Afro"

first occurred in English in 1890 with the founding of the Afro-American League in Ann Arbor, Michigan. By 1898 it had become commonplace, and by 1910 was adopted by the English, appearing in Sir H. H. Johnston's book *The Negro in the New World.* "Black" is a problematic reference to Africa because the Australoids in the Indian subcontinent, southeast and southwest (Yemen) Asia, and the Pacific islands are all "Black," but none of them Africans. Nor are all Africans descriptively black. As a signal of cultural difference, "Black" is too bound to its opposite, "non-Blackness" (the extent to which this is an effect of a particular ontology is elaborated in chapter 4 of this book). The terms "Afro" and "Black" are thus effects of the American experience, but they are disowned effects, with no historical domain or geographical field of operation. "African American," on the other hand, with its space rather than a hyphen, foregrounds the incongruity entailed in the notion of a cultural identity that is American without effecting America. "African American" pronounces the absurdity of conceiving the American story of cultural development as unilinear. Except when quotations require otherwise, African American will be employed from this point on in my text.

28. Kant presents a rather slim outline sketch of "the History of Reason" (*Die Geschichte der reinen Vernunft*) as the concluding chapter of *Critique of Pure Reason.* Although it is a much more substantial discussion of the subject, his subsequent 1794 essay in *Beliner Monatsschrift* (November), "Idea of a Universal History from a Cosmopolitan Point of View" ("Idee zu einer allgemeinen Geschichte in Weltbürgerlicher Absicht"), is no less theoretical in its scope.

29. For an insightful handling of Schelling's thinking on art see David Simpson's foreword to F. W. J. Schelling, *The Philosophy of Art,* trans. Douglas W. Stott (Minneapolis: University of Minnesota Press, 1989).

2. Critique of American Enlightenment

1. *The Slave's Narrative* is one of the last completed projects in Davis's illustrious scholarly career. He died two weeks after the book was contracted by Oxford University Press. It does indeed, as Gates hopes it will, stand as a testament to Davis's critical vision.

2. John W. Blassingame, *The Slave Community: Plantation Life in the Ante-Bellum South* (New York: Oxford University Press, 1972).

3. The key issue in these discussions is what theoretical model of the text is the appropriate basis for the analysis of slave narratives. Blassingame's critique of how historians in the field of the antebellum South failed to use slave narratives was primarily directed at the methodological tools of historians. It targeted the literary basis of historical analysis (i.e., methodologies of reading modeled on the written word). See John Blassingame, "Using the Testimony of Ex-slaves: Approaches and Problems," *Journal of Southern History* 41 (November 1975): 477.

4. Phillips first dismissed slave narratives as being of dubious value in *American Negro Slavery* (1918) and elaborated the grounds for their dismissal in terms of their questionable authenticity in *Life and Labor in the Old South* (1929) (Blassingame, *The Slave Community* vii).

5. Only thirty-four of the seventy-six were written before 1860; twenty-six of these, or 76 percent, were written by fugitive slaves.

6. The other two are material trace, which is the focus of archeology as well, and traditional material, taken to be information transmitted orally, or through practice, a euphemistic classification for the "preliterate" [see "History," *Encyclopaedia Britannica,* 15th ed. (1989), 20: 636]. The *Encyclopaedia Britannica's* classificatory schema, which is taken in large measure from Collingwood's *The Idea of History* (1946), reflects a historicist bias and gives ascendancy to the written document, because it is, on the one hand, more

verifiable than traditional sources, and on the other, more contextualized than material traces. This, of course, is the monumentalization of the document that Michel Foucault remarked as being already foreclosed on in his introduction to *The Archeology of Knowledge*. See Michel Foucault, *The Archeology of Knowledge*, trans. A. M. Sheridan Smith (New York: Pantheon Books, 1972).

7. The literary document is differentiated from the official in that it consists of events perceived through the eyes of an individual; the official consists of records produced in transacting business at any level from individual to international. Again this subdivision of the written document serves to present the possibility of historical objectivity, achieved in the neutrality of perspective, i.e., enforced methodological standards.

8. Henry Louis Gates, Jr., *Signifying Monkey: A Theory of Afro-American Literary Criticism* (New York: Oxford University Press, 1988), 130.

9. See Foucault, *Archeology of Knowledge*, 6-7.

10. Examples of this are the books by William Andrews, *To Tell a Free Story* (1986); Houston Baker, Jr., *The Journey Back* (1980) and *Blues, Ideology and Afro-American Literature* (1984); Henry Louis Gates, Jr., *The Slave's Narrative* (1985), *Signifying Monkey* (1988), and *Figures in Black* (1987); Valerie Smith, *Self-discovery and Authority in Afro-American Narrative*; and Robert Stepto, Jr., *From Behind the Veil* (1979).

11. As I argued in chapter 1, the 1977 Yale seminar on African American literary theory, at which Gates played a dominant part, established a school of thought about linguistic-based theories of literary history. Near the beginning of his introduction to *The Slave's Narrative*, "The Language of Slavery," Gates rehearses the principles on which he and Davis compiled the book. The first principle is that "[no] written text is a transparent rendering of 'historical reality' . . . the slave's narrative has *precisely* the identical 'documentary' status as does any other written account of slavery" (xi; emphasis in the original).

12. It is obvious at this point that it is African American literary theory that is enabled by "literary theory." The reciprocal nature of their dependencies, however, is discernible in the institutional history of theory. I've argued in the introduction that the emergence of Black studies in the midsixties facilitated the ascendancy of theory by opening up the issue of field delineation. Theory's translation into cultural studies has been achieved through the success of African American literary theory (among others, like feminist theory) in establishing a legitimate canon of texts.

13. See Wlad Godzich's foreword to Didier Coste, *Narrative as Communication* (Minneapolis: University of Minnesota Press, 1989). I am indebted to Didier Coste personally for first introducing me to this notion of the necessity of narrative form in 1984.

14. Stepto published *From Behind the Veil* in part to challenge what he perceived to be the prevalent way of teaching African American literature through non sequitur chronologies that trivialized African American literary developments by making them subservient to sociopolitical history and marginalized from other American literary developments. He presents the book in its introduction as a study that is intentionally "far more critical, historical and textual than bibliographical, chronological, and atextual" (ix).

15. Northrop Frye, *Anatomy of Criticism* (Princeton: Princeton University Press, 1957), 162.

16. Basic Eclectic Narrative is that in which external authenticating documents and strategies are appended to the tale. Basic Integrated Narrative is that in which the authenticating documents and strategies are integrated into the tale, formally becoming voices and/or characters of the tale. In the Generic Narrative, the authenticating documents and strategies are totally subsumed by the tale, so that the narrative becomes an identifiable generic text (e.g., autobiography). In the Authenticating Narrative the tale is subsumed by

the authenticating strategy, so that the narrative becomes an authenticating document for other generic texts (e.g., novels, histories) (*From Behind the Veil* 5).

17. Stepto gets this from Geoffrey Hartman's *Beyond Formalism* (New Haven: Yale University Press, 1970), in particular the chapter entitled "Towards Literary History" (356-86).

18. Cf. Geoffrey Hartman, *Saving the Text* (Baltimore: Johns Hopkins University Press, 1982), xx.

19. A good example of the effectiveness of such a tropology is Gates's developmental history of the trope of the Talking Book, whose revisions he follows through five slave narratives: those of James Albert Ukawsaw Gronniosaw (1770), John Marrant (1785), Ottobah Cugoano (1787), Olaudah Equiano (1789), and John Jea (1815). In summary, Gates abstracts principally from the narratives of Gronniosaw, Cugoano, Equiano, and Jea a story of the slave narrative's formal development, in accordance with a specific historical necessity: the slave's need to achieve humanity in writing. This necessity is articulated in the tropology of the slave narrative, beginning with Gronniosaw, who institutes the Talking Book as a metaphor for humanity and civility. Even though Gronniosaw's narrative is the second slave narrative published in English, preceded ten years earlier (1760) by the narrative of Briton Hammon, Gates holds it to inaugurate more clearly the genre of the slave narrative because of its author's use of the repeated figure of literacy training to unify his tale's structure (*Signifying Monkey* 132). This is followed by Cugoano's transposing of the metaphor as an allegory of story-telling (Marrant's narrative serves more or less as a bridge between Gronniosaw and Cugoano). Equiano then transposes Cugoano's allegory into the act of narrative self-fashioning, which is finally transposed by Jea as an allegory of reading. In the articulating of the trope's transpositions Gates subverts historiography's ideology of the past and articulates an alternative historiography of "Signifyin(g)," which is Gates's transcription of the same popular rhetorical practice generally called "signifying." The development of Signifyin(g) is achieved through the chain of improvisations on antecedent figures forged through Gates's reading of the five earliest English-language slave narratives. Jea's narrative is the final link in that chain; it is the culminating erasing improvisation because there are no subsequent Signifyin(g) plays made on his revision. Accepting this for the moment, Gates presents pragmatical reasons for no further revision on Jea's revision. Jea's "turn to the supernatural" put the trope completely out of range for subsequent nineteenth-century narratives more concerned with employing the figure of literacy as an indication of the African American's enlightened secular civility. This required that such narrators as Frederick Douglass figure a completely new original trope of literacy that would give them credibility in a way that Jea's figure of divinely inspired literacy could not. The post-Jea Signifyin(g)s, Douglass's in particular, "figured primarily in tropes of writing rather than speaking," constituting a "displacement of the eighteenth-century trope of the Talking Book." Yet, by the same token, narratives like Douglass's signify upon the same Great Chain of Being as did those of Gronniosaw, Cugoano, Equiano, and Jea. And they did so in the same manner by writing, and in that writing challenging the same received order of Western culture, "since writing, according to Hume, was the ultimate sign of difference between animal and human" (*Signifying Monkey* 167). Gates does not resolve or mitigate this inconsistency in his history of Signifyin(g); the erasure of the Talking Book with Jea's revision is merely presented as an arbitrarily determined disruption in the chain of Signifyin(g)s on the Western privileging of writing as the sign of civilization and culture. This determination is justified on religious grounds: Jea's representing the scene of literary instruction in terms of a supernatural redemption primarily for the converted Christian does not make for a believable narrative or narrator striving for secular freedom (see *Signifying Monkey*).

20. Antonius Gullielmus Amo, *Treatise on the Art of Philosophizing with Sobriety and Accuracy Composed in Accordance with His Academic Lectures Together with an Essay Concise and Exact on Criticism, Interpretation, Method: The Art of Disputation and Other Matters Dealt with in Logic* (Halle: Martin Luther University Halle-Wittenberg, 1968; originally published 1738), 233-41.

21. Amo exhibited sympathies for the philosophy of Christian Wolff throughout his professional career, even though he never studied with Wolff. Wolff had already been chased out of Halle by the Pietists the year before Amo's matriculation on 9 June 1727. Amo left Halle in 1739, the year before the king's prohibition against Wolff was lifted. There is no evidence of Amo's ever having corresponded with Wolff. On the other hand, there is also no evidence that Amo had any affiliation with the Francke Foundation. Locher is of the opinion that Amo's belonging to the Augsburg Confession made him as much an anathema to the Pietists as was Wolff. Amo defended his thesis on international law, *De jure Maurorum in Europa*, at Wittenberg in November 1729 with the Pietist Johan Peter von Ludwig as chair. On 2 September 1730, he was promoted to the academic degree of Magister of Philosophy and the Liberal Arts (which by 1731 was called a Doctor of Philosophy). He lectured at Halle on the political thought of Wolff until 1739, which as Locher notes was rather courageous given the king's prohibition on Wolff enforced at Halle until 1740. It may be because of this apparent Wolffianism that Amo left Halle under pressure from the Pietists in June 1739. He took up lecturing at the University of Jena in the Faculty of Philosophy on 17 July 1739.

22. In Homeric Greek *nomos* had the sense of field, pasture, or range, as in Herodotus's description of the functions of the gods, who are so called "because, putting them in order, they held all things and all *nomai*," meaning all fields of activity. *Nomos* also meant the human formulation of events normally occurring in the world (*Physis*) as custom and ritual, as in Herodotus's account of the sanction of custom.

23. See Wlad Godzich's foreword to Paul de Man, *Resistance to Theory* (Minneapolis: University of Minnesota Press, 1986), xiii.

24. This may appear somewhat confusing to us now because our conception of theory is determined by a different scheme of opposition. Since Kant the term "theory" has been used to mean a system of concepts that aims to give a global explanation to a realm or field of knowledge, and it is usually opposed to praxis by virtue of its being speculative knowledge.

25. The point is to discover in the oppositional politics of the slave narratives the traces of a critical reflection on representational being. As Gates writes in *The Slave's Narrative*: "Perhaps the most remarkable facet of the texts of the slaves in the South is the copious corpus of narrative that the black slave wrote 'Himself,' or 'Herself,' as the narratives' subtitles attest. When, in the history of slavery, have the enslaved reflected upon his [*sic*] own enslavement by 'representing' its hideous contours through the spoken and the written arts? Representing the institution of slavery, in the sense of mimesis, implies indictment, but it also implies something of the representativeness of the slave narrator himself vis-à-vis his 'experience' of slavery as well as his relationship to other slaves. To the day of his death, for example, Frederick Douglass was fairly popularly known as 'The Representative Colored Man of the United States.' Just *how* 'representative' was Frederick Douglass? The unmentioned term in this Emersonian description, however, was 'most'; Douglass apparently was held by his fellows to be most 'presentable.' And he was most presentable because of his unqualified abilities as a rhetorical artist. Douglass achieved a form of *presence* through the manipulation of rhetorical structures within a modern language" (xxiii).

26. Henry Louis Gates, Jr., *Figures in Black: Words, Signs, and the "Racial" Self* (New York: Oxford University Press, 1987), xxii.

27. When discussing the first moment of his critical development, "the Black Aesthetic," Gates summarizes the debate over the function of literature in relation to political struggle as entailing two positions. One held that Black literary criticism should valorize political and economic analysis, and the other held that there should be a Black Aesthetic that repudiates White literary methods and theories. From these two premises he delineates "all sorts of colorful and impassioned corollaries . . . notably that the history of black literature in this country splits along a great divide: those artists who represent 'the Black Experience' most realistically or mimetically, and those who represent it metaphorically or allegorically" (*Figures in Black* xxvi). This call for social realism betrays the extent to which the Black Aesthetics movement was Romantic: artistic expression, above all else, must reflect the history of (Black) consciousness. Such a consciousness is historicist rather than historical.

28. See chapter 4 of *Figures in Black*, "Frederick Douglass and the Language of Self": "When I choose to call these selves [of Douglass] fictive, I do not mean to suggest any sense of falsity or ill intent; rather, I mean by fictive the act of crafting or making by design, in this instance a process that unfolds in language, through the very discourse that Douglass employs to narrate his autobiographies. . . . To Douglass the autobiographer, his life was the vehicle for a social program. Accordingly, he served as editor and censor of even the smallest bits of data about his life until he rendered them in language as part of the public self that he spent forty-seven years retouching. . . . It is fairly simple to show that these lives of Douglass have at their foundation the idealist premise of the individual belonging to the realm of the transcendent, beyond further analysis" (103, 106, 112).

29. This is finally the sense of mimesis that Gates has in mind, and on which he amply elaborates in chapter 5 of *Signifying Monkey*, "Zora Neale Hurston and the Speakerly Text," where he artfully demonstrates the revising of the trope of the Talking Book, as the figure of the absented voice, into the trope of the Speakerly Text, as the figure of a present voice. This is done within the context of "the search for a voice in black letters [that] became a matter of grave concern among the black literati, [that] led to remarkably polemical debates over the precise register which an 'authentic' black voice would, or could, assume" (171). Gates characterizes the debate about register as having assumed two poles by the close of the nineteenth century. He holds that the first of these, which valued the extent to which the representations in literature imitated reality, was firmly established by the end of the Civil War; the second pole, more properly concerned with register as a question of the linguistic means by which a writer employs relations of meaning, and of discursive configuration, became predominant at the turn of the century. These poles eventually coalesce in an aesthetic confrontation over the appropriate narrative strategies of representation.

The political and epistemological stakes vested in this aesthetic confrontation are well summarized in W. E. B. Du Bois's article "Criteria of Negro Art" in *Crisis* 32 (1926): 290-97. That summary is useful for understanding the significance of Hurston's innovations in register, as well as the violently negative reaction they produced among certain African American writers and critics. For Du Bois, artists (and especially literary artists) were ideologues, not as producers of false consciousness, but as the producers of a whole new *body* of knowledge derived from the lived experience of the Negro. Literary artists were the manifestants of the Negro intelligentsia, the "Talented Tenth," who were to provide the prescription for the Negro's malaise. Artists were to serve the constitution and solidarity of the actual historical Negro community. Cultural production should generate "sound" cultural values, which would serve as the basis for a reeducation of the whole population, whose mentalities and habits were determined under a previous and now antiquated economy: feudalistic slavery. All of this was to be achieved through as accurate as possible

302   NOTES TO CHAPTER 2

representation of the objective reality of the Negro's unfailing moral strength in the face of the daily struggle with abjection at the hands of white America. Any such solidarity, grounded as it is in objective (realistic) representation, must construe the correct register for the authentic Negro voice as being that which assures the correspondence of representation to reality. The epistemological apparatus of such a realism must include a special relation between belief and its object, which enables the discernment of true and false beliefs, of fact and fiction. Combination of belief with its object obtains by natural and not merely logical means. Thus, artistic activity relies upon the assumption that a determination of the objective nature of things can be made.

This insistence on the correspondence of representation to reality resulted in a notion of social realism. As Gates remarks, the discursive medium through which that realism could be posited was found in Paul Lawrence Dunbar's use of "Black dialect" as the basis of poetic diction. Dunbar's use of dialectic facilitated the development of an aesthetic theory that "indissolubly linked" the mode of representation with the referent of representation. Once this was achieved, the debate over what linguistic means a writer should use for representation came to focus on the question of how the perceived antecedent properties of a given discourse affected its integration into the text. Gates situates his reading of Hurston's *Their Eyes Were Watching God* in the context of the concern with the political and ideological function of representation that he calls "mimetic principles," slipping back into an Aristotelian conception of narration as a third middle genre of rhetoric, in order to "show that Hurston's text is the first example ... of the speakerly text" (180). The "speakerly text" is that text "whose rhetorical strategy is designed to represent an oral literary tradition ... to emulate the phonetic, grammatical, and lexical patterns of actual speech and produce the illusion of oral narration" (180).

30. Ralph Ellison, "The Essential Ellison," interview, *Yard Bird Magazine* (1978): 155; emphasis in the original.

31. See Ellison's most recent book, *Going to the Territory* (New York: Random House, 1986), for a fuller sense of how this is his chief figure for African American literary expression and theory.

32. With considerable critical sophistication Gates names the movement of chiasmus at play in Ellison's figure of geospatial movement: "Ellison reverses Bontemps' claim about the narratives, detail by detail. Perhaps anticipating an Ellisonian revision ... Bontemps implies that the structural patterns implicit to the slave narrative were simultaneously formal *and* cultural; and whereas relations of content are readily initiated, borrowed, or derived, relations of form are not only implicitly ideological, but also shared, or 'collective,' despite the intention or conscious desires of an author. ... Bontemps argues that the evidence is to be found in these texts themselves. Where Ellison, curiously, places a priority upon 'experience,' Bontemps maintains that we know 'experience' through our canonical texts, which, taken together, will to the tradition what we think of as received *textual experience*" (*The Slave's Narrative* xx; emphasis in the original).

33. Ralph Ellison, "On Bird, Bird-Watching and Jazz," *Saturday Review* (July 28, 1962), reprinted in Ellison, *Shadow and Act* (New York: Random House, 1964), 231-32.

34. Ralph Ellison, "Blues People," *The New York Review* (February 6, 1964), reprinted in *Shadow and Act*, 249-50.

35. Ralph Ellison, "And Hickman Arrives," in *Black Writers of America*, eds. Richard Barksdale and Kenneth Kinnamon (New York: Macmillan, 1972), 704.

36. Gates has a different reading of this than I do. He reads "Patterns of movement" as Ellison's periphrasis of Bontemps. This enables him to read in Ellison's denial that *Invisible Man* has any necessary formal indebtedness to slave narrative a confirmation of Bon-

temps's view that all African American literature is formally indebted to slave narratives in some way.

37. See "A Song of Innocence," *The Iowa Review* (Spring 1970); "Cadillac Flambé," *American Review* (1973); "Juneteenth" and "The Roof, the Steeple and the People," *Quarterly Review of Literature* (1965 and 1960); and "It Always Breaks Out," *Partisan Review* (Spring 1963).

38. Ralph Ellison, "Society, Morality, and the Novel," *Going to the Territory* 239-40, 242.

39. F. O. Matthiessen, *American Renaissance* (New York: Oxford University Press, 1941).

40. Jonathan Arac, "F. O. Matthiessen and American Studies: Authorizing a Renaissance," *Critical Genealogies: Historical Situations for Postmodern Literary Studies* (New York: Columbia University Press, 1989), 157.

41. Arac attempts a redemption of "certain emphases and practices" of *American Renaissance* obscured in large part through Trilling's representation of Matthiessen's role in American studies, by finding in Matthiessen's "rejecting the cultural treasures of Holmes, Longfellow, and Lowell to rescue once-marginal writers as Emerson, Thoreau, Hawthorne, Melville, and Whitman," a resemblance to Walter Benjamin's canon-shifting interventionist strategy of fighting "for the oppressed past" of literary history in order to redeem what was stigmatized and suppressed as minor (Arac 174). As Arac also acknowledges, however, there is a fair amount of what Benjamin considered the "barbarism" of preserving cultural treasures in Matthiessen's defining a canon of American literature around these five authors (174).

42. In any event, Matthiessen felt that the answer to the question of why the popular taste of the nineteenth century was so poor lay outside the parameters of literary study and criticism: "Such material [as the popularity of women's sentimental novels] still offers a fertile field for the sociologist and for the historian of our taste" (xi). The sentimental novel and the slave narrative, therefore, are not even to be regarded in terms of their literariness, but rather in terms of their value as documents of historical taste, of importance to the historian and sociologist. This was a task beyond the concerns of *American Renaissance*, in which Matthiessen continues the cultural criticism based on combining moral and political virtues with New Critical formalism, which he began to develop in *The Achievements of T. S. Eliot* (1935). *American Renaissance* was explicitly proclaimed to be as historical as it was formalist. In it Matthiessen debunked the historian's bias that he attributes to some of Parrington's disciples, a bias that he feels divorces critical aesthetics from the history of ideas, and hence charges it with being mere "belletristic trifling" (ix). As Arac recounts, the very title of the book was related to the Communist party line of the Popular Front (which emphasized defending the cultural heritage, including the bourgeois-produced masterpieces) and indicated its profound political stakes.

43. Ralph Ellison, "Remembering Richard Wright" and "Going to the Territory," in *Going to the Territory* (198-216; 120-145).

44. This is a recurrent theme in most of Ellison's critical writings and interviews, e.g., "Beating That Boy," "The Art of Fiction," "A Very Stern Discipline," and "Perspective of Literature," and the central argument of one of his two essays completely dedicated to the topic of literary history, "Society, Morality and the Novel" and "The Novel as a Function of American Democracy," both of which are in *Going to the Territory* (239-74, 308-20).

45. For this and more complex reasons involving Genette's conception of narrative voice, Philippe Lejeune holds that the problems of autobiography must be considered in relation to the proper noun. See Philippe Lejeune, "The Autobiographical Contract," *French Literary Theory Today*, trans. R. Carter (Cambridge: Cambridge University Press, 1982), 198-200.

46. See Philippe Lejeune, *Le pacte autobiograpique* (Paris: Éditions de Seuil, 1975), 198-99.

47. It should also be obvious at this point that to reject theory as a vandalizing of African American culture is to hold forth a rather pathetic African American culture, a sort of massively disseminated kitsch.

48. At one level Gates is repeating the scholastic distinction between *exercite* and *signate*, whereby *exercite* refers to the effect, or exercise, of an act (say, seeing itself), and *signate* refers to the intention of the exercising agent. At another .level, the transformation into signification founds another intentional object: the meaning of the experience. It is this other intentional object that is at play in Gates's conception of figures as the constitutive field of experience.

49. In conjunction with Blassingame's efforts, the 1970s saw a small flourish of selective anthologies and historical studies of slave narratives, which, by and large, approached them in terms of their function as historical documents, as grounds for legitimate research dealing with how slaves lived, thought, and formed mental (discursive) representations of their own lived experience as slaves. See, for example, the work of Julius Lester, *Search for a New Land: History as Subjective Experience* (1969); Gilbert Osofsky, *Puttin' on Ole Massa* (1969); Stanley Feldstein, *Once a Slave* (1971); George P. Rawick, *From Sundown to Sunup: The Making of the Black Country* (1972); Stephen T. Butterfield, *Black Autobiography in America* (1974); Charles Perdue et al., eds., *Weevils in the Wheat* (1976); and Francis Smith Foster, *Witnessing Slavery* (1979). This flourish indicated a significant addition to the object field in the historiography of slavery, but it did not indicate that there had been a facile movement from one dominant methodological position on the reading of slave narratives to another. Most of these critical studies of slave narratives tended either to disregard or to obfuscate the problematics of meaning production, linguistic expression, entailed in slave narratives.

50. A degree of resemblance between this notion of theory and that found in I. A. Richards's *Principles of Literary Criticism* is vividly portrayed in the way Houston Baker, Jr.'s explicit privileging of the poetic image echoes a fundamental ontological presupposition implied in Richards's *Principles*, the notion that language can say any experience. As with Richards's notion of theory, this one too is predicated on the idea of a perpetual consciousness of the object and an experience of this consciousness. Paul de Man has already shown the "considerable difficulties" that Richards encounters when attempting to work out a correct form of this experience; see de Man, "The Dead-End of Formalist Criticism," *Blindness and Insight* (Minneapolis: University of Minnesota Press, 1983), 23. Chief among these difficulties is the questionable existential status of the originary experience. What in Baker's theory is taken as given, for example, "a self-conscious narrator of African ancestry," is shown to be a constructed narrative persona, constituted through the signifying functions of literature's linguistic structures; see Baker, "There Is No More Beautiful Way: Theory and the Poetics of Afro-American Women's Writing," *Afro-American Literary Study in the 1990s*, ed. Houston Baker and Patricia Redmond (Chicago: University of Chicago Press, 1989), 146-47. In this instance, instead of reflecting authorial experience, language is shown to constitute it, and a theory of constituting form is altogether different from a theory of signifying form (*Blindness and Insight* 232). Richards will be compelled by this view of language's constructive capacities to insist that criticism does not deal with any material object but with the experience (or consciousness) of the object. This originary mental experience is reflected in the substantial form that it is given in language. Form functions as a sign that refers back to the initial experience, thus legitimating form's treatment as a signifying object whose study will provide the contour of the initial experience of the object (*Blindness and Insight* 233). As the sign of the originary experience, form becomes the legitimate object of study. It thereby legitimatizes the development of a taxonomy of literary expression that will obfuscate the role of the critic in the constitution of the "originary"

experience, and so preserves the autonomous literary work, which otherwise threatens to dissolve in the notion of language's participatory constitution of the critical object.

3. Writing Culture in the Negro

1. Francis Bacon, *Novum Organum*, trans. R. Ellis and James Spedding (London: Routledge & Sons Ltd., 1861; originally published 1620). Gates reads this passage, along with one from Peter Heylyn's *Microcosmus* and one from Morgan Godwyn's *The Negro's and Indians Advocate*, as a representative example in support of his asserting that "since the Renaissance in Europe, the act of writing has been considered the visible sign of reason," and that "this association has been consistently invoked in Western aesthetic theory when discussing the enslavement and status of blacks" (*The Slave's Narrative*, xxiii-xxiv).

2. Morgan Godwyn, *The Negro's and Indians Advocate, Suing For their Admission into the Church. Or, a Persuasive to the Instructing and Baptizing the Negro's and Indians in our Plantations. Shewing that as the complying therewith can be no Prejudice to any Man's just Interest; so the willful Neglecting and Opposing of it, is no less than a manifest Apostacy from the Christian Faith* (London: J.D., 1680).

3. As a Christian religious tract, the ultimate purpose of Godwyn's text was evangelical, the preaching of the gospel to Negroes. In order to achieve this purpose, the objections (in particular the religious and moral objections of the planters) had to be overcome by persuasion through reason. Hence, the three general assertions according to which Godwyn ordered his book:

> 1. Chapter 1: "That *the* Negro's [*sic*] (both Slaves and others) have naturally an equal Right *with other Men to the* Exercise and Privileges *of* Religion; *of which 'tis most unjust in any part to deprive them.*"
>
> 2. Chapter 2: "*That the* profession of Christianity *absolutely obliging to the promoting of it,* no Difficulties *nor Inconveniences, how great soever, can excuse the* Neglect, *much less the* hindering *or* opposing *of it, which is in effect no better than a renunciation of that profession.*"
>
> 3. Chapter 3: "*That the Inconveniences here pretended for this Neglect, being* examined, *will be found nothing such, but rather the contrary.*" (Emphasis in the original.)

4. Janhneinz Jahn, *Neo-African Literature: A History of Black Writing* (New York: Grove Press, 1968), 15, 21.

5. The poetic success of Juan Latino, the professor of Rhetoric Greek and Latin at Granada, seems to have prompted a reappraisal of the Negro's image in Spanish Golden Age literature from that of ineloquent buffoon to erudite citizen, as evidenced in Lope de Vega's *La dama boba*, which did much to humanize the image of the Negro in Spanish theater. In 1620 Diego Jiménez de Enciso (1585-1634), a disciple of Lope de Vega, composed a play devoted to Latino, *La comedia famosa de Juan Latino*. Still, Latino's panegyric, which was directed at the power structure of the emerging Spanish state, by and large fit the pattern of sixteenth-century panegyric codified by Julius Caesar Scaliger (*Poetices libri septem;* Lyons, 1561), although two couplets in his "de faelicissima serenissimi Ferdinandi principis nativate" indicate racial pride and resentment of color-based discrimination. The most frequently discussed of his verses, however, is "Austriadis librio duo" (1572), dedicated to Don Juan of Austria for his role in defeating the Turkish navy at Lepanto.

6. English was not the sole language of expression by any means. Alvarenga Silva and Barbosa Caldas produced between them seven panegyrics in Portuguese between 1774 and 1798. The expression of contradiction was more prolific in English, however. Between

1746 and 1798, in addition to the already-mentioned poetry of Wheatley, the *Letters* of Sancho, and the four slave narratives of Hammon, Gronniosaw, Cugoano, and Equiano, there were twelve English-language writings produced by slaves. In 1746 Lucy Terry wrote a single poem of escape. In addition to her book of poems, Wheatley published an elegiac poem in 1770. Jupiter Hammon produced two versed broadsides, *An Evening Thought: Salvation by Christ with Penitential* (1761) and *An Address to Miss Phillis Wheatley, Ethiopian poetess, in Boston, who came from Africa at eight years of age, and soon will be acquainted with the gospel of Jesus Christ* (1778); two sermons, *An Address to the Negroes in the State of New York* and *A Winter Piece*; and a short piece consisting of an essay and poem, *An Evening Improvement. Shewing the Necessity of Beholding the Lamb of God, to which is added a Dialogue entitled. The Kind Master and Dutiful Servant* (1790). John Marrant's captivity and conversion narrative, *A Narrative of the Lord's wonderful dealings with John Marrant*, was published in 1785. Marrant also published a sermon (1789) and a journal (1790). The publication of Absalom Jones and Richard Allen's *Narrative of the Proceedings of the Black People during the Late Awful Calamity in Philadelphia in the Year 1793. A Refutation of Some Censures Thrown upon them in some late Publications* was in 1794, and Venture Smith's *A Narrative of the Life and Adventures of Venture Smith* appeared in 1798. During the eighteenth century, then, a total of eighteen prominent English-language writings were produced by African Americans and Anglo Africans. Thirteen of these were published in the twenty-eight years spanning 1770 and 1798.

7. James Albert Ukawsaw Gronniosaw, *A Narrative of the Most Remarkable Particulars in the Life of James Albert Gronniosaw, An African Prince, as Related by Himself* (Leeds: Davies and Booth, 1811).

8. Gates reads the trope of the Talking Book's emergence in this thought of Gronniosaw at this moment of abandonment and alienation; see *Signifying Monkey* 139.

9. Gates notes the following of Gronniosaw's conversion: "The Christian text that had once refused to acknowledge him he had by sixty mastered sufficiently not only to satisfy and persuade others by his eloquence 'that I was what I pretended to be,' but also to interweave within the fabric of his autobiographical text the warp and woof of Protestant Christianity and the strange passage from black man to white. The presence found in Gronniosaw's own text is generated by the voice, and face, of assimilation" (*Signifying Monkey* 139).

10. Ottobah Cugoano (né John Stuart), *Thoughts and Sentiments on the Evil and Wicked Traffick of the Slavery and Commerce of the Human Species, Humbly Submitted to the Inhabitants of Great-Britain, by Ottobah Cugoano, a Native of Africa* (London: Dawsons of Pall Mall, 1969).

11. Isabella to Ovando, 20 December 1503, *Colección de documentos inéditos relativos al descubrimiento, conquista y organización de las antiguas posesiones espannñolas*, ed. Joaquín Francisco Pacheco, 42 vols. (Madrid: Cárdenas and Mendoza, 1864-89), 31: 209-12; cited in Lesley B. Simpson, *The Encomienda in New Spain* (Berkeley: University of California Press, 1966), 13.

12. The Castilian *encomienda* was a temporary grant by the sovereign of territory, cities, towns, castles, and monasteries with the power of dominion. As this was granted as a charge of government by the Crown, the *encomendero* was to exercise the authority of the Crown; he was the royal representative in the area. The *encomienda* in Hispañola resulted in the Indians' being reduced to possessions of the land subject to the *encomenderos* who kidnapped and enslaved the natives as a sovereign right.

13. The Burgos Junta was not a *cortes* or any other kind of representative institution of the three Castilian estates—nobility, clergy, and town. It was an institution of professional lawyers in the service of the Catholic Monarchs, Ferdinand and Isabella.

14. The first letter written by Cortés to Charles V is not in either of the two known extant manuscript compilations of Cortés's *Cartas*, the Madrid manuscript and the Vienna Codex; it has never been found. See José Valero Silva, *El legalismo de Hernán Cortés como instrumento de su conquista* (Mexico: n.p., 1965), 31-35, cited in Hernán Cortés, *Letters from Mexico*, trans. Anthony Pagden (New Haven: Yale University Press), liv. The Vienna Codex, discovered by William Robertson in 1777 in the Österreichische Nationbibliothek in Vienna, contains what is commonly called the *Primera Relación* (the first narrative account, or first letter). This was not written by Cortés, nor is it the first letter to which he refers in his second letter. It is the letter sent by the municipal council of Vera Cruz to Charles V (*Carta de la Justicia y Regimiento de la Rica Villa de la Vera Cruz a la Reina Doña Juana y al Emperador Carlos V, su Hijo, en 10 de julio de 1519*) that gives the account of the circumstances of the expedition leading up to the popular incorporation of the *comunidad* and Cortés's appointment as *alcalde mayor*. The second letter, which was the first that Cortés wrote, provides a protoethnographic account of the material and religious culture of Yucatán, in further evidence that the interests of Vera Cruz are the emperor's, and that its principal agent, its *alcalde mayor*, is also the emperor's principal agent in Yucatán and so warranted designation as the *Adelantido* of Yucatán on behalf of *dominium jurisditionis*. In his descriptions of Mexico, Cortés is careful to draw analogies between the material culture of Mexico and that of African Spain. The principal Aztec cities of Cempoal and Tenochtitlán are compared to the principal Moorish cities of Granada, Seville, and Córdoba in terms of architecture and construction material; their inhabitants are compared to Africans in terms of intelligence and orderly conduct. By these analogies Motecuçoma's realm is represented as a highly cultured, materially wealthy, civil domain. Motecuçoma himself is translated by Cortés into the analogue of an African (Moorish) prince, so that his submission at Cortés's hand to Charles V is transcribed as an act of donation. That acknowledgment authorizes the literal translation of Tenochtitlán into an imperial capital, and Mexico into New Spain. These translations are legitimated by the emperor's decree of 15 October 1522, which named Cortés as *Adelantido* of New Spain. In other words, New Spain is a legal fiction (domain of villas) first brought into being in writing—*relaciones* being the authorized form for representing the acts and events of conquest, whose authority as knowledge-conveying was a function of writing as a disinterested medium of transmission. See Georges Baudot, *Utopie et Histoire au Mexique. Les premieres chroniquers de la civilisation mexicaine (1520-1560)* (Toulouse: Privat, 1976).

The Vienna Codex also contains the only known extant manuscript of the fifth letter. According to Pagden, a sixteenth-century copy of the fifth letter is at the John Carter Brown Library (lix). Pascual de Gayanos published all five letters together for the first time in 1866, based on the Madrid manuscript. In 1960 Manuel Alcalá published a new edition of all five texts, based on the Vienna Codex (Pagden lx). Pagden's own English-language translation of all five texts is also largely based on the Vienna Codex.

15. See, for example, Victor Frankl, "Imperio particular e imperio universal en las cartas de relación de Hernán Cortés," *Cuadernos Hispanoamericanos* (1963); and Manuel Alcalá, *César y Cortés* (Mexico City: Publicaciones de la Sociedad de Estudios Cortesianos, 1950).

16. See Eulalia Guzmán, *Relaciones de Hernán Cortés a Carlos V sobre la invasión de Anáhuac* (Mexico: Editorial Oribon, 1958).

17. Henry de Bracton, *De Legibus et Consuetudinibus Angliae*, ed. G. Woodbine (New Haven: Yale University Press, 1915-42), 2: 32-33. Hence Cortés's famous response to the emperor's man, Cristóbal de Tapia, "I obey but do not comply."

18. Given the Castilian monopoly of Indies exploration and trade, reinforced by Pope Alexander IV's 1493 bulls, receiving the license of conquest from the Spanish state presupposed membership in the Spanish nation.

19. As one of Vitoria's pupils, Melchor Cano, put it in 1546, Vitoria's argument rendered the Castilian Crown analogous to a beggar to whom alms were due, but who was not empowered to extract them; see Melchor Cano, *De dominio indorum*, fols. 301-3v, as cited in Anthony Pagden, "Dispossessing the Barbarian: The Language of Thomism and the Debate over the Property Rights of the American Indians," in *The Language of Political Theory in Early-Modern Europe*, ed. Anthony Pagden (London: Cambridge University Press, 1987), 89.

20. This view was also held by Vitoria's contemporary and fellow Dominican, Juan Maldonado. Addressing the University of Burgos in 1545, Maldonado described the Indians as ignorant "of the world not because they lacked reason, but because they lacked culture, not because they lacked the will to learn or a ready mind, but because they had neither tutors nor teachers" (Melchor Cano, *De dominio indorum*, as cited in Pagden, "Dispossessing the Barbarian," 89).

21. Nelson Goodman, *Ways of Worldmaking* (Indianapolis: Hackett, 1985), 20.

22. Olaudah Equiano, *The Interesting Narrative of the Life of Olaudah Equiano, or Gustavus Vassa, the African, Written by Himself*. In *The Classic Slave Narratives*, ed. Henry Louis Gates, Jr. (New York: Mentor Books, 1987).

23. After nearly seven months of enslavement in Africa with his birth name intact, Equiano apparently was first given an English name at some point en route to Virginia: "on board the *African Snow* I was called MICHAEL" (39). Once he reached Virginia he was called Jacob. He insisted on being Jacob when first onboard the *Industrious Bee*, but Pascal beat him into submission, and Gustavus Vassas remained his English name.

24. The term horror will not occur in the narrative again until chapter 2, where it is repeated continually from the moment of Equiano's first encounter with Whites when he was "quite overpowered with horror and anguish" (32).

25. Kant's theorizing on the experience of the sublime will crown these attempts. Through the unbridling of Imagination he demonstrates that cognition, even in the first instance of perception, is free from any natural determination.

26. Jean-Jacques Rousseau, *The Confessions of Jean-Jacques Rousseau*, trans. J. M. Cohen (New York: Penguin Books, 1953; originally published 1781). Rousseau remarks in book 7 of *Confessions:* "The true object of my confessions is to reveal my inner thoughts exactly in all the situations of my life. It is the history of my soul that I have promised to recount . . . " (262).

27. Rousseau opens the first part of his *Discours sur les sciences et les arts* with a lengthy reflection on the deceptive corruptibility of refined, civilized aesthetics. After calling on the arts and sciences to "claim their share in the salutary work of confusing appearance with being," he offers a supplementary thought (*une réflexion*) that plainly conveys the extent to which the constraints that define society are no more than pure relations of appearance that do not mirror man's true state of being. This he does by first opening his *Discourse* with an unambivalent rehearsal of the Enlightenment's commonplace positive assertions about emancipation through reason and the rule of law: the natural progress of man is grounded in his liberated reason; reason must displace, through the mediation of the liberal arts and sciences, the enslaving regression of doxa, and so emancipate man. However, the liberal arts and sciences that Rousseau describes, the very modes by which the Enlightenment would emancipate man from his enslavement to deceptive doxa, are then exposed—in their tendency to serve the social good in the provision of man's security and well-being in his common life—as reproducing an even more powerful deception than doxa: the deception of holding reality to be attainable through its appearances. Thus, the refined civilization of the Enlightenment, through "the effects of a taste acquired by liberal studies and improved by conversation with the world [promises] an air of philosophy

without pedantry . . . an address at once natural and engaging [but] appearance, in the guise of rigorous formalized method, obfuscates its dissimilarity from being." With this Enlightenment refinement, appearance comes to occupy all significance, such that the primal innocence of natural man whose expressions forever present the relation of appearance to being is lost. As far as Rousseau was concerned, the scandal was less the difference of appearance and being than the forgetting of the difference—a forgetting that he strove to overcome through embodying thought in writing. See Jean-Jacques Rousseau, *Discourse on the Sciences and Arts*, trans. and ed. Victor Gourevitch (New York: Perennial Library/ Harper & Row, 1986; originally published 1750), 4-11.

28. This act is clearly remarked in the slave narratives like those of Frederick Douglass, Mary Prince, and William (Box) Brown, where the slave steals her or himself in order to define and conserve the self.

29. Both Equiano and Douglass portray their people as existing in a state of illusionary ignorance. For Equiano, it is a state of blissful ignorance, idyllic in its "naturalness." For Douglass it is a function of survival, a protection against consciousness of how really bad their lot is (see chapter 3).

30. Paul de Man, *Allegory of Reading: Figural Language of Rousseau, Nietzsche, Rilke, and Proust* (New Haven: Yale University Press, 1979), 3.

31. This point is well illustrated in Valerie Smith's *Self-discovery and Authority in Afro-American Narrative* (Cambridge: Harvard University Press, 1987). In this work the concept of writing as being always in some way determined by experience, whose meaning is inextricably linked to the way it is embodied in language, is brought to bear on a reading of the narratives of Olaudah Equiano, Frederick Douglass, and Harriet Jacobs that tries to account for the complex generic situation of their production; see especially pages 6-7.

32. We need only recall that in his *Introduction to the Philosophy of History*, Hegel explicitly excludes Africa from the dialectic, on the grounds of the primitiveness of the Negro.

33. "Race has become a trope of ultimate, irreducible difference between cultures, linguistic groups, or adherents of specific belief systems which—more often than not—also have fundamentally opposed economic interest"; see Gates, "Writing 'Race' and the Difference It Makes," *Race Writing and Difference*, ed. Henry Louis Gates, Jr., special issue of *Critical Inquiry* 12, no. 1 (1985): 5.

34. This is not to suggest that African American literary theory will inevitably yield a doctrine of the black sign—negritude—that in turn will serve as the legitimating basis for asserting the autonomy of African American literary theory. Houston Baker, Jr., attributes the failure of the Black Aesthetics movement to such an attempt at legitimacy. The liberation of the black man from the suffocating categorical restrictions of modernity cannot be gained through self-recuperation via the aesthetic. To do so would amount to offering little more than the operation of a nonpredicative subject that could only entomb itself as pure *eidos*. Rather than overcoming the alienation brought on by the violence of Western culture, such a rarified black essence reinforces it by extending the distance between consciousness and reality.

35. The project of canon formation's investment in emancipatory gestures lies with this exploration of the "curious dialectic" between formal language and the inscription of metaphorical difference. As Gates states in *Black Literature and Literary Theory* (New York: Methuen, 1984), "to draw upon contemporary theories of reading, both to explicate discrete black texts and to define the precise structure of the Afro-American literary tradition itself by attempting to link in Geoffrey Hartman's phrase, the form of art and the form of its historical consciousness. I have been concerned, in other words, with that complex relationship between what is useful to call 'the representative' in black letters and its modes of representation, of mimesis" (3). Attention is paid to exposing language's culpability as the

sign of those insidious economies of subordination and exclusion that make the Negro what it is, but what interests Gates far more is inscription, viz., effecting an intervention into the nominal discourse of theory, wherein literacy becomes "the emblem that links" racial and economic alienation ("Writing 'Race' " 6).

36. Harold Bloom has read in Emerson's hypostatizing of literary expression a quest for the historicity of consciousness, which is a particular American burden that prefigures American cultural history such that all post-Emersonian poets are subject to the "same irreconcilable acceptance of negation"; see Bloom, *Anxiety of Influence: A Theory of Poetry* (New York: Oxford University Press, 1973), 137.

37. The question remains: If historicization is an inevitable process, and if field delimitation—equally essential for the instituting of an academic discipline—is predicated on it, how can a field be delimited in a way that foregrounds historicization, and so is highly instable without dissolving?

38. Gates has redrawn and charted this line of the trajectory in numerous tellings throughout his critical writings. The frequency and progressive refinement of his redrawing of this line attest to its importance for his ongoing attempt to define an African American literary theory. A discussion of this line of the trajectory was first published in his introduction to *The Slave's Narrative*, and it is retold with virtually no modification in his introduction to the 1987 anthology *The Classic Slave Narratives* (New York: Mentor, 1987). It later becomes abridged as the epigraph and subtext of the fourth chapter, "The Trope of the Talking Book," of his theoretical text *Signifying Monkey*, the second volume of a trilogy that treats the nature and function of African American literature and its criticism. Unquestionably the most polished and coherent telling occurs in the first chapter of *Figures in Black*, "Literary Theory and the Black Tradition," the first volume of this trilogy.

4. Critique of Genealogical Deduction

1. Insofar as it is exemplary of the fully developed slave narrative's formally describing the conditions of emancipation, Equiano's *The Interesting Narrative of the Life of Olaudah Equiano or Gustavus Vassa, the African, Written by Himself* is the prototypic text against which Frederick Douglass's 1845 *Narrative* links the acquisition of literacy to the process of liberation; see *The Classic Slave Narratives*, ed. Henry Louis Gates, Jr., xiii-xiv. And Douglass's text is held to be paradigmatic of the handling of this theme in subsequent African American narratives. For those who have tried to achieve the institutionalization of African American literature through the delimiting of a field and canon based on the slave narrative, it is in Douglass's slave narrative that identity, transcribed in the personal pronoun "I," first signifies the agency and collecting together of experience into significant representations constituting a manifestly complex formal discursive existence.

2. Caleb Bingham, *The Columbian Orator: Containing a Variety of Original and Selected Pieces; together with Rules; calculated to improve Youth and Others in the Ornamental and Useful Art of Eloquence* (Boston: Manning & Loring, 1804).

3. Douglass, in fact, attributes the second piece to the eighteenth-century British elocutionist, Thomas Sheridan, who, like Charles James Fox and William Pitt (two other orators included in Bingham's book whom Douglass claimed impressed him strongly), was an early opponent of slavery. Bingham only included one sample of oratory from Sheridan in *The Columbian Orator*, a fragment of a speech made before the British Parliament against one Mr. Taylor about a particular order of law. Bingham's *The Columbian Orator* was so popular a pedagogical tool in the first half of the nineteenth century that when Douglass acquired his secondhand copy from Mr. Knight of Thames Street in 1831 it was already in its seventeenth edition. None of these editions, however, contains a speech by Sheridan for

Catholic emancipation. Douglass's misattribution of this piece is not without consequence. Dickson J. Preston, in his *Young Frederick Douglass: The Maryland Years* (Baltimore: Johns Hopkins University Press, 1980), has drawn attention to the fact that *The Columbian Orator* was the principal source of Douglass's oratory stye. It was a book that Douglass kept with him from 1831 throughout his life, and he knew it well enough by 1835 to use it as a teaching text for some of his fellow slaves in the clandestine school he opened while hired out to work William Freedland's farm (Preston 96-100, 131). It is highly unlikely, then, that the misattribution was the result of the sort of lack of familiarity with a text scanned but not consumed that often leads to the misplacing of titles and authors. Douglass knew this book well. Preston corrects Douglass's misattribution without comment, appearing to treat it as the effect of a legitimate association of the work of Fox, Pitt, O'Connor, and Sheridan, based on their mutual commitment to individual freedom. In light of his own research, however, Preston's treatment of Douglass's attributing O'Connor's speech to Sheridan as an error of ideological association doesn't hold, particularly given the radical differences in length and topic between their respective representations in *The Columbian Orator*. I am inclined to read this "error" as a misnaming rather than a misattribution, that is, Douglass is signify(ing) on Sheridan. This reading is supported somewhat by the subsequent argument I make in this text for Douglass's engaging in a nonlogocentric writing. This is not the place for the sort of critical engagement with Sheridan's theory of language required in order to demonstrate adequately that it is the object of Douglass's critique. It is worth noting, however, that Sheridan in his *Lectures on Elocution* (London: Strahan, 1762) builds a study of elocution founded on John Locke's theory of language: words are the signs of ideas, and tones are the signs of passions.

4. Frederick Douglass, *Narrative of the Life of Frederick Douglass, an American Slave, Written by Himself* (New York: Signet Classics, 1968), 54-55; emphasis added.

5. Frederick Douglass, *My Bondage and My Freedom* (New York: Dover Publications Inc., 1969).

6. As already pointed out in chapter 3, the question of natural law and natural rights is always at issue in the writing of New World slave narratives.

7. In Gates's tropology of the Talking Book, Jea's slave narrative marks the erasure of the trope (see note 19 of chapter 2). Accordingly Gates defines Douglass's 1845 *Narrative* as the first of those post-Jea slave narratives that no longer employs the trope of the Talking Book. Taking Gates's example seriously, through his readings of Gronniosaw et al., of how an account of African American literary history is feasible through charting the modes of revision of one trope, I discover in Douglass's narrative the formal development of the same sort of nonrepresentational concept of literariness and literacy involved in Jea's concept of reading. That is to say that in Douglass's slave narrative it is possible to perceive the degree to which Jea's revision, rather than erasing the trope of the Talking Book, enhances its parodying effect. In this sense Douglass's text is an instance of Jea's bridge, as it were.

8. Immanuel Kant, *Observations on the Feelings of the Beautiful and Sublime*, trans. John Goldthwait (Berkeley: University of California Press, 1960), 113; quoted in *The Slave's Narrative* xxvi, with emphasis added by Gates.

9. In fact, Hume was not any more tactful than Kant in his judgment of Williams's writing verse in Latin. Humes's following assessment of the Negro's capacity for intellectual work is taken from his essay "Of National Characters," *Essays and Treatises on Several Subjects*, 4 vols. (Basel: J. J. Tourneissen, 1793): "I am apt to suspect the negroes and in general all the other species of men . . . to be naturally inferior to the whites. There never was a civilized nation of any other complexion than white, nor even any individual eminent either in action or speculation. No ingenious manufacturers amongst them, *no arts, no sci-*

ences. On the other hand, the most rude and barbarous of the Whites, such as the ancient Germans, the present Tartars, have still something eminent about them, in their valour, form of government, or some other particulars. Such a uniform and constant difference could not happen, in so many countries and ages, if *nature* had not made our original distinction betwixt these breeds of men. Not to mention our colonies, there are Negro slaves dispersed all over Europe, of which none ever discovered any symptoms of ingenuity. . . . In Jamaica, indeed they talk of one Negro as a man of parts and learning [Francis Williams]; but 'tis likely he is admired for very slender accomplishments, like a parrot who speaks a few words plainly" (3:252, n.1; emphasis in the original).

10. All German citations of the *Beobachtungen über das Gefühl des Schönen und Erhabenen* are from *Kants Werke*, ed. Ernst Cassirer, 11 vols. (1764; Berlin: Bruno Cassirer, 1914). Unless otherwise indicated, the English translations are from *Observations on the Feelings of the Beautiful and Sublime*, trans. John Goldthwait (Berkeley: University of California Press, 1960). The passage cited by Gates occurs in *Beobachtungen* 298, and *Observations* 113.

11. Kant remarked later in his life that the *Beobachtungen* was an empirical study in which he did not lay down a theory of aesthetic judgment; see *Kants gesammelte Schriften*, Königkich Preußische Akademie der Wissenschaften (Berlin: Walter Gruyter & Co., 1902), 1–192.

12. The German text of the first sentence of this passage reads as follows: "Die Negers von Afrika haben von der Natur kein Gefühl, welches über das Läppische stiege." In section 2 of *Observations*, "Of the Attributes of the Beautiful and Sublime in Man in General," Kant asserts that he who is *Läppische* ("trifling, silly, small as in foolish") has the feeling of the beautiful which lacks altogether any nobility. The lack of nobility is further compounded by the Negroes of Africa's having such a strong proclivity for ceaseless chatter "that they must be driven apart from each other with thrashings." In this regard the Negroes of Africa are like the driveling (*Faselt*) fool (*Albern*) of section 2. The lack of nobility is so great in the Negroes of Africa that they have absolutely no capacity for any feeling of the sublime. In this assessment of the Negroes of Africa Kant gives us almost a verbatim resume of Hume's argument that "Negroes [are] naturally inferior to the Whites."

13. Immanuel Kant, *Kritik der reinen Vernunft*, ed. Raymund Schmidt (1926; Hamburg: Felix Meiner Verlag, 1971), 51; B18. Henceforth referred to parenthetically as *KrV*. Unless otherwise indicated, English translations from the German, with occasional modifications of my own, are from *Critique of Pure Reason*, trans. Norman Kemp Smith (New York: St. Martin's Press, 1965), 55. Henceforth referred to parenthetically as *CPR*.

14. Immanuel Kant, *Prolegomena to Any Future Metaphysics*, trans. James Ellington (Indianapolis: Hackett, 1977), 11. The full German title and source of the citation is *Prolegomena zu einer jeden künftigen Metaphysik, die als Wissenschaft wird auftreten kännen*, in *Kants Werke*, ed. Ernst Cassirer, 4:1. I have modified the translation.

15. Immanuel Kant, *Metaphysical Foundations of Natural Science*, trans. James Ellington (Indianapolis: Hackett, 1985), 6. The German citations are from *Metaphysische Anfangsgründe der Naturwissenschaft*, in *Kants Werke*, ed. Ernst Cassirer, 4:371.

16. *Metaphysical Foundations of Natural Science* is ordered into four chapters: "Metaphysical Foundations of *Phoronomy*," "Metaphysical Foundations of *Dynamics*," "Metaphysical Foundations of *Mechanics*," and "Metaphysical Foundations of *Phenomenology*." The first chapter deals with the quantity of motion (e.g., velocity, rest, orientation), where motion is defined as the changing of a thing's external relations to a given space. The second chapter deals with matter in terms of force (*kraft*) of resistance: Kant delineates two kinds of force, attractive ("that moving force whereby a matter can be the cause of the approach of other matter to itself . . . or equivalently, whereby it resists the withdrawal of other matter from itself") and repulsive ("that whereby a matter can be the

cause of making other matter withdraw from itself . . . or equivalently, whereby it resists the approach of other matter to itself"). Both forces entail resistance, and the conjunction of that resistance enables matter. See *Metaphysical Foundations*: Explication 2, 482; Dynamics Explication 2, 498; Dynamics Proposition 2, 499; Dynamics Proposition 5, 508; and Dynamics Proposition 6, 510.

17. Later in this chapter I will address in more detail the relationship of the Labat story to Kant's assessment of the Negroes of Africa, but, because our attention has been initially drawn to the Labat story by Gates, it is sufficient at this moment to point out that the aesthetic judgment that Kant alleges that the Negroes of Africa lack has its basis in a transcendental principle. What Kant represents Negroes to be lacking is feeling (*Gefühl*), involving the purely indeterminate disinterested judgment that he calls "aesthetic judgment" in the *Critique of Judgment* (aesthetic in the sense of the judgment of taste as the pure form of judgment as the a priori basis of thought as well as intuition). The Negroes of Africa are not being represented as devoid of thought, but are held to be incapable of the purity of thought that expands the soul and liberates the Imagination from the limitations of sensible intuition, and which makes theoretical knowledge possible. That is to say that Negroes are represented as far too sensual to be capable of achieving that emancipation gained solely through Reason.

18. Although this sense of enthymeme is somewhat different from Aristotle's use of the term as a rhetorical syllogism, consisting of probable premises (Aristotle, *Rhetoric*, book 1, 1355a, 6–13; 1356b, 5; and book 2 1394a, 31; 1395b, 20; 1396b, 23; 1400b, 38), it stands in direct relation to his usage in the aspect of probability. In both the Aristotelian and post-Aristotelian logic of judgment, an enthymeme is a categorical syllogism in which the conclusion does not strictly follow from the premises but is merely made more possible by them.

19. I say in conclusion somewhat guardedly, because what Hume presents is a sequence of propositions that are merely probable and are meant to persuade if nothing else. Strictly speaking, Hume's argument is indeed an enthymeme in the Aristotelian sense.

20. Kant's transcendental critique was concerned with the Understanding that passes judgment on the nature of things experienced in the world, and even more particularly with the dynamics of the a priori knowledge by which the Understanding derives the principles of its judgment. Accordingly, the transcendental critique is a propaedeutic to the system of pure reason that he calls transcendental philosophy, which is the idea of a science for which the transcendental critique has to lay down the complete architectonic plan. The only reason that the transcendental critique is not the transcendental philosophy is that the latter would have to contain the whole of a priori human knowledge, whereas the transcendental critique is concerned only with a priori synthetic knowledge. Nevertheless, insofar as the transcendental critique contains all that is essential in the transcendental philosophy, it is the complete idea of that science, although it is not equivalent (*CPR* 61).

21. Dieter Henrich has already effectively argued that what Kant presents under the heading of "Deduction" is not a well-formed chain of syllogistic proof; see Dieter Henrich, "Kant's Notion of a Deduction and the Methodological Background of the First *Critique*," *Kant's Transcendental Deductions: The Three "Critiques" and the "Opus postumum,"* ed. Eckart Förster (Stanford: Stanford University Press, 1989), 57–68. As Henrich points out, Kant is quite explicit about his usage of deduction in the sense of an accounting of the genealogy of the categories of the Understanding, and that this accounting is in the manner and form of what came to be known by the eighteenth century as *Deduktionschriften* (deduction writing).

22. Terence Irwin, "Morality and Personality: Kant and Green," *Kant's Transcendental Deductions: The Three "Critiques" and the "Opus postumum,* ed. Eckart Förster, 31–56.

23. The table is divided into four heads, each of which contains three moments (*Momente*): (1) Quantity: Universal, Particular, Singular; (2) Quality: Affirmative, Negative, Infinite; (3) Relation: Categorical, Hypothetical, Disjunctive; (4) Modality: Problematic, Assertoric, Apodictic.

24. Kant understands the functions of both quantity and quality in the same fashion as the logicians of his period viewed the employment of judgments in syllogisms, with two important differences in technical distinction. According to the "Transcendental Logic," in the function of quantity, singular judgments (*judicia singularia*) are held to be distinct from general, or universal, judgments (*judicia communia*). With regard to quality, infinite judgments must be distinguished from those that are affirmative (*KrV* 93-94; *CPR* 107-8).

Concerning the third function, relation, for Kant all relations of thinking in judgment are either: (a) of the predicate to the subject (in this case only two concepts are being considered, i.e., categorical); (b) of the ground to its consequence (in this case two judgments are being considered, i.e., hypothetical); or (c) of the divided knowledge and of the members of the division, taken together, to each other (here several judgments are being considered in their relation to each other, i.e., disjunctive).

What is thought by the hypothetical judgment is only the logical sequence. The disjunctive judgment, however, does not involve the relation of logical sequence; rather, what is thought is logical opposition, and yet simultaneously community. This involves a plurality of parts in a sphere of knowledge whereby although the parts of that sphere are mutually exclusive of one another, when taken together they constitute the sum total of the divided sphere of knowledge.

Kant gives the following example for the hypothetical: "If there is a perfect justice, the obstinately wicked are punished" ("wenn eine volkommene Gerechtigkeit da ist, so wird der beharrlich Böse wird bestraft"). This contains in fact two propositions, i.e., "there is a perfect justice" and "the obstinately wicked are punished." Whether both these propositions are in themselves true is undetermined. No matter, it is only the logical sequence of the first to the second proposition that is being considered. The example Kant gives for the disjunctive is: "The world exists either through blind chance, or through inner necessity, or through an external cause" ("die Welt ist entweder durch einen blinden Zufall da, oder durch inner Notwendigkeit, oder durch ein äußere Ursache") (*KrV* 73; *CPR* 109).

According to the function of modality, the problematic judgment, in which affirmation or negation is merely possible, is that which expresses only purely logical possibility, making both hypothetical and disjunctive judgments problematic. The assertoric, in which affirmation or negation is viewed as real, deals with logical reality or truth. The apodictic, in which affirmation or negation is held to be necessary, addresses logical necessity.

25. Aristotle's ten categories were substance, quantity, quality, relation, place, time, position, state, action, and affection. Kant's argument against this classificatory scheme was that five of these were actually modes of pure sensibility (i.e., time, place, position, state, and substance), and that one, action, was an empirical concept.

26. As will be seen presently, for Kant, Imagination, unlike Understanding and Reason, has no proper domain in which its rules are delineated. This activity of *apprehension*, this *agencement*, is the function of *reproductive Imagination*. It is "reproductive" because it presupposes the impressions of appearance already being given through sensibility, making it wholly empirical (*KrV* 121; *CPR* 144).

27. If reproduction of representation occurred solely on the basis of Imagination's synthesizing activity, there would be no determinate assemblage of perception, but only an accidental collection that would not give rise to any determinate empirical knowledge.

28. In which case, even though there was an association of perceptions, it would be entirely indeterminate: perceptions would only be accidentally associable. Should associa-

tion not occur, which is possible under indeterminacy, this may very well occasion a heterogeneity of perception in which empirical consciousness would arise, but only in a state of fragmentation or separation without belonging to even a figurative apperception.

29. In a letter to Marcus Herz dated 26 May1789, Kant offers a precise sense of what he means by the Understanding: "I conceive of the Understanding as a special faculty and ascribe to it the concept of an object in general (a concept that even the clearest consciousness of our intuition would not at all disclose)"; see Immanuel Kant, "To Marcus Herz," letter 362 of *Kant: Philosophical Correspondence 1759–1799*, ed. and trans. Arnulf Zwieg (Chicago: University of Chicago Press, 1967), 153.

30. This exposition constitutes chapter 2 of "Transcendental Doctrine of Judgment," "The System of All Principles of Pure Understanding."

31. These four rubrics also serve as the subsection titles to section 3 of "System of All Principles of Pure Understanding," "Systematic Representation of all the Synthetic Principles of Pure Understanding" (*KrV* 161; *CPR* 196). In these subsections Kant presents the principles contained under each title and their proofs. The first two titles have single principles. The principle of axioms of intuition is, "All intuitions are extensive magnitudes" (*KrV* B202; *CPR* 197). The principle of anticipations of perceptions is, "In all appearances, the real that is an object of sensation has intensive magnitude, i.e., degree" (*KrV* 166; *CPR* 201). The single general principle of analogies of experience is, "Experience is possible only through the representation of a necessary connection of perceptions" (*KrV* B218; *CPR* 208). In addition to that principle there are three analogies each with its own principle. The principle of the first analogy is, "In all change of appearances substance is permanent; its quantum in nature is neither increased nor diminished" (*KrV* B224; *CPR* 212). The principle of the second analogy is, "All alterations take place in conformity with the law of causality" (*KrV* B232; *CPR* 218). The principle of the third analogy is, "All substances, insofar as they are perceived to coexist in space, are in thoroughgoing reciprocity or community [*Gemeinschaft*]" (*KrV* B256; *CPR* 233). As for the postulates of empirical thought in general, there are three principles: "(1) That which agrees with the formal conditions of experience is *possible*; (2) That which is bound up with the material conditions of experience is *actual*; and (3) That which in its connection with the actual is determined in accordance with universal conditions of experience, is (that is, exists as) *necessary*" (*KrV* B266; *CPR* 239).

32. "Ein jeder Gegenstand steht unter den notwendigen Bedingungen der synthetischen Einheit des Mannigfaltigen der Anschauung in einer möglichen Erfahrung" (*KrV* 158).

33. According to Kant's argument in "Transcendental Doctrine of Judgment," no synthetic proposition can be made merely from categories, because when intuition is absent from the judgment there is no means for going beyond a given concept or for connecting another concept with it. The intuitions in mind are outer intuitions, that is, intuitions in space and time that involve sensibility.

34. An idea of teleology is already implied in the *Critique of Pure Reason*.

35. The resulting relationship between the three faculties of cognition in the *Critique of Pure Reason* is such that the role of Understanding is to legislate and judge syntheses and schemata (in accordance with the categories), the role of Imagination is to synthesize and provide schemata, and the role of Reason is to reason and symbolize in such a way that knowledge has a maximum of systematic unity. This relation constitutes the famous *sensus communis logicus*, or the common sense of the faculties, in the theoretical interests of Reason.

36. "Die Menschheit in ihrer ganzen Vollkommenheit enthält . . . allein die Erweiterung aller zu dieser Natur gehörigen wesentlichen Eigenschaften, welche unseren Begriff von

derselben ausmachen [und] alles, was . . . zu der durchgängigen Bestimmung der Idee [der vollkommenen Menschheit] gehöret" (*KrV* 568).

37. Kant, *Anthropology from a Pragmatic Point of View*, trans. Mary Gregor (The Hague: Martinus Nijhoff, 1974), 56; emphasis in the original.

38. "Also sind synthetische Sätze a priori nicht bloß, wie wir behauptet haben, in Beziehung auf Gegenstände möglicher Erfahrung und zwar als Prinzipien der Möglichkeit dieser Erfahrung selbts tunlich und zulässig, sondern sie können auch auf Dinge überhaupt und sich selbts gehen; welche Folgerung beim Alten bewenden zu lassen" (*KrV* B410).

39. "Ist eine verborgen Kunst in den Tiefen der mensclichen Seels, deren wahre—Handgriffe wir der Hatur schwerlich jemals abraten und sie unverdeckt vor Augen legen werde" (*KrV* 141).

40. All German citations of this work are from *Kritik der Urteilskraft*, ed. Karl Vorländer (Hamburg: Felix Meiner Verlag, 1924); henceforth referred to parenthetically as *KU*. English translations are from *Critique of Judgment*, trans. Werner S. Pluhar (Indianapolis: Hackett, 1987); henceforth referred to parenthetically as *CJ*.

41. "Definieren soll, wie es der Ausdruck selbst gibt, eigentlich nur so viel bedeuten, als den ausführlichen Begriff eines Dinges innerhalb seiner Grenzen ursprünglich darstellen" (*KrV* 727).

42. The example Kant gives for such confusion is the various characteristics that can be represented in the concept of gold for different subjectivities: "One man may think, in addition to its weight, color, malleability, also its property of resisting rust, while another will perhaps know nothing of this quality" (*KrV* 727; *CPR* 586).

43. "Die deutsche Sprache hat für die Ausdrücke der Exposition, Explikation, Deklaration und Definition nichts mehr als ds eine Wort: Erklärung, und daher müssen wir schon von der Strenge der Foderung, da wir nämlich den philosophischen Erklärungen den Ehrennamen der Definition verweigerten, etwas ablassen und wollen diese ganze Anmerkiung darauf einschränken, daß philosophische Definition nur als Expositionen gegebener" (*KrV* 730).

44. What I wish to briefly draw attention to here is how in Kant's conception of judgmental illusion (appearance) is a problematic that is inherent to the formal properties of cognition. It appears that Imagination's indeterminacy is so threatening that the only way it can be accommodated to the architectonic is as a problematic that drives Understanding to an Ideal focus, albeit a merely postulated one. All such Ideal foci are nothing but merely postulated; and arguably, they are postulated in order to overcome the profound indeterminacy at work in experience. Through his attempt to ameliorate this indeterminacy and ground it in Reason, Kant plots a trajectory of thought that will lead to Hegel's denunciation of heterogeneity as the essential truth of cognition in favor of a primal homogeneity of reflectivity and Idea. But also in this conception of appearance as illusory and theoretically indeterminate, Kant anticipates Marx's critique of Hegel's ideology as illusion. By designating illusory appearance as an inevitable product of cognition's formal processes, Kant has already marked ideology as an essential aspect of human reality.

45. Gates shows that he is fully aware of how historical forms of African American resistance have been incapacitated by their dedication to the psychologism of subjective agency. A privileged example of this for Gates is what he terms "race and superstructure criticism": "What is wrong with employing race and superstructure as a critical premise? This theory of criticism sees language and literature as reflections of 'Blackness.' It postulates 'Blackness' as an entity, rather than a metaphor or sign. Thus the notion of a signified black element in literature retains a certain impressiveness insofar as it exists in some metaphysical kingdom halfway between a fusion of psychology and religion on the one

hand and the Platonic Theory of Ideas on the other. Reflections of this 'Blackness' are more or less literary according to the ideological posture of the critic. . . . In this criticism, rhetorical value judgments are closely related to social values. This method reconstitutes message, when what is demanded is an explication of a literary system" (39).

That critique notwithstanding, and in spite of his accurate characterization of the race and superstructure theory of criticism as being deterministic, demonstrating an "alarming disrespect for the diversity of the black experience itself and for the subtleties of close textual criticism," Gates's own perspective toward the sign maintains an extralinguistic site for agency (*Figures* 39–40). In Gates's theory of criticism that agency, delineated in the force of coherence, the "organizing principles by which a particular view of the world . . . really operates," affords a view of the "network of relations that form a particular aesthetic unity" (*Figures* 40–41). This is the crux of it: "unity" implies a perspective beyond the force, a world which is "maintained by a coherent social group" (*Figures* 41), a principle of *Gemeinschaft* (reciprocity). Which is how any structuralist approach must conceive of its analytical object. All aspects of movement and organization within the "structure" must be accounted for, requiring a system of typology, or poetics. Such a poetics of discourse, insofar as it seeks to discover the determining principle of coherence or community, replaces the psychologism of "man" with that of "culture."

46. In 1984 Allan Austin published a collection of such documents entitled, *African Muslims in Antebellum America: A Sourcebook* (New York: Garland, 1984). He provides a critical assessment of the publication circumstances and history of the Arabic manuscripts (or the translations of Arabic manuscripts) from fifteen American slave narrators. The manuscripts in Austin's collection are unedited and cover a diversity of generic forms, including the following types of Arabic texts: additional epistles of Ayyūb ibn Suleiman Diallo, written in 1734 after his return to Bundu, Futa Toro; the epistles, fragments of Scripture, and autobiographical sketch of 'Abdu-ur-Raḥmān, dated October 10, 1828; the epistles, aphorisms, and fragments of Scripture of 'Umar ibn Said and Abū Bakr as-Ṣiddiqi; and two pages from Ben Ali's manuscript. Along with these unedited Arabic manuscripts, there is a fragment from Bluett's *Memoirs of the Life of Job the Son of Solomon* (Ayyūb ibn Suleimān Diallo), and the English translations of the autobiographies of 'Umar ibn Said (dated 1831) and Abū Bakr as-Ṣiddiqi (written in 1825). The Arabic texts of both these autobiographies have been lost. Also included in the collection is one autobiography originally transcribed in English by Muḥammad Ali ibn Said, as well as numerous attendant documents of commentary, biographical and anthropological interest, and items of correspondence.

47. I have opted for the transliterated Arabic version of Ayyūb's name. To avoid confusion, however, in those instances where I am quoting his contemporaries who used Job Ben Solomon, I follow suit, as well as in those cases where he himself signed as Job Ben Solomon. There is an additional exception to this exception, where the referential confusion is intended. See "A Note on Transliteration" at the front of this book for explanation of my transcription of Arabic proper names.

48. British Public Records Office T, 70/302: 68. Cited in Douglas Grant, *The Fortunate Slave: An Illustration of African Slavery in the Early Eighteenth Century* (London: Oxford University Press, 1968), 88.

49. British Public Records Office T, 70/93: 243. Cited in Grant 89.

50. British Public Records Office T, 70/1424: 18. Cited in Grant 105.

51. Although Ayyūb's 1731 Arabic letter to his father did not lead to his immediate freedom, in the seven-month interim between April and November 1733 Ayyūb's Arabic literacy did gain him considerable honors. He was admitted into the membership of the Gentlemen's Society and into the company of England's intelligentsia. The Gentlemen's Society membership assured his inclusion in John Nichols's *Literary Anecdotes of the*

Eighteenth Century (1812), as well as Alexander Chalmer's *General Biographical Dictionary* (1816) and the *Biographie Universelle*.

52. This is borne out by the subsequent activities of the company agent Francis Moore, and the governor-general of James Fort, Richard Hull. Their activities in Bundu led to the French arrest of Ayyūb after his return to Bundu, which was explicitly justified on the fears that his rapport with the Royal African Company constituted a British incursion into French commercial territories.

53. William Andrews points out that a literary division of labor pervaded the relationship between the slave narrator and the amanuensis-editor from the earliest years of the genre; see William L. Andrews, "The First Fifty Years of Slave Narrative, 1760–1810," *The Art of Slave Narrative: Original Essays in Criticism and Theory*, eds. Darwin Turner and John Sekor (Urbana: Western Illinois University Press, 1982), 6-24.

54. Although slaves could engage in productive wage-labor (as in Douglass's being hired out), they were not productive in the strict sense, because they had no prior right to their labor. As property, they had no property rights, their labor was already entailed in their commodification. The issue of commodification and exchange value was crucial to the maintenance of the plantation economy. In those instances where slaves were able to exploit their own surplus value (their residual labor) in the cultivation of commodity crops, like Saint Dominque, the system was subverted substantially. Cf. Robin Blackburn, *The Overthrow of Colonial Slavery* (London: Routledge, 1988) and C. L. R. James, *Black Jacobins* (New York: Vintage-Random House, 1963).

55. A similar politics of identity is played with regard to ʿAbdu-ur-Rahmān, as well as Ayyūb. ʿAbdu-ur-Rahmān becomes a prince of the king of Timbuctou, and Ayyūb is recognized as a racial mediation between Arabo-Berber and Negro: a Fulani, also known in English as the Foulah.

56. This problem of denotation and thinking will be taken up at length in the conclusion of chapter 5.

57. Recall David Hume's response to Francis Williams's literacy.

5. Africa as a Paralogism

1. William B. Hodgson, *Notes on Northern Africa, the Sahara, and Soudan* (New York: Wiley and Putnam, 1844), 59. Unless otherwise indicated, all citations from work by Hodgson in this chapter refer to this source.

2. Dwight was born in 1796 in Brooklyn, New York. His father, Theodore Dwight, Sr. (1764–1846), was the founder in 1817 of the newspaper *The New York Daily Advertiser*, which became in 1836 *New York Daily Express*. His paternal uncle (Theodore, Sr.'s brother) was Timothy Dwight, the president of Yale, from which Theodore, Jr., graduated in 1814.

3. Reprinted in *The People of Africa*, 2d ed., ed. Henry Schieffelin (Ibadan: Ibadan University Press, 1974), 46–47.

4. As Austin reports, there is another article by Dwight entitled "An Account of the Serreculies, or Serrawallies, with hints respecting several other tribes or families of people composing the Foulah nation," to which reference is made in the 1845 transactions of the American Ethnological Society as a paper read before the society in that year (*The Transactions of the American Ethnological Society* 1 [1845]: xii). I have been unable as of yet to attain a copy of this paper from the Smithsonian, where the papers of the society are archived. It is clear that Austin did not see this paper either. There is very little basis for speculation about its content, whether it was essentially the same essay as "On the Sereculeh Nation in Negrita" or contained new materials. Even ten years later Dwight had not gone to Africa to conduct any fieldwork, so his sources remained secondary. Until this

essay, along with the rest of Dwight's work on the Muslim slaves he interviewed, is brought to light, the extent of what we can know about Kebe through literary sources is chiefly limited to two of Dwight's three published essays: the Lyceum paper and "Condition and Character of Negroes in Africa."

5. Abu 'Abdullah ibn Abdul-'Aẓiz al-Bak i, *Al-Masālik wa al-Mamālik* (Paris: Adrien-Massoneure, 1964).

6. For both of these chronicles, see Lamin Sanneh, *The Jakhanke Muslim Clerics: A Religious and Historical Study of Islam in Senegambia* (Lanham: University Press of America, 1989).

7. See Magbaily Fyle, *The Solima Yalunka Kingdom: Pre-Colonial Politics, Economics & Society* (Freetown, Sierra Leone: Nyakon Publishers, 1979).

8. Pere Jean Baptiste Labat, *Nouvelle relation de l'Afrique occidentale*, 5 vols. (Paris: Cavelier, 1728), 3:335.

9. Dwight reports that Kebe "performed two journeys, when quite young, to the *Jaliba* or Niger river, in one instance in company with an army of Mohamedans in a successful war upon an idolatrous nation, to convert them to Islamism" ("Condition and Character" 51–52). This is a problematical account, considering the time frame Dwight gives for Kebe's enslavement. In "On the Sereculeh Nation in Negrita" Dwight states that as of 1835 Kebe had been in slavery for thirty years. The same time-lapse was given by Breckenridge when he introduced Kebe to the American Colonization Society in January 1835. This would place Kebe's capture sometime around 1805. Yet in "Condition and Character," Dwight states that at his liberation in 1835, Kebe had been enslaved for forty years, which would make the year of his capture around 1795. Given the age Kebe started and completed his education (fourteen and twenty-one, respectively), and that he pursued his career for at least five, possibly seven years in the city of Kaba (Kebe) before being captured, Kebe was anywhere between twenty-six and twenty-eight years old at capture. Following the thirty-year time frame would mean that Kebe's birthdate was somewhere between 1779 (if he was twenty-six) and 1777 (if he was twenty-eight). By the forty-year time frame his birthdate was somewhere between 1769 (if he was twenty-six) and 1767 (if he was twenty-eight). Dwight provides a possible clue for determining the most probable time frame when he reports that Kebe was "quite young" on his first trip to the *Jaliba*. That being the "successful war raid against a neighboring idolatrous country to convert them," one must then determine what war that might have been.

In the immediate aftermath of the Jihad of Karamokho Alfa Ba (around 1730) the Foulah had achieved hegemony over the Djalonké of Djalonkédu and established the constitutional emirate of Futa Djallon. They also had sovereignty over the Djalonké of Solima, who peacefully submitted and broke bread with the Foulahs, and so were obliged to send their princes to Timbo and Lebe for Islamic education, and assist the Foulah in their military ventures. In the early 1760s war broke out between the Samaru of Sankara and the Wusulonké. This intermittent struggle lasted almost two decades. According to Arcin's chronology (which Tauxier followed, and Laing corroborated in his history of the Solimana), in 1763 the Solima Djalonké rebelled by refusing to send military support to Futa in its war against Konde Brima of Sankaran; see Andre Arcin, *Histoire de la Guinée Française* (Paris: Challamel, 1910); Louis Tauxier, *Moeurs et histoire des Peuls* (Paris: Payot, 1937); and Alexander Gordon Laing, *Travels in Timannee, Kooranko and Soolima Countries* (London: Longman, 1825). In response to this act of rebellion, the Foulah executed all but one, Asana Yira (Sori Wuleng), of the Solima elders and princes who were studying in Futa (Fyle 36). This led the Solimana's *kehleh mansa* (warlord), Tokba Asana (whom Arcin, Tauxier, and Laing identify as Tahabaire), to declare war on Futa Djallon and forge an alliance with Konde Brima. The first action of the new allies was to march on and take the

Futa capital of Timbo, during which its mosque, which housed the constitution, was burned (1763). In 1778 (again according to Arcin's chronology) Tokba Asana and Konde Brima launched a major expedition aimed at annihilating Futa Djallon once and for all. This led to the famous battle of the *Sirakouré* (Herico) River, in which the forces of Futa, under the command of Ibrahim Sori, defeated the combined might of Solimana and Saranka, and sacked Falaba. This would make Dwight's Jaliba actually Falaba, and the battle of Ibrahim Sori a more likely candidate for Kebe's youthful war trip. If Kebe was born in 1777/79, then by Arcin's chronology of Futa Djallon, he would have been no more than a year old. The forty-year time frame (1767/69) becomes more probable by default, making Kebe eleven or nine years of age at the battle of *Sirakouré*. This would make him eighteen or sixteen at his capture in 1795, which contradicts the account of his six to seven years of professional service prior to his capture.

There are acute problems with Arcin's and Laing's chronologies. Their dates for the Solimana rebellion, Asana/Brima expedition, and the subsequent Futa sacking of Falaba are at odds with the written chronicles (*tawārīkh*) and oral tradition of Futa Djallon, as well as those of the Solimana. On problems with Arcin's chronology, see *History of West Africa*, eds. J. F. A. Ajayi and Michael Crowder (London: Longman, 1976); for those of Laing, see Fyle. According to the *tawārīkh* and oral traditions, Tokba Asana's rebellion was not in 1763, but in 1778, which is when Timbo was sacked. In 1779 the combined Solimana Sankara forces made an unsuccessful attack on the Foulah religious center of Fugumba. In the year after this defeat, 1780, Tokba Asana became king (*manga*) of Solimana with the death of Yella Dansa, and the Solimana founded their capital beside a branch of the Mongo River, naming both the river and the city Falaba. In 1784 Falaba was attacked by Alifa Saidu (whose identity Laing confuses by transcribing his name as Salou), the son of Karamokho Alfa Ba, who disposed Ibrahim Sori for a short time as Almamy of Futa Djallon. The Foulah were repulsed by Asana (Laing correctly identifies Asana as the *manga* of Falaba at the time of this attack, although he erroneously gives the date as 1797; Walkenare placed the same attack on Falaba in 1795; Terry Alford in his biography of Ibrahim Sori's son 'Abdu-ur-Raḥmān Ibrahima, *Prince among Slaves*, follows Laing's chronology in reporting these events). This disaster led to Ibrahim Sori's reinstatement as Almamy of Futa Djallon, with the major expedition of Tokba Asana and Konde Brima following in 1788, resulting in Sori's victory at *Sirakouré*, the deaths of both Asana and Brima, and the Futa sacking of Falaba. According to the *tawārīkh* chronology of Futa and Solimana, if Kebe was born in 1777/79 he would have been eleven or nine at the time of this battle. If he was born in 1767/69, then he would have been twenty-one or nineteen. Given that he is supposed to have completed his professional studies at the latter age, and that the war raid was to have occurred sometime before he started his professional training, it seems that the forty-year time frame is the most probable. This would also support Kebe's own account of the reason for the trip on which he was captured into slavery. As a turbaned Jakhanké *fiqhi*, Kebe would have been opposed in principle to armed struggle, preferring instead the peaceful dissemination of Islam. In this spirit, to speak of jihad is to speak of revival through scholarship and devotion, not armed war.

10. Reported in the society's *Transactions* of January 1835.

11. *Inventaire de la bibliothèque 'Umarienne de Ségu* (conservé à la Bibliothèque Nationale, Paris), eds. Noureddine Ghali and Sidi Mohamed Mahibou (Paris: Éditions du Centre National de la Recherche Scientifique, 1985). Henceforth referred to parenthetically as *IBUS*, followed by index reference number.

12. M. Hiskett has provided an annotated translation of Abdullah's manuscript in his article "Material Relating to the State of Learning among the Fulani before Their Jihad," *Journal of African History* 19 (1967).

13. Austin erroneously identifies two of these, reading *Nahayi* as "*Nahw* (grammar)," and *Alsára* as "*Surahs*, or chapters of *The Qur'an*."

14. Some philosophical orientalists, such as the American Rescher and the Germans, van Ess and Gätje, as a result of their encountering the term *ma'nā* (from which derives *'ilm-ul-ma'āni*, i.e., rhetoric) in the philosophical texts of al-Fārabī, trace a connection between the Arabic term *ma'na* and the classical Greek *lektòn* through the translation of Greek philosophy into Arabic.

15. Immanuel Kant, *De Mundi sensibilis atque intelligibilis forma et principiis*, in *Kants gesammelte Schriften*, 2:412.

16. In the course of these efforts numerous manuscripts and Arabic writing samples were collected and commented on. Some of these are presented in Austin's collection. More writing fragments are also available in the Hodgson Archives in Savannah, Georgia, and at the Philadelphia Philosophical Society.

17. These are the views which Fredrika Bremer attributes to Couper in her essay "The Institution of Slavery as a Benefit," in *Homes of the New World: Impressions of America*, trans. Mary Botham Howitt (New York: Harper & Brothers, 1853), 488–91. Bremer is very specific about Couper's general views about "the negro race," views that were close to her own: "But as Mr. C[ouper], on the question of slavery, unites with the good party in the South, who regard the colonization of Africa by the liberated negro slaves as the final result and object of the institution of slavery, it was any thing [*sic*] but difficult for me to converse with him on this subject, and that which naturally belongs to it. Neither could I do other than agree with him in the views he expressed regarding the peculiar faculties of the negro race and their future destiny, because they accord with my own observations. . . . Mr. C[ouper] regards slavery in America as a school for the children of Africa, in which they may be educated for self-government on the soil of Africa. He is inclined to look at the institution of slavery as a benefit to them."

As reported by numerous visitors to Hopeton, from Captain Basil Hall to John D. Legare, editor of the *Southern Agriculturalist*, Couper was quite methodical about actualizing the "benefits" of the institution. A severely self-disciplined man, he managed his "people" in a systematic way geared toward obedience, attention, honesty, and orderly behavior. Departure from these parameters of good behavior was promptly punished. It is the opinion of Legare that such punishment was "moderate," an assessment easily enough understood when it is recalled on what side of the stick he stood; see *Southern Agriculturalist* 6 (April 1833): 157–58. The humaneness of this system of punishment derived from its effective control of passion, the passion to which the Negro was natively inclined, passions that Couper sought to control to the extent that he maintained a low protein diet among his slaves in order to rid them of their predilection toward "Crimes of a savage nature" (from the journal of Fanny Kembel Butler, cited in Austin, 360).

18. Marie Armand Pascal d'Avezac-Macaya was vice president of the Société Ethnologique de Paris, the first professional society for what was then the new science of anthropology, and a corresponding member of the American Ethnological Society. According to P. C. Lloyd, d'Avezac was the first ethnographer to make systematic use of the list of professionally oriented desiderata that the Société published in the form of a field questionnaire in 1841. This is held to be the first of such research tools used in ethnology.

19. In *A Theory of Semiotics*, Umberto Eco outlines a typology of modes of sign production that takes into account four parameters: (1) the physical labor to produce expressions; (2) the relation between the abstract type of expression and its token; (3) the type of continuum or material substance to be shaped in order to produce physically an expression; and

(4) the mode and complexity of the articulation. Cf. Umberto Eco, "Producing Signs," in *On Signs*, ed. Marshall Blonsky (Baltimore: Johns Hopkins University Press, 1985), 179.

20. When Ivor Wilks reproduces a portion of Couper's letter in Curtin's *Africa Remembered* he regulates the spellings according to current conventions of English transliteration and orthography, producing *Timbuktu, Jenne,* and *Segu;* see Ivor Wilks, "Sāliḥ Bilalī of Massina," in *Africa Remembered: Narratives by West Africans from the Era of the Slave Trade,* ed. Philip Curtin (Madison: University of Wisconsin Press, 1967), 147–51, passim.

21. All of these letters are reprinted as "The Letters of Major Alexander Gordon Laing," in *Missions to the Niger* (Cambridge: Cambridge University Press, 1964–66), 228–29, 296, 301, 302.

22. David Prescott Barrows, *Berbers and Blacks: Impressions of Morocco, Timbuktu, and Western Sudan* (Westport, Conn.: Negro University Press, 1927), viii.

23. Numerous other examples of the same problem include names such as *Zāgha, Dia, Jagha,* and their cognates, *Zāghawī, Diahinké,* and *Jahinke*. All of these refer to the same metropolis and the same societal grouping.

24. As a point of information, in the case of the Foulah that Tom knew, there was an orthography as well. It was not Latin, however, but Arabic.

25. Marie Armand Pascal d'Avezac-Macaya, "Notice sur le pays et le peuple des Yébous, en Afrique," *Mémoires de la Société Ethnologique* 2, no. 2 (1845): 1–10, 13–27, 30–46, 53–105.

26. Hans Wellisch, "General Principles for the Conversion of One Written Language into Another," *International Systems for the Transliteration of Cyrillic Characters* (Geneva: n.p., 1957).

27. Nancy Kobrin, "Moses on the Margin: A Critical Transcription and Semiotic Analysis of Eight Aljamiado Legends of the Morisco Figura of Muucaa" (Ph.D. diss., University of Minnesota, 1984), 21.

28. Heinrich Barth, *Travels and Discoveries in North and Central Africa, 1849–55* (New York: Harper & Brothers, 1859), 5–6.

29. Sékéné Mody Cissoko, *Tombouctou et l'empire Songhay: epanouissement de Soudan Nigérien aux XVe-XVIe siècle* (Paris: Les nouvelles éditions africaines, 1980).

30. Felix Dubois, *Timbuctoo the Mysterious,* trans. Diana White (New York: Negro University Press, 1896), 232.

31. See Delheur's *Dictionnaire Mozabite-Français* (Paris: Société d'études linguistiques et anthropologiques de France, 1964).

32. Noah Webster, *Dissertations on the English Language: With Notes Historical and Critical, to which is added by way of Appendix an Essay on a Reformed Mode of Spelling, with Dr. Benjamin Franklin's Arguments on that Subject* (Boston: Isaiah Thomas and Co., 1789); see Scholar Press Facsimile, *English Linguistics 1500–1800,* ed. R. C. Alston (Menston, England: The Scholar Press Ltd., 1967), 54.

33. This thesis was to govern all of Webster's subsequent writings on language, including his views on orthography, which are clearly put down in the appendix published with the *Dissertations,* "An Essay on a Reformed Mode of Spelling, with Dr. Benjamin Franklin's Arguments on that Subject." Not only was orthography to be regularized in order to preserve a distinctly American language, but it was to be based on the standardized American tongue, an American pronunciation. Indeed the two go hand in hand: a regularized orthography "would lessen the trouble of writing, and much more, of learning the [American English] language; it would reduce the true pronunciation to a certainty; and while it would assist foreigners and our children in acquiring the language, it would render the pronunciation uniform, in different parts of the country, and almost prevent the possibility of changes. . . . Correct orthography would render the pronunciation of the lan-

guage, as uniform as the spelling in books. A general uniformity thro the United States, would be the event of such a reformation [of orthography] as I am here recommending. All persons, of every rank, would speak with some degree of precision and uniformity" (*Dissertations* 394–95).

A footnote from Webster is attached to this passage, where he writes: "I once heard Dr. Franklin remark that 'those people spell best who do not know how to spell'; that is, they spell as their ears dictate, without being guided by rules, and thus fall into a regular orthography." A correct orthography based on pronunciation would fix in literature that pronunciation, making it the (de facto) standard.

6. Designating Ben Ali's Manuscript Arabic

1. There has been some confusion over Ben Ali's name. In a paper given before the Ethnological Society of New York (precursor to the American Ethnological Society), Hodgson modifies Couper's orthography, writing Bul-Ali as "Ben-ali" ("The Gospels: Written in the Negro Patois of English with Arabic Characters" 3). Benjamin Goulding, in his affidavit, spells the name "Ben Ali"; in a letter dated 21 October 1931 to the head librarian at Georgia State Law Library, Ella May Thornton, he writes that his father called him "Ben (meaning Sun) Ali, [a] corruption of Allah, meaning God." Goulding is somewhat in error. Ben means son, not sun; and Ali is a proper noun, making the name, as Harold Glidden notes in a letter to Thornton in 1950, "Son of Ali." In his 1931 letter, Goulding further states that he never heard his father speak of Ben Ali as Belali. In her description of the manuscript in *Law Library Journal* (1955), Thornton refers to the manuscript's author by the three names Bilali, Bu Allah, and Ben Ali. Austin's fixing on Bilali is fanciful. The Belali name appears to be attributable to an error made by Georgia Bryan Conrad in her *Reminiscences of a Southern Woman*. It is repeated in Wylly's *History of Sapelo*, and a variant of it is given in Ivor Wilks' contribution to Philip Curtin's *Africa Remembered*, "Salih Bilali of Massina." Not only is there no evidence to support this misnaming, but it contradicts the reports of those who either had some direct contact with the manuscript's author or were in close and regular contact with him—i.e., Hodgson, Dwight, and Goulding. The Buallah or Bu Allah error is traced to Lovell. The *Drums and Shadow* interview with Katie Brown, a purported descendant of the author, presents scanty information. Moreover, in light of the problems of transcription and interpretation entailed in the W.P.A. slave narrative project, as Blassingame points out, it would be premature to hold that interview as definitive report on the manuscript's author. What this name actually was is up for grabs; for the moment I have opted to follow Goulding's and Greenberg's readings and will refer to the author as Ben Ali.

2. A typographical error on the cover sheet of a copy of this paper archived in the William Hodgson Archives, American Philosophical Society, gives the date of this paper as 1857.

3. In addition to this paper, another possible reference was made to Ben Ali by Marie Armand Pascal d'Avezac-Macaya, who was the vice president of the Société Ethnologique de Paris, as well as a corresponding member of the American Ethnological Society, in his "Notice sur le pays et le peuple des Yébous, en Afrique," published in *Mémoires de la Société Ethnologique* 2, no. 2 (1845): 1–10, 13–27, 30–46, 53–105. In a footnote d'Avezac states that while his monograph was in press, Hodgson had sent word to him that he "intends to take advantage of the presence in the United States of a literate Foulah with whom he has already begun a correspondence in Arabic, in order to obtain the elements of an ethnological introduction, a vocabulary and an essay on grammar" ("Notice" 27; my translation). This problematical footnote is made somewhat more so by P. C. Lloyd's identifying the

Foulah mentioned in the note as being the same Sali-bul-Ali of Couper's letter. Given the coincidence of the publication dates for the "Notice" and Hodgson's *Notes*, 1841 and 1844 respectively, the fact that Hodgson's collected papers show correspondence only with two other Arabic literate slaves besides Tom—Spalding's bul-Ali and an unnamed slave of Captain David Anderson (Hodgson Archives)—both of which were carried out in English through intermediaries, it would seem that the Foulah in d'Avezac's note indicates Couper's Tom and not Ben Ali. This might be the likely case, except that Hodgson's *Notes* provides the most obvious reason for Tom's not being the slave in question. Couper's letter states plainly that although Tom "reads Arabic," he "does not write it" (69).

4. In common law, an affidavit is a legal document of evidence: a written statement, or a transcribed assertion, given in evidence specific of facts and signed before either an officer of the court or an officer of the state who is empowered to administer oaths (e.g., a notary public). In the United States an affidavit is an admissible court instrument and may be used in juridical proceedings when it recites a record of the facts or events deposed along with the place where the statement was given, an oath of intent to present truthful testimony (e.g., "the affiant being first sworn, or duly sworn, says . . . "), the affiant's signature, and the official's jurat attesting to the fact that the instrument was properly sworn to and signed in the official's presence. These formalities give an official assurance, backed by the court and the state, that the instrument is genuine in its form as an oath. The oath gives assurance that the statements of the facts are true as far as official formalities are concerned. This is not to say that it assures that the statements are true per se, but rather that the affiant makes them true under penalty of law. Should they be proved false then the instrument constitutes a false testimony, which is the felony of perjury, punishable under the law. Because affidavits are not subject to cross-examination (when they are, as in interlocutory civil proceedings, they are called depositions), the law courts usually decline to receive them in lieu of oral testimony.

5. Joel Chandler Harris, *The Story of Aaron (So Named) the Son of Ben Ali: Told by his Friends and Acquaintances* (1896; Boston: Houghton, Mifflin and Company, 1900).

6. What remains of Thornton's correspondence concerning *Ben Ali's Diary* is currently archived with the manuscript in the Goulding Collection, Hargrett Rare Books and Manuscript Library, University of Georgia Library, Athens, Georgia.

7. Joseph Greenberg, "The Decipherment of the 'Ben Ali Diary,' a Preliminary Statement," *Journal of Negro History* 25 (July 1940): 372–74.

8. Abu Muḥammad 'Abdullah ibn Abī Zaid Al-Qairawänï, *ar-risālat-ul-Fiqhīyyah*, ed. al-Hādī Humī and Muḥammad Abū al-Ajfān (327 A.H./A.D. 945; Beirut: Dār-ul-Gharb-il-Islām ī, 1406 A.H./A.D. 1986). In subsequent chapters citations of this work will use the abbreviation *RF*.

9. In addition there was Hillelson's *Hints for the Guidance of Officers and Officials of the Sudan Government in the Study of the Arabic Language* (Khartoum: n.p., 1925) and his *Sudan Arabic Texts with Translation and Glossary* (Cambridge: Cambridge University Press, 1935). Also available was Allan Worsley's *Sudanese Grammar* (London: Society for Promoting Christian Knowledge, 1925) and G. S. M. Burton's *Sudan Arabic Note-Book* (London: McCorquodale, 1934). There was also the fieldwork published in the journal *Sudan Notes and Research*, such as R. Davies, "Vocabulary of Sudan Arabic," *Sudan Notes and Research* 9 (1925): 131–36, and R. Davis, "Sudan Arabic," *Sudan Notes and Research* 10 (1927): 211–19.

10. To which should be added Askell Benton, *Notes on Some Languages of the Western Sudan* (London: n.p., 1912); Decorse and Maurice Gaudefroy-Demombynes, *Rabah et les Arabes du Chari: Documents arabes et vocabulaire* (Paris: Guilmoto, 1905); Maurice Delafosse, *Essai sur le peuple et la langue Sara* (Paris: n.p., 1898); R. Derendinger, "Notes sur les dialectes arabe de Tchad," *Revue Africaine* 56 (1912): 339–70, and *Vocabulaire pratique de dialect*

arabe centre-africain (Paris: Tournon, 1923); J. Lukas, "Beiträge zur Kenntnis der Sprachen von Wadai," *Journal de la société des africanistes* 3 (1933): 25–55, "The Linguistic Situation in the Lake Chad Area," *Africa* 9 (1936): 332–49, and *Zentralsudanische Studien* (Hamburg: n.p., 1937); G. Muraz, *Vocabulaire du patois arabe tchadien ou "Tourkou" et les dialectes sara-madjin-ngaye et saram'bbaye (S.O. de Tchad)* (Paris: Lavauzelle, 1932); Diedrich Westermann, "Die westlichen Sudansprachen und ihre Beziehungen zum Bantu," *Mitteilungen des Seminars für Orientalische Sprachen* 29 (1927).

11. Jean Catineau, in "La dialectologie arabe," *Orbis* 4 (1955): 149–69, notes the universality of the merging of the emphatics. Charles Ferguson finds this common enough to make it feature 14 of his presumed Arabic koine; see "The Arabic Koine," *Linguistics* 35 (1959): 616–30. Even Joshua Blau and Ariel Bloch, who dispute Ferguson's koine theory, favoring instead a theory of linguistic drift and intercommunication, acknowledge the merging of the emphatic interdentals as a definitive element of most modern Arabic dialects. For Blau, see *The Emergence and Linguistic Background of Judeo-Arabic: A Study of the Origins of Middle Arabic* (New York: Oxford University Press, 1965); and *On Pseudo-Corrections in Some Semitic Languages* (Jerusalem: The Israel Academy of Sciences and Humanities, 1970). For Bloch, see "The Vowel of the Imperfect Performatives in the Old Dialects of Arabic," *ZDMG* 117 (1967): 22–29; and "Morphological Doublets in Arabic Dialects," *Journal of Semitic Studies* 16 (1971): 53–73. Moreover, Alan Kaye finds this to be a feature of most Sudan Arabic dialects, including the Chadian Arabic dialects as far west as Nigeria and Niger; see *Chadian and Sudanese Arabic in Light of Comparative Arabic Dialectology* (The Hague: Mouton, 1976).

12. I owe a tremendous debt to Cherno Uthman Diallo of Dakar, Senegal, for providing me with much of the information on Fulani Arabic presented in this paragraph. The generosity with which he shared his time and knowledge with me while we were both residents of Rabat, Morocco, during the months of January through March 1989 bore fruit.

13. The Ben Ali manuscript has some features of pseudo-correction (Blau 1970) that might be indicative of elements shared with Chadian Arabic (Kaye 1976). Moreover, the interchangeability of L/ ل and Ḍ/ ض clearly points to the absence of a stable phonemic referent, which would indicate the absence of any emphatic interdentals in Fulani Arabic. The significance of the Ben Ali manuscript for the linguistic study of the defusion of Arabic vernaculars in Africa is made more apparent when it is recognized that Ben Ali's writing is not an anomaly, but is part (albeit a distant and problematic part) of an established general African-Arabic literacy.

14. I am indebted to Nancy Kobrin for pointing out to me, through the example of another instance of Arabic diglossia in the West (the romance language of *Aljamia*, which was written in Spain in Arabic script during the fifteenth and sixteenth centuries), that "transcription under diglossia functions in the interpenetration and overlapping of languages." See Kobrin, "Moses on the Margin," 19.

15. In 1983 (8 November) Mae Ruth Green, librarian in charge of the Ben Ali manuscript at the Georgia State Law Library, wrote to Glidden and inquired about the translation he had mentioned to Thornton. Glidden responded on 7 December 1983, saying: "I never published this material because at the time I was dealing with it there was little interest in it. The situation has changed in this respect and perhaps the time has come to put it into print." My personal correspondence with Glidden has proved to be no more fruitful.

16. Roland Barthes has already shown the extent to which the class distinctions of reader/consumer and author are reinforced within this scheme. The problematic of the "idle" intransitive reader, equated with being "serious," as distinct from the functioning transitive writer may have been formulated along Barthes's lines. But neglected is the equally, if not

more so, intransitive "author," who is intransitive through the loss of ownership, the alienation from labor. It is the distributor, reproducer, who owns and determines the event.

17. Indeed it seems as though Glidden will take the secret of his purported translation to the grave with him. And in a personal interview with Muḥammad al-Ahari, Greenberg admitted that the speculations he made about the manuscript in his *Journal of Negro History* article were based on the fragments that Nigerian scholars translated for him, and that he was unable to translate the bulk of the text. (From a personal interview with Muḥammad al-Ahari, 15 March 1990.)

7. Reading the Sign's Indeterminate Corpora

1. Abdullah Laroui, *The Crisis of the Arab Intellectual: Traditionalism or Historicism?* trans. Diarmid Cammell (Berkeley: University of California Press, 1976), 5.

2. I have learned since completing this book that the Africanist Bradford G. Martin has completed a partial translation of the Ben Ali manuscript, and has carefully studied the material condition of its paper. It is his conclusion that the manuscript is written on Italian paper, produced sometime in the eighteenth century, and shipped to Africa. Martin's findings will be published in a forthcoming issue of the *Georgia Historical Society Journal*.

3. Here the س (sīn) of سيّدنا (sayyidnā) is displaced by ش (shīn), producing شيّدنا (shayyidnā), "our master."

4. Again, ش (shīn) displaces another grapheme, this time ص (ṣād), producing شحبِه (shaḥbihi) instead of صحبِه (ṣaḥbihi), "his companions."

5. The definite article "al/ الـ " and the initial grapheme "U/ أ " are displaced in the first term, giving سـتاد (stādh) instead of الاسـتاد (al-ustādh). In the second term, ك (kāf) displaces ق (qāf), producing الفَكيه (al-fakīh) instead of الفَقيه (al-faqīh).

6. ك (kāf) displaces ق (qāf), and the long vowel, Ā/ ا , disappears, producing كَلَ (kala) instead of قَالَ (qāla), "he said."

7. الكعب (al-kaʿab) usually refers to the ankle joint. In the discourse of *fiqh*, and in al-Qairawānī's *ar-Risāla*, the elbow is indicated by the term المرفق (al-mirfaq). In fact *ar-Risāla* reads: " المرفقيْن الى (ila-īl-mirfaqaini)" (until the two elbows) (*RF* 95).

8. Although ركبَة (ruqba) usually does refer to the knee, the standard Malikite prescription is to wash the foot to the heel: " عَقبيْه يَعْرك (yaʿruk ʿaqibaihi)" (he rubs his heels) (*RF* 97).

9. This edited Standard Arabic version of Ben Ali's manuscript is expurgated. In order to facilitate making the Ben Ali text accessible, I have adhered to contemporary grammatical and stylistic conventions by and large; however, I have retained the manuscript's consistent use of the third-person masculine imperfect form of the verb, even where current convention calls for the imperative form. The consequence is that the edited Standard Arabic text entails the same ambiguity in narrative perspective as the manuscript. I do not want to lose sight of this problematic of narrative perspective, because, as I will argue presently, the legibility of the Ben Ali manuscript requires a failure to definitively determine its circuit of exchange.

10. Here Ben Ali makes a series of deviations common in both SCA and Chadian Arabic (Kaye 1976). In the word *ashhadu* أشـهَـد ("I bear witness") he displaces the grapheme هـ (hā') and displaces the ش (shīn) with س (sīn), producing *ashadu;* / اسـحـد. In the following word, *anna* / أنّ ("that"), he displaces the أ (hamza) with ع (ʿain), inserts an additional *hamza* before the ʿain, and displaces the grapheme ن (nūn) with the indefinite nominative case ending ـًا (an) producing *aʿan* / عـأـًا instead of *anna* / أنّ .

11. Here Ben Ali has added the first-person plural suffix "nā / نَا" , writing "a 'an nā / اعّنَا ".

12. The standard spelling is al-adhān.

13. Ben Ali's text conflates the imperative verb ḥiya/ حَيّ ("come") with the preposition 'alā/ علَى ("on"), getting one word, ḥiy'al/ حَيّعَل. The manuscript gives ṣalaḥ/ صلاح ("propriety, righteousness"), instead of the appropriate term, ṣalāh/ صلاة ("prayer"), with "h" transliterating the muted ة (tā' marbūṭa; also called hā' ta' nīth, which is transliterated as "at" in constructs), because of the weak third radical.

14. The appropriate phrase here is ḥiya 'alā al-falāh / حَيّ افلاح ("come to success"), with a penultimate long vowel Ā followed حر. (ḥā'). The Ben Ali manuscript's ḥiy'al al-fā Allah / الفا اللّه is not simply an instance of phonetic substitution or displacement; it reflects a profound indeterminacy of reference.

15. Here the silenced consonant و (waw) has been displaced by ع ('u); otherwise it is written as naum / نوم .

16. This is written in the margin of page 10 of the manuscript. It is in the predominant hand of the text, and appears to be a correction of the irregularly spelled ash-shalāh/ الشلاة .

17. Here Ben Ali has returned the displaced ن (nūn) of anna ("that") and added an initial hamza, as well as left the 'ain without ligature, writing a'anā/ اعنا.

18. Besides the text's usual conflation of the imperative verb ḥiya / حَيّ ("come") with the preposition 'alā/ علَى ("on") getting one word, ḥiy'al / حَيّعَل, the "broken alif" of ḥiy'al / علَى is displaced by the long vowel Ā.

19. Muḥammad b. 'Abd-ur-Raḥmān al-'Uthmānī, īḍah al ta'añf bi-ba'dfaḍa'il al-'ilm al shañf, Princeton University Library, Yahuda Ms. 4293; quoted in Jonathan Berkey, Transmission of Knowledge in Medieval Cairo: A Social History of Islamic Education (Princeton: Princeton University Press, 1992), 26.

20. Substantial historical work has been done on the structure of classical Islamic learning since Greenberg published his article on the Ben Ali manuscript. Of particular significance is the work of George Makdisi, The Rise of Colleges: Institutions of Learning in Islam and the West (Edinburgh, 1981); Georges Vajda, "De la transmission orale du savoir dans l'Islam traditionnel," L'Arabisant 4 (19975): 2–8; A. L. Tibawi, "Origin and Character of Al-Madrasah," Bulletin of the School of Oriental and African Studies 25 (1962): 225–38; Muhsin Mahdi, "The Book and the Master as Poles of Cultural Change in Islam," Islam and Cultural Change in the Middle Ages, ed. Speros Vryonis (Wiesbaden: n.p., 1975); and Jonathan Berkey, Transmission of Knowledge in Medieval Cairo. On the history of Islamic education in West Africa in the seventeenth through nineteenth centuries, see M. Hiskett, "Materials Relating to the State of Learning among the Fulani," Bulletin of the School of Oriental and African Studies 19 (1957); The Sword of Truth: The Life and Times of Shehu Usuman dan Fodio (New York: Oxford University Press, 1973); and "The Arabic Literature of Nigeria to 1804," Bulletin of the School of Oriental and African Studies 25 (1962). Also on Islamic learning in Africa, see Elias N. Saad, Social History of Timbuktu (Cambridge: Cambridge University Press, 1983); and Lamin Sanneh, The Jakhanke Muslim Clerics.

21. These epistles could address specific questions of law, such as al-Maghīlī's Replies, which is an epistle sent to Askīa al-Hajj Muḥammad by al-Maghīlī, in response to the former's questions regarding the proper juridical basis for state hegemony. Or they could address general issues of worship and ritual praxis, such as in al-Qairawānī's ar-Risāla, which instructs the believers in the intricacies of quotidian ritual, from prayer and ablution to the question of whether or not it was lawful to enslave Muslims.

22. According to al-Baghdādī, al-Farq bain al-farq (32), Abū Ḥanifa was the first semiotician (kalāmī) among the fuqahā' (scientists). 'Ali Sām ībn-Nashār is even more laudatory; because Abū Ḥanifa was one of the tābi'i-n (the generation of the children of Muḥam-

mad's companions) who received many transmissions directly from Muḥammad's companions, an-Nashār regards Abū Ḥanifa's efforts as the historical beginning of the Sunna methods of `ilm-ul-kalām (an-Nashār, Nashā't-ul-fikr-il-Falsifi - fil-Islam 234).

23. Ibn Khaldūn, al-Muqaddamma (Beirut: Dār-ul-Qalam, 1978), 464. The term used by Ibn Khaldūn for "the ascension of Allah to the throne" is al-istiwā'; it refers to the issue of whether or not it can be determined how Allah ascended the throne (see Qur'an: Suras al-Baqara, 28; Yunis, 3; and al-A'arāf, 54). The issue of al-istiwā' was an aspect of a paramount problematic for the early as well as later Mutakallimūn (the practitioners of 'ilm-ul-kalām, or semioticians), that being the nature of Allah's discourse: Does Allah discourse, and is the Qur'an as that discourse created or eternal?

The predecessors (as-Salaf) to which ibn Khaldūn refers are the first three generations of Muslims, specifically the companions of Muḥammad, their children, and their grandchildren who were adherents of Qur'an and Sunna, and whose consensus in turn became valid.

24. Ibn Taymīya, al-Farqān bain al-haq wa al-bātil 137, 142; Ibn Kathīr, Tārīkh Ibn Kathīr, 9:350; and Adh-Dhabī, Mīzān-ul-a'atidal, 1:158.

25. For examples and discussions of such confusion, see Jamāl-ul-Din al-qāsmī ad-Dimashqī, Tārīkh-ul-jahamīa wa al-mu`tazila 6; Imām Aḥmad ib Ḥanbal; al-Bukhārī; and ibn Taymīa.

26. al-Baghdādī, al-Farq bain al-farq.

27. al-Ghazalī, Kitāb al-iqtisad fil-i'tiqad (Beirut: Dar-ul-Imana, 1969), 141. Henceforth referred to parenthetically as KII.

28. This reading of al-Ghazalī's doctrine of signs as being analogous to the Stoics' finds support in C. H. M. Versteegh's Greek Elements in Arabic Linguistic Thinking (Leiden: Brill, 1977), particularly in chapter 10, "The Stoic Component in the Theory of Meaning," 179–90. Versteegh's focus is on linguistic matters, therefore his concentration is almost exclusively on grammatical and philological sources at the expense of philosophical texts. What this amounts to, in relation to the argument that the Stoics' concept of lektòn was appropriated by Arabic scholars, is his dismissal of the arguments by Rescher, van Ess, and Gätje that trace a connection between the Arabic term ma'nan (signification, meaning, thought) and lektòn through the translation of Greek philosophy into Arabic. He dismisses this view on the grounds that their research is based wholly on the occurrence of the term ma'nan in philosophical texts, when in fact it first occurred in earlier grammatical texts, i.e., Sībawaihi's kitāb.

Versteegh attempts to trace a connection between the Greek term lektòn and the Arabic term ma'nan that can be proven primarily through the direct transmission of Greek grammatical concepts to early Arabic grammarians. What compels him to venture this attempt is a striking similarity in opposition between the Greek grammarians' pair, phônè (sound) and semainòmenon, and the Arabic grammarians' pair, lafẓ (the singular of alfāẓ) and ma'nan. The opposition in both pairs is between the materiality of expression and the process of signification. Versteegh is convinced that there must be a point of historical contact between the two grammars, because the basis for the Greek grammarians' oppositional dyad is in the Stoic theories of signification. He fails to find such a direct contact, however, asserting that: "There is no direct proof, apart from resemblance in meaning (the verb 'anā could translate the Greek verb légein, to intend), that ma'nan was a calque of the Stoic lektòn" (emphasis in the original). Instead, he makes a great deal out of the evidence for the translating of the Greek term pâgmata into ma'na. This translation occurs, in fact, in two translations of philosophical texts: al-Fārābī's translation of the term in Aristotle's De Interpretatione, and Jābir ibn Hayyān's translation of the same passage. Nonetheless, Versteegh argues that there is a link between the word ma'nan and the Stoic term prâgmata

on the basis of five points: (1) *prâgmata* and *lektòn* were synonymous for the Stoics; (2) the Stoics distinguished between meaning and thought such that *lektòn* was extramental but not an event or object; (3) there was a confusion about the precise meaning of the word *lektòn*, which was held to be equivalent with "thought"; (4) al-Fārābī's erroneous translation of Aristotle's *prâgmata* as *ma'nan* is evidence of the Greek term's being understood to mean something extramental; and (5) there is ample evidence that *ma'nan* was generally held as being extramental, and in the case of the *mu'tazila*, specifically Mu'ammar (d. 220 A.H./A.D. 835), it was something nonphysical within objects.

The chief flaw in this argument is Versteegh's failure to establish any clear evidence of even one instance where *ma'nan* is a translation of the Stoic *prâgmata/lektòn*. At best he finds that "'Abd-ul-Jabbār's assertion that 'there is no connection between the expression [`*ibāra*] [and] of that thought,' expressed in a somewhat crude way the essence of the Stoic theory that there is no identity of thought and speech." Moreover, the correlation of *prâgmata* and *ma'nan* rests entirely on the same philosophical sources that Versteegh sought to avoid.

In spite of its difficulties, Versteegh's text does point out an important conceptual problem. In attempting to discover through translation the influence of one doctrine of signs on another, instead Versteegh finds *in* translation a problem of signification: What does *ma'nan* mean? This relationship between signification and translation is not a function of lost material, but rather a function of the Western conception of semiotics, which subtends Versteegh's analysis of the extant Arabic texts, causing him to misread al-Ghazalī as being indebted to the Stoics for his doctrine of the sign.

29. Quoted in 'Abdu-ur-Rahman Jalal-ul-Din As-Sayītī, *al-Mazhir fi 'ulūm al-lugha wa Anwā'ihā*, eds. Muḥammad Aḥmad Jād-ul-Muwalī et al. (1285; Beirut: Dar-ul-Fikr, 1986), 137–38.

30. Abu Mansūr Muḥammad b. Aḥmad al-Azharī, *tahdhīb-ul-lugha*, ed. Rashīd 'Abdu-ur-Rahman al-'Ubaidī (Cairo: al-hiyat-ul-misriyat-ul-'amat-ul-kitāb, 1975), 7.

31. There is a dialectic at work in al-Haithm's saying, "The *mu'jam* of *al-khaṭṭ* refers to [the act] of writing with diacritics. We say, '*a'jamtu al-kitāb*' [the book], i.e., 'we obscure its obscurity'; and we do not say, '*ajamtuhu*,' i.e., 'we obscured it.' " Written discourse becomes elucidated by an act of obscuring. Because vowels in Arabic writing are separate from the consonants, the unmarked, nonsigned text is open to any combination of "mispronunciations" and mistakes in meaning: in its simple form writing displaces the vocality of speech. The function of diacritics is to replace what has been displaced by writing, to negate the effect of writing's absenting of vocality, which is why al-Haithm's play with words has the negative produce the positive. His playing is determined by the grammar of morphology, according to which *a'ajamtu* has the paradigmatic weight of *af'altu*, indicating augmentation, the process of becoming, and agency. In this way, it is tantamount to the displacement of displacement. This is what ibn Janī had in mind when he wrote: "Yet, they were named thusly: *al-hurūf al-mu'jam*, because, when individually articulated, if their phonetics were modified some would be obscured [*a'jamat*] and some neglected. . . . Thus, the function of displacement and obscurity is displaced . . . by way of *i'jām* [diacritics]" (*Sar as-snā'ahu* 40).

32. Blau's theory that modern Arabic dialect variation is informed by Arabic dialect variation that existed prior to Islam and was widespread through the Islamic expansions seems more plausible than Ferguson's theory of a universal koine (Ferguson 1959). Not only is there the impressive textual indication of persistent dialect variation in the Judeo-Arabic and Christian Arabic writings of medieval Egypt and Syria (Blau 1965, 1970), but there is also the neglected early modern texts of Sudan Colloquial Arabic (Al-Amīn 1923, Hillelson 1935, Kayes 1976).

33. Abū Muḥammad ʿAbdullah ibn Muslim ibn Qutaibah, *Adab-ul-Kātib*, ed. Muḥammad ad-Dālī (1300; Beirut: Muʾsasah ar-Risāla, 1985).

34. Abu Bakr Muḥammad b. Yahya aṣ-Ṣūlī, *Adāb-ul-kitāb* (Rabat: n.p., n.d.), 31–32.

35. Hence, my reading of the Ben Ali manuscript gets caught up in those of Harris and Greenberg.

36. See Fairūzābādi's *al-qāmūs al-muhīt*, (fasl al-khā', bāb-ul-tā).

37. Jacques Derrida, "Otobiographies: The Teaching of Nietzsche and the Poetics of the Proper Name," *The Ear of the Other: Otobiography, Transference, Translation.* Trans. Avital Ronell (New York: Schocken Books, 1984), 4.

38. In defining autobiography in these terms, Georg Mish (*Geschichte der Autobiographie*) evokes Hegel's state in Reason in History.

39. It becomes extremely difficult and problematical to assert even a formal difference in perspective between autobiographical and speculative philosophical reflection. In both instances, perspective is the narrative effect of a subject engendering in a specific rhetorical movement its site, position, of viewing exteriority and interiority through verbal deictics. For the narrative subject of speculation in the autobiographical, reflection = narrative as a historical dynamic development; in speculative reflection there is an inscribing of the economy of mastery and control that sustains the comprehensivity of narrative in the form of autocritical analysis as a historical totality. After Kant, philosophical reflection can no longer attempt, by means of introspection, a static representation of the personality. On the contrary, like autobiography, philosophy (which in the wake of Kant is no longer system-building) has its main stake in a certain authenticating genealogy of discourse, the developmental history of thought and writing that transcribes the experience of materiality as having universal , as in historical, meaning. In philosophy writing, which like autobiography is narrative, experience is not only transcribable into narrative agency, but it is purely an effect of this transcription.

40. Recall al-Ghazalī's attempt to preserve the concept of literality of the Qur'an by releasing it from ideology into propositional inference (*KII* 258–59).

41. *al-muʾjam al-wasīt*, bāb-ul-kāf: "al-kitāb."

42. For the grammarians, the locator's locution (*khiṭāba*), is defined as "a type of discourse in which the locator is at rest, or present" (*Adāb-ul-wasīṭ* 23).

43. These are أَنْتَ, *anta* (you, m.); أَنْتِ, *anti* (you, f.); أَنْتُمَا, *antumā* (you, dual); أَنْتُمْ, *antum* (you, m. pl.); and أَنْتُنَّ, *antunna* (you, f. pl.).

44. Both the direct object and the genitive suffixes employ the same graphemic markers, the difference being that when attached to verbs they serve as direct objects, and when attached to nouns as genitive pronouns. These markers are كَ, *ka* (your, m.); كِ, *ki* (your, f.); كُمَا, *kumā* (your, dual); كُمْ, *kum* (your, m. pl.); and كُنَّ, *kunna* (your, f. pl.).

45. As I've already indicated in note 9 of this chapter, in the edited Standard Arabic text of the manuscript I have retained the manuscript's employment of the third-person masculine singular imperfect verb form, where current convention calls for the imperative form.

8. Critique of Hypotyposis

1. Yuri Lotman, "Theses on the Semiotic Study of Cultures," *A Tell Tale Sign*, ed. Thomas Sebeok (Lisse: Peter de Ridder, 1975), 81.

2. Wlad Godzich, "The Construction of Meaning," 391; emphasis in the original.

3. See Aristotle, *De Interpretatione*, trans. Harold P. Cooke, vol. 1 of *Aristotle*, Loeb Classic Library (1938; Cambridge: Harvard University Press, and London: Heinemann, 1983), 115.

4. The other two branches are *physica* (natural philosophy) and *practica* (ethics); see John Locke, *Essay Concerning Humane Understanding*, ed. Alexander Campbell Fraser, 2 vols. (1690; 1894; New York: Dover, 1959), book 4, chapter 21, section 4, 461–62.

5. The Italian semiotician Luigi Romeo has proposed that the history of semiotics is actually the history of humanity par excellence, because it seeks to map the historical emergence and development of all human sign systems, and it is the concept of the sign that marks the emergence of *Homo*. Thus, for Romeo, *Homo* and *Homo semeioticus* are one and the same entity. This view of humanity as *Homo semeioticus* stems from Romeo's analysis of *ars semeiotica* (τεχνη σημειωτιχη) as a sine qua non for the understanding of *ars gramatica*. See Luigi Romeo, "The Derivation of 'Semiotics' through the History of the Discipline," *Semiosis* (1977): 37; and "*Homo Semeioticus* So Far," *Ars Semeiotica* 3, no. 1 (1980): 101–5.

Epilogue

1. Nelson George, *The Death of Rhythm and Blues* (New York: E. P. Dutton, 1989).

Index

'Abd-ur-Rahmān Ibrahima, 23; writings of, 187, 219, 275
Abū Bakr as-Ṣiddiqi (of Jamaica): autobiography of, 153, 154, 219
Abū Ḥanīfa, 248, 250
Abū 'Ubaid, 254, 256, 259
Adab-ul-kātib, 259
aesthemata, 47
aesthesis, 45–46, 83
aesthetics, 8, 14, 20, 46, 57, 70, 82, 181, 301–2 n. 29; in Ellison's literary theory, 55, 59, 60; Kant's theory of, 24; Schelling's *Philosophy of Art*, 24, 26; Gronniosaw's empiricist, 70; and translation of *Ben Ali's Diary*, 226; and semiotics, 257, 290; and Aztec civilization, 82; Romantic concept of, 8, 308–9 n. 27; *sensus communis aesthetica*, 182
African American literary history, 8, 16, 38–40, 50, 59; as a viable academic discipline, 18, 21; and *la pensée de libertinage érudit*, 63
African American literary theory: Yale seminar on (1977), 3, 4, 36; connection with structuralist and poststructuralist theory, 36; and the laws of cultural expression, 40; Yale school of, 18, 20, 37, 61, 92–93, 94, 96; and the reorganization of knowledge, 20; and ethical ethnic formalism, 92
African American literature, 1, 2, 10; and literary historiography of culture, 8; excluded from the field of American literary history, 58; slave narratives as paradigm of, 38, 92 (*see also* Diallo, Ayyūb ibn Suleimān); as a historical development, 40 (*see also* Stepto, Robert; historiography); theoretical rigor in the handling of, 16–18; as a normative object of analysis, 20; institutional marginalization of, 42 (*see also* Ellison, Ralph; literary genealogy)
African American studies (*see also* Black studies): collaboration with critical theory, 2; Yale Afro-American Studies Program, 1, 4–8, 20; and the institutional history of the humanities in North America, 8, 10, 11, 17, 19, 24; in collaboration with theory, 2, 17; and Allan Bloom 11, 290
African-Arabic: New World slave narratives, 2, 20, 22–24, 148, 167, 275, 285; literacy, 160, 165–66, 172; orthography, 187, 266; dialectology, 219
agencement, 135, 136, 260, 273
agency, 37, 45, 47, 77, 89, 249, 281; cognitive, 28, 52, 107; indeterminate, 121, 145, 262–263 (*see also* Imagination); narrative, 52, 60, 96, 145, 148, 185, 257, 263; writing for, 160, 268; as symbolic economy, 266; and political function of liberal arts, 287
Ahl-Diakha (*see also* Diakha), 168, 172
a'jam, 256, 257, 260
Alexander IV, Pope, 72, 74
Alfīyat al-ma'ani, 172
Álvares, Afonso, 67
American Ethnological Society, 153, 156, 198, 201; interest in New World African-Arabic texts, 166, 186–87, 194
American literary history, 8, 20, 22, 38, 54, 96; periodization model, 56, 58–59
American Renaissance: and the emergence of American studies, 55–56; as an idealized period of cultural unity, 57
American studies, 8, 10, 22, 55–56, 58, 94
Amo, Antonius Gullielmus, 44, 47, 67–68, 102, 300 nn. 20, 21
apperception, 25, 63, 98; as heterogeneous from perception, 89; in Frederick Douglass's *Narrative*, 104; Kant's designation of, 122–24, 126; and the possibility of synthetic judgments, 127, 132, 133; transcendental, 122; and human identity, 130–31; Imagination's indeterminacy, 136, 140, 145

Ronald A. T. Judy is assistant professor of comparative literature and cultural theory at the University of Pittsburgh.

Wahneema Lubiano teaches English and Afro-American studies at Princeton University. Her work has been published in journals such as *Cultural Critique* and *American Literary History*.

(Dis)Forming the American Canon